Cultural Interface of India with Southeast Asia

Cultural Interface of India with Southeast Asia

Dr Prem Shankar Choudhary

MD Publications Pvt Ltd
New Delhi
www.mdppl.com

Published by :

MD Publications Pvt Ltd
'MD House', 11, Darya Ganj
New Delhi - 110 002
Phone : +91-11-41563325 (Customer Service)
+91-11-41562846 (Editorial)
E-mail (orders): contact@mdppl.com
Website: www.mdppl.com

ISBN : 978-81-7533-169-3

Published and Printed by Mrs. Rajni Gupta on behalf of **MD Publications Pvt Ltd** at Times Press, New Delhi.

CONTENTS

PREFACE

Southeast Asia or Southeastern Asia is a subregion of Asia, consisting of the countries that are geographically south of China, east of India and north of Australia. Southeast Asia consists of two geographic regions: the Asian mainland, and island arcs and archipelagoes to the east and southeast. The mainland section consists of Cambodia, Laos, Myanmar, Thailand and Vietnam. The maritime section consists of Brunei, East Timor, Indonesia, Malaysia, the Philippines and Singapore.

The history of Southeast Asia has been characterized as interaction between regional players and foreign powers. Though 11 countries currently make up the region, the history of each country is intertwined with all the others. For instance, the Malay empires of Srivijaya and Malacca covered modern day Indonesia, Malaysia, and Singapore while the Burmese, Thai, and Khmer peoples governed much of Indochina.

Southeast Asian countries have made a political association called the ASEAN (Association of Southeast Asian Nations). All of the above are members of the Association of Southeast Asian Nations (ASEAN), except East Timor (also known as Timor Leste), which is an ASEAN candidate state. The area, together with part of South Asia, was widely known as the East Indies or simply the Indies until the twentieth century. Christmas Island and the Cocos (Keeling) Islands are considered part of Southeast Asia though they are governed by Australia.

During the 1990s, Southeast Asia emerged as the fastest growing economy in the world. Its successes have made some to call Southeast Asia as an economic miracle and "Four Asian Tigers". India has maintained good relations with the Southeast Asian countries. This book traces historical, political, cultural and economic condition of this region and India's relations with these countries.

I am very grateful to Mr. Pranav Gupta, Director, MD Publications Pvt Ltd for his cooperation and support for this book.

Dr Prem Shankar Choudhary

1

INDIA: HISTORY, GEOGRAPHY, CULTURE AND ECONOMY

India, officially the Republic of India, is a country in South Asia. It is a parliamentary federal republic consisting of 28 states and 7 union territories. It is the seventh largest country by geographical area, the second most populous country, and the most populous democracy in the world. Bounded by the Indian Ocean on the south, the Arabian Sea on the west, and the Bay of Bengal on the east, India has a coastline of 7,517 kilometers (4,671 mi). It borders Pakistan to the west; China, Nepal, and Bhutan to the north-east; and Bangladesh and Burma to the east. India is in the vicinity of Sri Lanka, the Maldives, and Indonesia in the Indian Ocean.

Home to the Indus Valley Civilization and a region of historic trade routes and vast empires, the Indian subcontinent was identified with its commercial and cultural wealth for much of its long history. Four major world religions, Hinduism, Buddhism, Jainism and Sikhism originated here, while Zoroastrianism, Judaism, Christianity and Islam arrived in the first millennium CE and shaped the region's diverse culture. Gradually annexed by the British East India Company from the early eighteenth century and colonised by the United Kingdom from the mid-nineteenth century, India became a modern nation state in 1947 after a struggle for independence that was marked by widespread nonviolent resistance.

India has the world's twelfth largest economy at market exchange rates and the fourth largest in purchasing power. Economic reforms have transformed it into the second fastest growing large economy; however, it still suffers from high levels of poverty, illiteracy, and malnutrition. A pluralistic, multilingual, and multiethnic society, India is also home to a diversity of wildlife in a variety of protected habitats.

HISTORY OF INDIA

The history of India begins with the Indus Valley Civilization, which spread and flourished in the north-western part of the Indian subcontinent, from c. 3300 to 1300 BCE. Its Mature Harappan period lasted from 2600-1900 BCE. This Bronze Age civilization collapsed at the beginning of the second millennium BCE and was followed by the Iron Age Vedic period, which extended over much of the Indo-Gangetic plains and which witnessed the rise of major kingdoms known as the Mahajanapadas. In one of these kingdoms Magadha, Mahavira and Gautama Buddha were born in the 6th century BCE, who propagated their Shramanic philosophies among the masses.

Later, successive empires and kingdoms ruled the region and enriched its culture– from the Achaemenid Persian empire around 543 BCE, to Alexander the Great in 326 BCE. The Indo-Greek Kingdom, founded by Demetrius of Bactria, included Gandhara and Punjab from 184 BCE; it reached its greatest extent under Menander, establishing the Greco-Buddhist period with advances in trade and culture.

The subcontinent was united under the Maurya Empire during the 4th and 3rd centuries BCE. It subsequently became fragmented, with various parts ruled by numerous Middle kingdoms for the next ten centuries. Its northern regions were united once again in the 4th century CE, and remained so for two centuries thereafter, under the Gupta Empire. This period, of Hindu religious and intellectual resurgence, is known among its admirers as the "Golden Age of India." During the same time, and for several centuries afterwards, Southern India, under the rule of the Chalukyas, Cholas, Pallavas and Pandyas, experienced its own golden age, during which Indian civilization, administration, culture, and religion (Hinduism and Buddhism) spread to much of south-east Asia.

Islam arrived on the subcontinent in 712 CE, when the Arab general Muhammad bin Qasim conquered Sindh and Multan in southern Punjab, setting the stage for several successive Islamic invasions between the 10th and 15th centuries CE from Central Asia, leading to the formation of Muslim empires in the Indian subcontinent, including the Ghaznavid, the Ghorid, the Delhi Sultanate and the Mughal Empire. Mughal rule came to cover most of the northern parts of the subcontinent. Mughal rulers introduced middle-eastern art and architecture to India. In addition to the Mughals, several independent Hindu kingdoms, such as the Maratha Empire, the Vijayanagara Empire and various Rajput kingdoms, flourished contemporaneously, in Western and Southern India respectively. The Mughal Empire suffered a gradual decline in the early eighteenth century, which provided opportunities for the Afghans, Balochis and Sikhs to exercise control over large areas in the northwest of the subcontinent until the British East India Company gained ascendancy over South Asia.

Beginning in the mid-18th century and over the next century, India was gradually annexed by the British East India Company. Dissatisfaction with Company rule led to the First War of Indian Independence, after which India was directly administered by the British Crown and witnessed a period of both rapid development of infrastructure and economic decline.

During the first half of the 20th century, a nationwide struggle for independence was launched by the Indian National Congress, and later joined by the Muslim League. The subcontinent gained independence from Great Britain in 1947, after being partitioned into the dominions of India and Pakistan. Pakistan's eastern wing became the nation of Bangladesh in 1971.

Pre-Historic Era

Stone Age

Isolated remains of *Homo erectus* in Hathnora in the Narmada Valley in Central India indicate that India might have been inhabited since at least the Middle Pleistocene era, somewhere between 200,000 to 500,000 years ago. The Mesolithic period in the Indian subcontinent covered a timespan of around 25,000 years, starting around 30,000 years ago. Modern humans seem to have settled the subcontinent towards the end of the last Ice Age, or approximately 12,000 years ago. The first confirmed permanent settlements appeared 9,000 years ago in the Rock Shelters of Bhimbetka in modern Madhya Pradesh. Early Neolithic culture in South Asia is represented by the Mehrgarh findings (7000 BCE onwards) in present day Balochistan, Pakistan. Traces of a Neolithic culture have been found submerged in the Gulf of Khambat, radiocarbon dated to 7500 BCE. Late Neolithic cultures sprang up in the Indus Valley region between 6000 and 2000 BCE and in southern India between 2800 and 1200 BCE.

The region of the subcontinent that is now the country of Pakistan has been inhabited continuously for at least two million years. The ancient history of the region includes some of South Asia's oldest settlements and some of its major civilizations.

The earliest archaeological site in Pakistan is the palaeolithic hominid site in the Soan River valley. Village life began with the Neolithic site of Mehrgarh, while the first urban civilization of the region was the Indus Valley Civilization, with major sites at Mohenjo Daro and Harappa.

Bronze Age

The Bronze Age on the Indian subcontinent began around 3300 BCE with the beginning of the Indus Valley Civilization. Inhabitants of the ancient Indus river valley, the Harappans, developed new techniques in metallurgy and produced copper, bronze, lead and tin.

The Indus Valley Civilization which flourished from about 2600 BCE to 1900 BCE marked the beginning of the urban civilization on the subcontinent. The ancient civilization included urban centers such as Harappa and Mohenjo-daro (in modern day Pakistan), Dholavira and Lothal (in modern day India). It was centred on the Indus River and its tributaries, and extended into the Ghaggar-Hakra River valley, the Ganges-Yamuna Doab, Gujarat, and northern Afghanistan.

The civilization is noted for its cities built of brick, road-side drainage system and multi-storied houses. Among the settlements were the major urban centres of Harappa and Mohenjo-daro, as well as Dholavira, Ganweriwala, Lothal, Kalibangan and Rakhigarhi. It is thought by some that geological disturbances and climate change, leading to a gradual deforestation may ultimately have contributed to the civilization's downfall. The decline of the Indus Valley Civilization also included a break down of urban society and of the use of distinctively urban traits such as the use of writing and seals.

Iron Age

The Iron Age in the Indian subcontinent succeeds the Late Harappan (Cemetery H) culture, also known as the last phase of the Indus Valley Tradition. The cultures of the Punjab and Rajasthan in this phase spread eastward across the Gangetic plain. For this reason, the succession of Iron Age cultures of northern India and Pakistan are also known as the Indo-Gangetic Tradition.

The Painted Gray Ware culture (ca 1200-800 BCE) and the Northern Black Polished Ware culture (ca 700-300 BCE) belong to the "Regionalization Era" of the Indo-Gangetic Tradition. This corresponds to the later phase of the Vedic period and Mahajanapadas and the rise of the Maurya Empire. Chandragupta Maurya and Ashoka the Great belong to this period.

The earliest Iron Age site in South India is Hallur. India enters the classical period from the 6th century BC with the births of Mahavira and Gautama Buddha, followed by the Sanskrit grammar of Panini, the Edicts of Ashoka, and the emerging Middle kingdoms of India.

Vedic period

The Vedic culture is the Indo-Aryan culture associated with the Hindu sacred texts of Vedas, which were orally composed in Vedic Sanskrit. Vedas are some of the oldest extant texts. This period lasted from about 1500 BCE to 500 BCE, and during which time the definitions of much of latter Indian language, culture and most importantly, religion were laid down. However, the timing of this period is disputed by some nationalist Indian historians who posit the earlier date of 3000 BCE. Properly speaking, the first 500 years (1500–1000 BCE) of the Vedic Age correspond to Bronze Age India and the next 500 years (1000–500 BCE) to Iron Age India. Many scholars today postulate an Indo-Aryan migration into India, proposing that early Indo-Aryan speaking tribes migrated into the north-west regions of the Indian subcontinent in the early 2nd millennium BCE. Some scholars postulate these Indo-Aryan tribes as originating in Central Asia and Afghanistan from where they migrated east into India, and west into Mesopotamia and finally assimilating with them whilst spreading their language and culture. This has been opposed by the proponents of Out of India theory, who claim Aryans were indigenous to the Indian subcontinent. It is to be noted that the 19th century "Aryan Invasion theory" has long been abandoned by scholars. Instead the various scenarios of an "Aryan Immigration" are presently researched.

Early Vedic society consisted of largely pastoral groups, with late Harappan urbanization being abandoned for unknown reasons. After the Rigveda, Aryan society became increasingly agricultural, and was socially organized around the four Varnas. In addition to the principal texts of Hinduism (the Vedas), the epics (the Ramayana and Mahabharata) are said to have their ultimate origins during this period. Early Indo-Aryan presence probably corresponds, in part, to the presence of Ochre Coloured Pottery in archaeological findings. The kingdom of the Kurus corresponds to the Black and Red Ware and Painted Gray Ware culture and the beginning of the Iron Age in Northwestern India, around 1000 BCE (roughly contemporaneous with the composition of the Atharvaveda, the first Indian text to mention Iron, as úyâma ayas, literally "black metal"). The Painted Grey Ware culture spanning much of Northern India were prevalent from about 1100 to 600 BCE. This later period also corresponds with a change in outlook towards the prevalent tribal system of living leading to establishment of kingdoms called *Mahajanapadas*.

The Mahajanapadas

In the later Vedic Age, a number of small kingdoms or city states had covered the subcontinent, many mentioned during Vedic, early Buddhist and Jaina literature as far back as 1000 BCE. By 500 BCE, sixteen monarchies and 'republics' known as the *Mahajanapadas* — Kasi, Kosala, Anga, Magadha, Vajji (or Vriji), Malla, Chedi, Vatsa (or Vamsa), Kuru, Panchala, Machcha (or Matsya), Surasena, Assaka, Avanti, Gandhara, Kamboja — stretched across the Indo-Gangetic plains from modern-day Afghanistan to Bengal and Maharastra. This period was that of the second major urbanisation in India after the Indus Valley Civilization. Many smaller clans mentioned within early literature seem to have been present across the rest of the subcontinent. Some of these kings were hereditary; other states elected their rulers. The educated speech at that time was Sanskrit, while the dialects of the general population of northern India are referred to as Prakrits. Many of the sixteen kingdoms had coalesced to four major ones by 500/

400 BCE, that is by the time of Siddhartha Gautama. These four were Vatsa, Avanti, Kosala and Magadha.

Hindu rituals at that time were complicated and conducted by the priestly class. It is thought that the Upanishads, late Vedic texts dealing mainly with incipient philosophy, were composed in the later Vedic Age and early in this period of the *Mahajanapadas* (from about 600-400 BCE). Upanishads had a substantial effect on Indian philosophy, and were contemporary to the development of Buddhism and Jainism, indicating a golden age of thought in this period. It is believed that in 537 BCE, Siddhartha Gautama attained the state of "enlightenment", and became known as the 'Buddha'—the awakened one. Around the same time, Mahavira (the 24th Jain Tirthankara according to Jains) propagated a similar theology, that was to later become Jainism. However, Jain orthodoxy believes it predates all known time. The Vedas are believed to have documented a few Jain Tirthankars, and an ascetic order similar to the sramana movement. The Buddha's teachings and Jainism had doctrines inclined toward asceticism, and were preached in Prakrit, which helped them gain acceptance amongst the masses. They have profoundly influenced practices that Hinduism and Indian spiritual orders are associated with namely, vegetarianism, prohibition of animal slaughter and ahimsa (non-violence).

While the geographic impact of Jainism was limited to India, Buddhist nuns and monks eventually spread the teachings of Buddha to Central Asia, East Asia, Tibet, Sri Lanka and South East Asia.

Persian and Greek invasions

Much of the northwestern Indian Subcontinent (present day Eastern Afghanistan and Pakistan) came under the rule of the Persian Achaemenid Empire in c. 520 BCE during the reign of Darius the Great, and remained so for two centuries thereafter. In 334 BCE, Alexander the Great conquered Asia Minor and the Achaemenid Empire, reaching the north-west frontiers of the Indian subcontinent. There, he defeated King Puru in the Battle of the Hydaspes (near modern-day Jhelum, Pakistan) and conquered much of the Punjab; however, Alexander's troops refused to go beyond the Hyphases (Beas) River near modern day Jalandhar, Punjab. Alexander left many Macedonian veterans in the conquered regions; he himself turned back and marched his army southwest.

The Persian and Greek invasions had important repercussions on Indian civilization. The political systems of the Persians was to influence future forms of governance on the subcontinent, including the administration of the Mauryan dynasty. In addition, the region of Gandhara, or present-day eastern Afghanistan and north-west Pakistan, became a melting pot of Indian, Persian, Central Asian and Greek cultures and gave rise to a hybrid culture, Greco-Buddhism, which lasted until the 5th century CE and influenced the artistic development of Mahayana Buddhism.

The Magadha Empire

Amongst the sixteen Mahajanapadas, the kingdom of Magadha rose to prominence under a number of dynasties. According to tradition, the Haryanka dynasty founded the Magadha Empire in 684 BC whose capital was Rajagriha, later Pataliputra, near the present day Patna. This dynasty was succeeded by the Shishunaga dynasty which, in turn, was overthrown by the Nanda dynasty in 424 BCE. The Nandas were followed by the Maurya dynasty.

Maurya Dynasty

In 321 BCE, exiled general Chandragupta Maurya, under direct patronage of the genius of Chanakya, founded the Maurya dynasty after overthrowing the reigning king Dhana Nanda. Most of the subcontinent was united under a single government for the first time under the Maurya rule. Mauryan empire under Chandragupta would not only conquer most of the Indian subcontinent, but also push its boundaries into Persia and Central Asia, conquering the Gandhara region. Chandragupta Maurya is credited for the spread of Jainism in southern Indian region.

Chandragupta was succeeded by his son Bindusara, who expanded the kingdom over most of present day India, barring Kalinga, and the extreme south and east, which may have held tributary status. Bindusara's kingdom was inherited by his son Ashoka the Great who initially sought to expand his kingdom. In the aftermath of the carnage caused in the invasion of Kalinga, he renounced bloodshed and pursued a policy of non-violence or ahimsa after converting to Buddhism. The Edicts of Ashoka are the oldest preserved historical documents of India, and from Ashoka's time, approximate dating of dynasties becomes possible. The Mauryan dynasty under Ashoka was responsible for the proliferation of Buddhist ideals across the whole of East Asia and South-East Asia, fundamentally altering the history and development of Asia as a whole. Ashoka's grandson Samprati adopted Jainism and helped spread Jainism.

Post Mauryan Magadha Dynasties

The Sunga Dynasty was established in 185 BCE, about fifty years after Ashoka's death, when the king Brihadratha, the last of the Mauryan rulers, was murdered by the then commander-in-chief of the Mauryan armed forces, Pusyamitra Sunga. The Kanva dynasty replaced the Sunga dynasty, and ruled in the eastern part of India from 71 BCE to 26 BCE. In 30 BCE, the southern power swept away both the Kanvas and Sungas. Following the collapse of the Kanva dynasty, the Satavahana dynasty of the Andhra kingdom replaced the Magadha kingdom as the most powerful Indian state.

Early Middle Kingdoms—the Golden Age

The middle period was a time of notable cultural development. The Satavahanas, also known as the Andhras, were a dynasty which ruled in Southern and Central India starting from around 230 BCE. Satakarni, the sixth ruler of the Satvahana dynasty, defeated the Sunga dynasty of North India. Gautamiputra Satakarni was another notable ruler of the dynasty. Kuninda Kingdom was a small Himalayan state that survived from around the 2nd century BCE to roughly the 3rd century CE. The Kushanas invaded north-western India about the middle of the 1st century CE, from Central Asia, and founded an empire that eventually stretched from Peshawar to the middle Ganges and, perhaps, as far as the Bay of Bengal. It also included ancient Bactria (in the north of modern Afghanistan) and southern Tajikistan. The Western Satraps (35-405 CE) were Saka rulers of the western and central part of India. They were the successors of the Indo-Scythians and contemporaneous with the Kushans who ruled the northern part of the Indian subcontinent, and the Satavahana (Andhra) who ruled in Central India.

Different empires such as the Pandyan Kingdom, Early Cholas, Chera dynasty, Kadamba Dynasty, Western Ganga Dynasty, Pallavas and Chalukya dynasty dominated the southern part of the Indian peninsula, at different periods of time. Several southern kingdoms formed overseas empires that stretched across South East Asia. The kingdoms warred with each other and Deccan states, for domination of the south. Kalabhras, a Buddhist kingdom, briefly interrupted the usual domination of the Cholas, Cheras and Pandyas in the South.

Northwestern Hybrid Cultures

The north-western hybrid cultures of the subcontinent included the *Indo-Greeks*, the *Indo-Scythians*, the *Indo-Parthians*, and the *Indo-Sassinids*. The first of these, the Indo-Greek Kingdom, founded when the Greco-Bactrian king Demetrius invaded the region in 180 BCE, extended over various parts of present-day Afghanistan and Pakistan. Lasting for almost two centuries, it was ruled by a succession of more than 30 Greek kings, who were often in conflict with each other. The Indo-Scythians were a branch of the Indo-European Sakas (Scythians), who migrated from southern Siberia first into Bactria, subsequently into Sogdiana, Kashmir, Arachosia, Gandhara and finally into India; their kingdom lasted from the middle of the 2nd century BCE to the 1st century BCE. Yet another kingdom, the Indo-Parthians (also known as Pahlavas) came to control most of present-day Afghanistan and northern Pakistan, after fighting many local rulers such as the Kushan ruler Kujula Kadphises, in the Gandhara region. The Sassanid empire of Persia, who were contemporaries of the Guptas, expanded into the region of present-day Pakistan, where the mingling of Indian and Persian cultures gave birth to the Indo-Sassanid culture.

Roman Trade with India

Roman trade with India started around 1 CE following the reign of Augustus and his conquest of Egypt, theretofore India's biggest trade partner in the West.

The trade started by Eudoxus of Cyzicus in 130 BCE kept increasing, and according to Strabo (II.5.12.), by the time of Augustus up to 120 ships were setting sail every year from Myos Hormos to India. So much gold was used for this trade, and apparently recycled by the Kushans for their own coinage, that Pliny (NH VI.101) complained about the drain of specie to India:

> "India, China and the Arabian peninsula take one hundred million sesterces from our empire per annum at a conservative estimate: that is what our luxuries and women cost us. For what percentage of these imports is intended for sacrifices to the gods or the spirits of the dead?"
>
> —*Pliny, Historia Naturae 12.41.84.*

These trade routes and harbour are described in detail in the 1st century CE Periplus of the Erythraean Sea.

Gupta Dynasty

In the 4th and 5th centuries, the Gupta Dynasty unified northern India. During this period, known as India's Golden Age of Hindu renaissance, Hindu culture, science and political administration reached new heights. Chandragupta I, Samudragupta, and Chandragupta II were the most notable rulers of the Gupta dynasty. The Vedic Puranas are also thought to have been written around this period. The empire came to an end with the attack of the Huns from central Asia. After the collapse of the Gupta Empire in the 6th century, India was again ruled by numerous regional kingdoms. A minor line of the Gupta clan continued to rule Magadha after the disintegration of the empire. These Guptas were ultimately ousted by the Vardhana king Harsha, who established an empire in the first half of the seventh century.

The White Huns, who seem to have been part of the Hephthalite group, established themselves in Afghanistan by the first half of the fifth century, with their capital at Bamiyan. They were responsible for the downfall of the Gupta dynasty, and thus brought an end to what historians consider a golden age in northern India. Nevertheless, much of the Deccan and southern India were largely unaffected by this state of flux in the north.

Late Middle Kingdoms—the Classical Age

The classical age in India began with the resurgence of the north during Harsha's conquests around the 7th century, and ended with the fall of the Vijayanagar Empire in the South, due to pressure from the invaders to the north in the 13th century. This period produced some of India's finest art, considered the epitome of classical development, and the development of the main spiritual and philosophical systems which continued to be in Hinduism, Buddhism and Jainism.

King Harsha of Kannauj succeeded in reuniting northern India during his reign in the 7th century, after the collapse of the Gupta dynasty. His kingdom collapsed after his death. From the 7th to the 9th century, three dynasties contested for control of northern India: the Pratiharas of Malwa and later Kannauj; the Palas of Bengal, and the Rashtrakutas of the Deccan. The Sena dynasty would later assume control of the Pala kingdom, and the Pratiharas fragmented into various states. These were the first of the Rajputs, a series of kingdoms which managed to survive in some form for almost a millennium until Indian independence from the British. The first recorded Rajput kingdoms emerged in Rajasthan in the 6th century, and small Rajput dynasties later ruled much of northern India. One Rajput of the Chauhan dynasty, Prithviraj Chauhan, was known for bloody conflicts against the encroaching Islamic Sultanates. The Shahi dynasty ruled portions of eastern Afghanistan, northern Pakistan, and Kashmir from the mid-seventh century to the early eleventh century. Whilst the northern concept of a pan-Indian empire had collapsed at the end of Harsha's empire, the ideal instead shifted to the south.

The Chalukya Empire ruled parts of southern and central India from 550 to 750 from Badami, Karnataka and again from 970 to 1190 from Kalyani, Karnataka. The Pallavas of Kanchi were their contemporaries further to the south. With the decline of the Chalukya empire, their feudatories, Hoysalas of Halebidu, Kakatiya of Warangal, Seuna Yadavas of Devagiri and a southern branch of the Kalachuri divided the vast Chalukya empire amongst themselves around the middle of 12th century. Later during the middle period, the Chola kingdom emerged in northern Tamil Nadu, and the Chera kingdom in Kerala. By 1343 A.D., all these kingdoms had ceased to exist giving rise to the Vijayanagar empire.

Southern Indian kingdoms of the time expanded their influence as far as Indonesia, controlling vast overseas empires in Southeast Asia. The ports of southern India were involved in the Indian Ocean trade, chiefly involving spices, with the Roman Empire to the west and Southeast Asia to the east. Literature in local vernaculars and spectacular architecture flourished till about the beginning of the 14th century when southern expeditions of the sultan of Delhi took their toll on these kingdoms. The Hindu Vijayanagar dynasty[Karnata Rajya] came into conflict with Islamic rule (the Bahmani Kingdom) and the clashing of the two systems, caused a mingling of the indigenous and foreign culture that left lasting cultural influences on each other. The Vijaynagar Empire eventually declined due to pressure from the first Delhi Sultanates who had managed to establish themselves in the north, centered around the city of Delhi by that time.

The Islamic Sultanates

After the Arab invasion of India's ancient western neighbour Persia, expanding forces in that area were keen to invade India, which was the richest classical civilization, with a flourishing international trade and the only known diamond mines in the world. After resistance for a few centuries by various north Indian kingdoms, short lived Islamic empires (Sultanates) got established and spread across the northern subcontinent over a period of a few centuries. But, prior to Turkic invasions, Muslim trading communities had flourished throughout coastal South India, particularly in Kerala, where they arrived in small numbers, mainly from the Arabian peninsula, through trade links via the Indian Ocean. However, this had marked the introduction of an Abrahamic Middle Eastern religion in Southern India's pre-existing dharmic Hindu culture, often in puritanical form. Later, the Bahmani Sultanate and Deccan sultanates flourished in the south.

Delhi Sultanate

In the 12th and 13th centuries, Arabs, Turks and Afghans invaded parts of northern India and established the Delhi Sultanate at the beginning of the 13th century, in the former Rajput holdings. The subsequent Slave dynasty of Delhi managed to conquer large areas of northern India, approximate to the ancient extent of the Guptas, while the Khilji Empire was also able to conquer most of central India, but were ultimately unsuccessful in conquering and uniting most of the subcontinent. The Sultanate ushered in a period of Indian cultural renaissance. The resulting "Indo-Muslim" fusion of cultures left lasting syncretic monuments in architecture, music, literature, religion, and clothing. It is surmised that the language of Urdu (literally meaning "horde" or "camp" in various Turkic dialects) was born during the Delhi Sultanate period as a result of the inter-mingling of the local speakers of Sanskritic prakrits with the Persian, Turkish and Arabic speaking immigrants under the Muslim rulers. The Delhi Sultanate is the only Indo-Islamic empire to stake a claim to enthroning one of the few female rulers in India, Razia Sultan (1236-1240).

A Turco-Mongol conqueror Timur began a trek starting in 1398 to invade the reigning Sultan Nasir-u Din Mehmud of the Tughlaq Dynasty in the north Indian city of Delhi. The Sultan's army was defeated on December 17, 1398. Timur entered Delhi and the city was sacked, destroyed, and left in ruins.

The Mughal Era

In 1526, Babur, a Timurid (Turco-Persian) descendant of Timur and Genghis Khan, swept across the Khyber Pass and established the Mughal Empire, which lasted for over 200 years. The Mughal Dynasty ruled most of the Indian subcontinent by 1600; it went into a slow decline after 1707 and was finally defeated during the *1857 war of independence* also called the Indian rebellion of 1857. This period marked vast social change in the subcontinent as the Hindu majority were ruled over by the Mughal emperors, some of whom showed religious tolerance, liberally patronising Hindu culture, and some of whom destroyed historical temples and imposed taxes on non-Muslims. During the decline of the Mughal Empire, which at its peak occupied an area slightly larger than the ancient Maurya Empire, several smaller empires rose to fill the power vacuum or themselves were contributing factors to the decline. The Mughals were perhaps the richest single dynasty to have ever existed. In 1739, Nader Shah defeated the Mughal army at the huge Battle of Karnal. After this victory, Nader captured and sacked Delhi, carrying away many treasures, including the Peacock Throne.

During the Mughal era, the dominant political forces consisted of the Mughal Empire and its tributaries and, later on, the rising successor states–including the Maratha confederacy–who fought an increasingly weak and disfavoured Mughal dynasty. The Mughals, while often employing brutal tactics to subjugate their empire, had a policy of integration with Indian culture, which is what made them successful where the short-lived Sultanates of Delhi had failed. Akbar the Great was particularly famed for this. Akbar declared "Amari" or non-killing of animals in the holy days of Jainism. He rolled back the *Jazia Tax* for non-Muslims. The Mughal Emperors married local royalty, allied themselves with local Maharajas, and attempted to fuse their Turko-Persian culture with ancient Indian styles, creating unique Indo-Saracenic architecture. It was the erosion of this tradition coupled with increased brutality and centralisation that played a large part in their downfall after Aurangzeb, who unlike previous emperors, imposed relatively non-pluralistic policies on the general population, that often inflamed the majority Hindu population.

Post-Mughal Regional Kingdoms

The post-Mughal era was dominated by the rise of the Maratha suzerianity as other small regional states (mostly post-Mughal tributary states) emerged, and also by the increasing activities of European powers. The Maratha Kingdom was founded and consolidated by Shivaji. By the 18th century, it had transformed itself into the Maratha Empire under the rule of the Peshwas. By 1760, the Empire had stretched across practically the entire subcontinent. This expansion was brought to an end by the defeat of the Marathas by an Afghan army led by Ahmad Shah Abdali at the Third Battle of Panipat (1761). The last Peshwa, Baji Rao II, was defeated by the British in the Third Anglo-Maratha War.

Mysore was a kingdom of southern India, which was founded around 1400 CE by the Wodeyar dynasty. The rule of the Wodeyars was interrupted by Hyder Ali and his son Tippu Sultan. Under their rule Mysore fought a series of wars sometimes against the combined forces of the British and Marathas, but mostly against the British with some aid or promise of aid from the French. Hyderabad was founded by the Qutb Shahi dynasty of Golconda in 1591. Following a brief Mughal rule, Asif Jah, a Mughal official, seized control of Hyderabad declaring himself Nizam-al-Mulk of Hyderabad in 1724. It was ruled by a hereditary Nizam from 1724 until 1948. Both Mysore and Hyderabad became princely states in British India.

The Punjabi kingdom, ruled by members of the Sikh religion, was a political entity that governed the region of modern day Punjab. This was among the last areas of the subcontinent to be conquered by the British. The Anglo-Sikh wars marked the downfall of the Sikh Empire. Around the 18th century modern Nepal was formed by Gorkha rulers, and the Shahs and the Ranas very strictly maintained their national identity and integrity.

Colonial Era

Vasco da Gama's maritime success to discover for Europeans a new sea route to India in 1498 paved the way for direct Indo-European commerce. The Portuguese soon set up trading-posts in Goa, Daman, Diu and Bombay. The next to arrive were the Dutch, the British—who set up a trading-post in the west-coast port of Surat in 1619—and the French. The internal conflicts among Indian Kingdoms gave opportunities to the European traders to gradually establish political influence and appropriate lands. Although these continental European powers were to control various regions of southern and eastern India during the ensuing century, they would eventually lose all their territories in India to the British islanders, with the exception of the French outposts of Pondicherry and Chandernagore, the Dutch port of Travancore, and the Portuguese colonies of Goa, Daman, and Diu.

The British East India Company had been given permission by the Mughal emperor Jahangir in 1617 to trade in India. Gradually their increasing influence led the *de-jure* Mughal emperor Farrukh Siyar to grant them *dastaks* or permits for duty free trade in Bengal in 1717. The Nawab of Bengal Siraj Ud Daulah, the *de facto* ruler of the Bengal province, opposed British attempts to use these permits. This led to the Battle of Plassey in 1757, in which the 'army' of East India Company, led by Robert Clive, defeated the Nawab's forces. This was the first political foothold with territorial implications that the British acquired in India. Clive was appointed by the Company as its first 'Governor of Bengal' in 1757. After the Battle of Buxar in 1764, the Company acquired the civil rights of administration in Bengal from the Mughal Emperor Shah Alam II; it marked the beginning of its formal rule, which was to engulf eventually most of India and extinguish the Moghul rule and dynasty itself in a century. The East

India Company monopolized the trade of Bengal. They introduced a land taxation system called the Permanent Settlement which introduced a feudal like structure in Bengal. By the 1850s, the East India Company controlled most of the Indian sub-continent, which included present-day Pakistan and Bangladesh. Their policy was sometimes summed up as Divide and Rule, taking advantage of the enmity festering between various princely states and social and religious groups.

The first major movement against the British Company's high handed rule resulted in the Indian Rebellion of 1857, also known as the "Indian Mutiny" or "Sepoy Mutiny" or the "First War of Independence". After a year of turmoil, and reinforcement of the East India Company's troops with British soldiers, the British overcame the rebellion. The nominal leader of the uprising, the last Mughal emperor Bahadur Shah Zafar, was exiled to Burma, his children were beheaded and the Moghul line abolished. In the aftermath all power was transferred from the East India Company to the British Crown, which began to administer most of India as a colony; the Company's lands were controlled directly and the rest through the rulers of what it called the Princely states.

The British Raj

The British East India Company had been given permission by the Mughal emperor Jahangir in 1617 to trade in India. Gradually their increasing influence led the *de-jure* Mughal emperor Farrukh Siyar to grant them *dastaks* or permits for duty free trade in Bengal in 1717. The Nawab of Bengal Siraj Ud Daulah, the *de facto* ruler of the Bengal province, opposed British attempts to use these permits. This led to the Battle of Plassey in 1757, in which the 'army' of East India Company, led by Robert Clive, defeated the Nawab's forces. This was the first political foothold with territorial implications that the British acquired in India. Clive was appointed by the Company as its first 'Governor of Bengal' in 1757. After the Battle of Buxar in 1764, the Company acquired the civil rights of administration in Bengal from the Mughal Emperor Shah Alam II; it marked the beginning of its formal rule, which was to engulf eventually most of India and extinguish the Moghul rule and dynasty itself in a century. The East India Company monopolized the trade of Bengal. They introduced a land taxation system called the Permanent Settlement which introduced a feudal like structure in Bengal. By the 1850s, the East India Company controlled most of the Indian sub-continent, which included present-day Pakistan and Bangladesh. Their policy was sometimes summed up as Divide and Rule, taking advantage of the enmity festering between various princely states and social and religious groups.

The first major movement against the British Company's high handed rule resulted in the Indian Rebellion of 1857, also known as the "Indian Mutiny" or "Sepoy Mutiny" or the "First War of Independence". After a year of turmoil, and reinforcement of the East India Company's troops with British soldiers, the British overcame the rebellion.

The nominal leader of the uprising, the last Mughal emperor Bahadur Shah Zafar, was exiled to Burma, his children were beheaded and the Moghul line abolished. In the aftermath all power was transferred from the East India Company to the British Crown, which began to administer most of India as a colony; the Company's lands were controlled directly and the rest through the rulers of what it called the Princely states.

INDIAN INDEPENDENCE MOVEMENT

The term "Indian independence movement" is diffuse, incorporating various national and regional campaigns, agitations and efforts of both Nonviolent and Militant philosophy and involved a wide spectrum of political organizations, philosophies, and movements which had the common aim of ending the British Colonial Authority as well as other colonial administrations in South Asia. The initial resistance to the movement can be traced back to the very beginnings of Colonial Expansion in Karnataka by the Portuguese in the 16th century and by the British East India Company in Bengal, in the middle and late 1700s. The first organised militant movement was in Bengal, that later took political stage in the form of mainstream movement from the latter part of the 1800s was increasingly led by the leaders of the then newly formed Indian National Congress with prominent moderate leaders seeking only their basic rights to appear for civil services examinations and more rights, economic in nature, for the people of the soil. They used moderate methods of prayer, petition and the press (3p's).

Beginning of early 1900s saw a more radical approach towards political independence proposed by leaders as the Lal Bal Pal and Sri Aurobindo. Militant nationalism also emerged in the first decades, culminating in the failed Indo-German Pact and Ghadar Conspiracy during the World War I. The end of the war saw the Congress adopt the policies of nonviolent agitation and civil disobedience led by Mahatma Gandhi. Other leaders, such as Netaji Subhash Chandra Bose, later came to adopt a military approach to the movement. The World War II period saw the peak of the movements like INA movement led by Netaji Subhas Chandra Bose from East Asia and Quit India movement.

India remained a Dominion of The Crown until 26 January 1950, when it adopted its Constitution to proclaim itself a Republic. Pakistan proclaimed itself a Republic in 1956 but faced a number of internal power struggles that has seen suspensions of democracy. In 1971, the Pakistani Civil War culminating in the 1971 War saw the splintering-off of East Pakistan into the nation of Bangladesh.

The independence movement also served as a major catalyst for similar movements in other parts of the world, leading to the eventual disintegration and dismantling of the British Empire and its replacement with the Commonwealth of Nations. Gandhi's philosophy of nonviolent resistance inspired the American Civil Rights Movement (1955-1968) led by Martin Luther King, Jr., the quest for democracy in Myanmar led by Aung San Suu Kyi and the African National Congress's struggle against apartheid in South Africa led by Nelson Mandela. However not all these leaders adhered to Gandhi's strict principle of nonviolence and nonresistance.

European Rule

European traders came to Indian shores with the arrival of the Portuguese explorer Vasco da Gama in 1498 at the port of Calicut in search of the lucrative spice trade. After the 1757 Battle of Plassey, during which the British army under Robert Clive defeated the Nawab of Bengal, the British East India Company established itself. This is widely seen as the beginning of the British Raj in India. The Company gained administrative rights over Bengal, Bihar, and Orissa in 1765 after the Battle of Buxar. They then annexed Punjab in 1849 after the death of Maharaja Ranjit Singh in 1839 and the First Anglo-Sikh War (1845–1846) and then the Second Anglo-Sikh War (1848–49).

The British parliament enacted a series of laws to handle the administration of the newly-conquered provinces, including the Regulating Act of 1773, the India Act of 1784, and the Charter Act of 1813; all enhanced the British government's rule. In 1835 English was made the medium of instruction. Western-educated Hindu elites sought to rid Hinduism of controversial social practices, including the *varna* (caste) system, child marriage, and *sati*. Literary and debating societies initiated in Bombay and Madras became fora for open political discourse. The educational attainment and skillful use of the press by these early reformers created the growing possibility for effecting broad reforms within colonial India, all without compromising larger Indian social values and religious practices.

Even while these modernising trends influenced Indian society, Indians increasingly despised British rule. The memoirs of Henry Ouvry of the 9th Lancers record many "a good thrashing" to careless servants. A spice merchant, Frank Brown, wrote to his nephew that stories of maltreatment of servants had not been exaggerated and that he knew people who kept orderlies "purposely to thrash them". As the British increasingly dominated the continent, they grew increasingly abusive of local customs by, for example, staging parties in mosques, dancing to the music of regimental bands on the terrace of the Taj Mahal, using whips to force their way through crowded bazaars (as recounted by General Henry Blake), and mistreating sepoys. In the years after the annexation of Punjab in 1849, several mutinies among sepoys broke out; these were put down by force.

Regional Movements Prior to 1857

Several regional movements against foreign rule were staged in various parts of pre-1857 India. However, they were not united and were easily controlled by the foreign rulers. Examples include the rebellion of Abbakka Rani in Karnataka from 1555 to 1570 against the Portuguese, Sannyasi Rebellion in Bengal in the 1770s, the 1787 ethnic revolt against Portuguese control of Goa known as the Conspiracy Of The Pintos, the revolt of Titumir in Bengal in 1830's and uprisings by South Indian local chieftains like Veerapandya Kattabomman against British rule. Other movements included the Santal Rebellion and the resistance offered to the British by Titumir in Bengal, the Kittur Rebellion led by Rani Chennamma in Karnataka, Polygar Wars in Tamil Nadu, Kutch Rebellion in Saurashtra.

The Indian Rebellion of 1857

The Indian Rebellion of 1857 was a period of uprising in the northern and central India against British rule in 1857–58. The rebellion was the result of decades of ethnic and cultural differences between Indian soldiers and their British officers. The indifference of the British towards Indian rulers like the Mughals and ex-Peshwas and the annexation of Oudh were political factors triggering dissent amongst Indians. Dalhousie's policy of annexation, the doctrine of lapse or escheat, and the projected removal of the descendants of the Great Mughal from their ancestral palace to the Qutb, near Delhi also angered some people. The specific reason that triggered the rebellion was the rumoured use of cow and pig fat in 557 calibre Pattern 1853 Enfield (P/53) rifle cartridges. Soldiers had to break the cartridges with their teeth before loading them into their rifles. So if there was cow and pig fat, it would be offensive to Hindu and Muslim soldiers, respectively. In February 1857, sepoys (Indian soldiers in the British army) refused to use their new cartridges. The British claimed to have replaced the cartridges with new ones and tried to make sepoys make their own grease from beeswax and vegetable oils, but the rumour persisted.

In March 1857, Mangal Pandey, a soldier of the 34th Native Infantry in Barrackpore, attacked his British sergeant and wounded an adjutant. General Hearsay, who said Pandey was in some kind of "religious frenzy," ordered a jemadar to arrest him but the jemadar refused. Mangal Pandey was hanged on 7 April along with the jemadar. The whole regiment was dismissed as a collective punishment. On May 10, when the 11th and 20th Cavalry assembled, they broke rank and turned on their commanding officers. They then liberated the 3rd Regiment, and on 11 May the sepoys reached Delhi and were joined by other Indians. The Red Fort, the residence of the last Mughal emperor Bahadur, was attacked and captured by the sepoys. They demanded that he reclaim his throne. He was reluctant at first, but eventually agreed to the demands and became the leader of the rebellion.

Soon, the revolt spread throughout northern India. Revolts broke out in places like Meerut, Jhansi, Kanpur, Lucknow etc. The British were slow to respond, but eventually responded with brute force. British moved regiments from the Crimean War and diverted European regiments headed for China to India. The British fought the main army of the rebels near Delhi in Badl-ke-Serai and drove them back to Delhi before laying siege on the city. The siege of Delhi lasted roughly from 1 July to 31 August. After a week of street fighting, the British retook the city. The last significant battle was fought in Gwalior on 20 June 1858. It was during this battle that Rani Lakshmi Bai was killed. Sporadic fighting continued until 1859 but most of the rebels were subdued. Some notable leaders were Ahmed Ullah, an advisor of the ex-King of Oudh; Nana Sahib; his nephew Rao Sahib and his retainers, Tantia Topi and Azimullah Khan; the Rani of Jhansi; Kunwar Singh; the Rajput chief of Jagadishpur in Bihar; Firuz Saha, a relative of the Mughal Emperor, Bahadur Shah and Pran Sukh Yadav who along with Rao Tula Ram of Rewari fought with Britishers at Nasibpur, Haryana.

Aftermath

The war of 1857 was a major turning point in the history of modern India. The British abolished the British East India Company and replaced it with direct rule under the British crown. A Viceroy was appointed to represent the Crown. In proclaiming the new direct-rule policy to "the Princes, Chiefs, and Peoples of India," Queen Victoria promised equal treatment under British law, but Indian mistrust of British rule had become a legacy of the 1857 rebellion.

The British embarked on a program in India of reform and political restructuring, trying to integrate Indian higher castes and rulers into the government. They stopped land grabs, decreed religious tolerance and admitted Indians into the civil service, albeit mainly as subordinates. They also increased the number of British soldiers in relation to native ones and allowed only British soldiers to handle artillery. Bahadur Shah was exiled to Rangoon, Burma where he died in 1862, finally bringing the Mughal dynasty to an end. In 1877, Queen Victoria took the title of Empress of India.

Rise of Organized Movements

The decades following the Sepoy Rebellion were a period of growing political awareness, manifestation of Indian public opinion and emergence of Indian leadership at national and provincial levels. Dadabhai Naoroji formed East India Association in 1867, and Surendranath Banerjee founded Indian National Association in 1876. Inspired by a suggestion made by A.O. Hume, a retired British civil servant, seventy-three Indian delegates met in Bombay in 1885 and founded the Indian National Congress. They were mostly members of the upwardly mobile and successful western-educated provincial elites, engaged in professions such as law, teaching, and journalism. At its inception, the Congress had no well-defined ideology and commanded few of the resources essential to a political organization. It functioned more as a debating society that met annually to express its loyalty to the British Raj and passed numerous resolutions on less controversial issues such as civil rights or opportunities in government, especially the civil service. These resolutions were submitted to the Viceroy's government and occasionally to the British Parliament, but the Congress's early gains were meagre. Despite its claim to represent all India, the Congress voiced the interests of urban elites; the number of participants from other economic backgrounds remained negligible.

The influences of socio-religious groups such as *Arya Samaj* (started by Swami Dayanand Saraswati) and *Brahmo Samaj* (founded, among others, by Raja Ram Mohan Roy) became evident in pioneering reform of Indian society. The inculcation of religious reform and social pride was fundamental to the rise of a public movement for complete nationhood. The work of men like Swami Vivekananda, Ramakrishna Paramhansa, Sri Aurobindo, Subramanya Bharathy, Bankim Chandra Chatterjee, Sir Syed Ahmed Khan, Rabindranath Tagore and Dadabhai Naoroji spread the passion for rejuvenation and freedom.

By 1900, although the Congress had emerged as an all-India political organization, its achievement was undermined by its singular failure to attract Muslims, who felt that their representation in government service was inadequate. Attacks by Hindu reformers against religious conversion, cow slaughter, and the preservation of Urdu in Arabic script deepened their concerns of minority status and denial of rights if the Congress alone were to represent the people of India. Sir Syed Ahmed Khan launched a movement for Muslim regeneration that culminated in the founding in 1875 of the Muhammadan Anglo-Oriental College at Aligarh, Uttar Pradesh (renamed Aligarh Muslim University in 1921). Its objective was to educate wealthy students by emphasizing the compatibility of Islam with modern western knowledge. The diversity among India's Muslims, however, made it impossible to bring about uniform cultural and intellectual regeneration.

Rise of Indian Nationalism

The first spurts of nationalistic sentiment that rose amongst Congress members were when the desire to be represented in the bodies of government, to have a say, a vote in the lawmaking and issues of administration of India. Congressmen saw themselves as loyalists, but wanted an active role in governing their own country, albeit as part of the Empire. This trend was personified by Dadabhai Naoroji, who went as far as contesting, successfully, an election to the British House of Commons, becoming its first Indian member.

Bal Gangadhar Tilak was the first Indian nationalist to embrace *Swaraj* as the destiny of the nation. Tilak deeply opposed the British education system that ignored and defamed India's culture, history and values. He resented the denial of freedom of expression for nationalists, and the lack of any voice or role for ordinary Indians in the affairs of their nation. For these reasons, he considered Swaraj as the natural and only solution. His popular sentence "Swaraj is my birthright, and I shall have it" became the source of inspiration for Indians.

In 1907, the Congress was split into two. Tilak advocated what was deemed as *extremism*. He wanted a direct assault by the people upon the British Raj, and the abandonment of all things British. He was backed by rising public leaders like Bipin Chandra Pal and Lala Lajpat Rai, who held the same point of view. Under them, India's three great states–Maharashtra, Bengal and Punjab shaped the demand of the people and India's nationalism. Gokhale criticized Tilak for encouraging acts of violence and disorder. But the Congress of 1906 did not have public membership, and thus Tilak and his supporters were forced to leave the party.

But with Tilak's arrest, all hopes for an Indian offensive were stalled. The Congress lost credit with the people, A Muslim deputation met with the Viceroy, Minto (1905–10), seeking concessions from the impending constitutional reforms, including special considerations in government service and electorates. The British recognised some of Muslim League's petitions by increasing the number of elective offices reserved for Muslims in the Government of India Act 1909. The Muslim League insisted on its separateness from the Hindu-dominated Congress, as the voice of a "nation within a nation."

Partition of Bengal

In 1905, Curzon, the Viceroy and Governor-General (1899–1905), ordered the partition of the province of Bengal for improvements in administrative efficiency in that huge and populous region, where the Bengali Hindu intelligentsia exerted considerable influence on local and national politics. The partition outraged Bengalis. Not only had the government failed to consult Indian public opinion, but the action appeared to reflect the British resolve to divide and rule. Widespread agitation ensued in the streets and in the press, and the Congress advocated boycotting British products under the banner of *swadeshi*. People showed unity by tying Rakhi on each other's wrists and observing *Arandhan* (not cooking any food).

During the partition of Bengal new methods of struggle were adopted. These led to swadeshi and boycott movements. The Congress-led boycott of British goods was so successful that it unleashed anti-British forces to an extent unknown since the Sepoy Rebellion. A cycle of violence and repression ensued in some parts of the country. The British tried to mitigate the situation by announcing a series of constitutional reforms in 1909 and by appointing a few moderates to the imperial and provincial councils. In what the British saw as an additional goodwill gesture, in 1911 King-Emperor George V visited India for a *durbār* (a traditional court held for subjects to express fealty to their ruler), during which he announced the reversal of the partition of Bengal and the transfer of the capital from Calcutta to a newly planned city to be built immediately south of Delhi, which later became New Delhi. However, ceremony of transfer on 23 December 1912 was marked by the attempt to assassinate the then Viceroy, Lord Hardinge, in what came to be known as the Delhi-Lahore conspiracy.

World War I

World War I began with an unprecedented outpouring of loyalty and goodwill towards the United Kingdom from within the mainstream political leadership, contrary to initial British fears of an Indian revolt. India contributed massively to the British war effort by providing men and resources. About 1.3 million Indian soldiers and labourers served in Europe, Africa, and the Middle East, while both the Indian government and the princes sent large supplies of food, money, and ammunition. However, Bengal and Punjab remained hotbeds of anti colonial activities. Terrorism in Bengal, increasingly closely linked with the unrests in Punjab, was significant enough to nearly paralyse the regional administration. Also from the beginning of the war, expatriate Indian population, notably from United States, Canada, and Germany, headed by the Berlin Committee and the Ghadar Party, attempted to trigger insurrections in India on the lines of the 1857 uprising with Irish Republican, German and Turkish help in a massive conspiracy that has since come to be called the Hindu German conspiracy. This conspiracy also attempted to rally Afghanistan against British India. A number of failed attempts were made at mutiny, of which the February mutiny plan and the Singapore mutiny remains most notable. This movement was suppressed by means of a massive international counter-intelligence operation and draconian political acts (including the Defence of India act 1915) that lasted nearly ten years.

In the aftermath of the WW I, high casualty rates, soaring inflation compounded by heavy taxation, a widespread influenza epidemic, and the disruption of trade during the war escalated human suffering in India. The Indian soldiers smuggled arms into India to overthrow the British rule. The prewar nationalist movement revived as moderate and extremist groups within the Congress submerged their differences in order to stand as a unified front. In 1916, the Congress succeeded in forging the Lucknow Pact, a temporary alliance with the Muslim League over the issues of devolution of political power and the future of Islam in the region.

The British themselves adopted a "carrot and stick" approach in recognition of India's support during the war and in response to renewed nationalist demands. In

August 1917, Edwin Montagu, the secretary of state for India, made the historic announcement in Parliament that the British policy for India was "increasing association of Indians in every branch of the administration and the gradual development of self-governing institutions with a view to the progressive realization of responsible government in India as an integral part of the British Empire." The means of achieving the proposed measure were later enshrined in the Government of India Act 1919, which introduced the principle of a dual mode of administration, or diarchy, in which both elected Indian legislators and appointed British officials shared power. The act also expanded the central and provincial legislatures and widened the franchise considerably. Diarchy set in motion certain real changes at the provincial level: a number of non-controversial or "transferred" portfolios, such as agriculture, local government, health, education, and public works, were handed over to Indians, while more sensitive matters such as finance, taxation, and maintaining law and order were retained by the provincial British administrators.

Gandhi Arrives in India

Mahatma Gandhi had been a prominent leader of the anti-Apartheid movement in South Africa, and had been a vocal opponent of basic discrimination and abusive labour treatment as well as suppressive police control such as the Rowlatt Acts. During these protests, Gandhi had perfected the concept of *satyagraha,* which had been inspired by the philosophy of Baba Ram Singh (famous for leading the Kuka Movement in the Punjab in 1872). The end of the protests in South Africa saw oppressive legislation repealed and the release of political prisoners by General Jan Smuts, head of the South African Government of the time.

Gandhi, a stranger to India and its politics after twenty years, had initially entered the fray not with calls for a nation-state, but in support of the unified commerce-oriented territory that the Congress Party had been asking for. Gandhi believed that the industrial development and educational development that the Europeans had brought with them were required to alleviate many of India's problems. Gopal Krishna Gokhale, a veteran Congressman and Indian leader, became Gandhi's mentor. Gandhi's ideas and strategies of non-violent civil disobedience initially appeared impractical to some Indians and Congressmen. In Gandhi's own words, "civil disobedience is civil breach of unmoral statutory enactments." It had to be carried out non-violently by withdrawing cooperation with the corrupt state. Gandhi's ability to inspire millions of common people became clear when he used satyagraha during the anti-Rowlatt Act protests in Punjab.

Gandhi's vision would soon bring millions of regular Indians into the movement, transforming it from an elitist struggle to a national one. The nationalist cause was expanded to include the interests and industries that formed the economy of common Indians. For example, in Champaran, Bihar, the Congress Party championed the plight of desperately poor sharecroppers and landless farmers who were being forced to pay oppressive taxes and grow cash crops at the expense of the subsistence crops which formed their food supply. The profits from the crops they grew were insufficient to provide for their sustenance.

The Rowlatt Act and its Aftermath

The positive impact of reform was seriously undermined in 1919 by the Rowlatt Act, named after the recommendations made the previous year to the Imperial Legislative Council by the Rowlatt Commission, which had been appointed to investigate what was termed the "seditious conspiracy" and the German and Bolshevik involvement in the militant movements in India. The Rowlatt Act, also known as the Black Act, vested the Viceroy's government with extraordinary powers to quell sedition by silencing the press, detaining the political activists without trial, and arresting any individuals suspected of sedition or treason without a warrant. In protest, a nationwide cessation of work (*hartal*) was called, marking the beginning of widespread, although not nationwide, popular discontent. The agitation unleashed by the acts culminated on 13 April 1919, in the Jallianwala Bagh massacre (also known as the Amritsar Massacre) in Amritsar, Punjab. The British military commander, Brigadier-General Reginald Dyer, blocked the main entrance, and ordered his soldiers to fire into an unarmed and unsuspecting crowd of some 5,000 men, women and children. They had assembled at Jallianwala Bagh, a walled in courtyard in defiance of the ban. A total of 1,651 rounds were fired, killing 379 people (as according to an official British commission; Indian estimates ranged as high as 1,499) and wounding 1,137 in the episode, which dispelled wartime hopes of home rule and goodwill in a frenzy of post-war reaction.

The Non-cooperation Movements

It can be argued that the independence movement, even towards the end of First World War, was far removed from the masses of India, focusing essentially on a unified commerce-oriented territory and hardly a call for a united nation. That came in the 1930s with the entry of Mohandas Karamchand Gandhi into Indian Politics in 1915.

The first Non-cooperation Movement

The first satyagraha movement urged the use of Khadi and Indian material as alternatives to those shipped from Britain. It also urged people to boycott British educational institutions and law courts; resign from government employment; refuse to pay taxes; and forsake British titles and honours. Although this came too late to influence the framing of the new Government of India Act of 1919, the movement enjoyed widespread popular support, and the resulting unparalleled magnitude of disorder presented a serious challenges to foreign rule. However, Gandhi called off the movement following the Chauri Chaura incident, which saw the death of twenty-two policemen at the hands of an angry mob.

In 1920, the Congress was reorganized and given a new constitution, whose goal was *Swaraj* (independence). Membership in the party was opened to anyone prepared to pay a token fee, and a hierarchy of committees was established and made responsible for discipline and control over a hitherto amorphous and diffuse movement. The party was transformed from an elite organization to one of mass national appeal and participation.

Gandhi was sentenced in 1922 to six years of prison, but was released after serving two. On his release from prison, he set up the Sabarmati Ashram in Ahmedabad, on the banks of river Sabarmati, established the newspaper *Young India*, and inaugurated a series of reforms aimed at the socially disadvantaged within Hindu society–the rural poor, and the untouchables.

This era saw the emergence of new generation of Indians from within the Congress Party, including C. Rajagopalachari, Jawaharlal Nehru, Vallabhbhai Patel, Subhash Chandra Bose and others- who would later on come to form the prominent voices of the Indian independence movement, whether keeping with Gandhian Values, or diverging from it.

The Indian political spectrum was further broadened in the mid-1920s by the emergence of both moderate and militant parties, such as the Swaraj Party, Hindu Mahasabha, Communist Party of India and the Rashtriya Swayamsevak Sangh. Regional political organizations also continued to represent the interests of non-Brahmins in Madras, Mahars in Maharashtra, and Sikhs in Punjab. However, brahmins like Mahakavi Subramanya Bharathi, Vanchinathan and Neelakanda Brahmachari played a major role from Tamil Nadu in both freedom struggle and fighting for equality for all castes and communities.

Purna Swaraj

Following the rejection of the recommendations of the Simon Commission by Indians, an all-party conference was held at Bombay in May 1928. This was meant to instil a sense of resistance among people. The conference appointed a drafting committee under Motilal Nehru to draw up a constitution for India. The Calcutta session of the Indian National Congress asked the British government to accord dominion status to India by December 1929, or a countrywide civil disobedience movement would be launched. By 1929, however, in the midst rising political discontent and increasingly violent regional movements, the call for complete independence from Britain began to find increasing grounds within the Congress leadership. Under the presidency of Jawaharlal Nehru at its historic Lahore session in December 1929, The Indian National Congress adopted a resolution calling for complete independence from the British. It authorised the Working Committee to launch a civil disobedience movement throughout the country. It was decided that 26 January 1930 should be observed all over India as the *Purna Swaraj* (total independence) Day. Many Indian political parties and Indian revolutionaries of a wide spectrum united to observe the day with honour and pride.

Salt March and Civil Disobedience

Gandhi emerged from his long seclusion by undertaking his most famous campaign, a march of about 400 kilometres from his commune in Ahmedabad to Dandi, on the coast of Gujarat between 12 March and 6 April 1930. The march is usually known as the *Dandi March* or the *Salt Satyagraha*. At Dandi, in protest against British taxes on salt, he and thousands of followers broke the law by making their own salt from seawater.

In April 1930 there were violent police-crowd clashes in Calcutta. Approximately over 100,000 people were imprisoned in the course of the Civil disobedience movement (1930-31), while in Peshawar unarmed demonstrators were fired upon in the Qissa Khwani bazaar massacre. The latter event catapulted the then newly formed Khudai Khidmatgar movement (founder Khan Abdul Ghaffar Khan, the *Frontier Gandhi*) onto the National scene. While Gandhi was in jail, the first Round Table Conference was held in London in November 1930, without representation from the Indian National Congress. The ban upon the Congress was removed because of economic hardships caused by the satyagraha. Gandhi, along with other members of the Congress Working Committee, was released from prison in January 1931.

In March of 1931, the Gandhi-Irwin Pact was signed, and the government agreed to set all political prisoners free (Although, some of the key revolutionaries were not set free and the death sentence for Bhagat Singh and his two comrades was not taken back which further intensified the agitation against Congress not only outside it but with in the Congress it self). In return, Gandhi agreed to discontinue the civil disobedience movement and participate as the sole representative of the Congress in the second Round Table Conference, which was held in London in September 1931. However, the conference ended in failure in December 1931. Gandhi returned to India and decided to resume the civil disobedience movement in January 1932.

For the next few years, the Congress and the government were locked in conflict and negotiations until what became the Government of India Act of 1935 could be hammered out. By then, the rift between the Congress and the Muslim League had become unbridgeable as each pointed the finger at the other acrimoniously. The Muslim League disputed the claim of the Congress to represent all people of India, while the Congress disputed the Muslim League's claim to voice the aspirations of all Muslims.

Elections and the Lahore Resolution

The Government of India Act 1935, the voluminous and final constitutional effort at governing British India, articulated three major goals: establishing a loose federal structure, achieving provincial autonomy, and safeguarding minority interests through separate electorates. The federal provisions, intended to unite princely states and British India at the centre, were not implemented because of ambiguities in safeguarding the existing privileges of princes. In February 1937, however, provincial autonomy became a reality when elections were held; the Congress emerged as the dominant party with a clear majority in five provinces and held an upper hand in two, while the Muslim League performed poorly.

In 1939, the Viceroy Linlithgow declared India's entrance into World War II without consulting provincial governments. In protest, the Congress asked all of its elected representatives to resign from the government. Jinnah, the president of the Muslim League, persuaded participants at the annual Muslim League session at Lahore in 1940 to adopt what later came to be known as the Lahore Resolution, demanding the division of India into two separate sovereign states, one Muslim, the other Hindu; sometimes referred to as Two Nation Theory. Although the idea of Pakistan had been introduced as early as 1930, very few had responded to it. However, the volatile political climate and hostilities between the Hindus and Muslims transformed the idea of Pakistan into a stronger demand.

Revolutionary Activities

Apart from a few stray incidents, the armed rebellion against the British rulers was not organized before the beginning of the 20th century. The Indian revolutionary underground began gathering momentum through the first decade of 1900s, with groups arising in Maharastra, Bengal, Orissa, Bihar, Uttar Pradesh, Punjab, and the then Madras Presidency including what is now called South India. More groups were scattered around India. Particularly notable movements arose in Bengal, especially around the Partition of Bengal in 1905, and in Punjab. In the former case, it was the educated, intelligent and dedicated youth of the urban Middle Class *Bhadralok* community that came to form the "Classic" Indian revolutionary, while the latter had an immense support base in the rural and Military society of the Punjab. Organisations like Jugantar and Anushilan Samiti had emerged in the 1900s. The revolutionary philosophies and movement made their presence felt during the 1905 Partition of Bengal. Arguably, the initial steps to organize the revolutionaries were taken by Aurobindo Ghosh, his brother Barin Ghosh, Bhupendranath Datta etc. when they formed the Jugantar party in April 1906. Jugantar was created as an inner circle of the Anushilan Samiti which was already present in Bengal mainly as a revolutionary society in the guise of a fitness club.

The Anushilan Samiti and Jugantar opened several branches throughout Bengal and other parts of India and recruited young men and women to participate in the revolutionary activities. Several murders and looting were done, with many revolutionaries being captured and imprisoned. The Jugantar party leaders like Barin Ghosh and Bagha Jatin initiated making of explosives. Amongst a number of notable events of political terrorism were the Alipore bomb case, the Muzaffarpur killing tried several activists and many were sentenced to deportation for life, while Khudiram Bose was hanged. The founding of the India House and The Indian Sociologist under Shyamji Krishna Varma in London in 1905 took the radical movement to Britain itself. On 1 July 1909, Madan Lal Dhingra, an Indian student closely identified with India House in London shot dead William Hutt Curzon Wylie, a British M.P. in London. 1912 saw the Delhi-Lahore Conspiracy planned under Rash Behari Bose, an erstwhile Jugantar member, to assassinate the then Viceroy of India Charles Hardinge. The conspiracy culminated in an attempt to Bomb the Viceregal procession on 23 December 1912, on the occasion of transferring the Imperial Capital from Calcutta to Delhi. In the aftermath of this event, concentrated police and intelligence efforts were made by the British Indian police to destroy the Bengali and Punjabi revolutionary underground, which came under intense pressure for sometime. Rash Behari successfully evaded capture for nearly three years. However, by the time that WW I opened in Europe, the revolutionary movement in Bengal (and Punjab) had revived and was strong enough to nearly paralyse the local administration.

During the First World War, the revolutionaries planned to import arms and ammunitions from Germany and stage an armed revolution against the British.

The Ghadar Party operated from abroad and cooperated with the revolutionaries in India. This party was instrumental in helping revolutionaries inside India catch hold of foreign arms.

After the First World War, the revolutionary activities began to slowly wane as it suffered major setbacks due to the arrest of prominent leaders. In the 1920s, some revolutionary activists began to reorganize. Hindustan Socialist Republican Association was formed under the leadership of Chandrasekhar Azad. Bhagat Singh and Batukeshwar Dutt threw a bomb inside the Central Legislative Assembly on 8 April 1929 protesting against the passage of the Public Safety Bill and the Trade Disputes Bill. Following the trial (Central Assembly Bomb Case), Bhagat Singh, Sukhdev and Rajguru were hanged in 1931. Allama Mashriqi founded Khaksar Tehreek in order to direct particularly the Muslims towards the independence movement.

Surya Sen, along with other activists, raided the Chittagong armoury on 18 April 1930 to capture arms and ammunition and to destroy government communication system to establish a local governance. Pritilata Waddedar led an attack on a European club in Chittagong in 1932, while Bina Das attempted to assassinate Stanley Jackson, the Governor of Bengal inside the convocation hall of Calcutta University. Following the Chittagong armoury raid case, Surya Sen was hanged and several others were deported for life to the Cellular Jail in Andaman. The Bengal Volunteers started operating in 1928. On 8 December 1930, the Benoy-Badal-Dinesh trio of the party entered the secretariat Writers' Building in Kolkata and murdered Col. N. S. Simpson, the Inspector General of Prisons.

On 13 March 1940, Udham Singh shot Michael O'Dwyer, generally held responsible for the Amritsar Massacre, in London. However, as the political scenario changed in the late 1930s — with the mainstream leaders considering several options offered by the British and with religious politics coming into play — revolutionary activities gradually declined. Many past revolutionaries joined mainstream politics by joining Congress and other parties, especially communist ones, while many of the activists were kept under hold in different jails across the country.

The Climax: War, Quit India, INA and Post-war Revolts

Indians throughout the country were divided over World War II, as Linlithgow, without consulting the Indian representatives had unilaterally declared India a belligerent on the side of the allies. In opposition to Linlithgow's action, the entire Congress leadership resigned from the local government councils. However, many wanted to support the British war effort, and indeed the British Indian Army was one of the largest volunteer forces during the war. Especially during the Battle of Britain, Gandhi resisted calls for massive civil disobedience movements that came from within as well as outside his party, stating he did not seek India's freedom out of the ashes of a destroyed Britain. However, like the changing fortunes of the war itself, the movement for freedom saw the rise of two movements that formed the climax of the 100-year struggle for independence.

The first of these, the Azad Hind movement led by Netaji Subhash Chandra Bose, saw its inception early in the war and sought help from the Axis Powers. The second saw its inception in August 1942 led by Gandhi and began following failure of the Cripps' mission to reach a consensus with the Indian political leadership over the transfer of power after the war.

The Indian National Army

The arbitrary entry of India into the war was strongly opposed by Subhash Chandra Bose, who had been elected President of the Congress twice, in 1937 and 1939. After lobbying against participation in the war, he resigned from Congress in 1939 and started a new party, the All India Forward Bloc. When war broke out, the Raj had put him under house arrest in Calcutta in 1940. However, at the time the war was at its bloodiest in Europe and Asia, he escaped and made his way through Afghanistan to Germany to seek Axis help to raise an army to fight the shackles of the Raj. Here, he raised with Rommel's Indian POWs what came to be known as the Free India Legion. This came to be the conceptualisation in embryonic form of Bose's dream of raising a liberation Army to fight the Raj. However, the turn of tides in the Battlefields of Europe saw Bose make his way ultimately to Japanese South Asia where he formed what came to be known as the Azad Hind Government as the Provisional Free Indian Government in exile, and organized the Indian National Army with Indian POWs and Indian expatriates at South-East Asia, with the help of the Japanese. Its aim was to reach India as a fighting force that would build on public resentment to inspire revolts among Indian soldiers to defeat the Raj.

The INA was to see action against the allies, including the British Indian Army, in the forests of in Arakan, Burma and Assam, laying siege on Imphal and Kohima with the Japanese 15th Army. During the war, the Andaman and Nicobar islands were captured by the Japanese and handed over by them to the INA; Bose renamed them *Shahid* (Martyr) and *Swaraj* (Independence).

The INA would ultimately fail, owing to disrupted logistics, poor arms and supplies from the Japanese, and lack of support and training. The supposed death of Bose is seen as culmination of the entire Azad Hind Movement. Following the surrender of Japan, the troops of the INA were brought to India and a number of them charged with treason. However, Bose's audacious actions and radical initiative had by this time captured the public imagination and also turned the inclination of the native soldiers of the British Indian Forces from one of loyalty to the crown to support for the soldiers that the Raj deemed as collaborators.

After the war, the stories of the Azad Hind movement and its army that came into public limelight during the trials of soldiers of the INA in 1945 were seen as so inflammatory that, fearing mass revolts and uprisings — not just in India, but across its empire — the British Government forbade the BBC from broadcasting their story. Newspapers reported the summary execution of INA soldiers held at Red Fort. During and after the trial, mutinies broke out in the British Indian Armed forces, most notably in the Royal Indian Navy which found public support throughout India, from Karachi to Bombay and from Vizag to Calcutta. Many historians have argued that it was the INA and the mutinies it inspired among the British Indian Armed forces that were the true driving force behind India's final independence.

Quit India

The Quit India Movement *(Bharat Chhodo Andolan)* or the *August Movement* was a civil disobedience movement in India launched in August 1942 in response to Gandhi's call for immediate independence of India and against sending Indians to the World War II.

At the outbreak of war, the Congress Party had during the Wardha meeting of the working-committee in September 1939, passed a resolution conditionally supporting the fight against fascism, but were rebuffed when they asked for independence in return. In March 1942, faced with an increasingly dissatisfied sub-continent only reluctantly participating in the war, and deteriorations in the war situation in Europe and South East Asia, and with growing dissatisfactions among Indian troops- especially in Europe- and among the civilian population in the sub-continent, the British government sent a delegation to India under Stafford Cripps, in what came to be known as the Cripps' Mission. The purpose of the mission was to negotiate with the Indian National Congress a deal to obtain total co-operation during the war, in return of progressive devolution and distribution of power from the crown and the Viceroy to elected Indian legislature. However, the talks failed, having failed to address the key demand of a timeframe towards self-government, and of definition of the powers to be relinquished, essentially portraying an offer of limited dominion-status that was wholly unacceptable to the Indian movement. To force the Raj to meet its demands and to obtain definitive word on total independence, the Congress took the decision to launch the Quit India Movement.

The aim of the movement was to bring the British Government to the negotiating table by holding the Allied War Effort hostage. The call for determined but passive resistance that signified the certitude that Gandhi foresaw for the movement is best described by his call to *Do or Die,* issued on 8 August at the Gowalia Tank Maidan in Bombay, since re-named *August Kranti Maidan* (August Revolution Ground). However, almost the entire Congress leadership, and not merely at the national level, was put into confinement less than twenty-four hours after Gandhi's speech, and the greater number of the Congress khiland were to spend the rest of the war in jail.

On August 8, 1942, the Quit India resolution was passed at the Bombay session of the All India Congress Committee (AICC). The draft proposed that if the British did not accede to the demands, a massive Civil Disobedience would be launched. However, it was an extremely controversial decision. At Gowalia Tank, Mumbai, Gandhi urged Indians to follow a non-violent civil disobedience. Gandhi told the masses to act as an independent nation and not to follow the orders of the British. The British, already alarmed by the advance of the Japanese army to the India–Burma border, responded the next day by imprisoning Gandhi at the Aga Khan Palace in Pune. The Congress Party's Working Committee, or national leadership was arrested all together and imprisoned at the Ahmednagar Fort. They also banned the party altogether. Large-scale protests and demonstrations were held all over the country. Workers remained absent en masse and strikes were called. The movement also saw widespread acts of sabotage, Indian under-ground organisation carried out bomb attacks on allied supply convoys, government buildings were set on fire, electricity lines were disconnected and transport and communication lines were severed. The Congress had lesser success in rallying other political forces, including the Muslim League under a single mast and movement. It did however, obtain passive support from a substantial Muslim population at the peak of the movement.

The British swiftly responded by mass detentions. A total over 100,000 arrests were made nationwide, mass fines were levied, bombs were airdropped and demonstrators were subjected to public flogging. The movement soon became a leaderless act of defiance, with a number of acts that deviated from Gandhi's principle of non-violence. In large parts of the country, the local underground organisations took over the movement. However, by 1943, *Quit India* had petered out.

RIN Mutiny

The Royal Indian Navy Mutiny (the RIN Mutiny or the Bombay Mutiny) encompasses a total strike and subsequent mutiny by the Indian sailors of the Royal Indian Navy on board ship and shore establishments at Bombay (Mumbai) harbour on 18 February 1946. From the initial flashpoint in Bombay, the mutiny spread and found support through India, from Karachi to Calcutta and ultimately came to involve 78 ships, 20 shore establishments and 20,000 sailors.

The RIN Mutiny started as a strike by ratings of the Royal Indian Navy on the 18th February in protest against general conditions. The immediate issues of the mutiny were conditions and food, but there were more fundamental matters such as racist behaviour by British officers of the Royal Navy personnel towards Indian sailors, and disciplinary measures being taken against anyone demonstrating pro-nationalist sympathies. By dusk on 19 February, a Naval Central Strike committee was elected. Leading Signalman M.S Khan and Petty Officer Telegraphist Madan Singh were unanimously elected President and Vice-President respectively.

The strike found immense support among the Indian population already in grips with the stories of the Indian National Army. The actions of the mutineers were supported by demonstrations which included a one-day general strike in Bombay. The strike spread to other cities, and was joined by the Air Force and local police forces. Naval officers and men began calling themselves the Indian National Navy and offered left-handed salutes to British officers. At some places, NCOs in the British Indian Army ignored and defied orders from British superiors. In Madras and Pune, the British garrisons had to face revolts within the ranks of the British Indian Army. Widespread rioting took place from Karachi to Calcutta. Famously the ships hoisted three flags tied together — those of the Congress, Muslim League, and the Red Flag of the Communist Party of India (CPI), signifying the unity and demarginalisation of communal issues among the mutineers.

Independence, 1947 to 1950

On 3 June 1947, Viscount Louis Mountbatten, the last British Governor-General of India, announced the partitioning of the British Indian Empire into a secular India and a Muslim Pakistan. On 14 August 1947, Pakistan was declared a separate nation from them. At midnight, on 15 August 1947, India became an independent nation. Violent clashes between Hindus, Muslims, and Sikhs followed. Prime Minister Nehru and Deputy Prime Minister Sardar Vallabhbhai Patel invited Mountbatten to continue as Governor General of India. He was replaced in June 1948 by Chakravarti Rajagopalachari. Patel took on the responsibility of unifying 565 princely states, steering efforts by his "iron fist in a velvet glove" policies, exemplified by the use of military force to integrate Junagadh, Jammu and Kashmir, and Hyderabad state (Operation Polo) into India.

The Constituent Assembly completed the work of drafting the constitution on 26 November 1949; on 26 January 1950 the Republic of India was officially proclaimed. The Constituent Assembly elected Dr. Rajendra Prasad as the first President of India, taking over from Governor General Rajgopalachari. Subsequently, a free and sovereign India absorbed three other territories: Goa (from Portuguese control in 1961), Pondicherry (which the French ceded in 1953–1954) and Sikkim which was absorbed in 1975. In 1952, India held its first general elections, with a voter turnout exceeding 62%).

Partition of India

The Partition of India was the partition of the British Indian Empire which led to the creation, on August 14, 1947 and August 15, 1947, respectively, of the sovereign states of the Dominion of Pakistan (later Islamic Republic of Pakistan and People's Republic of Bangladesh) and the Union of India (later Republic of India). "Partition" here refers not only to the division of the Bengal province of British India into East

Pakistan and West Bengal (India), and the similar partition of the Punjab province into Punjab (West Pakistan) and Punjab (India), but also to the respective divisions of other assets, including the British Indian Army, the Indian Civil Service and other administrative services, the railways, and the central treasury.

The secession of Bangladesh from Pakistan in 1971 is not covered by the term *Partition of India,* nor is the earlier separation of Burma (from the administration of British India, or the even earlier separation of Ceylon (now Sri Lanka). Ceylon, part of the Madras Presidency of British India from 1795 until 1798, became a separate Crown Colony in 1798. Burma, gradually annexed by the British during 1826–86 and governed as a part of the British Indian administration until 1937, was directly administered thereafter. Burma was granted independence on January 4, 1948 and Ceylon on February 4, 1948. The Kingdom of Sikkim was established as a princely state after the *Anglo-Sikkimese Treaty* of 1861, however, the issue of sovereignty was left undefined. In 1947, Sikkim became an independent kingdom under the suzerainty of India and remained so until 1975 when it was absorbed into India as the 22nd state.

The remaining countries of present-day South Asia are Nepal, Bhutan, and the Maldives. The first two, Nepal and Bhutan, having signed treaties with the British designating them as *independent states,* were never a part of British India, and therefore their borders were not affected by the partition. The Maldives, which became a protectorate of the British crown in 1887 and gained its independence in 1965, was also unaffected by the partition.

Partition was accompanied by the largest and most rapid population transfer in history, with 17.9 million people leaving their homes. Of these, only 14.5 million arrived, suggesting that 3.4 million went "missing".

Pakistan and India

Two self governing countries legally came into existence at the stroke of midnight on 15 August 1947. The ceremonies for the transfer of power were held a day earlier in Karachi, at the time the capital of the new state of Pakistan, so that the last British Viceroy, Louis Mountbatten, could attend both the ceremony in Karachi as well as the ceremony in Delhi. However another reason for this arrangement was to make it not appear that Pakistan was seceding from a sovereign India. Therefore Pakistan celebrates Independence Day on August 14, while India celebrates it on August 15.

Another reason for Pakistan celebrating independence on August 14 is the adoption of new standard time in Pakistan after partition.The new standard time of Pakistan is behind Indian standard time by 30 minutes, so technically on the stroke of midnight falling between August 14 and 15, when India and Pakistan were "created" and "got independence", it was still 11:30 PM of 14 August in the Pakistan (West Pakistan to be specific). Although there is no evidence that the Pakistani government asked the general public to set their clocks to the new standard time, as there were far more pressing tasks at hand just after independence.

Background

1920–1932

The All India Muslim League (AIML) was formed in Dhaka in 1906 by Muslims who were suspicious of the mainstream, secular but Hindu-majority Indian National Congress. A number of different scenarios were proposed at various times. Among the first to make the demand for a separate state was the writer/philosopher Allama Iqbal, who, in his presidential address to the 1930 convention of the Muslim League said that he felt a separate nation for Muslims was essential in an otherwise Hindu-dominated subcontinent. The Sindh Assembly passed a resolution making it a demand in 1935. Iqbal, Jouhar and others then worked hard to draft Mohammad Ali Jinnah, who had till then worked for Hindu-Muslim unity, to lead the movement for this new nation. By 1930, Jinnah had begun to despair of the fate of minority communities in a united India and had begun to argue that mainstream parties such as the Congress, of which he was once a member, were insensitive to Muslim interests. The 1932 communal award which seemed to threaten the position of Muslims in Hindu-majority provinces catalysed the resurgence of the Muslim League, with Jinnah as its leader. However, the League did not do well in the 1937 provincial elections, demonstrating the hold of the conservative and local forces at the time.

1932–1942

In 1940, Jinnah made a statement at the Lahore conference, which seemed to be calling for a separate Muslim 'nation'. However, the document was ambiguous and opaque, and did not evoke a Muslim nation in a territorial sense. This idea, though, was taken up by Muslims and particularly Hindus in the next seven years, and given a more territorial element. All Muslim political parties including the Khaksar Tehrik of Allama Mashriqi (Mashriqi was arrested on March 19, 1940) opposed the partition of India

Hindu organisations such as the Hindu Mahasabha, though against the division of the country, were also insisting on the same chasm between Hindus and Muslims. In 1937 at the 19th session of the Hindu Mahasabha held at Ahmedabad, Veer Savarkar in his presidential address asserted:

> "India cannot be assumed today to be Unitarian and homogeneous nation, but on the contrary there are two nations in the main — the Hindus and the Muslims."

Most of the Congress leaders were secularists and resolutely opposed the division of India on the lines of religion. Mohandas Gandhi and Allama Mashriqi believed that Hindus and Muslims could and should live in amity. Gandhi opposed the partition, saying,

"My whole soul rebels against the idea that Hinduism and Islam represent two antagonistic cultures and doctrines. To assent to such a doctrine is for me a denial of God."

For years, Gandhi and his adherents struggled to keep Muslims in the Congress Party (a major exit of many Muslim activists began in the 1930s), in the process enraging both Hindu Nationalists and Indian Muslim Nationalists. (Gandhi was assassinated soon after Partition by Hindu Nationalist Nathuram Godse, who believed that Gandhi was appeasing Muslims at the cost of Hindus.) Politicians and community leaders on both sides whipped up mutual suspicion and fear, culminating in dreadful events such as the riots during the Muslim League's *Direct Action Day* of August 1946 in Calcutta, in which more than 5,000 people were killed and many more injured. As public order broke down all across northern India and Bengal, the pressure increased to seek a political partition of territories as a way to avoid a full-scale civil war.

1942–1946

Until 1946, the definition of Pakistan as demanded by the League was so flexible that it could have been interpreted as a sovereign nation Pakistan, or as a member of a confederated India.

Some historians believe Jinnah intended to use the threat of partition as a bargaining chip in order to gain more independence for the Muslim dominated provinces in the west from the Hindu dominated center.

Other historians claim that Jinnah's real vision was for a Pakistan that extended into Hindu-majority areas of India, by demanding the inclusion of the East of Punjab and West of Bengal, including Assam, all Hindu-majority country. Jinnah also fought hard for the annexation of Kashmir, a Muslim majority state with Hindu ruler; and the accession of Hyderabad and Junagadh, Hindu-majority states with Muslim rulers.

The British colonial administration did not directly rule all of "India". There were several different political arrangements in existence: Provinces were ruled directly and the Princely States with varying legal arrangements, like paramountcy.

The British Colonial Administration consisted of Secretary of State for India, the India Office, the Governor-General of India, and the Indian Civil Service.

The Indian Political Parties were (alphabetically) All India Muslim League, Communist Party of India, Hindu Mahasabha, Indian National Congress Khaksar Tehrik, and the Unionist Muslim League (mainly in the Punjab).

The Partition: 1947

Mountbatten Plan

The actual division between the two new dominions was done according to what has come to be known as the *3rd June Plan* or *Mountbatten Plan.*

The border between India and Pakistan was determined by a British Government-commissioned report usually referred to as the Radcliffe Line after the London lawyer, Sir Cyril Radcliffe, who wrote it. Pakistan came into being with two non-contiguous enclaves, East Pakistan (today Bangladesh) and West Pakistan, separated geographically by India. India was formed out of the majority Hindu regions of the colony, and Pakistan from the majority Muslim areas.

On July 18, 1947, the British Parliament passed the Indian Independence Act that finalized the partition arrangement. The Government of India Act 1935 was adapted to provide a legal framework for the two new dominions. Following partition, Pakistan was added as a new member of the United Nations. The union formed from the combination of the Hindu states assumed the name *India* which automatically granted it the seat of British India (a UN member since 1945) as a successor state. The 625 Princely States were given a choice of which country to join.

Geography of the partition: the Radcliffe Line

The Punjab — the region of the five rivers east of Indus: Jhelum, Chenab, Ravi, Beas, and Sutlej — consists of interfluvial *doabs,* or tracts of land lying between two confluent rivers. These are the *Sind-Sagar* doab (between Indus and Jhelum), the *Jech* doab (Jhelum/Chenab), the *Rechna* doab (Chenab/Ravi), the *Bari* doab (Ravi/Beas), and the *Bist* doab (Beas/Sutlej). In early 1947, in the months leading up to the deliberations of the Punjab Boundary Commission, the main disputed areas appeared to be in the *Bari* and *Bist* doabs, although some areas in the *Rechna* doab were claimed by the Congress and Sikhs. In the *Bari* doab, the districts of Gurdaspur, Amritsar, Lahore, and Montgomery were all disputed. All districts (other than Amritsar, which was 46.5% Muslim) had Muslim majorities; albeit, in Gurdaspur, the Muslim majority, at 51.1%, was slender. At a smaller area-scale, only three *tehsils* (sub-units of a district) in the *Bari* doab had non-Muslim majorities. These were: Pathankot (in the extreme north of Gurdaspur, which was not in dispute), and Amritsar and Tarn Taran in Amritsar district. In addition, there were four Muslim-majority tehsils east of Beas-Sutlej (with two where Muslims outnumbered Hindus and Sikhs together).

Before the Boundary Commission began formal hearings, governments were set up for the East and the West Punjab regions. Their territories were provisionally divided by "notional division" based on simple district majorities. In both the Punjab and Bengal, the Boundary Commission consisted of two Muslim and two non-Muslim judges with Sir Cyril Radcliffe as a common chairman. The mission of the Punjab commission was worded generally as: "To demarcate the boundaries of the two parts of the Punjab, on the basis of ascertaining the contiguous majority areas of Muslims and non-Muslims. In doing so, it will take into account other factors." Each side (the Muslims and the Congress/Sikhs) presented its claim through counsel with no liberty to bargain. The judges too had no mandate to compromise and on all major issues they "divided two and two, leaving Sir Cyril Radcliffe the invidious task of making the actual decisions."

Independence and Population Exchanges

Massive population exchanges occurred between the two newly-formed states in the months immediately following Partition. Once the lines were established, about 14.5 million people crossed the borders to what they hoped was the relative safety of religious majority. Based on 1951 Census of displaced persons, 7,226,000 Muslims went to Pakistan from India while 7,249,000 Hindus and Sikhs moved to India from Pakistan immediately after partition. About 11.2 million or 78% of the population transfer took place in the west, with Punjab accounting for most of it; 5.3 million Muslims moved from India to West Punjab in Pakistan, 3.4 million Hindus and Sikhs moved from Pakistan to East Punjab in India; elsewhere in the west 1.2 million moved in each direction to and from Sind.

The newly formed governments were completely unequipped to deal with migrations of such staggering magnitude, and massive violence and slaughter occurred on both sides of the border. Estimates of the number of deaths range around roughly 500,000, with low estimates at 200,000 and high estimates at 1,000,000.

Punjab

The Indian state of Punjab was created in 1947, when the Partition of India split the former Raj province of Punjab between India and Pakistan. The mostly Muslim western part of the province became Pakistan's Punjab Province; the mostly Sikh and Hindu eastern part became India's Punjab state. Many Hindus and Sikhs lived in the west, and many Muslims lived in the east, and so the partition saw many people displaced and much intercommunal violence. Lahore and Amritsar were at the center of the problem, the British were not sure where to place them–make them part of India or Pakistan. The British did make a decision to hand both cities to Pakistan, but due to lack of control and regulation for the border Amritsar became part of India whilst Lahore became part of Pakistan.

Bengal

The province of Bengal was divided into the two separate entities of West Bengal belonging to India, and East Bengal belonging to Pakistan. East Bengal was renamed East Pakistan in 1955, and later became the independent nation of Bangladesh after the Bangladesh Liberation War of 1971.

Sindh

Hindu Sindhis expected to stay in Sindh following Partition, as there was good relations between Hindu and Sindhi Muslims. At the time of Partition there were 1,400,000 Hindu Sindhis though most were concentrated in the cities such as Hyderabad, Karachi, Shikarpur and Sukhur; in a space of less than a year approximately 1,200,000 of them were forced to leave for India due to violence as more Muslims started to pour into Sindh and looting the homes of Hindus. Thus Hindus were forced to leave their homes and businesses behind. Of all the Partition victims, the Hindu Sindhis were the worst effected as they not only lost homes, but also a homeland. Unlike the Punjabi, there was part of Punjab both in India and Pakistan, but all of Sindh was allotted to Pakistan..

Perspectives

The Partition was a highly controversial arrangement, and remains a cause of much tension on the subcontinent today. British Viceroy Louis Mountbatten has not only been accused of rushing the process through, but also is alleged to have influenced the Radcliffe Line in India's favour since everyone agreed India would be a more desirable country for most. However, the commission took so long to decide on a final boundary that the two nations were granted their independence even before there was a defined boundary between them. Even then, the members were so distraught at their handiwork (and its results) that they refused compensation for their time on the commission.

Some critics allege that British haste led to the cruelties of the Partition. Because independence was declared *prior* to the actual Partition, it was up to the new governments of India and Pakistan to keep public order. No large population movements were contemplated; the plan called for safeguards for minorities on both sides of the new state line. It was an impossible task, at which both states failed. There was a complete breakdown of law and order; many died in riots, massacre, or just from the hardships of their flight to safety. What ensued was one of the largest population movements in recorded history. According to Richard Symonds

> "at the lowest estimate, half a million people perished and twelve million became homeless".

However, some argue that the British were forced to expedite the Partition by events on the ground., Law and order had broken down many times before Partition, with much bloodshed on both sides. A massive civil war was looming by the time Mountbatten became Viceroy. After World War II, Britain had limited resources, perhaps insufficient to the task of keeping order. Another view point is that while Mountbatten may have been too hasty he had no real options left and achieved the best he could under difficult circumstances. Historian Lawrence James concurs that in 1947 Mounbatten was left with no option but to cut and run. The alternative being getting involved in a potentially bloody civil war from which it would be difficult to get out.

Conservative elements in England consider the partition of India to be the moment that the British Empire ceased to be a world power, following Curzon's dictum that "While we hold on to India, we are a first-rate power. If we lose India, we will decline to a third-rate power." The 'flick' of the pen with which Clement Atlee signed the independence treaty is, where remembered, considered sadly; not for the loss of India, but for the loss of what holding India meant.

Delhi Punjabi Refugees

An estimated 25 million people–Hindus, Muslims and Sikhs -(1947-present) crossed the newly carved borders to reach their new homelands. These estimates are based on comparisons of decadal censuses from 1941 and 1951 with adjustments for normal population growth in the areas of migration. In northern India–undivided Punjab and North Western Frontier Province (NWFP)–nearly 12 million were forced to move from as early as March 1947 following the Rawalpindi violence. Delhi received the highest number of refugees for a single city–the population of Delhi grew rapidly in 1947 from under 1 million (917.939) to a little less than 2 million (1.744.072) between the period 1941-1951 (Census of India, 1941 and 1951).

The refugees were housed in various historical and military locations such as the Old Fort (Purana Qila), Red Fort (Red Fort), and military barracks in Kingsway (around the present Delhi university). The latter became the site of one of the largest refugee camps in northern India with more than 35,000 refugees at any given time besides Kurukshetra camp near Panipat. The camp sites were later converted into permanent housing through extensive building projects undertaken by the Government of India from 1948 onwards. A number of housing colonies in Delhi came up around this period like Lajpat Nagar, Rajinder Nagar, Nizamuddin, Punjabi Bagh, Rehgar Pura, Jungpura and Kingsway. A number of schemes such as provision of education, employment opportunities, easy loans to start businesses etc. were provided for the refugees at all-India level. The Delhi refugees, however, able to make use of these facilities much better than their counterparts elsewhere.

Refugees Settled in India

Many Sikhs and Hindu Punjabis settled in the Indian parts of Punjab and Delhi. Hindus migrating from East Pakistan (now Bangladesh) settled across Eastern India and Northeastern India, many ending up in close-by states like West Bengal, Assam, and Tripura. Some migrants were sent to the Andaman islands.

Hindu Sindhis found themselves without a homeland. The responsibility of rehabilitating them was borne by their government. Refugee camps were set up for Hindu Sindhis. However non sindhi Hindus had very little help from the Government of India and many never received compensation of any sort from the Indian Government.

Many refugees overcame the trauma of poverty. The loss of a homeland has had a deeper and lasting effect on their Sindhi culture,it may be in decline in India.

In late 2004, the Sindhi diaspora vociferously opposed a Public Interest Litigation in the Supreme Court of India which asked the government of India to delete the word "Sindh" from the Indian National Anthem (written by Rabindranath Tagore prior the partition) on the grounds that it infringed upon the sovereignty of Pakistan.

Refugees Settled in Pakistan

Refugees or Muhajirs in Pakistan came from various parts of India. There was a large influx of Punjabi Muslims from East Punjab fleeing the riots. Despite severe physical and economic hardships, East Punjabi refugees to Pakistan did not face problems of cultural and linguistic assimilation after partition. However, there were many Muslim refugees who migrated to Pakistan from other Indian states. These refugees came from many different ethnic groups and regions in India, including Rajasthan, Uttar Pradesh (then known as "United Provinces of Agra and Awadh", or UP), Madhya Pradesh (then Central Province or "CP"), Gujarat, Bihar, what was then the princely state of Hyderabad and so on. The descendants of these non-Punjabi refugees in Pakistan often refer to themselves as Muhajir whereas the assimilated Punjabi refugees no longer make that political distinction. Large numbers of non-Punjabi refugees settled in Sindh, particularly in the cities of Karachi and Hyderabad. They are united by their refugee status and their native Urdu language and are a strong political force in Sindh.

History of Indian Republic

The History of the Republic of India began on August 15, 1947 when India became an independent Dominion within the British Commonwealth. Concurrently the Muslim-majority northwest and east of British India was separated into the Dominion of Pakistan. Lord Louis Mountbatten, and later Chakravarti Rajagopalachari served in the office of the Governor General of India. Jawaharlal Nehru became the first Prime Minister of

India and Sardar Vallabhbhai Patel became the Deputy Prime Minister of India and its Minister of Home Affairs.

1947–1950

Independent India's first years were marked with turbulent events — a massive exchange of population with Pakistan, the Indo-Pakistani War of 1947 and the integration of over 500 princely states to form a united nation.

Aftermath of Partition

An estimated 3.5 million Hindus and Sikhs living in West Punjab, NWFP, Baluchistan, East Bengal and Sind migrated to India in fear of domination and suppression in Muslim Pakistan. Communal violence killed an estimated 1 million Hindus, Muslims and Sikhs, and gravely destabilized both Dominions along their Punjab and Bengal boundaries, and the cities of Calcutta, Delhi and Lahore. The violence was stopped by early September owing to the cooperative efforts of both Indian and Pakistani leaders, and especially due the efforts of Mohandas Gandhi, the leader of the Indian freedom struggle, who undertook a *fast-unto-death* in Calcutta and later in Delhi to calm people and emphasize peace despite the threat to his life. Both Governments constructed large relief camps for incoming and leaving refugees, and the Indian Army was mobilized to provide humanitarian assistance on a massive scale. The assassination of Mahatma Gandhi on January 30, 1948 was a major setback to the young nation. Gandhi was murdered by Nathuram Vinayak Godse, allegedly affiliated with the Hindu nationalist movement, who held him responsible for partition and charged that Gandhi was appeasing Muslims. More than one million people flooded the streets of Delhi to follow the procession to cremation grounds and pay their last respects.

In 1949, India recorded close to 1 million Hindu refugees flooded into West Bengal and other states from East Pakistan, owing to communal violence, intimidation and repression from Muslim authorities. The plight of the refugees outraged Hindus and Indian nationalists, and the refugee population drained the resources of Indian states, who were unable to absorb them. While not ruling out war, Prime Minister Nehru and Sardar Patel invited Liaquat Ali Khan for talks in Delhi. Although many Indians termed this appeasement, Nehru signed a pact with Liaquat Ali Khan that pledged both nations to the protection of minorities and creation of minority commissions. Although opposed to the principle, Patel decided to back this Pact for the sake of peace, and played a critical role in garnering support from West Bengal and across India, and enforcing the provisions of the Pact. Khan and Nehru also signed a trade agreement, and committed to resolving bilateral disputes through peaceful means. Steadily, hundreds of thousands of Hindus returned to East Pakistan, but the thaw in relations did not last long, primarily owing to the Kashmir dispute.

Union's Integration

British India consisted of 17 provinces and 562 princely states. The provinces were given to India or Pakistan, in some cases in particular – Punjab and Bengal – after being partitioned. The princes of the princely states, however, won the right to either remain independent or join either nation. Thus India's leaders faced the prospect of inheriting a nation fragmented between medieval-era kingdoms and provinces organized by colonial powers. Under the leadership of Sardar Vallabhbhai Patel, the new Government of India employed political negotiations backed with the option (and, on several occasions, the use) of military action to ensure the primacy of the Central government and of the Constitution then being drafted.

There were three States that proved more difficult to integrate than others:

1. Junagadh—a December 1947 plebiscite resulted in a 99% vote to merge with India, annulling the controversial accession to Pakistan, which was made despite the people of the state being overwhelmingly Hindu.
2. Hyderabad—Patel ordered the Indian army to depose the government of the Nizam after the failure of negotiations, which was done between September 13 – September 17, 1948. It was incorporated as a state of India the next year.
3. The area of Kashmir in the far north of the subcontinent quickly became a source of controversy that erupted into the First Indo-Pakistani War which lasted from 1947 to 1949. Eventually a United Nations-overseen ceasefire was agreed that left India in control of two thirds of the contested region.The Controversy arose because Jawaharlal Nehru had agreed to give a plebiscite to the State. But due to Pakistan's forced attempt to integrate Kashmir, it was helped and integrated by India, the plebiscite never being held. The Indian Constitution came into force in Kashmir on 26th January 1957 with special clauses for the state.

Constitution

The Constituent Assembly adopted the Constitution of India, drafted by a committee headed by B. R. Ambedkar, on November 26, 1949. India became a federal, democratic republic after its Constitution came into effect on January 26, 1950. Rajendra Prasad became the first President of India.

1950s and 1960s

India held its first national elections under the Constitution in 1952, where a turnout of over 60% was recorded. The Congress Party won an overwhelming majority, and Jawaharlal Nehru began a second term as Prime Minister. President Prasad was also elected to a second term by the electoral college of the first Parliament of India.

Nehru administration (1952–1964)

Prime Minister Nehru led the Congress to major election victories in 1957 and 1962. The Parliament passed extensive reforms that increased the legal rights of women in Hindu society, and further legislated against caste discrimination and untouchability. Nehru advocated a strong initiative to enroll India's children to complete primary education, and thousands of schools, colleges and institutions of advanced learning, such as the Indian Institutes of Technology were founded across the nation. Nehru advocated a socialist model for the economy of India — no taxation for Indian farmers, minimum wage and benefits for blue-collar workers, and the nationalization of heavy industries such as steel, aviation, shipping, electricity and mining. An extensive public works and industrialization campaign resulted in the construction of major dams, irrigation canals, roads, thermal and hydroelectric power stations.

States reorganization

Potti Sreeramulu's *fast-unto-death,* and consequent death for the demand of an Andhra State in 1953 sparked a major re-shaping of the Indian Union. Nehru appointed the *States Reorganization Commission,* upon whose recommendations, the States Reorganization Act was passed in 1956. Old states were dissolved and new states created on the lines of shared linguistic and ethnic demographics. The separation of Kerala and the Telugu-speaking regions of Madras State enabled the creation of an exclusively Tamil-speaking state of Tamil Nadu. On May 1, 1960, the states of Maharashtra and Gujarat were created out of the Bombay state. The creation of Punjabi Suba on November 1, 1966, an exclusively Punjabi speaking state of Punjab (India), occurred after a long struggle.

Foreign policy and military conflicts

Nehru's foreign policy was the inspiration of the Non-Aligned Movement, of which India was a co-founder. Nehru maintained friendly relations with both the United States and the Soviet Union, and encouraged the People's Republic of China to join the global community of nations. In 1956, when the Suez Canal Company was seized by the Egyptian government, an international conference voted 18-4 to take action against Egypt. India was one of the 4 backers of Egypt, along with Indonesia, Sri Lanka, and the USSR. India had controversially opposed the partition of Palestine and the 1956 invasion of the Sinai by Israel, Britain and France, but did not oppose the Chinese occupation of Tibet and the suppression of a pro-democracy movement in Hungary by the Soviet Union. Although Nehru disavowed nuclear ambitions for India, Canada and France aided India in the development of nuclear power stations for electricity. India also negotiated an agreement in 1960 with Pakistan on the just use of the waters of seven rivers shared by the countries. Nehru had visited Pakistan in 1953, but owing to political turmoil in Pakistan, no headway was made on the Kashmir dispute.

India has fought a total of four wars/military conflicts with its rival nation Pakistan, two in this period. In the Indo-Pakistani War of 1947 fought over Kashmir, Pakistan occupied one third of Kashmir (which India claims as its territory), and India occupied three fifths (which Pakistan claims as its territory). In the Indo-Pakistani War of 1965 India attacked Pakistan on all fronts after attempts by Pakistani troops to infiltrate into Indian controlled Kashmir. #In 1961, after continual petitions for a peaceful handover, India invaded and annexed the Portuguese colony of Goa on the west coast of India.

In 1962 China and India engaged in the brief Sino-Indian War over the border in the Himalayas. The war was a complete rout for the Indians and led to a refocusing on arms build-up and an improvement in relations with the United States. While China withdrew from occupied lands in the northeast, it continues to occupy Aksai Chin in Kashmir. China disputes India's sovereignty over Arunachal Pradesh and until recently, Sikkim.

Post-Nehru India

Jawaharlal Nehru died on May 27, 1964. Lal Bahadur Shastri succeeded him as Prime Minister. In 1965 in the Second Kashmir War India and Pakistan again went to war, but without any definitive outcome or alteration of the Kashmir boundary. The Tashkent Agreement was signed under the mediation of the Soviet government, but Shastri died on the night after the signing ceremony. A leadership election resulted in the elevation of Indira Gandhi, Nehru's daughter who had been serving as Minister for Information and Broadcasting, as the third Prime Minister. She defeated right-wing leader Morarji Desai. The Congress Party won a reduced majority in the 1967 elections owing to widespread disenchantment over rising prices of commodities, unemployment, economic stagnation and a food crisis. Indira Gandhi had started on a rocky note after agreeing to a devaluation of the Indian rupee, which created much hardship for Indian businesses and consumers, and the import of wheat from the U.S. fell through due to political disputes.

Morarji Desai entered Gandhi's government as Deputy Prime Minister and Finance Minister, and with senior Congress politicians attempted to constrain Gandhi's authority. But following the counsel of her political advisor P. N. Haksar, Gandhi resuscitated her popular appeal by a major shift towards socialist policies. She successfully ended the privy purse guarantee for former Indian royalty, and waged a major offensive against party hierarchy over the nationalization of India's banks. Although resisted by Desai and India's business community, the policy was popular with the masses. When Congress politicians attempted to oust Gandhi by suspending her Congress membership, Gandhi was empowered with a large exodus of MPs to her own Congress (R). The bastion of the freedom struggle, the Indian National Congress had split in 1969. Gandhi continued to govern with a slim majority.

1970s

In 1971, Indira Gandhi and her Congress (R) were returned to power with a massively increased majority. The nationalization of banks was carried out, and many other socialist economic and industrial policies enacted. India intervened in Bangladesh Liberation War a civil war taking place in Pakistan's Bengali half, after millions of refugees had fled the persecution of the Pakistani army. The clash resulted in the independence of East Pakistan, which became known as Bangladesh, and Prime Minister Indira Gandhi's elevation to immense popularity. Relations with the United States grew strained, and India signed a 20-year treaty of friendship with the Soviet Union–breaking explicitly for the first time from non-alignment. In 1974, India tested its first nuclear weapon in the desert of Rajasthan. Meanwhile, in the Indian protectorate of Sikkim, a referendum was held that resulted in a vote to formally join India and depose the Chogyal. On 26 April 1975, Sikkim formally became India's 21st state.

Green Revolution and Operation Flood

India's population passed the 500 million mark in the early 1970s, but its long-standing food crisis was resolved with greatly improved agricultural productivity due to the Green revolution. India's government sponsored modern agricultural implements, new varieties of generic seeds and increased financial assistance to farmers that increased the yield of food crops such as wheat, rice and corn, as well as commercial crops like cotton, tea, tobacco and coffee. Increased agricultural productivity expanded across the states of the Indo-Gangetic plains and the Punjab. Under Operation Flood, the Government encouraged the production of milk, which increased greatly, and improved rearing of livestock across India. This enabled India to become self-sufficient in feeding its own population, ending two decades of food imports.

Indo-Pakistan War of 1971

The Indo-Pakistan War of 1971 was the third in four wars fought between the two nations. In this war, fought over the issue of the Independence of East Pakistan from Pakistan into the nation of Bangladesh India decisively defeated Pakistan resulting in the independence of Bangladesh from Pakistani control.

Indian Emergency

Economic and social problems, as well as allegations of corruption caused increasing political unrest across India, culminating in the Bihar Movement. In 1974, the Allahabad High Court found Indira Gandhi guilty of misusing government machinery for election purposes. Opposition parties conducted nationwide strikes and protests demanding her immediate resignation. Various political parties united under Jaya Prakash Narayan to resist what he termed Mrs. Gandhi's dictatorship. Leading strikes across India that paralyzed its economy and administration, Narayan even called for the Army to oust Mrs. Gandhi. In 1975, Mrs. Gandhi advised President Fakhruddin Ali Ahmed to declare a state of emergency under the Constitution, which allowed the Central government to assume sweeping powers to defend law and order in the nation. Explaining the breakdown of law and order and threat to national security as her primary reasons, Mrs. Gandhi suspended many civil liberties and postponed elections at national and state levels. Non-Congress governments in Indian states were dismissed, and opposition political leaders and activists imprisoned. Strikes and public protests were outlawed in all forms.

India's economy benefited from an end to paralyzing strikes and political disorder. Indira announced a 20-point programme which enhanced agricultural and industrial production, increasing national growth, productivity and job growth. But many organs of government and many Congress politicians were accused of corruption and authoritarian conduct. Police officers were accused of arresting and torturing innocent people. Indira's son and political advisor, Sanjay Gandhi was accused of committing gross excesses–Sanjay was blamed for the Health Ministry carrying out forced vasectomies of men and sterilization of women as a part of the initiative to control population growth, and for the demolition of slums in Delhi near the Turkmen Gate, which left thousands of people dead and many more displaced.

Janata Interlude

Indira called for elections in 1977, only to suffer a humiliating electoral defeat at the hands of the Janata Party, an amalgamation of opposition parties. Morarji Desai became the first non-Congress Prime Minister of India. The Desai administration established tribunals to investigate Emergency-era abuses, and

Indira and Sanjay Gandhi were arrested after a report from the Shah Commission. But in 1979, the coalition crumbled and Charan Singh formed an interim government. The Janata party had become intensely unpopular due to its internecine warfare, and the fact that it offered no leadership on solving India's serious economic and social problems.

1980s

Indira Gandhi and her Congress (I) party were swept back into power with a large majority in January, 1980. But the rise of an insurgency in Punjab would jeopardize India's security. In Assam, there were many incidents of communal violence between native villagers and refugees from Bangladesh, as well as settlers from other parts of India. When Indian forces, undertaking Operation Bluestar, raided the hideout of Khalistan militants in the Golden Temple in Amritsar, the inadvertent deaths of civilians and damage to the temple building inflamed tensions in the Sikh community across India. The Government used intensive police operations to crush militant operations, but it resulted in many incidents of abuse of civil liberties. Northeast India was paralyzed owing to the ULFA's clash with Government forces. On October 31, 1984, the Prime Minister's own Sikh bodyguards killed her, and communal violence erupted in Delhi and parts of Punjab, causing the deaths of thousands of people along with terrible pillage, arson and rape. Government investigation has failed to date to discover the causes and punish the perpetrators, but public opinion blamed Congress leaders for directing attacks on Sikhs in Delhi.

Rajiv Gandhi administration

The Congress party chose Rajiv Gandhi, Indira's older son as the next Prime Minister. Rajiv had been elected to Parliament only in 1982, and at 40, was the youngest national political leader and Prime Minister ever. But his youth and inexperience were an asset in the eyes of citizens tired of the inefficacy and corruption of career politicians, and looking for newer policies and a fresh start to resolve the country's long-standing problems. The Parliament was dissolved, and Rajiv led the Congress party to its largest majority in history (over 450 seats out of 545 possible), reaping a sympathy vote over his mother's assassination.

Rajiv Gandhi initiated a series of reforms–the license raj was loosened, and government restrictions on foreign currency, travel, foreign investment and imports decreased considerably. This allowed private businesses to use resources and produce commercial goods without government bureaucracy interfering, and the influx of foreign investment increased India's national reserves. As Prime Minister, Rajiv broke from his mother's precedent to improve relations with the United States, which increased economic aid and scientific cooperation. Rajiv's encouragement of science and technology resulted in a major expansion of the telecommunications industry, India's space program and gave birth to the software industry and information technology sector.

India in 1987 brokered an agreement between the Government of Sri Lanka and the LTTE insurgency that had torn apart the island for over a decade. Rajiv sent Indian troops to enforce the agreement and disarm the Tamil rebels, but the Indian Peace Keeping Force, as it was known, became entangled in outbreaks of violence–ultimately ending up fighting the Tamil rebels itself, and becoming a target of attack from Sri Lankan nationalists. VP Singh withdrew the IPKF in 1990, but thousands of Indian soldiers had died. Rajiv's departure from socialist policies did not sit well with the masses, who did not benefit from the innovations. Unemployment was a serious problem, and India's burgeoning population added ever-increasing needs for diminishing resources. Rajiv Gandhi's image as an honest politician (he was nicknamed *Mr. Clean* by the press) was shattered when the Bofors scandal broke, revealing that senior government officials had taken bribes over defence contracts by a Swedish guns producer.

Janata Dal

Elections in 1989 gave Rajiv's Congress a plurality, a far cry from the awesome majority which propelled him to power. Power came instead to his former finance and defence minister, VP Singh. Singh had been moved from the Finance ministry to the Defence ministry after he unearthed some scandals which made the Congress leadership uncomfortable. Singh then unearthed the Bofors scandal, and was sacked from the party and office. Becoming a popular crusader for reform and clean government, Singh led the Janata Dal coalition to a majority. He was supported by BJP and the leftist parties from outside. Becoming Prime Minister, Singh made an important visit to the Golden Temple shrine, to heal the wounds of the past. He started to implement the controversial Mandal commission report, to increase the quota in reservation for low caste Hindus. The BJP protested these implementations, and took its support back, following which he resigned. Chandra Shekhar split to form the Janata Dal (Socialist), supported by Rajiv's Congress. This new government also collapsed in a matter of months, when congress withdrew its support.

1990s

On May 21, 1991, while Rajiv Gandhi campaigned in Tamil Nadu on behalf of Congress (I), a Liberation Tigers of Tamil Eelam (LTTE) female suicide bomber killed him and many others, setting off the bomb in her belt by leaning forward while garlanding him. In the elections, Congress (I) won 244 parliamentary seats and put together a coalition, returning to power under the leadership of P.V. Narasimha Rao. This Congress-led government, which served a full 5-year term, initiated a gradual process of economic liberalisation and reform, which has opened the Indian economy to global trade and investment. India's domestic politics also took new shape, as traditional alignments by caste, creed, and ethnicity gave way to a plethora of small, regionally-based political parties. But India was rocked by communal violence between Hindus and Muslims that killed over 10,000 people, following the Babri Mosque demolition by Hindu mobs in the course of the Ram Janmabhoomi dispute in Ayodhya in 1992. The final months of the Rao-led government in the spring of 1996 suffered the effects of several major political corruption scandals, which contributed to the worst electoral performance by the Congress Party in its history.

Era of Coalitions

The Bharatiya Janata Party (BJP) emerged from the May 1996 national elections as the single-largest party in the Lok Sabha but without enough strength to prove a majority on the floor of that Parliament. Under Prime Minister Atal Bihari Vajpayee, the BJP coalition lasted in power 13 days. With all political parties wishing to avoid another round of elections, a 14-party coalition led by the Janata Dal emerged to form a government known as the United Front. A United Front government under former Chief Minister of Karnataka H.D. Deve Gowda lasted less than a year. The leader of the Congress Party withdrew his support in March 1997. Inder Kumar Gujral replaced Deve Gowda as the consensus choice for Prime Minister of a 16-party United Front coalition.

In November 1997, the Congress Party again withdrew support for the United Front. New elections in February 1998 brought the BJP the largest number of seats in Parliament (182), but this fell far short of a majority. On March 20, 1998, the President inaugurated a BJP-led coalition government with Vajpayee again serving as Prime Minister. On May 11 and 13, 1998, this government conducted a series of underground nuclear tests, prompting President of the United States Bill Clinton and Japan to impose economic sanctions on India pursuant to the 1994 Nuclear Proliferation Prevention Act.

Into the 21st Century

In April 1999, the BJP-led coalition government fell apart, leading to fresh elections in September. In May and June 1999, India discovered an elaborate campaign of terrorist infiltration that resulted in the Kargil War in Kashmir, derailing a promising peace process that had begun only three months earlier when Prime Minister Vajpayee visited Pakistan, inaugurating the Delhi-Lahore bus service. Indian forces killed infiltrators, who included Pakistani soldiers, and reclaimed important border posts in high-altitude warfare. In the same year, India's population exceeded 1 billion.

Soaring on popularity earned following the successful conclusion of the Kargil conflict, the National Democratic Alliance–a new coalition led by the BJP–gained a majority to form a government with Vajpayee as Prime Minister in October 1999. The NDA government's credibility was adversely affected by reports of intelligence failures that led to the Kargil incursions going undetected, as well as allegations that the Defence Minister George Fernandes took bribes over the purchase of coffins for soldiers who died in the battle. The Tehelka scandal exposed the BJP party chief taking unaccounted contributions in return for promised favours, and the CBI chargesheeted senior BJP leaders for inciting the demolition of the Babri mosque. In 2002, tensions increased over the Ram Janmabhoomi dispute when the Vishwa Hindu Parishad threatened to defy the Government, vowing to perform a religious ceremony on the disputed site. 59 Hindu activists died returning from the site when a train carriage took fire a month later, in Godhra, Gujarat. This sparked off the 2002 Gujarat violence, leading to the deaths of thousands of Hindus and Muslims. The BJP-led state government, and its chief minister Narendra Modi were accused of not doing enough to stop Hindu mobs in attacking Muslims.

But throughout 2003, India's speedy economic progress, political stability and a rejuvenated peace initiative with Pakistan increased the Government's popularity. In January 2004 Vajpayee recommended early dissolution of the Lok Sabha and General elections. The Congress Party-led alliance won an upset victory in elections held in May 2004. Manmohan Singh became the Prime Minister, after the Congress President Sonia Gandhi, the widow of Rajiv Gandhi declined to take the office, in order to defuse the controversy about whether her Italian birth should be considered a disqualification for the Prime Minister's post. The Congress formed a coalition with socialist and regional parties, and enjoys the outside support of India's Communist parties. Manmohan Singh is the first Sikh to date to hold India's most powerful office. Singh has continued economic liberalization, although the need for support from Indian socialists and communists has forestalled further privatization. The 21st century saw India, improve relations, with many countries including the United States, the European Union, and the People's Republic of China. The Economy of India, has accelarated growing at 9% per year. India, is now being looked at as a potential superpower.

Terrorism, has increased in India too. Bomb Blasts in leading cities like, Mumbai, New Delhi, Jaipur, Bangalore, Hyderabad, etc. has been very common.

Economic Transformation

Under the policies initiated by Late Prime Minister Narasimha Rao and his Finance minister Manmohan Singh, India's economy expanded rapidly. The Rao administration initiated the privatization of large, inefficient and loss-inducing government corporations. The UF government had attempted a progressive budget that encouraged reforms, but the 1997 Asian financial crisis and political instability created economic stagnation. The

Vajpayee administration continued with privatization, reduction of taxes, a sound fiscal policy aimed at reducing deficits and debts and increased initiatives for public works. The Golden Quadrilateral project aimed to link India's corners with a network of modern highways. Cities like Bangalore, Hyderabad, Pune and Ahmedabad have risen in prominence and economic importance, became centres of rising industries and destination for foreign investment and firms. Strategies like forming *Special Economic Zones*–tax amenities, good communications infrastructure, low regulation–to encourage industries has paid off in many parts of the country.

A rising generation of well-educated and skilled professionals in scientific sectors of industry began propelling the Indian economy, as the information technology industry took hold across India with the proliferation of computers. The new technologies increased the efficiency of activity in almost every type of industry, which also benefitted from the availability of skilled labor. Foreign investment and outsourcing of jobs to India's labor markets further enhanced India's economic growth. A large middle-class has arisen across India, which has increased the demand, and thus production of a wide array of consumer goods. Unemployment is steadily declining, and poverty has fallen to approximately 22%. Gross Domestic Product growth increased to beyond 7%. While serious challenges remain, India is enjoying a period of economic expansion that has propelled it to the forefront of the world economy, and has correspondingly increased its influence in political and diplomatic terms.

GEOGRAPHY OF INDIA

The **geography** of India is diverse, with landscape ranging from snow-capped mountain ranges to deserts, plains, rainforests, hills, and plateaus. India comprises most of the Indian subcontinent situated on the Indian Plate, the northerly portion of the Indo-Australian Plate. Having a coastline of over 7,000 kilometres (4,350 mi), most of India lies on a peninsula in Southern Asia that protrudes into the Indian Ocean. India is bounded in the southwest by the Arabian Sea and in the east and southeast by the Bay of Bengal.

The fertile Indo-Gangetic Plain occupies most of northern, central, and eastern India, while the Deccan Plateau occupies most of southern India. To the west of the country is the Thar Desert, which consists of a mix of rocky and sandy desert. India's east and northeastern border consists of the high Himalayan range. The highest point in India is disputed owing to a territorial dispute with Pakistan; according to India's claim, the highest point (located in the disputed Kashmir region) is K2, at 8,611 metres (28,251 ft). The highest point in undisputed Indian territory is Kangchenjunga, at 8,598 m (28,209 ft). Climate ranges from equatorial in the far south, to Alpine in the upper reaches of the Himalayas.

India is bordered by Pakistan to the northwest, China, Bhutan and Nepal to the north, Myanmar to the east and Bangladesh to the east of West Bengal. Sri Lanka, the Maldives and Indonesia are island nations to the south of India. Sri Lanka is separated from India by a narrow channel of sea formed by Palk Strait and the Gulf of Mannar.Politically, India is divided into 28 states, and seven federally administered union territories. The political divisions generally follow linguistic and ethnic boundaries rather than geographic transitions.

India lies to the north of the equator between 8°4' and 37°6' north latitude and 68°7' and 97°25' east longitude. It is the seventh-largest country in the world, with a total land area of 3,287,263 square kilometres (1,269,219 sq mi). India measures 3,214 km (1,997 mi) from north to south and 2,993 km (1,860 mi) from east to west. It has a land frontier of 15,200 km (9,445 mi) and a coastline of 7,517 km (4,671 mi).

India is bounded to the southwest by the Arabian Sea, to the southeast by the Bay of Bengal, and the Indian Ocean to the south. To the north, northeast, and northwest are the Himalayas. Cape Comorin constitutes the southern tip of the mainland Indian peninsula, which narrows before ending in the Indian Ocean. The southernmost part of India is Indira Point in the Andaman and Nicobar Islands in the Bay of Bengal. The territorial waters of India extend into the sea to a distance of twelve nautical miles measured from the appropriate baseline.

India is divided into 28 states (which are further subdivided into districts), seven union territories. States have their own elected government, while union territories are governed by an administrator appointed by the union government.

India is divided into seven physiographic regions. They are

1. The northern mountains including the Himalayas, which includes the Kuen Lun and the Karakoram ranges and the northeast mountain ranges.
2. Indo-Gangetic plains
3. Thar Desert
4. Central Highlands and Deccan Plateau
5. East Coast
6. West Coast
7. Bordering seas and islands

Mountains

A great arc of mountains, composed of the Himalaya, Hindu Kush, and Patkai ranges, define the Indian subcontinent. These mountains were formed by the ongoing tectonic collision of the Indian Plate with the Eurasian Plate which started some 50 million years ago. These mountain ranges are home to some of the world's tallest mountains and act as a natural barrier to cold polar winds. They also facilitate the monsoons winds drive climate in India. Rivers that originate in these mountains provide water to the fertile Indo-Gangetic plains. These mountains are recognised by biogeographers as the boundary between two of the earth's great ecozones; the temperate Palearctic that covers most of Eurasia, and the tropical and subtropical Indomalaya ecozone that includes the Indian subcontinent extending into Southeast Asia and Indonesia. Historically, these ranges have also served as barriers to invaders.

India has nine major mountain ranges having peaks of over 1,000 m (3,281 ft). The Himalayas are the only mountain ranges to have snow-capped peaks. These ranges are:

1. Aravalli Range
2. Eastern Ghats
3. Himalayas
4. Patkai
5. Vindhya Range
6. Western Ghats (*Sahyadri*)
7. Satpura Range
8. Karakoram
9. Kunlun

The Himalaya mountain range is the world's highest mountain range. They form India's northeastern border, separating it from the rest of Asia. The Himalayas are also one of the world's youngest mountain ranges, and extend almost uninterrupted for a distance of 2,500 m (8,202 ft), covering an area of 500,000 km (193,051 sq mi). The Himalayas extend from the state of Jammu and Kashmir in the west to the state of Arunachal Pradesh in the east. These states along with Himachal Pradesh, Uttarakhand, and Sikkim lie mostly in the Himalayan region. Some of the Himalayan peaks range over 7,000 m (22,966 ft) and the snow line ranges between 6,000 m (19,685 ft) in Sikkim to around 3,000 m (9,843 ft) in Kashmir. Kangchenjunga, which lies on the Sikkim–Nepal border, is the highest point in the area administered by India. Most peaks in the Himalayas remain snowbound throughout the year.

The Shiwalik, or lower Himalaya, consists of smaller hills towards the Indian side. Most of the rock formations are young and highly unstable, with landslides being a regular phenomenon during the rainy season. Many of India's hill stations are located on this range. The climate varies from subtropical in the foothills to alpine at the higher elevations of these mountain ranges.

The mountains on India's eastern border with Myanmar are called as the Patkai or the Purvanchal. They were created by the same tectonic processes that resulted in the formation of the Himalaya. The features of the Patkai ranges are conical peaks, steep slopes and deep valleys. The Patkai ranges are not as rugged or tall as the Himalayas. There are three hill ranges that come under the Patkai: The Patkai-Bum, the Garo–Khasi–Jaintia, and the Lushai hills. The Garo–Khasi range is in the state of Meghalaya. Mawsynram,a village near Cherrapunji lying on the windward side of these hills, has the distinction of being the wettest place in the world, receiving the highest annual rainfall.

The Vindhya range runs across most of central India, covering a distance of 1,050 km (652 mi). The average elevation of these hills is 3,000 m (9,843 ft). They are believed to have been formed by the wastes created by the weathering of the ancient Aravali mountains. It geographically separates northern India from southern India. The western end of the range lies in eastern Gujarat, near its border with the state of Madhya Pradesh, and the range runs east and north almost meeting the Ganges River at Mirzapur.

The Satpura Range is a range of hills in central India. It begins in eastern Gujarat near the Arabian Sea coast, then runs east across Maharashtra, Madhya Pradesh and ends in the state of Chhattisgarh. It extends for a distance of 900 km (559 mi) with many of its peaks rising above 1,000 m (3,281 ft). It is triangular in shape, with its apex at Ratnapuri and the two sides being parallel to the Tapti and Narmada rivers. It runs parallel to the Vindhya Range, which lies to the north, and these two east-west ranges divide the Indo-Gangetic plain of northern India from the Deccan Plateau lying in the south. The Narmada runs in the depression between the Satpura and Vindhya ranges, and drains the northern slope of the Satpura range, running west towards the Arabian Sea.

The Aravali Range is the oldest mountain range in India, running from northeast to southwest across Rajasthan in western India, extending approximately 500 km (311 mi). The northern end of the range continues as isolated hills and rocky ridges into Haryana, ending near Delhi. The highest peak is Mount Abu, rising to 1,722 m (5,650 ft), lying near the southwestern extremity of the range, close to the border with Gujarat. The Aravali Range is the eroded stub of an ancient folded mountain system that was once snow-capped. The range rose in a Precambrian event called the Aravali-Delhi orogen. The range joins two of the ancient segments that make up the Indian craton, the Marwar segment to the northwest of the range, and the Bundelkhand segment to the southeast.

The Western Ghats or Sahyadri mountains run along the western edge of India's Deccan Plateau, and separate it from a narrow coastal plain along the Arabian Sea. The range starts south of the Tapti River near the Gujarat–Maharashtra border, and runs approximately 1,600 km (994 mi) across the states of Maharashtra, Goa, Karnataka,

Kerala, and Tamil Nadu, almost to the southern tip of the Indian peninsula. The average elevation is around 1,000 m (3,281 ft). The Anai Mudi in the Anaimalai Hills at 2,695 m (8,842 ft)in Kerala is the highest peak in the Western Ghats.

The Eastern Ghats are a discontinuous range of mountains, which have been eroded and cut through by the four major rivers of southern India, the Godavari, Mahanadi, Krishna, and Kaveri. These mountain ranges extend from West Bengal in the north, through Orissa and Andhra Pradesh to Tamil Nadu in the south. They run parallel to the Bay of Bengal. Though not as tall as the Western Ghats, though some of its peaks are over 1,000 m (3,281 ft) in height. The Eastern Ghats meet with the Western Ghats meet at the Nilgiri hills in Tamil Nadu.

Indo-Gangetic plain

The Indo-Gangetic plains are large floodplains of the Indus and the Ganga-Brahmaputra river systems. They run parallel to the Himalaya mountains, from Jammu and Kashmir in the west to Assam in the east, draining the states of Punjab, Haryana, parts of Rajasthan, Uttar Pradesh, Bihar, Jharkhand and West Bengal. The plains encompass an area of 700,000 km^2 (270,000 mile^2) and vary in width through their length by several hundred kilometres. Major rivers that form a part of this system are the Ganga (Ganges) and Indus River along with their tributaries; Beas, Yamuna, Gomti, Ravi, Chambal, Sutlej and Chenab.

The great plains are sometimes classified into four divisions:

- The **Bhabar** belt—This is adjacent to the foothills of the Himalayas and consists of boulders and pebbles which have been carried down by the river streams. As the porosity of this belt is very high, the streams flow underground. The bhabar is generally narrow about 7-15 km wide.
- The **Terai** belt—This belt lies next to the Bhabar region and is composed of newer alluvium. The underground streams reappear in this region. The region is excessively moist and thickly forested. It also receives heavy rainfall throughout the year and is populated with a variety of wildlife.
- The **Bangar** belt—It consists of older alluvium and forms the alluvial terrace of the flood plains. In the Gangetic plains, it has a low upland covered by laterite deposits.
- The **Khadar** belt—It lies in lowland areas after the Bangar belt. It is made up of fresh newer alluvium which is deposited by the rivers flowing down the plain.

The Indo-Gangetic belt is the world's most extensive expanse of uninterrupted alluvium formed by the deposition of silt by the numerous rivers. The plains are flat and mostly treeless, making it conducive for irrigation through canals. The area is also rich in ground water sources.

The plains are one of the world's most intensely farmed areas. Crops grown on the Indo-Gangetic Plain are primarily rice and wheat, grown in rotation. Other crops include maize, sugarcane and cotton. Also known as the Great Plains, the Indo-Gangetic plains rank among the world's most densely populated areas.

The Desert

The Thar Desert (also known as the *Great Indian Desert*) is a hot desert that forms a significant portion of western India. Spread over four states in India—Punjab, Haryana, Rajasthan, and Gujarat it covers an area of 208,110 km^2 (80,350 mile^2). The desert continues into Pakistan as the Cholistan Desert. Most of the Thar Desert is situated in Rajasthan, covering 61% of its geographic area. Most of the desert is rocky, with a small part of the extreme west of the desert being sandy.

The origin of the Thar Desert is uncertain. Some geologists consider it to be 4,000 to 10,000 years old, whereas others state that aridity began in this region much earlier. The area is characterised by extreme temperatures of above 45 °C (113 °F) in summer to below freezing in winters. Rainfall is precarious and erratic, ranging from below 120 mm (4.72 inches) in the extreme west to 375 mm (14.75 inches) eastward. The lack of rainfall is mainly due to the unique position of the desert with respect to the Aravalli range. The desert lies in the rain shadow area of the Bay of Bengal arm of the southwest monsoon. The parallel nature of the range to the Arabian Sea arm also means that the desert does not receive much rainfall.

The soils of the arid region are generally sandy to sandy-loam in texture. The consistency and depth vary according to the topographical features. The low-lying loams are heavier and may have a hard pan of clay, calcium carbonate or gypsum. Because of the low population density, the effect of the population on the environment is relatively less compared to the rest of India.

Highlands

The Central Highlands are composed of three main plateaus—the Malwa Plateau in the west, the Deccan Plateau in the south, (covering most of the Indian peninsula), and the Chota Nagpur Plateau in Jharkhand towards the east.

The Deccan Plateau is a large triangular plateau, bounded by the Vindhyas to the north and flanked by the Eastern and Western Ghats. The Deccan covers a total area of 1.9 million km^2 (735,000 mile^2). It is mostly flat, with elevations ranging from 300 to 600 m (1,000 to 2,000 ft).

The name *Deccan* comes from the Sanskrit word *dakshina,* which means "the south". The plateau slopes gently from west to east and gives rise to several peninsular rivers such as the Godavari, the Krishna, the Kaveri and the Narmada. This region is mostly semi-arid as it lies on the leeward side of both Ghats. Much of the Deccan is covered by thorn scrub forest scattered with small regions of deciduous broadleaf forest. Climate ranges from hot summers to mild winters.

The Chota Nagpur Plateau is a plateau in eastern India, which covers much of Jharkhand state as well as adjacent parts of Orissa, Bihar, and Chhattisgarh. The total area of Chota Nagpur Plateau is approximately 65,000 km^2 (25,000 mile^2). The Chota Nagpur Plateau is made up of three smaller plateaus, the Ranchi, Hazaribagh, and Kodarma plateaus. The Ranchi plateau is the largest of the plateaus, with an average elevation of 700 m (2,300 ft). Much of the plateau is forested, covered by the Chota Nagpur dry deciduous forests. The plateau is famous for its vast reserves of ores and coal. Besides the Great Indian peninsula, the Kathiawar Peninsula in Gujarat is another large peninsula of India.

East Coast

The Eastern Coastal Plain is a wide stretch of land lying between the Eastern Ghats and the Bay of Bengal. It stretches from Tamil Nadu in the south to West Bengal in the north. Deltas of many of India's rivers form a major portion of these plains. The Mahanadi, Godavari, Kaveri and Krishna rivers drain these plains. The region receives both the Northeast and Southwest monsoon rains with its annual rainfall averaging between 1,000 mm (40 in) and 3,000 mm (120 in). The width of the plains varies between 100 to 130 km (62 to 80 miles).

The plains are divided into six regions: The Mahanadi delta; the southern Andhra Pradesh plain; the Krishna Godavari deltas; the Kanyakumari coast; Coromandel Coast and sandy coastal.

West Coast

The Western Coastal Plain is a narrow strip of land sandwiched between the Western Ghats and the Arabian Sea. The strip begins in Gujarat in the north and extends across the states of Maharashtra, Goa, Karnataka and Kerala. The plains are narrow, and range from 50 to 100 km (30 to 60 miles) in width.

Small rivers and numerous backwaters inundate the region. The rivers, which originate in the Western Ghats, are fast flowing and are mostly perennial. The fast flowing nature of the rivers results in the formation of estuaries rather than deltas. Major rivers flowing into the sea are the Tapi, Narmada, Mandovi and Zuari.

The coast is divided into three regions. The northern region of Maharashtra and Goa is known as the Konkan Coast, the central region of Karnataka is known as the Kanara Coast and the southern coastline of Kerala is known as the Malabar Coast. Vegetation in this region is mostly deciduous. The Malabar Coast has its own unique ecoregion known as the Malabar Coast moist forests.

Islands

India has two major offshore island possessions: the Lakshadweep islands and the Andaman and Nicobar Islands. Both these island groups are administered by the Union government of India as Union Territories.

The Lakshadweep islands lie 200 to 300 km (124 to 186 miles) off the coast of Kerala in the Arabian Sea. It consists of twelve coral atolls, three coral reefs, and five banks. Ten of these islands are inhabited.

The Andaman & Nicobar Islands are located between 6 and 14 North latitude and 92 and 94 East longitude. The Andaman and Nicobar islands consist of 572 isles which lie in the Bay of Bengal, near the Myanmar coast. It is located 1255 km (780 miles) from Kolkata (Calcutta) and 193 km (120 miles) from Cape Negrais in Myanmar. The territory consists of two island groups, the Andaman Islands and the Nicobar Islands. The Andaman islands consist of 204 islands having a total length of 352 km (220 miles). The Nicobar Islands, which lie south of the Andamans, consist of twenty-two islands with a total area of 1,841 km^2 (710 $mile^2$). The highest point is Mount Thullier at 642 m (2,140 ft). Indira Point, India's southernmost land point is situated in the Nicobar islands, and lies just 189 km (117 miles) from the Indonesian island of Sumatra to the southeast.

Significant islands just off the Indian coast include Diu, a former Portuguese enclave; Majuli, Asia's largest freshwater island; Salcette Island, India's most populous island, on which Mumbai (Bombay) city is located; Elephanta in Bombay Harbour; and Sriharikota barrier island in Andhra Pradesh.

Rivers

All major rivers of India originate from one of the three main watersheds. They are:

1. The Himalaya and the Karakoram ranges
2. Vindhya and Satpura range in central India
3. Sahyadri or Western Ghats in western India

The Himalayan river networks are snow-fed and have a continuous flow throughout the year. The other two networks are dependent on the monsoons and shrink into rivulets during the dry season.

Twelve of India's rivers are classified as major, with the total catchment area exceeding 2,528,000 km^2 (976,000 mile^2).

Himalayan rivers or the northern rivers that flow westward into Pakistan are the Indus, Beas, Chenab, Ravi, Sutlej, and Jhelum.

The Ganga-Brahmaputra-Meghana system has the largest catchment area of 1,100,000 km^2 (424,700 mile^2). The river Ganga originates at the Gangotri Glacier in Uttarakhand. It flows in a south easterly direction, draining into Bangladesh. The Yamuna and Gomti rivers also arise in the Western Himalayas and join the Ganga river in the plains. The Brahmaputra, another tributary of the Ganga originates in Tibet and enters India in the far eastern state of Arunachal Pradesh. It then proceeds westwards, unifying with the Ganga in Bangladesh.

The Chambal, another tributary of the Ganga originates from the Vindhya-Satpura watershed. The river flows eastward. Westward flowing rivers from this watershed are the Narmada (also called Nerbudda) and Tapti (also spelled Tapi) rivers which drain into the Arabian Sea in Gujarat. The river network that flows from east to west constitutes 10% of the total outflow.

The Western Ghats are the source of all Deccan rivers. Major rivers in the Deccan include the Mahanadi River through the Mahanadi River Delta, Godavari River, Krishna River, and Kaveri River (also spelled Cauvery), all draining into the Bay of Bengal. These rivers constitute 20% of India's total outflow.

Bodies of Water

Major gulfs include the Gulf of Cambay, Gulf of Kutch and the Gulf of Mannar. Straits include the Palk Strait which separates India from Sri Lanka and the Ten Degree Channel, separating the Andamans from the Nicobar Islands and the Eight Degree Channel separating the Laccadive and Amindivi Islands from Minicoy Island towards the south. Important capes include the Cape Comorin, the southern tip of mainland India, Indira Point, the southernmost location of India, Rama's Bridge and Point Calimere. Arabian Sea is to the west of India. Bay of Bengal is to the eastern side of India while India Ocean is to the South of India.

Smaller seas include the Laccadive Sea and the Andaman Sea. There are four coral reefs in India and are located in; the Andaman and Nicobar Islands, Gulf of Mannar, Lakshadweep and Gulf of Kutch.

Important lakes include Chilka Lake, the country's largest saltwater lake in Orissa; Kolleru Lake in Andhra Pradesh; Loktak Lake in Manipur, Dal Lake in Kashmir, Sambhar Lake in Rajasthan, and the Sasthamkotta Lake in Kerala.

Wetlands

Wetlands are lands transitional between aquatic and territorial system where water table is usually near the water surface and land is covered by shallow water. They also act as a buffer against the devastating effect of hurricanes and cyclones, thereby stabilizing the shoreline. It also helps in keeping a check on sea and soil erosion. India's wetland ecosystem is widely distributed from the cold and arid; from ones in the Ladakh region in the state of Jammu and Kashmir to the ones in the wet and humid climate of peninsula India. Most of the wetlands are directly or indirectly linked to India's river networks. In 1987, National Wetland Conservation Programme was initiated by the government for wetland conservation. Under this programme, the Indian government has identified a total of 71 wetlands for conservation.

Mangrove forests occur all along the Indian coastline, in sheltered estuaries, creeks, backwaters, salt marshes and mudflats. The mangrove area covers a total of 4 461 km^2 (1,722 $mile^2$) which comprises 7% of the world's total mangrove cover. The Andaman and Nicobar Islands; the Sundarbans; Gulf of Kutch; deltas of the Mahanadi, Godavari and Krishna; and parts of Maharashtra, Karnataka and Kerala have large mangrove covers. Most of the identified wetlands adjoin or are parts of sanctuaries, national parks and are thus protected.

The Sundarbans

The Sundarbans delta is the largest mangrove forest in the world. It lies at the mouth of the Ganges and is spread across areas of Bangladesh and West Bengal, India. The Bangladeshi and Indian portions of the jungle are listed in the UNESCO world heritage list separately as the Sundarbans and Sundarbans National Park respectively, though they are parts of the same forest. The Sundarbans are intersected by a complex network of tidal waterways, mudflats and small islands of salt-tolerant mangrove forests, and presents an excellent example of ongoing ecological processes.

The area is known for its wide range of fauna. The most famous among these is the Bengal Tiger, but numerous species of birds, spotted deer, crocodiles and snakes also inhabit it. It is estimated that there are now 400 Bengal tigers and about 30,000 spotted deer in the area.

Rann of Kutch

The Rann of Kutch is a marshy region located in the Gujarat state of India, which borders the Sindh region of Pakistan. The name *Rann* comes from the Hindi word *ran* meaning "salt marsh." It occupies a total area of 27 900 km^2 (10,800 $mile^2$).

The region was originally a part of the Arabian Sea. Geologic forces, most likely by earthquakes, resulted in the damming up of the region, turning it into a large saltwater lagoon. This area gradually filled with silt thus turning it into a seasonal salt marsh. During the monsoons, the area turns into a shallow marsh, often flooding to knee-depth. After the monsoons, the region turns dry and becomes parched.

Soil

Soils in India can be classified into 8 categories namely, alluvial soil, black soil, red soil, laterite soil, forest soil, arid & desert soil, saline & alkaline soil, and finally peaty & organic soil. Of the above eight varieties, the first 4 constitute nearly 80% of total land surface. Alluvial soil constitute the largest soil group in India. It is derived from deposition of silt carried by numerous rivers. Alluvial soils are generally fertile but they lack nitrogen and tend to be phosphoric. These are found in the Great Northern plains from Punjab to Assam valley.

Black soil are well developed in the Deccan lava region of Maharashtra, Gujarat, and Madhya Pradesh. These contain high percentage of clay and are thus moisture retentive. Because of these properties they are preferred for dry farming and growing cotton, linseed etc.

Red soil have a wide diffusion of iron content and are found in Tamil Nadu, Karnataka plateau, and Andhra plateau. The central highlands from Aravallis to Chota Nagpur plateau also have significant tracts of red soil. These are deficient in nitrogen, phosphorus and humus.

Laterite soils are formed in tropical regions with heavy rainfall. Heavy rainfall results in leaching out all soluble material of top layer of soil. These are generally found in Western ghats, Eastern ghats and hilly areas of northeastern states which receive very heavy rainfall.

Forest soils occur on the slopes of mountains and hills in Himalayas, Western Ghats and Eastern Ghats. These generally consist of large amounts of dead leaves and other organic matter called humus. These scils are used for tea and coffee plantations.

Climate

The climate of India is comprised of a wide range of weather conditions across a vast geographic scale and varied topography, making generalisations difficult. Based on the Köppen system, India hosts six major climatic subtypes, ranging from arid desert in the west, alpine tundra and glaciers in the north, and humid tropical regions supporting rainforests in the southwest and the island territories. Many regions have starkly different microclimates. The nation has four seasons: winter (January–February), summer (March–May), a monsoon (rainy) season (June–September), and a post-monsoon period (October–December).

India's unique geography and geology strongly influence its climate; this is particularly true of the Himalayas in the north and the Thar Desert in the northwest. The Himalayas act as a barrier to the frigid katabatic winds flowing down from Central Asia. Thus, North India is kept warm or only mildly cooled during winter; in summer, the same phenomenon makes India relatively hot. Although the Tropic of Cancer—the boundary between the tropics and subtropics—passes through the middle of India, the whole country is considered to be tropical.

Summer lasts between March and June in most parts of India. Temperatures exceed 40 °C (104 °F) during the day. The coastal regions exceed 30 °C (86 °F) coupled with high levels of humidity. In the Thar desert area temperatures can exceed 45 °C (113 °F).

Summer is followed by the southwest monsoon rains that provide most of India with its rainfall. The rain-bearing clouds are attracted to the low-pressure system created by the Thar Desert. The official date for the arrival of the monsoon is 1 June, when the monsoon crosses the Kerala coast. The southwest monsoon splits into two arms, the Bay of Bengal arm and the Arabian Sea arm. The Bay of Bengal arm moves northwards crossing northeast India in early June. It then progresses eastwards, crossing Delhi by June 29. The Arabian Sea arm moves northwards and deposits much of its rain on the windward side of Western Ghats. By early July, most of India receives rain from the monsoons.

The monsoons start retreating by August from northern India and by October from Kerala. This short period after the retreat is known as the retreat of the monsoons and is characterised by still weather. By November, winter starts setting in the northern areas.

Winters start in November in northern India and late December in southern India. Winters in peninsula India see mild to warm days and cool nights. Further north the temperature is cooler. Temperatures in some parts of the Indian plains sometimes fall below freezing. Most of northern India is plagued by fog during this season.

The highest temperature recorded in India was 50.6 °C (123.08 °F) in Alwar in 1955. The lowest was "45 °C ("49 °F) in Kashmir. Recent claims of temperatures touching 55 °C (131 °F) in Orissa have been met with some scepticism by the Indian Meteorological Department, largely on the method of recording of such data.

Geology

India has a varied geology spanning the entire spectrum of the geological time period. India's geological features are classified based on their era of formation.

The Precambrian formations of Cudappah and Vindhyan systems are spread out over the eastern and southern states. A small part of this period is spread over western and central India.

The Paleozoic formations from the Cambrian, Ordovician, Silurian and Devonian system are found in the Western Himalaya region in Kashmir and Himachal Pradesh.

The Mesozoic Deccan Traps formation is seen over most of the northern Deccan. Geologists believe that the Deccan Traps were the result of sub-aerial volcanic activity. The Trap soil is black in colour and conducive to agriculture. The Carboniferous system, Permian System, Triassic and Jurassic systems are seen in the western Himalayas. The Jurassic system is also seen in Rajasthan.

Tertiary imprints are seen in parts of Manipur, Nagaland, parts of Arunachal Pradesh and along the Himalayan belt. The Cretaceous system is seen in central India in the Vindhyas and part of the Indo-Gangetic plains.

The Gondowana system is also seen in the Narmada River area in the Vindhyas and Satpuras. The Eocene system is seen in the western Himalayas and Assam. Oligocene formations are seen in Kutch and in Assam.

The Pleistocene system is found over central India. It is rich in minerals such as lignite, iron ore, manganese, and aluminium. The Andaman and Nicobar Island groups are thought to have been formed in this era by volcanoes. The Himalayas are a result of the convergence and deformation of the Indo-Australian and Eurasian Plates. Their continued convergence raises the height of the Himalayas by 1 cm each year.

Natural Resources

India is particularly rich in a variety of natural resources. Along with 56% arable land, it has significant sources of coal (fourth-largest reserves in the world), iron ore, manganese, mica, bauxite, titanium ore, chromite, natural gas, diamonds, petroleum, limestone. India is self-sufficient in thorium, mined along shores of Kerala, possessing 24% of the world's known and economically available thorium.

Petroleum is found off the coast of Maharashtra, Gujarat and in Assam, but meets only 40% of India's demand. Increasing amounts of natural gas are being discovered regularly especially off the coast of Andhra Pradesh. Uranium is mined in Andhra Pradesh and gold in the Kolar gold mine in Karnataka.

Natural Disasters

Natural disasters cause massive losses of Indian life and property. Droughts, flash floods, cyclones, avalanches, landslides brought on by torrential rains, and snowstorms pose the greatest threats. Other dangers include frequent summer dust storms, which usually track from north to south; they cause extensive property damage in North India and deposit large amounts of dust from arid regions. Hail is also common in parts of India, causing severe damage to standing crops such as rice and wheat.

In the Lower Himalaya, landslides are common. The young age of the region's hills result in labile rock formations, which are susceptible to slippages. Parts of the Western Ghats also suffer from low-intensity landslides. Avalanches occur in Kashmir, Himachal Pradesh, and Sikkim. Floods are the most common natural disaster in India. The heavy southwest monsoon rains cause the Brahmaputra and other rivers to distend their banks, often flooding surrounding areas. Though they provide rice paddy farmers with a largely dependable source of natural irrigation and fertilisation, the floods can kill thousands and displace millions. Excess, erratic, or untimely monsoon rainfall may also wash away or otherwise ruin crops. Almost all of India is flood-prone, and extreme precipitation events, such as flash floods and torrential rains, have become increasingly common in central India over the past several decades, coinciding with rising temperatures. Mean annual precipitation totals have remained steady owing to the declining frequency of weather systems that generate moderate amounts of rain.

Indian agriculture is heavily dependent on the monsoon as a source of water. In some parts of India, the failure of the monsoons result in water shortages, resulting in below-average crop yields. This is particularly true of major drought-prone regions such as southern and eastern Maharashtra, northern Karnataka, Andhra Pradesh, Orissa, Gujarat, and Rajasthan. In the past, droughts have periodically led to major Indian famines, including the Bengal famine of 1770, in which up to one third of the population in affected areas died; the 1876–1877 famine, in which over five million people died; the 1899 famine, in which over 4.5 million died; and the Bengal famine of 1943, in which over five million died from starvation and famine-related illnesses.

According to earthquake hazard zoning of India, tectonic plates beneath the earth's surface are responsible for yearly earthquakes along the Himalayan belt and in northeast India. This region is classified as a Zone V, indicating that it is a very high-risk area. Parts of western India, around the Kutch region in Gujarat and Koyna in Maharashtra, are classified as a Zone IV region (high risk). Other areas have a moderate to low risk chance of an earthquake occurring.

Tropical cyclones, which are severe storms spun off from the Intertropical Convergence Zone, may affect thousands of Indians living in coastal regions. Cyclones bring with them heavy rains, storm surges, and winds that often cut affected areas off from relief and supplies. In the North Indian Ocean Basin, the cyclone season runs from April to December, with peak activity between May and November. Each year, an average of eight storms with sustained wind speeds greater than 63 kilometres per hour (39 mph) form; of these, two strengthen into true tropical cyclones, which have sustained gusts greater than 117 km/h (73 mph). On average, a major (Category 3 or higher) cyclone develops every other year. In terms of damage and loss of life, Cyclone

05B, a supercyclone that struck Orissa on 29 October 1999, was the worst in more than a quarter century.

A tsunami caused by the 2004 Indian Ocean earthquake struck the Andaman and Nicobar Islands and India's east coast resulting in the deaths of an estimated 10,000. Until then India was thought to have negligible activity related to tsunamis, though there is historical anecdotal evidence of its occurrence in the past.

India has one active volcano: the Barren Island volcano which last erupted in May 2005. There is also a dormant volcano called the Narcondum and a mud volcano at Baratang. All these volcanoes lie in the Andaman Islands.

GOVERNMENT AND POLITICS OF INDIA

The Constitution of India, the longest and the most exhaustive constitution of any independent nation in the world, came into force on January 26, 1950. The preamble of the constitution defines India as a sovereign, socialist, secular, democratic republic. India has a quasi-federal form of government and a bicameral parliament operating under a Westminster-style parliamentary system. It has three branches of governance: the Legislature, Executive, and Judiciary.

The President of India is the official head of state elected indirectly by an electoral college for a five-year term. The Prime Minister is, however, the *de facto* head of government and exercises most executive powers. The Prime Minister is appointed by the President and, by convention, is the candidate supported by the party or political alliance holding the majority of seats in the lower house of Parliament.

The legislature of India is the bicameral Parliament, which consists of the upper house called the Rajya Sabha (Council of States) and the lower house called the Lok Sabha (House of People). The Rajya Sabha, a permanent body, has 245 members serving staggered six year terms. Most are elected indirectly by the state and territorial legislatures in proportion to the state's population. The 543 of the Lok Sabha's 545 members are directly elected by popular vote to represent individual constituencies for five year terms. The other two members are nominated by the President from the Anglo-Indian community if, in his opinion, the community is not adequately represented.

The executive branch consists of the President, Vice-President, and the Council of Ministers (the Cabinet being its executive committee) headed by the Prime Minister. Any minister holding a portfolio must be a member of either house of parliament. In the Indian parliamentary system, the executive is subordinate to the legislature, with the Prime Minister and his Council being directly responsible to the lower house of the parliament.

India has a unitary three-tier judiciary, consisting of the Supreme Court, headed by the Chief Justice of India, twenty-one High Courts, and a large number of trial courts. The Supreme Court has original jurisdiction over cases involving fundamental rights and over disputes between states and the Centre, and appellate jurisdiction over the High Courts. It is judicially independent, and has the power to declare the law and to strike down union or state laws which contravene the Constitution. The role as the ultimate interpreter of the Constitution is one of the most important functions of the Supreme Court.

India, at the federal level, is the most populous democracy in the world. For most of its democratic history, the federal government has been led by the Indian National Congress (INC). State politics have been dominated by several national parties including the INC, the Bharatiya Janata Party (BJP), the Communist Party of India (Marxist) (CPI(M)), and various regional parties. From 1950 to 1990, barring two brief periods, the INC enjoyed a parliamentary majority. The INC was out of power between 1977 and 1980, when the Janata Party won the election owing to public discontent with the "Emergency" declared by the then Prime Minister Indira Gandhi. In 1989, a Janata Dal-led National Front coalition in alliance with the Left Front coalition won the elections but managed to stay in power for only two years.

The years 1996–1998 were a period of turmoil in the federal government with several short-lived alliances holding sway. The BJP formed a government briefly in 1996, followed by the United Front coalition. In 1998, the BJP formed the National Democratic Alliance (NDA) with several regional parties and became the first non-Congress government to complete a full five-year term. In the 2004 Indian elections, the INC won the largest number of Lok Sabha seats and formed a government with a coalition called the United Progressive Alliance (UPA), supported by various left-leaning parties and members opposed to the BJP.

DEMOGRAPHY

With an estimated population of 1.13 billion, India is the world's second most populous country. Almost 70% of Indians reside in rural areas, although in recent decades migration to larger cities has led to a dramatic increase in the country's urban population. India's largest cities are Mumbai (formerly Bombay), Delhi, Kolkata (formerly Calcutta), Chennai (formerly Madras), Bengaluru (formerly Bangalore), Hyderabad and Ahmedabad.

India is the second most culturally, linguistically and genetically diverse geographical entity after the African continent. India is home to two major linguistic families: Indo-Aryan (spoken by about 74% of the population) and Dravidian (spoken by about 24%).

Other languages spoken in India come from the Austro-Asiatic and Tibeto-Burman linguistic families. Hindi, with the largest number of speakers, is the official language of the union. English, which is extensively used in business and administration, has the status of a 'subsidiary official language.' The constitution also recognises in particular 21 other languages that are either abundantly spoken or have classical status. The number of dialects in India is as high as 1,652.

Over 800 million Indians (80.5%) are Hindu. Other religious groups include Muslims (13.4%), Christians (2.3%), Sikhs (1.9%), Buddhists (0.8%), Jains (0.4%), Jews, Zoroastrians, Bahá'ís and others. Tribals constitute 8.1% of the population.

India's literacy rate is 64.8% (53.7% for females and 75.3% for males). The state of Kerala has the highest literacy rate (91%); Bihar has the lowest (47%). The national human sex ratio is 944 females per 1,000 males. India's median age is 24.9, and the population growth rate of 1.38% per annum; there are 22.01 births per 1,000 people per year.

INDIAN CULTURE

The culture of India has been shaped by the long history of India, its unique geography and the absorption of customs, traditions and ideas from some of its neighbors as well as by preserving its ancient heritages, which were formed during the Indus Valley Civilization and evolved further during the Vedic age, rise and decline of Buddhism, Golden age, Muslim conquests and European colonization. India's great diversity of cultural practices, languages, customs, and traditions are examples of this unique co-mingling over the past five millennia.

India is also the birth place of several religious systems such as Hinduism, Jainism, Buddhism, and Sikhism. The various religions and traditions of India that were created by these amalgamations have influenced other parts of the world too.

Language

The great number of languages in India have added to the diverse cultures and traditions at both regional and national levels. 216 languages are spoken by a group of more than 10,000 people; however there are many others which are spoken by fewer than 10,000 people. All together, there are 415 living languages in India. The Constitution of India has stipulated the usage of Hindi and English to be the two official languages of communication for the Union Government. Individual state's own internal communications are done in the state's language. The two major linguistic families in India are those of the Indo-Aryan languages and the Dravidian languages, the former being largely confined to northern, western, central and eastern India and the latter to southern India. The next largest language family in India is the Austro-Asiatic language group, which contains the Munda languages of central and eastern India, the Khasian languages of northeastern India, and the Nicobarese languages of the Nicobar Islands. The fourth largest language family in India is the Tibeto-Burman languages, which are themselves a subgroup of the larger Sino-Tibetan language family.

Literature

History

The earliest literary traditions were oral and have been passed down as such. Later, though, they were transcribed. Many of them derive from Hindu tradition and are represented by texts in Sanskrit such as the Vedas, the epics of the Mahabharata and Ramayana. Other are in Sangam literature from the beginning of the Common Era, and in Kannada such as the writings *Prabhrita* (650 CE) and *Chudamani* (*Crest Jewel*- 650 CE or earlier; a 96,000 verse commentary on logic). Furthermore, many Buddhist sutras and Jain works are in Prakrit languages like Pali (c. 250 BCE) and Ardhamagadhi, and later on in Sanskrit. All these represent some of India's oldest literary traditions.

During the period of the Delhi sultanate (after 1200 CE) and in the subsequent Mughal era, Islamic culture has influenced medieval Indian literature. This was especially due to the increased influence of Persian, including the work of famous poets such as Amir Khusro.

During the period of English colonial rule, modern literature exemplified by the works of Rabindranath Tagore, Subramania Barathi, Kuvempu, Bankim Chandra Chattopadhyay, Michael Madhusudan Dutt, Munshi Premchand, Muhammad Iqbal, Devaki Nandan Khatri became prominent. In contemporary India, writers like Girish Karnad, Agyeya, Nirmal Verma, Kamleshwar, Vaikom Muhammad Basheer, Indira Goswami, Mahasweta Devi, Amrita Pritam, Maasti Venkatesh Ayengar, Qurratulain Hyder and Thakazhi Sivasankara Pillai, to name but a few, have been the recipients of critical acclaim.

Poetry

India has strong traditions of poetry ever since the Rigveda, as well as prose compositions. Poetry is often closely related to musical traditions, and much of poetry can be attributed to religious movements. Writers and philosophers were often also skilled poets. In modern times, poetry has served as an important non-violent tool of nationalism during the Indian freedom movement. A famous modern example of this tradition can be found in such figures as Rabindranath Tagore and K. S. Narasimhaswamy in modern times and poets such as Basava (*vachanas*), Kabir and

Purandaradasa (*padas* and *devaranamas*) in medieval times, as well as the epics of ancient times. Two examples of poetry from Tagore's Gitanjali serve as the national anthems of both India and Bangladesh.

Epics

The Ramayana and Mahabharata are the oldest preserved and still well-known epics of India; some of their versions have been adopted as the epics of Southeast Asian countries like Thailand, Malaysia and Indonesia. In addition, there are five epics in the classical Tamil language -they being Silappadhikaram, Manimegalai, Jeevaga-chintamani, Valayaapathi, Kundalakesi. Other regional variations of them as well as unrelated epics include the Tamil Kamba Ramayanam, in Kannada, the Pampa Bharata by Adikavi Pampa, Torave Ramayana by Kumara Valmiki and Karnata Bharata KathaManjari by Kumaravyasa, Hindi Ramacharitamanasa, Malayalam Adhyathmaramayanam.

Performing arts

Music

The music of India includes multiples varieties of religious, folk, popular, pop, and classical music. The oldest preserved examples of Indian music are the melodies of the Samaveda that are still sung in certain Vedic Shrauta sacrifices. India's classical music tradition is heavily influenced by Hindu texts. It includes Carnatic and Hindustani music and is noted for the use of several Raga, has a history spanning millennia, and, developed over several eras, remains instrumental to the religious inspiration, cultural expression and pure entertainment. Alongside distinctly subcontinental forms, there are some similarities with other types of Oriental music.

Purandaradasa is considered the "father of carnatic music" (*Karnataka sangeeta pitamaha*). He concluded his songs with a salutation to Lord Purandara Vittala and is believed to have composed as many as 475,000 songs in the Kannada language. However, only about 1000 are known today.

Dance

Indian dance too has diverse *folk* and *classical* forms. Among the well-known folk dances are the *bhangra* of the Punjab, the *bihu* of Assam, the *chhau* of Jharkhand and Orissa, the *ghoomar* of Rajasthan, the *dandiya* and *garba* of Gujarat, the *Yakshagana* of Karnataka and *lavani* of Maharashtra. Eight dance forms, many with narrative forms and mythological elements, have been accorded classical dance status by India's *National Academy of Music, Dance, and Drama*. These are: *bharatanatyam* of the state of Tamil Nadu, *kathak* of Uttar Pradesh, *kathakali* and *mohiniattam* of Kerala, *kuchipudi* of

Andhra Pradesh, *manipuri* of Manipur, *odissi* of the state of Orissa and the *sattriya* of Assam.

Martial arts

Kalarippayattu or Kalari for short is one of the world's oldest martial art. It is preserved in texts such as the Mallapurana. Kalari and other later formed martial arts have been assumed by some to have traveled to China, like Buddhism, and eventually developing into Kung-fu. Other later martial arts are Gatka,Pehlwani,and Malla-yuddha. There have been many great practitioners of Indian martial Arts including Bodhidharma who supposedly brought Indian martial arts to China.

Drama and theater

Indian drama and theater has a long history alongside its music and dance. Kalidasa's plays like Shakuntala and Meghadoota are some of the older plays, following those of Bhasa. One of the oldest surviving theatre tradition of the world is the 2000 year old Kutiyattam of Kerala. It strictly follows the Natya Shastra. The dramas of Bhasa are very popular in this art form. *Nâtyâchârya* (late) Padma Shri Mâni Mâdhava Châkyâr- the unrivaled maestro of this art form and *Abhinaya,* revived the age old drama tradition from extinction. He was known for mastery of Rasa Abhinaya. He started to perform the Kalidasa plays like Abhijñânaúâkuntala, Vikramorvaúîya and Mâlavikâgnimitra ; Bhasa's Swapnavâsavadatta and Pancharâtra; Harsha's Nagananda in Kutiyattam form.

The tradition of folk theater is popular in most linguistic regions of India. In addition, there is a rich tradition of puppet theater in rural India, going back to at least the second century BCE. (It is mentioned in Patanjali's commentary on Panini). Group Theater is also thriving in the cities, initiated by the likes of Gubbi Veeranna Utpal Dutt, Khwaja Ahmad Abbas, K. V. Subbanna and still maintained by groups like Nandikar, Ninasam and Prithvi Theatre.

Painting

The earliest Indian paintings were the rock paintings of pre-historic times, the petroglyphs as found in places like Bhimbetka, some of which go back to the Stone Age. Ancient texts outline theories of darragh and anecdotal accounts suggesting that it was common for households to paint their doorways or indoor rooms where guests resided.

Cave paintings from Ajanta, Bagh, Ellora and Sittanavasal and temple paintings testify to a love of naturalism. Most early and medieval art in India is Hindu, Buddhist or Jain. A freshly made coloured flour design (Rangoli) is still a common sight outside the doorstep of many (mostly South Indian) Indian homes.

Madhubani painting, Mysore painting, Rajput painting, Tanjore painting, Mughal painting are some notable Genres of Indian Art; while Raja Ravi Varma, Nandalal Bose, Geeta Vadhera,Jamini Roy and B.Venkatappa are some modern painters. Among the present day artists, Atul Dodiya, Bose Krishnamacnahri, Devajyoti Ray and Shibu Natesan represent a new era of Indian art where global art shows direct amalgamation with Indian classical styles. These recent artists have acquired international recognition. Devajyoti Ray's paintings have been acquired by the National Fine Arts Museum in Cuba and so have been the works of some of the new generation artists.

Jehangir Art Gallery, Mumbai, Mysore Palace has on display several good Indian paintings.

Sculpture

The first sculptures in India date back to the Indus Valley civilization, where stone and bronze figures have been discovered. Later, as Hinduism, Buddhism, and Jainism developed further, India produced some extremely intricate bronzes as well as temple carvings. Some huge shrines, such as the one at Ellora were not constructed by using blocks but carved out of solid rock.

Sculptures produced in the northwest, in stucco, schist, or clay, display a very strong blend of Indian and Classical Hellenistic or possibly even Greco-Roman influence. The pink sandstone sculptures of Mathura evolved almost simultaneously. During the Gupta period (4th to 6th century) sculpture reached a very high standard in execution and delicacy in modeling. These styles and others elsewhere in India evolved leading to classical Indian art that contributing to Buddhist and Hindu sculpture throughout Southeast Central and East Asia.

ECONOMY OF INDIA

The economy of India, measured in USD exchange-rate terms, is the twelfth largest in the world, with a GDP of around $1 trillion (2008). It recorded a GDP growth rate of 9.1% for the fiscal year 2007–2008 which makes it the second fastest big emerging economy, after China, in the world. At this rate of sustained growth many economists forecast that India would, over the coming decades, have a more pronounced economic effect on the world stage. Despite this phenomenal rate of growth, India's large population has a per capita income of $2,659, measured by PPP, and $978, measured in nominal terms (revised 2007 estimate). The World Bank classifies India as a low-income economy.

India's economy is diverse, encompassing agriculture, handicrafts, textile, manufacturing, and a multitude of services. Although two-thirds of the Indian workforce still earn their livelihood directly or indirectly through agriculture, services are a growing sector and play an increasingly important role in India's economy. The advent of the digital age, and the large number of young and educated populace fluent in English, is gradually transforming India as an important 'back office' destination for global outsourcing of customer services and technical support. India is a major exporter of highly-skilled workers in software and financial services, and software engineering. Other sectors like manufacturing, pharmaceuticals, biotechnology, nanotechnology, telecommunication, shipbuilding, aviation, tourism and retailing are showing strong potentials with higher growth rates.

India followed a socialist-inspired approach for most of its independent history, with strict government control over private sector participation, foreign trade, and foreign direct investment. However, since the early 1990s, India has gradually opened up its markets through economic reforms by reducing government controls on foreign trade and investment. The privatisation of publicly owned industries and the opening up of certain sectors to private and foreign interests has proceeded slowly amid political debate.

India faces a fast-growing population and the challenge of reducing economic and social inequality. Poverty remains a serious problem, although it has declined significantly since independence.

India's economic history can be broadly divided into three eras, beginning with the pre-colonial period lasting up to the 17th century. The advent of British colonisation started the colonial period in the 17th century, which ended with independence in 1947. The third period stretches from independence in 1947 until now.

Pre-colonial

The citizens of the Indus Valley civilisation (based around the river Indus in modern day Pakistan and Northern and Western India), a permanent and predominantly urban settlement that flourished between 2800 BC and 1800 BC, practised agriculture, domesticated animals, used uniform weights and measures, made tools and weapons, and traded with other cities. Evidence of well planned streets, a drainage system and water supply reveals their knowledge of urban planning, which included the world's first urban sanitation systems and the existence of a form of municipal government.

The 1872 census revealed that 99.3% of the population of the region constituting present-day India resided in villages, whose economies were largely isolated and self-sustaining, with agriculture the predominant occupation. This satisfied the food requirements of the village and provided raw materials for hand-based industries, such as textiles, food processing and crafts. Although many kingdoms and rulers issued coins, barter was prevalent. Villages paid a portion of their agricultural produce as revenue to the rulers, while its craftsmen received a part of the crops at harvest time for their services.

Religion, especially Hinduism, and the caste and the joint family systems, played an influential role in shaping economic activities. The caste system functioned much like medieval European guilds, ensuring the division of labour, providing for the training of apprentices and, in some cases, allowing manufacturers to achieve narrow specialization. For instance, in certain regions, producing each variety of cloth was the speciality of a particular sub-caste.

Textiles such as muslin, Calicos, shawls, and agricultural products such as pepper, cinnamon, opium and indigo were exported to Europe, the Middle East and South East Asia in return for gold and silver.

Assessment of India's pre-colonial economy is mostly qualitative, owing to the lack of quantitative information. One estimate puts the revenue of Akbar's Mughal Empire in 1600 at £17.5 million, in contrast with the total revenue of Great Britain in 1800, which totalled £16 million. India, by the time of the arrival of the British, was a largely traditional agrarian economy with a dominant subsistence sector dependent on primitive technology. It existed alongside a competitively developed network of commerce, manufacturing and credit. After the fall of the Mughals, India was administered by Maratha Empire. The maratha empire's budget in 1740s, at its peak, was Rs. 100 million. After the loss at Panipat, the maratha empire disintegrated into confederate states of Gwalior, Baroda, Indore, Jhansi, Nagpur, Pune and Kolhapur. Gwalior state had a budget of Rs. 30M. However, at this time, British East India company entered the Indian political theatre. Until, 1857, when India was firmly under the British crown, the country remained in a state of political instability due to internecine wars and conflicts.

Colonial

Colonial rule brought a major change in the taxation environment from revenue taxes to property taxes resulting in mass impoverishment and destitution of the great majority of farmers. It also created an institutional environment that, on paper, guaranteed property rights among the colonizers, encouraged free trade, and created a single currency with fixed exchange rates, standardized weights and measures, capital markets, a well developed system of railways and telegraphs, a civil service that aimed to be free from political interference, and a common-law, adversarial legal system. India's colonisation by the British coincided with major changes in the world economy—industrialisation, and significant growth in production and trade. However, at the end of colonial rule, India inherited an economy that was one of the poorest in the developing world, with industrial development stalled, agriculture unable to feed a rapidly growing population, one of the world's lowest life expectancies, and low rates of literacy.

An estimate by Cambridge University historian Angus Maddison reveals that India's share of the world income fell from 22.6% in 1700, comparable to Europe's share of 23.3%, to a low of 3.8% in 1952. While Indian leaders during the Independence struggle, and left-nationalist economic historians have blamed colonial rule for the dismal state of India's economy in its aftermath, a broader macroeconomic view of India during this period reveals that there were sectors of growth and decline, resulting from changes brought about by colonialism and a world that was moving towards industrialisation and economic integration.While the exact sectors of growth and decline is of questionable importance, the overall effect of the changes brought about by colonialism, and India's degree of industrialisation and economic integration of India under the British rule on India's economy can be assessed from the kind of economy India inherited after the end of the colonial rule in India.

Independence to 1991

Indian economic policy after independence was influenced by the colonial experience (which was seen by Indian leaders as exploitative in nature) and by those leaders' exposure to Fabian socialism. Policy tended towards protectionism, with a strong emphasis on import substitution, industrialization, state intervention in labour and financial markets, a large public sector, business regulation, and central planning. Jawaharlal Nehru, the first prime minister, along with the statistician Prasanta Chandra Mahalanobis, carried on by Indira Gandhi formulated and oversaw economic policy. They expected favourable outcomes from this strategy, because it involved both public and private sectors and was based on direct and indirect state intervention, rather than the more extreme Soviet-style central command system. The policy of concentrating simultaneously on capital- and technology-intensive heavy industry and subsidising manual, low-skill cottage industries was criticized by economist Milton Friedman, who thought it would waste capital and labour, and retard the development of small manufacturers.

India's low average growth rate from 1947–80 was derisively referred to as the Hindu rate of growth, because of the unfavourable comparison with growth rates in other Asian countries, especially the "East Asian Tigers".

After 1991

In the late 80s, the government led by Rajiv Gandhi eased restrictions on capacity expansion for incumbents, removed price controls and reduced corporate taxes. While this increased the rate of growth, it also led to high fiscal deficits and a worsening current account. The collapse of the Soviet Union, which was India's major trading partner, and the first Gulf War, which caused a spike in oil prices, caused a major balance-of-payments crisis for India, which found itself facing the prospect of defaulting on its loans. In response, Prime Minister Narasimha Rao along with his finance minister Manmohan Singh initiated the economic liberalisation of 1991. The reforms did away with the Licence Raj (investment, industrial and import licensing) and ended many public monopolies, allowing automatic approval of foreign direct investment in many sectors. Since then, the overall direction of liberalisation has remained the same, irrespective of the ruling party, although no party has tried to take on powerful lobbies such as the trade unions and farmers, or contentious issues such as reforming labour laws and reducing agricultural subsidies.

Since 1990 India has emerged as one of the wealthiest economies in the developing world; during this period, the economy has grown constantly, but with a few major setbacks. This has been accompanied by increases in life expectancy, literacy rates and food security.

While the credit rating of India was hit by its nuclear tests in 1998, it has been raised to investment level in 2007 by S&P and Moody's. In 2003, Goldman Sachs predicted that India's GDP in current prices will overtake France and Italy by 2020, Germany, UK and Russia by 2025 and Japan by 2035. By 2035, it was projected to be the third largest economy of the world, behind US and China.

Currency System

The rupee is the only legal tender accepted in India. The exchange rate as of May 23, 2008 is about 38.695 to a US dollar, 67.335 to a Euro, and 82.004 to a UK pound. The Indian rupee is accepted as legal tender in the neighboring Nepal and Bhutan, both of which peg their currency to that of the Indian rupee. The rupee is divided into 100 paise. The highest-denomination banknote is the 1,000 rupee note; the lowest-denomination coin in circulation is the 25 paise coin.

Natural Resources

India's total cultivable area is 1,269,219 km^2 (56.78% of total land area), which is decreasing due to constant pressure from an ever growing population and increased urbanisation.

India has a total water surface area of 314,400 km^2 and receives an average annual rainfall of 1,100 mm. Irrigation accounts for 92% of the water utilisation, and comprised 380 km^2 in 1974, and is expected to rise to 1,050 km^2 by 2025, with the balance accounted for by industrial and domestic consumers. India's inland water resources comprising rivers, canals, ponds and lakes and marine resources comprising the east and west coasts of the Indian ocean and other gulfs and bays provide employment to nearly 6 million people in the fisheries sector. In 2008, India had the world's third largest fishing industry.

India's major mineral resources include Coal (fourth-largest reserves in the world), Iron ore, Manganese, Mica, Bauxite, Titanium ore, Chromite, Natural gas, Diamonds, Petroleum, Limestone and Thorium (world's largest along Kerala's shores). India's oil reserves, found in Bombay High off the coast of Maharashtra, Gujarat, and in eastern Assam meet 25% of the country's demand.

Rising energy demand concomitant with economic growth has created a perpetual state of energy crunch in India. India is poor in oil resources and is currently heavily dependent on coal and foreign oil imports for its energy needs. Though India is rich in Thorium, but not in Uranium, which it might get access to if a nuclear deal with US comes to fruition. India is rich in certain energy resources which promise significant future potential–clean / renewable energy resources like solar, wind, biofuels (jatropha, sugarcane).

Physical Infrastructure

Development of infrastructure was completely in the hands of the public sector and was plagued by corruption, bureaucratic inefficiencies, urban-bias and an inability to scale investment.

India's low spending on power, construction, transportation, telecommunications and real estate, at $31 billion or 6% of GDP in 2002 had prevented India from sustaining higher growth rates. This had prompted the government to partially open up infrastructure to the private sector allowing foreign investment which has helped in a sustained growth rate of close to 9% for the past six quarters. India holds second position in the world in roadways' construction, more than twice that of China. As of 2005 the electricity production was at 661.6 billion kWh with oil production standing at 785,000 bbl/day. India's prime import partners are: China 8.7%, US 6%, Germany 4.6%, Singapore 4.6%, Australia 4% as of 2006 CIA FactBook As of 15 January 2007, there were 2.10 million broadband lines in India. Low tele-density is the major hurdle for slow pickup in broadband services. Over 76% of the broadband lines were via DSL and the rest via cable modems.

Financial Institutions

India inherited several institutions, such as the civil services, Reserve Bank of India, railways, etc., from its British rulers. Mumbai serves as the nation's commercial capital, with the Reserve Bank of India (RBI), Bombay Stock Exchange (BSE) and the National Stock Exchange (NSE) located here. The headquarters of many financial institutions are also located in the city.

The RBI, the country's central bank was established on 1 April 1935. It serves as the nation's monetary authority, regulator and supervisor of the financial system, manager of exchange control and as an issuer of currency. The RBI is governed by a central board, headed by a governor who is appointed by the Central government of India. The BSE Sensex or the BSE Sensitive Index is a value-weighted index composed of 30 companies with April 1979 as the base year (100). These companies have the largest and most actively traded stocks and are representative of various sectors, on the Exchange. They account for around one-fifth of the market capitalisation of the BSE. The Sensex is generally regarded as the most popular and precise barometer of the Indian stock markets. Incorporated in 1992, the National Stock Exchange is one of the largest and most advanced stock markets in India. The NSE is the world's third largest stock exchange in terms of transactions. There are a total of 23 stock exchanges in India, but the BSE and NSE comprise 83% of the volumes. The Securities and Exchange Board of India (SEBI), established in 1992, regulates the stock markets and other securities markets of the country.

Sectors

Agriculture

India ranks second worldwide in farm output. Agriculture and allied sectors like forestry, logging and fishing accounted for 16.6% of the GDP in 2007, employed 60% of the total workforce and despite a steady decline of its share in the GDP, is still the largest economic sector and plays a significant role in the overall socio-economic development of India. Yields per unit area of all crops have grown since 1950, due to the special emphasis placed on agriculture in the five-year plans and steady improvements in irrigation, technology, application of modern agricultural practices and provision of agricultural credit and subsidies since Green revolution in India. However, international comparisons reveal that the average yield in India is generally 30% to 50% of the highest average yield in the world.

The low productivity in India is a result of the following factors:

- Illiteracy, general socio-economic backwardness, slow progress in implementing land reforms and inadequate or inefficient finance and marketing services for farm produce.
- The average size of land holdings is very small (less than 20,000 m^2) and is subject to fragmentation, due to land ceiling acts and in some cases, family disputes. Such small holdings are often over-manned, resulting in disguised unemployment and low productivity of labour.
- Adoption of modern agricultural practices and use of technology is inadequate, hampered by ignorance of such practices, high costs and impracticality in the case of small land holdings.

- Irrigation facilities are inadequate, as revealed by the fact that only 52.6% of the land was irrigated in 2003–04, which result in farmers still being dependent on rainfall, specifically the Monsoon season. A good monsoon results in a robust growth for the economy as a whole, while a poor monsoon leads to a sluggish growth. Farm credit is regulated by NABARD, which is the statutory apex agent for rural development in the subcontinent.

Industry

India is fourteenth in the world in factory output. They together account for 27.6% of the GDP and employ 17% of the total workforce. However, about one-third of the industrial labour force is engaged in simple household manufacturing only.

Economic reforms brought foreign competition, led to privatisation of certain public sector industries, opened up sectors hitherto reserved for the public sector and led to an expansion in the production of fast-moving consumer goods.

Post-liberalisation, the Indian private sector, which was usually run by oligopolies of old family firms and required political connections to prosper was faced with foreign competition, including the threat of cheaper Chinese imports. It has since handled the change by squeezing costs, revamping management, focusing on designing new products and relying on low labour costs and technology.

Services

India is fifteenth in services output. It provides employment to 23% of work force, and it is growing fast, growth rate 7.5% in 1991–2000 up from 4.5% in 1951–80. It has the largest share in the GDP, accounting for 55% in 2007 up from 15% in 1950. Business services (information technology, information technology enabled services, business process outsourcing) are among the fastest growing sectors contributing to one third of the total output of services in 2000. The growth in the IT sector is attributed to increased specialisation, availability of a large pool of low cost, but highly skilled, educated and fluent English-speaking workers. On the supply side and on the demand side, increased demand from foreign consumers interested in India's service exports or those looking to outsource their operations. India's IT industry, despite contributing significantly to its balance of payments, accounted for only about 1% of the total GDP or 1/50th of the total services.

Socio-economic Characteristics

Poverty

Large numbers of India's people live in abject poverty. Wealth distribution in India is improving since the liberalization and with the end of the socialist rule termed as the license raj. While poverty in India has reduced significantly, official figures estimate that 27.5% of Indians still lived below the national poverty line in 2004-2005. A 2007 report by the state-run National Commission for Enterprises in the Unorganised Sector (NCEUS) found that 65% of Indians, or 750 million people, lived on less than 20 rupees per day with most working in "informal labour sector with no job or social security, living in abject poverty."

Since the early 1950s, successive governments have implemented various schemes, under planning, to alleviate poverty, that have met with partial success. All these programmes have relied upon the strategies of the *Food for work* programme and *National Rural Employment Programme* of the 1980s, which attempted to use the unemployed to generate productive assets and build rural infrastructure. In August 2005, the Indian parliament passed the *Rural Employment Guarantee Bill*, the largest programme of this type in terms of cost and coverage, which promises 100 days of minimum wage employment to every rural household in 200 of India's 600 districts. The question of whether economic reforms have reduced poverty or not has fuelled debates without generating any clear cut answers and has also put political pressure on further economic reforms, especially those involving the downsizing of labour and cutting agricultural subsidies.

Occupations and Unemployment

Agricultural and allied sectors accounted for about 57% of the total workforce in 1999–2000, down from 60% in 1993–94. While agriculture has faced stagnation in growth, services have seen a steady growth. Of the total workforce, 8% is in the organised sector, two-thirds of which are in the public sector. The NSSO survey estimated that in 1999–2000, 106 million, nearly 10% of the population were unemployed and the overall unemployment rate was 7.32%, with rural areas doing marginally better (7.21%) than urban areas (7.65%).

Unemployment in India is characterized by chronic underemployment or disguised unemployment. Government schemes that target eradication of both poverty and unemployment (which in recent decades has sent millions of poor and unskilled people into urban areas in search of livelihoods) attempt to solve the problem, by providing financial assistance for setting up businesses, skill honing, setting up public sector enterprises, reservations in governments, etc. The decreased role of the public sector after liberalization has further underlined the need for focusing on better education and has also put political pressure on further reforms.

Regional Imbalance

One of the critical problems facing India's economy is the sharp and growing regional variations among India's different states and territories in terms of per capita income, poverty, availability of infrastructure and socio-economic development.

The five-year plans have attempted to reduce regional disparities by encouraging industrial development in the interior regions, but industries still tend to concentrate around urban areas and port cities. After liberalization, the more advanced states are better placed to benefit from them, with infrastructure like well developed ports, urbanisation and an educated and skilled workforce which attract manufacturing and service sectors. The union and state governments of backward regions are trying to reduce the disparities by offering tax holidays, cheap land, etc., and focusing more on sectors like tourism, which although being geographically and historically determined, can become a source of growth and is faster to develop than other sectors.

DEMOGRAPHICS

With an estimated population of 1.13 billion, India is the world's second most populous country. Almost 70% of Indians reside in rural areas, although in recent decades migration to larger cities has led to a dramatic increase in the country's urban population. India's largest cities are Mumbai (formerly Bombay), Delhi, Kolkata (formerly Calcutta), Chennai (formerly Madras), Bengaluru (formerly Bangalore), Hyderabad and Ahmedabad.

India is the second most culturally, linguistically and genetically diverse geographical entity after the African continent. India is home to two major linguistic families: Indo-Aryan (spoken by about 74% of the population) and Dravidian (spoken by about 24%). Other languages spoken in India come from the Austro-Asiatic and Tibeto-Burman linguistic families. Hindi, with the largest number of speakers, is the official language of the union. English, which is extensively used in business and administration, has the status of a 'subsidiary official language.' The constitution also recognises in particular 21 other languages that are either abundantly spoken or have classical status. The number of dialects in India is as high as 1,652.

Over 800 million Indians (80.5%) are Hindu. Other religious groups include Muslims (13.4%), Christians (2.3%), Sikhs (1.9%), Buddhists (0.8%), Jains (0.4%), Jews, Zoroastrians, Bahá'ís and others. Tribals constitute 8.1% of the population.

India's literacy rate is 64.8% (53.7% for females and 75.3% for males). The state of Kerala has the highest literacy rate (91%); Bihar has the lowest (47%). The national human sex ratio is 944 females per 1,000 males. India's median age is 24.9, and the population growth rate of 1.38% per annum; there are 22.01 births per 1,000 people per year.

2

HISTORY OF SOUTHEAST ASIAN NATIONS

The history of Southeast Asia has been characterized as interaction between regional players and foreign powers. Though 11 countries currently make up the region, the history of each country is intertwined with all the others. For instance, the Malay empires of Srivijaya and Malacca covered modern day Indonesia, Malaysia, and Singapore while the Burmese, Thai, and Khmer peoples governed much of Indochina. At the same time, opportunities and threats from the east and the west shaped the direction of Southeast Asia. The history of the countries within the region only started to develop independently of each other after European colonialization was at full steam between the 17th and the 20th century.

Evidences suggest that the earliest non-aboriginal Southeast Asians came from southern China and were Austronesian speakers. Contemporary research by anthropologists, linguists (Blust, Reid, Ross, Pawley), and archaeologists (Bellwood) suggests that the inhabitants of the Malay Archipelago migrated from southern China to islands of the Philippines around 2,500 BCE and later spread to modern day Malaysia and Indonesia.

The earliest population of Southeast Asia was animist before Hinduism and Buddhism were exported from the Indian subcontinent. Islam arrived mostly through Indian Muslims and later dominated much of the archipelago around the 13th century while Christianity came along when European colonization started around the 16th century.

During the classical age, the existence of Southeast Asia had been known to the Greeks. The Greek astronomer Ptolemy in his *Geographia* named the Malay Peninsula as *Aurea Chersonesus* (Golden Peninsula) while Java was called *Labadius*. Labadius was probably a corruption of Sanskrit *Yavadvipa* which refers to the same island. An ancient Hindu text may have earlier referred to Southeast Asia as *Suvarnabhumi* which means land of gold.

The region has been an important source of spices and this was one of the reasons European explorers were attracted to the Far East. During the colonization period, states of the region became important assets to the British, the Dutch and the French. British Malaya for instance was the world's largest producer of tin and rubber while the Dutch East Indies was the source of Dutch's wealth.

During the 1990s, Southeast Asia emerged as the fastest growing economy in the world. Its successes have made some to call Southeast Asia as an economic miracle and "Four Asian Tigers". Though the Asian Financial Crisis struck in the late 1990s and left many crippled, the economy of the region has started to pick up again at a more sustainable rate as demand from the United States and People's Republic of China soar.

PREHISTORY

Paleolithic

Before the latest ice period, much of the archipelago was not under water. Sometime around the Pleistocene period, the Sunda Shelf was flooded as thawing occurred and thus revealing current geographical features. The area's first known human-like inhabitant some 500,000 years ago was "Java Man" (first classified as Pithecanthropus erectus, then subsequently named a part of the species Homo erectus). Recently discovered was a species of human, dubbed "Flores Man" (Homo floresiensis), a miniature hominid that grew only three feet tall. Flores Man seems to have shared some islands with Java Man until only 10,000 years ago, when they became extinct.

The oldest human settlement in Malaysia has been discovered in Niah Caves. The human remains found there have been dated back to 40,000 BC. Another remain dated back to 9,000 BC dubbed the "Perak Man" and tools as old as 75,000 years have been discovered in Lenggong, Malaysia.

Mesolithic and early agricultural societies

Agriculture was a natural development based on necessity. Before agriculture, hunting and gathering sufficed to provide food. The chicken and pig were domesticated here, millennia ago. So much food was available that people could gain status by giving food away in feasts and festivals, where all could eat their fill. These *big men* (Malay: *orang kaya*) would work for years, accumulating the food (wealth) needed for the festivals provided by the *orang kaya*. These individual acts of generosity or kindness are remembered by the people in their oral histories, which serves to provide *credit* in more dire times. These customs ranged throughout Southeast Asia, stretching, for example, to the island of Papua. The agricultural technology was exploited after population pressures increased to the point that systematic intensive farming was required for mere survival, say of yams (in Papua) or rice (in Indonesia). Rice paddies are well-suited for the monsoons of Southeast Asia. The rice paddies of Southeast Asia have existed for millennia, with evidence for their existence coeval with the rise of agriculture in other parts of the globe.

Yam cultivation in Papua, for example, consists of placing the tubers in prepared ground, heaping vegetation on them, waiting for them to propagate, and harvesting them. This work sequence is still performed by the women in the traditional societies of Southeast Asia; the men might perform the heavier duties of preparing the ground, or of fencing the area to prevent predation by pigs.

The earliest known community in Thailand–dated 3,000 BC–was located in Ban Chiang. From Burma around 1,500 BC, the Mon and ancestors of the Khmer people started to move in while the Tai people later came from southern China to reside in the mainland in the first millennium AD.

Early Metal Phases in Southeast Asia

It was around 2,500 BC that the Austronesian people started to populate the archipelago and introduced primitive ironworks technology that they had mastered to the region.

By around the 5th century BC, people of the Dong Son culture, who lived in what is now Vietnam, had mastered basic metal working. Their works are the earliest known metal object to be found by archeologists in Southeast Asia.

Ancient and Classical Kingdoms

Southeast Asia has been inhabited since prehistoric times. The communities in the region evolved to form complex cultures with varying degrees of influence from India and China.

The ancient kingdoms can be grouped into two distinct categories. The first is agrarian kingdoms. Agrarian kingdoms had agriculture as the main economic activity. Most agrarian states were located in mainland Southeast Asia. Examples are the Ayutthaya Kingdom, based on the Chao Phraya River delta and the Khmer Empire on the Tonle Sap. The second type is maritime states. Maritime states were dependent on sea trade. Malacca and Srivijaya were maritime states.

A succession of trading systems dominated the trade between China and India. First, goods were shipped through Funan to the Isthmus of Kra, portaged across the narrow, and then transhipped for India and points west. Around the sixth century, CE merchants began sailing to Srivijaya where goods were transhipped directly. The limits of technology and contrary winds during parts of the year made it difficult for the ships of the time to proceed directly from the Indian Ocean to the South China Sea. The third system involved direct trade between the Indian and Chinese coasts.

Very little is known about Southeast Asian religious beliefs and practices before the advent of Indian merchants and religious influences from the second century BCE onwards. Prior to the 13th century, Buddhism and Hinduism were the main religions in Southeast Asia.

The first dominant power to arise in the archipelago was Srivijaya in Sumatra. From the fifth century CE, the capital, Palembang, became a major seaport and functioned as an entrepot on the Spice Route between India and China. Srivijaya was also a notable center of Vajrayana Buddhist learning and influence. Srivijaya's wealth and influence faded when changes in nautical technology in the tenth century CE enabled Chinese and Indian merchants to ship cargo directly between their countries and also enabled the Chola state in southern India to carry out a series of destructive attacks on Srivijaya's possessions, ending Palembang's entrepot function.

In the Philippines, the Laguna Copperplate Inscription dating from 900 CE relates a granted debt from a *Maharlika* caste nobleman named *Namwaran* who lived in the Manila area. This document shows strong Srivijayan influence, and mentions a leader of Medan, Sumatra. Java was dominated by a kaleidoscope of competing agrarian kingdoms including the Sailendras, Mataram, and finally Majapahit.

European Colonization

Europeans first came to Southeast Asia in the sixteenth century. It was the lure of trade that brought Europeans to Southeast Asia while missionaries also tagged along the ships as they hoped to spread Christianity into the region.

Portugal was the first European power to establish a bridgehead into the lucrative Southeast Asia trade route with the conquest of the Sultanate of Malacca in 1511. The Netherlands and Spain followed and soon superseded Portugal as the main European powers in the region. The Dutch took over Malacca from the Portuguese in 1641 while Spain began to colonize the Philippines (named after Phillip II of Spain) from 1560s. Acting through the Dutch East India Company, the Dutch established the city of Batavia (now Jakarta) as a base for trading and expansion into the other parts of Java and the surrounding territory.

Britain, in the form of the British East India Company, came relatively late onto the scene. Starting with Penang, the British began to expand their Southeast Asian empire. They also temporarily possessed Dutch territories during the Napoleonic Wars, In 1819 Stamford Raffles established Singapore as a key trading post for Britain in their rivalry with the Dutch. However, their rivalry cooled in 1824 when an Anglo-Dutch treaty demarcated their respective interests in Southeast Asia. From the 1850s onwards, the pace of colonization shifted to a significantly higher gear.

This phenomenon, denoted New Imperialism, saw the conquest of nearly all Southeast Asian territories by the colonial powers. The Dutch East India Company and British East India Company were dissolved by their respective governments, who took over the direct administration of the colonies. Only Thailand was spared the experience of foreign rule, although, Thailand itself was also greatly affected by the power politics of the Western powers.

By 1913, the British occupied Burma, Malaya and the Borneo territories, the French controlled Indochina, the Dutch ruled the Netherlands East Indies while Portugal managed to hold on to Portuguese Timor. In the Philippines, Filipino revolutionaries declared independence from Spain in 1898 but was handed over to the United States despite protests as a result of the Spanish-American War.

Colonial rule had a profound effect on Southeast Asia. While the colonial powers profited much from the region's vast resources and large market, colonial rule did develop the region to a varying extent. Commercial agriculture, mining and an export based economy developed rapidly during this period. Increased labor demand resulted in mass immigration, especially from British India and China, which brought about massive demographic change. The institutions for a modern nation state like a state bureaucracy, courts of law, print media and to a smaller extent, modern education, sowed the seeds of the fledgling nationalist movements in the colonial territories.

Decolonization

In the inter-war years, these nationalist movements grew and often clashed with the colonial authorities when they demanded self-determination.

With the rejuvenated nationalist movements in wait, the Europeans returned to a very different Southeast Asia after World War II. Indonesia declared independence in 17 August 1945 and subsequently fought a bitter war against the returning Dutch; the Philippines were granted independence in 1946; Burma secured their independence from Britain in 1948, and the French were driven from Indochina in 1954 after a bitterly fought war against the Vietnamese nationalists. The newly-established United Nations provided a forum both for nationalist demands and for the newly demanded independent nations.

During the Cold War, countering the threat of communism was a major theme in the decolonization process. After suppressing the communist insurrection during the Malayan Emergency from 1948 to 1960, Britain granted independence to Malaya and later, Singapore, Sabah and Sarawak in 1957 and 1963 respectively within the framework of the Federation of Malaysia. In one of the most bloody single incidents of violence in Cold War Southeast Asia, General Suharto seized power in Indonesia in

1965 and initiated a massacre of approximately 500,000 alleged members of the Indonesian Communist Party (PKI). Recent evidence from the US National Security Archive published by George Washington University suggests this massacre was carried out with the support of the United States embassy in Jakarta, which supplied lists of names of suspected PKI members to Suharto.

The United States intervention against communist forces in Indochina during a conflict commonly referred to in the United States as the Vietnam War meant that Vietnam, Laos and Cambodia had to go through a prolonged and protracted war in their route to independence.

In 1975, Portuguese rule ended in East Timor. However, independence was short-lived as Indonesia annexed the territory soon after. Finally, Britain ended its protectorate of the Sultanate of Brunei in 1984, marking the end of European rule in Southeast Asia.

Contemporary Southeast Asia

Modern Southeast Asia has been characterized by high economic growth by most countries and closer regional integration. Indonesia, Malaysia, the Philippines, Singapore and Thailand have traditionally experienced high growth and are commonly recognized as the more developed countries of the region. As of late, Vietnam too had been experiencing an economic boom. However, Myanmar, Cambodia, Laos and the newly independent East Timor are still lagging economically.

On August 8, 1967, Association of Southeast Asian Nations (ASEAN) was founded by Thailand, Indonesia, Malaysia, Singapore, and the Philippines. Since Cambodian admission into the union in 1999, East Timor is the only Southeast Asian country that is not part of ASEAN, although plans are under way for eventual membership. The association aims to enhance cooperation among Southeast Asian community. ASEAN Free Trade Area has been established to encourage greater trade among ASEAN members. ASEAN has also been a front runner in greater integration of Asia-Pacific region through East Asia Summits.

HISTORY OF CAMBODIA

Archaeological evidence indicates that parts of the region now called Cambodia were inhabited from around 1000-2000 BCE by a Neolithic culture that may have migrated from South Eastern China to the Indochinese Peninsula. By the first century CE, the inhabitants had developed relatively stable, organized societies which had far surpassed the primitive stage in culture and technical skills. The most advanced groups lived along the coast and in the lower Mekong River valley and delta regions in houses constructed on stilts where they cultivated rice, fished and kept domesticated animals.

Recent research has unlocked the discovery of artificial circular earthworks dating to Cambodia's Neolithic era.

The Khmer people were one of the first inhabitants of South East Asia. They were also among the first in South East Asia to adopt religious ideas and political institutions from India and to establish centralized kingdoms surrounding large territories. The earliest known kingdom in the area, Funan, flourished from around the first to the sixth century AD. This was succeeded by Chenla, which controlled large parts of modern Cambodia, Vietnam, Laos, and Thailand.

The golden age of Khmer civilization, however, was the period from the ninth to the thirteenth centuries, when the kingdom of Kambuja, which gave Kampuchea, or Cambodia, its name, ruled large territories from its capital in the region of Angkor in western Cambodia.

Under Jayavarman VII (1181–ca. 1218), Kambuja reached its zenith of political power and cultural creativity. Jayavarman VII gained power and territory in a series of successful wars against its close enemies; the Cham and the Vietnamese. Following Jayavarman VII's death, Kambuja experienced a gradual decline. Important factors were the aggressiveness of neighboring peoples (especially the Thai, or Siamese), chronic interdynastic strife, and the gradual deterioration of the complex irrigation system that had ensured rice surpluses. The Angkorian monarchy survived until 1431, when the Thai captured Angkor Thom and the Cambodian king fled to the southern part of the country.

Dark Ages

The fifteenth to the nineteenth centuries were a period of continued decline and territorial loss. Cambodia enjoyed a brief period of prosperity during the sixteenth century because its kings, who built their capitals in the region southeast of the Tonle Sap along the Mekong River, promoted trade with other parts of Asia. This was the period when Spanish and Portuguese adventurers and missionaries first visited the country. However, the Thai conquest of the new capital at Lovek in 1594 marked a downturn in the country's fortunes and Cambodia. Becoming a pawn in power struggles between its two increasingly powerful neighbors, Siam and Vietnam. Cambodia remained a protectorate of Siam. Vietnam's settlement of the Mekong Delta led to its annexation of that area at the end of the seventeenth century. Cambodia thereby lost some of its richest territory and was cut off from the sea. Because of current king's brother, prince Ang whom allowed the Vietnamese to settle and take over the last portion which was left of Cambodia's soil to the sea. Such foreign encroachments continued through the first half of the nineteenth century because Vietnam was determined to absorb Khmer land and to force the inhabitants to accept Vietnamese culture.

French Colonial Period

In 1863, King Norodom signed an agreement with the French to establish a protectorate over his kingdom. The state gradually came under French colonial domination.

During World War II, the Japanese allowed the French government (based at Vichy) that collaborated with the republican opponents and attempted to negotiate acceptable terms for independence from the French.

Cambodia's situation at the end of the war was chaotic. The Free French, under General Charles de Gaulle, were determined to recover Indochina, though they offered Cambodia and the other Indochinese protectorates a carefully circumscribed measure of self-government. Convinced that they had a "civilizing mission," they envisioned Indochina's participation in a French Union of former colonies that shared the common experience of French culture.

Sihanouk's "royal crusade for independence" resulted in grudging French acquiescence to his demands for a transfer of sovereignty. A partial agreement was struck in October 1953. Sihanouk then declared that independence had been achieved and returned in triumph to Phnom Penh.

First Administration of Sihanouk

As a result of the Geneva Conference on Indochina, Cambodia was able to bring about the withdrawal of the Viet Minh troops from its territory and to withstand any residual impingement upon its sovereignty by external powers.

Neutrality was the central element of Cambodian foreign policy during the 1950s and 1960s. By the mid-1960s, parts of Cambodia's eastern provinces were serving as bases for North Vietnamese Army and Viet Cong (NVA/VC) forces operating against South Vietnam, and the port of Sihanoukville was being used to supply them. As NVA/VC activity grew, the United States and South Vietnam became concerned, and in 1969, the United States began a fourteen month long series of bombing raids targeted at NVA/VC elements, contributing to destabilization. Prince Sihanouk, fearing that the conflict between communist North Vietnam and South Vietnam might spill over to Cambodia, steadfastly opposed the bombing campaign by the United States along the Vietnam-Cambodia border and inside Cambodian territory.

Prince Sihanouk wanted Cambodia to stay out of the North Vietnam-South Vietnam conflict and was very critical of the United States government and its allies (the South Vietnamese government). The United States claims that the bombing campaign took place no further than ten, and later twenty miles (32 km) inside the Cambodian border, areas where the Cambodian population had been evicted by the NVA. Prince Sihanouk, facing internal struggles of his own, due to the rise of the Khmer Rouge, did not want Cambodia to be involved in the conflict. Sihanouk wanted the United States and its allies (South Vietnam) to keep the war away from the Cambodian border. Not only did Sihanouk try to keep the communist North Vietnamese soldiers from entering Cambodia territory, but he also did not allow the United States to use Cambodian air space and airports for military purposes. This upset the United States greatly. The United States saw Prince Sihanouk as a North Vietnamese sympathizer and a thorn on the United States, and using the CIA, it began plans to get rid of Sihanouk.

Throughout the 1960s, domestic Cambodian politics became polarized. Opposition to the government grew within the middle class and leftists including Paris-educated leaders like Son Sen, Ieng Sary, and Saloth Sar (later known as Pol Pot), who led an insurgency under the clandestine Communist Party of Kampuchea (CPK). Sihanouk called these insurgents the Khmer Rouge, literally the "Red Khmer." But the 1966 national assembly elections showed a significant swing to the right, and General Lon Nol formed a new government, which lasted until 1967. During 1968 and 1969, the insurgency worsened. In August 1969, Lon Nol formed a new government. Prince Sihanouk went abroad for medical reasons in January 1970.

The Khmer Republic and the War

In March 1970, while Prince Sihanouk was absent, General Lon Nol deposed Prince Sihanouk in a coup d'état [a Military Coup] planned by the CIA. Lon Nol assumed the power after the military coup and allied Cambodia with the United States. Son Ngoc Thanh announced his support for the new government. On October 9, the Cambodian monarchy was abolished, and the country was renamed the Khmer Republic.

Hanoi rejected the new republic's request for the withdrawal of NVA troops. 2,000–4,000 Cambodians who had gone to North Vietnam in 1954 reentered Cambodia, backed by North Vietnamese soldiers. In response, the United States moved to provide material assistance to the new government's armed forces, which were engaged against both CPK insurgents and NVA forces.

In April 1970, US President Nixon announced to the American public that US and South Vietnamese ground forces had entered Cambodia in a campaign aimed at destroying NVA base areas in Cambodia. The US had already been bombing Cambodia for well over a year by that point.

Although a considerable quantity of equipment was seized or destroyed by US and South Vietnamese forces, containment of North Vietnamese forces proved elusive. The

North Vietnamese moved deeper into Cambodia to avoid US and South Vietnamese raids. NVA units overran many Cambodian army positions while the CPK expanded their small-scale attacks on lines of communication.

The Khmer Republic's leadership was plagued by disunity among its three principal figures: Lon Nol, Sihanouk's cousin Sirik Matak, and National Assembly leader In Tam. Lon Nol remained in power in part because none of the others were prepared to take his place. In 1972, a constitution was adopted, a parliament elected, and Lon Nol became president. But disunity, the problems of transforming a 30,000-man army into a national combat force of more than 200,000 men, and spreading corruption weakened the civilian administration and army.

The Communist insurgency inside Cambodia continued to grow, aided by supplies and military support from North Vietnam. Pol Pot and Ieng Sary asserted their dominance over the Vietnamese-trained communists, many of whom were purged. At the same time, the Communist Party of Kampuchea forces became stronger and more independent of their Vietnamese patrons. By 1973, the CPK were fighting battles against government forces with little or no North Vietnamese troop support, and they controlled nearly 60% of Cambodia's territory and 25% of its population.

The government made three unsuccessful attempts to enter into negotiations with the insurgents, but by 1974, the CPK were operating openly as divisions, and some of the NVA combat forces had moved into South Vietnam. Lon Nol's control was reduced to small enclaves around the cities and main transportation routes. More than 2 million refugees from the war lived in Phnom Penh and other cities.

On New Year's Day 1975, Communist troops launched an offensive which, in 117 days of the hardest fighting of the war, collapsed the Khmer Republic. Simultaneous attacks around the perimeter of Phnom Penh pinned down Republican forces, while other CPK units overran fire bases controlling the vital lower Mekong resupply route. A US-funded airlift of ammunition and rice ended when Congress refused additional aid for Cambodia. The Lon Nol government in Phnom Penh surrendered on April 17—5 days after the US mission evacuated Cambodia.

Democratic Kampuchea (the Khmer Rouge/Red Khmer Age)

Immediately after its victory, the CPK ordered the evacuation of all cities and towns, sending the entire urban population into the countryside to work as farmers, as the CPK was trying to reshape society into a model that Pol Pot had conceived.

Thousands starved or died of disease during the evacuation and its aftermath. Many of those forced to evacuate the cities were resettled in newly created villages, which lacked food, agricultural implements, and medical care. Many who lived in cities had lost the skills necessary for survival in an agrarian environment. Thousands starved before the first harvest. Hunger and malnutrition—bordering on starvation—were constant during those years. Most military and civilian leaders of the former regime who failed to disguise their pasts were executed.

Within the CPK, the Paris-educated leadership—Pol Pot, Ieng Sary, Nuon Chea, and Son Sen—were in control. A new constitution in January 1976 established Democratic Kampuchea as a Communist People's Republic, and a 250-member Assembly of the Representatives of the People of Kampuchea (PRA) was selected in March to choose the collective leadership of a State Presidium, the chairman of which became the head of state.

Prince Sihanouk resigned as head of state on April 4. On April 14, after its first session, the PRA announced that Khieu Samphan would chair the State Presidium for a 5-year term. It also picked a 15-member cabinet headed by Pol Pot as prime minister. Prince Sihanouk was put under virtual house arrest.

The new government sought to completely restructure Cambodian society. Remnants of the old society were abolished and religion, particularly Buddhism and Catholicism, was suppressed. Agriculture was collectivized, and the surviving part of the industrial base was abandoned or placed under state control. Cambodia had neither a currency nor a banking system.

Life in 'Democratic Kampuchea' was strict and brutal. In many areas of the country people were rounded up and executed for speaking a foreign language, wearing glasses, scavenging for food, and even crying for dead loved ones. Former businessmen and bureaucrats were ruthlessly hunted down and killed along with their entire families; the Khmer Rouge feared that they held beliefs that could lead them to oppose their regime. A few Khmer Rouge loyalists were even killed for failing to find enough 'counter-revolutionaries' to execute.

Solid estimates of the numbers who died between 1975 and 1979 are not available, but it is likely that hundreds of thousands were brutally executed by the regime. Hundreds of thousands died of starvation and disease (both under the CPK and during the Vietnamese invasion in 1978). Some estimates of the dead range from 1 to 3 million, out of a 1975 population estimated at 7.3 million. The CIA estimated 50,000–100,000 were executed and 1.2 million died from 1975 to 1979.

Democratic Kampuchea's relations with Vietnam and Thailand worsened rapidly as a result of border clashes and ideological differences. While communist, the CPK was fiercely pro-Cambodia, and most of its members who had lived in Vietnam were purged. Democratic Kampuchea established close ties with the People's Republic of China, and the Cambodian-Vietnamese conflict became part of the Sino-Soviet rivalry, with Moscow backing Vietnam. Border clashes worsened when Democratic Kampuchea military attacked villages in Vietnam. The regime broke off relations with Hanoi in December 1977, protesting Vietnam's alleged attempt to create an Indochina Federation. In mid-1978, Vietnamese forces invaded Cambodia, advancing about 30 miles (48 km) before the arrival of the rainy season.

The reasons for Chinese support of the CPK was to prevent a pan-Indochina movement, and maintain Chinese military superiority in the region. The Soviet Union supported a strong Vietnam to maintain a second front against China in case of hostilities and to prevent further Chinese expansion. Since Stalin's death, relations between Mao-controlled China and the Soviet Union were lukewarm at best. In the late 1970s and early 1980s, China and Vietnam would fight the brief Sino-Vietnamese War over the issue.

In December 1978, Vietnam announced formation of the Kampuchean United Front for National Salvation (KUFNS) under Heng Samrin, a former DK division commander. It was composed of Khmer Communists who had remained in Vietnam after 1975 and officials from the eastern sector—like Heng Samrin and Hun Sen—who had fled to Vietnam from Cambodia in 1978. In late December 1978, Vietnamese forces launched a full invasion of Cambodia, capturing Phnom Penh on January 7, 1979 and driving the remnants of Democratic Kampuchea's army westward toward Thailand.

People's Republic of Kampuchea (Vietnamese Occupation)

On January 10, 1979, Communist Vietnam installed Heng Samrin as head of state in the new People's Republic of Kampuchea (PRK). The Vietnamese army continued its pursuit of Pol Pot's Khmer Rouge forces. At least 600,000 Cambodians displaced during the Pol Pot era and the Vietnamese invasion began streaming to the Thai border in search of refuge. The international community responded with a massive relief effort coordinated by the United States through UNICEF and the World Food Program. More than $400 million was provided between 1979 and 1982, of which the United States contributed nearly $100 million. At one point, more than 500,000 Cambodians were living along the Thai-Cambodian border and more than 100,000 in holding centers inside Thailand.

Modern Cambodia

On October 23, 1991, the Paris Conference reconvened to sign a comprehensive settlement giving the UN full authority to supervise a cease-fire, repatriate the displaced Khmer along the border with Thailand, disarm and demobilize the factional armies, and prepare the country for free and fair elections. Prince Sihanouk, President of the Supreme National Council of Cambodia (SNC), and other members of the SNC returned to Phnom Penh in November 1991, to begin the resettlement process in Cambodia. The UN Advance Mission for Cambodia (UNAMIC) was deployed at the same time to maintain liaison among the factions and begin demining operations to expedite the repatriation of approximately 370,000 Cambodians from Thailand.

On March 16, 1992, the UN Transitional Authority in Cambodia (UNTAC) arrived in Cambodia to begin implementation of the UN Settlement Plan. The UN High Commissioner for Refugees began fullscale repatriation in March 1992. UNTAC grew into a 22,000-strong civilian and military peacekeeping force to conduct free and fair elections for a constituent assembly.

Over 4 million Cambodians (about 90% of eligible voters) participated in the May 1993 elections, although the Khmer Rouge or Party of Democratic Kampuchea (PDK), whose forces were never actually disarmed or demobilized, barred some people from participating. Prince Ranariddh's FUNCINPEC Party was the top vote recipient with a 45.5% vote, followed by Hun Sen's Cambodian People's Party and the Buddhist Liberal Democratic Party, respectively. FUNCINPEC then entered into a coalition with the other parties that had participated in the election. The parties represented in the 120-member assembly proceeded to draft and approve a new constitution, which was promulgated September 24, 1993. It established a multiparty liberal democracy in the framework of a constitutional monarchy, with the former Prince Sihanouk elevated to King. Prince Ranariddh and Hun Sen became First and Second Prime Ministers, respectively, in the Royal Cambodian Government (RGC). The constitution provides for a wide range of internationally recognized human rights.

On October 4, 2004, the Cambodian National Assembly ratified an agreement with the United Nations on the establishment of a tribunal to try senior leaders responsible for the atrocities committed by the Khmer Rouge. Donor countries have pledged the $43 million international share of the three-year tribunal budget, while the Cambodian government's share of the budget is $13.3 million. The tribunal plans to begin trials of senior Khmer Rouge leaders in 2008.

HISTORY OF INDONESIA

Indonesia is an archipelagic country of 17,508 islands (6,000 inhabited) stretching along the equator in South East Asia. The country's strategic sea-lane position fostered inter-island and international trade; trade has since fundamentally shaped Indonesian history. The area is populated by peoples of various migrations, creating a diversity of cultures, ethnicities, and languages.

Fossilised remains of *Homo erectus,* popularly known as the "Java Man", suggest the Indonesian archipelago was inhabited two million to 500,000 years ago. Austronesian people, who form the majority of the modern population, were originally from Taiwan and arrived in Indonesia around 2000 BCE. From the seventh century CE, the powerful Srivijaya naval kingdom flourished bringing Hindu and Buddhist influences with it. The agricultural Buddhist Sailendra and Hindu Mataram dynasties subsequently thrived and declined in inland Java. The last significant non-Muslim kingdom, the Hindu Majapahit kingdom, flourished from the late 13th century, and its influence stretched over much of Indonesia. The earliest evidence of Islamised populations in Indonesia dates to the 13th century in northern Sumatra; other Indonesian areas gradually adopted Islam which became the dominant religion in Java and Sumatra by the end of the 16th century. For the most part, Islam overlaid and mixed with existing cultural and religious influences.

Europeans arrived in Indonesia from the 16th century seeking to monopolise the sources of valuable nutmeg, cloves, and cubeb pepper in Maluku. In 1602 the Dutch established the Dutch East India Company (VOC) and became the dominant European power. Following bankruptcy, the VOC was formally dissolved in 1800, and the government of the Netherlands established the Dutch East Indies as a nationalised colony. By the early 20th century Dutch dominance extended to what was to become Indonesia's current boundaries. The Japanese invasion and subsequent occupation during WWII ended Dutch rule, and encouraged the previously suppressed Indonesian independence movement. Two days after the surrender of Japan in August 1945, nationalist leader, Sukarno, declared independence and was appointed president. The Netherlands tried to reestablish their rule, but a bitter armed and diplomatic struggle ended in December 1949, when in the face of international pressure, the Dutch formally recognised Indonesian independence.

An attempted coup in 1965 led to a violent army-led anti-communist purge in which over half a million people were killed. Politically, General Suharto, out-manoeuvred President Sukarno, and was formally appointed president in March 1968. His New Order administration garnered the favour of the West whose investment in Indonesia was a major factor in the subsequent three decades of substantial economic growth. In the late 1990s, however, Indonesia was the country hardest hit by the East Asian Financial Crisis which led to popular protests and Suharto's resignation on 21 May 1998. The *Reformasi* era following Suharto's resignation, has led to a strengthening of democratic processes, including a regional autonomy program, the secession of East Timor, and the first direct presidential election in 2004. Political and economic instability, social unrest, corruption, natural disasters, and terrorism have slowed progress. Although relations among different religious and ethnic groups are largely harmonious, acute sectarian discontent and violence remain problems in some areas.

Prehistory

Geologically the area of modern Indonesia appeared sometime around the Pleistocene period, when it was still linked with the Asian mainland. The archipelago formed during the thaw after the latest ice age. Fossilised remains of *Homo erectus*, popularly known as the "Java Man", suggest the Indonesian archipelago was inhabited two million to 500,000 years ago. Recent discoveries on the island of Flores were dubbed "Flores Man" (*Homo floresiensis*), a miniature hominoid that grew only three feet tall, although whether this is a separate species is in dispute. Nevertheless, Flores Man seems to have shared some islands with Java Man until only 10,000 years ago, when they became extinct.

Austronesian people, who form the majority of the modern population, migrated to South East Asia from Taiwan. They arrived in Indonesia around 2000 BCE, and confined the native Melanesian peoples to the far eastern regions as they expanded. Dong Son culture spread to Indonesia bringing with it techniques of wet-field rice cultivation, ritual buffalo sacrifice, bronze casting, megalithic practises, and *ikat* weaving methods. Ideal agricultural conditions, and the mastering of wet-field rice cultivation as early as the eighth century BCE, allowed villages, towns, and small kingdoms to flourish by the first century CE.

Pre-colonial Civilisations

Early kingdoms

The earliest archeological record from the present era is from the Ujung Kulon National Park, West Java, where an early Hindu archeological relic of a Ganesha statue from the 1st century AD was found on the summit of Mount Raksa in Panaitan Island.

There is also archeological evidence of a kingdom in Tatar Sunda / Sunda Territory (West Java) dating from the 2nd century, and according to Dr Tony Djubiantono, the head of Bandung Archeology Agency, Jiwa Temple in Batujaya, Karawang, West Java was also built around this time.

Three rough plinths dating from the beginning of the fourth century are found in Kutai, East Kalimantan, near Mahakam River. The plinths bear an inscription in the Pallava script of India reading "A gift to the Brahmin priests". In addition, the "Batu Tulis" monument (a huge black boulder) near Bogor, West Java, dates from around 450. On this monument, King Purnavarna inscribed his name and made an imprint of his footprints, as well as his elephant's footprints. The accompanying inscription reads, "Here are the footprints of King Purnavarna, the heroic conqueror of the world". This inscription is in Sanskrit and is still clear after 1500 years.

A number of Hindu and Buddhist states flourished and declined across Indonesia. By the time of the European Renaissance, the two largest islands in what is now Indonesia, Java and Sumatra had already seen over a millennium of civilization and two major empires. One such early kingdom was Tarumanagara, which flourished between 358 and 669 AD. Located in Sunda (modern-day West Java) and near what is now Jakarta, its fifth-century king, Purnawarman, produced the earliest known inscriptions in Java. Purnawarman apparently built a canal that changed the course of the Cakung River, and drained a coastal area for agriculture and settlement. In his stone inscriptions, Purnawarman associated himself with Vishnu, and Brahmins ritually secured the hydraulic project.

The political history of Indonesia during the fourteenth and fifteen centuries is not well known due to scarcity of evidence. Two major states dominated this period; Majapahit in East Java, the greatest of the pre-Islamic Indonesian states, and Malacca on the west coast of the Malay Peninsula, arguably the greatest of the Muslim trading empires.

Kingdom of Mataram

Mataram was an Indianized kingdom based in Central Java (the area surrounding modern-day Yogyakarta) between the 8th and 10th centuries. The centre of the kingdom was moved from Central Java to East Java by Mpu Sindok. The move may have been caused by an eruption of the volcano Mount Merapi, or a power struggle.

The first king of Mataram was Sri Sanjaya, who drove the Sailendras from Java and left inscriptions in stone. The monumental Hindu temple of Prambanan in the vicinity of Yogyakarta was built by Daksa. Dharmawangsa ordered the translation of the Mahabharata into Old Javanese in 996.

The kingdom collapsed into chaos at the end of Dharmawangsa's reign under military pressure from Srivijaya. Airlangga, a son of Udayana of Bali and a relative of Dharmawangsa re-established the kingdom (including Bali) under the name of Kahuripan.

Srivijaya Empire

Srivijaya (-*sri* meaning glitters or radiant, -*jaya* meaning success or excellence) was an ancient Malay kingdom on the island of Sumatra which influenced much of the Maritime Southeast Asia. From the seventh century CE, the powerful Srivijaya naval kingdom flourished as a result of trade and the influences of Hinduism and Buddhism that were imported with it.

Srivijaya was centred in the coastal trading center of present day Palembang. The empire was a thalassocracy and did not extend its influence far beyond the coastal areas of the islands of Southeast Asia. Srivijaya was organised in three main zones — the estuarine capital region centred on Palembang, the Musi River basin which served as hinterland, and rival estuarine zones capable of forming rival power centres. The capital zone was administered directly by the ruler. The hinterland zone remained under its own local datus or chiefs who were organized into a network of allegiance to the maharaja. Force was the dominant element in the empire's relations with rival river systems such as the Batang Hari river basin centred on Jambi. The ruling lineage intermarried with and allied with the Sailendras of Central Java.

Although historical records and archaeological evidence are scarce, it appears that by the seventh century, Srivijaya established suzerainty over large areas of Sumatra, western Java, and much of the Malay Peninsula. Dominating the Malacca and Sunda straits, Srivijaya controlled both the Spice Route traffic and local trade, charging a toll on passing ships, and remained a formidable sea power until the thirteenth century. This spread the Malay culture throughout Sumatra, the Malay Peninsula, and western Borneo.

A stronghold of Vajrayana Buddhism, Srivijaya attracted pilgrims and scholars from other parts of Asia. These included the Chinese monk Yijing, who made several lengthy visits to Sumatra on his way to study at Nalanda in India in 671 and 695, and the eleventh-century Buddhist scholar Atisha, who played a major role in the development of Vajrayana Buddhism in Tibet. Travellers to these islands mentioned that gold coinage was in use on the coasts, but not inland.

In 1068, Rajendra Chola, the Chola king of Tamil Nadu, conquered Kedah from Srivijaya. The Cholas continued a series of raids and conquests throughout what is now Indonesia and Malaysia for the next 20 years. Although the Chola invasion was ultimately unsuccessful, it gravely weakened the Srivijayan hegemony and enabled the formation of regional kingdoms based, like Kediri, on intensive agriculture rather than coastal and long distance trade.

Srivijaya influence waned by the 11th century. The island was in frequent conflict with the Javanese kingdoms, first Singhasari and then Majapahit. Islam eventually made its way to the Aceh region of Sumatra, spreading its influence through contacts with Arabs and Indian traders. By the late 13th century, the kingdom of Pasai (in northern Sumatra) converted to Islam. At the same time Srivijaya was briefly a tributary of the Khmer empire and later the Sukhothai kingdom. The last inscription dates to 1374, in a crown prince, Ananggavarman, is mentioned.

Srivijaya had ceased to exist by 1414, when Parameswara, the kingdom's last prince, converted to Islam and founded the Sultanate of Malacca on the Malay peninsula.

Singhasari and Majapahit

The Singhasari and Majapahit kingdoms both rose in eastern Java and assumed the territory of Srivijaya. Singhasari was a kingdom located in east Java between 1222 and 1292.

The Hindu Majapahit kingdom was founded in eastern Java in the late 13th century, and under Gajah Mada it experienced what is often referred to as a "Golden Age" in Indonesian history, when its influence extended to much of southern Malay Peninsula, Borneo, Sumatra, and Bali from about 1293 to around 1500.

The founder of the Majapahit Empire, Kertarajasa, was the son-in-law of the ruler of the Singhasari kingdom, also based in Java. After Singhasari drove Srivijaya out of Java altogether in 1290, the rising power of Singhasari came to the attention of Kublai Khan in China and he sent emissaries demanding tribute. Kertanagara, ruler of the Singhasari kingdom, refused to pay tribute and the Khan sent a punitive expedition which arrived off the coast of Java in 1293. By that time, a rebel from Kediri, Jayakatwang, had killed Kertanagara. The Majapahit founder allied himself with the Mongols against Jayakatwang and, once the Singhasari kingdom was destroyed, turned and forced his Mongol allies to withdraw in confusion.

Gajah Mada, an ambitious Majapahit prime minister and regent from 1331 to 1364, extended the empire's rule to the surrounding islands. A few years after Gajah Madah's death, the Majapahit navy captured Palembang, putting an end to the Srivijayan kingdom. Although the Majapahit rulers extended their power over other islands and destroyed neighbouring kingdoms, their focus seems to have been on controlling and gaining a larger share of the commercial trade that passed through the archipelago. About the time Majapahit was founded, Muslim traders and proselytisers began entering the area.

After peaking the 1300s, Majapahit power began to decline with a war over succession that started in 1401 and went on for four years. Majapahit found itself unable to control the rising power of the Sultanate of Malacca. Dates for the end of the Majapahit Empire range from 1478 to 1520. A large number of courtiers, artisans, priests, and members of the royalty moved east to the island of Bali at the end of Majapah existence.

The Spread of Islam

Although Muslim traders first traveled through South East Asia early in the Islamic era, the earliest evidence of Islamized populations in Indonesia dates to the 13th century in northern Sumatra. Although it is known that the spread of Islam began in the west of the archipelago, the fragmentary evidence does not suggest a rolling wave of conversion through adjacent areas; rather, it suggests the process was complicated and slow. The spread of Islam was driven by increasing trade links outside of the archipelago;

in general, traders and the royalty of major kingdoms were the first to adopt the new religion.

Other Indonesia areas gradually adopted Islam, making it the dominant religion in Java and Sumatra by the end of the 16th century. For the most part, Islam overlaid and mixed with existing cultural and religious influences, which shaped the predominant form of Islam in Indonesia, particularly in Java. Only Bali retained a Hindu majority. In the eastern archipelago, both Christian and Islamic missionaries were active in the 16th and 17th centuries, and, currently, there are large communities of both religions on these islands.

Sultanate of Mataram

Sultanate of Mataram was the third Sultanate in Java. The first was Demak Bintoro and the second was Pajang

According to Javanese records, Kyai Gedhe Pamanahan became the ruler of the Mataram area some time in the 1570s with the support of the kingdom of Pajang to the east, near the current site of Surakarta (Solo). Pamanahan was often referred to as Kyai Gedhe Mataram after his ascension.

Pamanahan's son, Panembahan Senapati Ingalaga, replaced his father on the throne around 1584. Under Senapati the kingdom grew substantially through regular military campaigns against Mataram's neighbors. Shortly after his accession, for example, he conquered his father's patrons in Pajang.

The reign of Panembahan Seda ing Krapyak (*c.* 1601-1613), the son of Senapati, was dominated by further warfare, especially against powerful Surabaya, already a major center in East Java. The first contact between Mataram and the Dutch East India Company (VOC) occurred under Krapyak. Dutch activities at the time were limited to trading from limited coastal settlements, so their interactions with the inland Mataram kingdom were limited, although they did form an alliance against Surabaya in 1613. Krapyak died that year.

Krapyak was succeeded by his son, who is known simply as Sultan Agung ("Great Sultan") in Javanese records. Agung was responsible for the great expansion and lasting historical legacy of Mataram due to the extensive military conquests of his long reign from 1613 to 1646.

After years of war Agung finally conquered Surabaya. The city was taken not through outright military invasion, but instead because Agung surrounded it on land and sea, starving it into submission. With Surabaya brought into the empire, the Mataram kingdom encompassed all of central and eastern Java, and Madura; only in the west did Banten and the Dutch settlement in Batavia remain outside Agung's control. He tried repeatedly in the 1620s and 1630s to drive the Dutch from Batavia, but his armies had met their match, and he was forced to share control over Java.

In 1645 he began building Imogiri, his burial place, about fifteen kilometers south of Yogyakarta. Imogiri remains the resting place of most of the royalty of Yogyakarta and Surakarta to this day. Agung died in the spring of 1646, with his image of royal invincibility shattered by his losses to the Dutch, but he did leave behind an empire that covered most of Java and stretched to its neighboring islands.

Upon taking the throne, Agung's son Susuhunan Amangkurat I tried to bring long-term stability to Mataram's realm, murdering local leaders that were insufficiently deferential to him, and closing ports so he alone had control over trade with the Dutch.

By the mid-1670s dissatisfaction with the king fanned into open revolt, beginning at the margins and creeping inward. Raden Trunajaya, a prince from Madura, lead a revolt fortified by itinerant fighters from faraway Makassar that captured the king's court at Mataram in mid-1677. The king escaped to the north coast with his eldest son, the future king Amangkurat II, leaving his younger son Pangeran Puger in Mataram. Apparently more interested in profit and revenge than in running a struggling empire, the rebel Trunajaya looted the court and withdrew to his stronghold in East Java leaving Puger in control of a weak court.

Amangkurat I died just after his expulsion, making Amangkurat II king in 1677. He too was nearly helpless, though, having fled without an army or treasury to build one. In an attempt to regain his kingdom, he made substantial concessions to the Dutch, who then went to war to reinstate him. For the Dutch, a stable Mataram empire that was deeply indebted to them would help ensure continued trade on favorable terms. They were willing to lend their military might to keep the kingdom together. Dutch forces first captured Trunajaya, then forced Puger to recognize the sovereignty of his elder brother Amangkurat II.

The Sultanate of Banten

In 1524-25, Sunan Gunung Jati from Cirebon, together with the armies of Demak Sultanate, seized the port of Banten from the Sunda kingdom, and established The Sultanate of Banten. This was accompanied by Muslim preachers and the adoption of Islam amongst the local population. At its peak in the first half of the seventeenth century, the Sultanate lasted from 1526 to 1813 AD. The Sultanate left many archaeological remains and historical records.

Colonial Era

Beginning in the sixteenth century, successive waves of Europeans—the Portuguese, Spanish, Dutch and British—sought to dominate the spice trade at its sources in India and the 'Spice Islands' (Maluku) of Indonesia. This meant finding a way to Asia to cut out Muslim merchants who, with their Venetian outlet in the Mediterranean, monopolised spice imports to Europe. Astronomically priced at the time, spices were highly coveted not only to preserve and make poorly preserved meat palatable, but also as medicines and magic potions.

The arrival of Europeans in South East Asia is often regarded as the watershed moment in its history. Other scholars consider this view untenable, arguing that European influence during the times of the early arrivals of the sixteenth and seventeenth centuries was limited in both area and depth. This is in part due to Europe not being the most advanced or dynamic area of the world in the early fifteenth century. Rather, the major expansionist force of this time was Islam; in 1453, for example, the Ottoman Turks conquered Constantinople, while Islam continued to spread through Indonesia and the Philippines. European influence, particularly that of the Dutch, would not have its greatest impact on Indonesia until the eighteenth and nineteenth centuries.

The Portuguese

Europeans were, however, making technological advances; new found Portuguese expertise in navigation, ship building and weaponry allowed them to make daring expeditions of exploration and expansion. Starting with the first exploratory expeditions sent from newly-conquered Malacca in 1512, the Portuguese were the first Europeans to arrive in Indonesia, and sought to dominate the sources of valuable spices and to extend their Roman Catholic missionary efforts. Initial Portuguese attempts to establish a coalition and peace treaty in 1512 with Sunda Kingdom at Kalapa, failed due hostilities amongst other indigenous Javan kingdoms. The Portuguese turned east to Maluku, which comprised a varied collection of principalities and kingdoms that were occasionally at war with each other but maintained significant inter-island and international trade. Through both military conquest and alliance with local rulers, they established trading posts, forts, and missions in eastern Indonesia including the islands of Ternate, Ambon, and Solor. The height of Portuguese missionary activities, however, came at the latter half of the sixteenth century, after the pace of their military conquest in the archipelago had stopped and their east Asian interest was shifting to Japan, Macau and China; and sugar in Brazil and the Atlantic slave trade in turn further distracted their Indonesian efforts.

The Portuguese presence in Indonesia was reduced to Solor, Flores and Timor in modern day Nusa Tenggara, following defeat in 1575 at Ternate at the hands of indigenous Ternateans, Dutch conquests in Ambon, north Maluku and Banda, and a general failure for sustained control of trade in the region. In comparison with the original Portuguese ambition to dominate Asian trade, their influences on Indonesian culture are small: the romantic *keroncong* guitar ballads; a large number of Indonesian words which reflect Portuguese's role as the 'lingua franca' of the archipelago alongside Malay; and many family names in eastern Indonesia such as da Costa, Dias, de Fretes, Gonsalves, etc. The most significant impacts of the Portuguese arrival were the disruption and disorganisation of the trade network mostly as a result of their conquest of Malacca, and the first significant plantings of Christianity in Indonesia. There have continued to be Christian communities in eastern Indonesia through to contemporary times, which has contributed to a sense of shared interest with Europeans, particularly among the Ambonese.

Dutch East-India Company

The Dutch followed the Portuguese aspirations, courage, brutality and strategies but brought better organisation, weapons, ships, and superior financial backing. Although they failed to gain complete control of the Indonesian spice trade, they had much more success than the previous Portuguese efforts. Beginning in 1602 with the founding of the Dutch East India Company, the Dutch took three centuries to establish themselves as rulers of what is now Indonesia, exploiting the fractionalisation of the small kingdoms that had replaced Majapahit. Unlike the Portuguese, the Dutch established a permanent foothold in Java, from which the Dutch ultimately established a land-based colonial empire known as the Dutch East Indies into one of the world's richest colonial possessions. Although the full extent of the colonial territory was not established until the early Twentieth century, it was these boundaries that formed the modern nation of Indonesia that was declared in 1945. Portuguese Timor, however, remained under Portuguese rule until 1975 when it was invaded and occupied, and declared the Indonesia province of East Timor until 1999.

In the 17th and 18th centuries the Dutch East Indies were not controlled directly by the Dutch government, but by a joint-stock trading company, the Dutch East India Company (in Dutch: *Verenigde Oostindische Compagnie* or VOC). The VOC had been awarded a monopoly on trade and colonial activities in the region by the Dutch parliament in 1602, but had no territory of its own in Java. In 1619, the Company conquered the Javanese city of Jayakarta, burned it to the ground and then founded the city of Batavia (present-day Jakarta), modelling it on Amsterdam.

A primary aim of the VOC was the maintenance of its monopoly of the spice trade in the archipelago. It did this through the use and threatened use of violence against the peoples of the spice-producing islands, and against non-Dutch outsiders who attempted to trade with them. For example, when the people of the Banda Islands continued to sell nutmeg to English merchants, the Dutch killed or deported virtually the entire population and repopulated the islands with VOC indentured servants and slaves who worked in the nutmeg groves. The VOC became deeply involved in the internal politics of Java in this period, and fought in a number of wars involving the leaders of Mataram and Banten (Bantam).

Dutch state rule

After the VOC was dissolved in 1800 following bankruptcy, and after a short British rule under Thomas Stamford Raffles, the Dutch state took over the VOC possessions in 1816. For most of the colonial period, Dutch control over these territories was tenuous; only in the early 20th century did Dutch dominance extend to what was to become Indonesia's current boundaries. A Javanese uprising was crushed in the Java War of 1825-1830. After 1830 a system of forced cultivations was introduced on Java, the Cultivation System (in Dutch: *cultuurstelsel*). This system brought the Dutch and their Indonesian collaborators enormous wealth. The cultivation system was a government monopoly and was abolished in a more liberal period after 1870.

During Dutch rule, several important treaties that delineate modern Indonesian borders were signed. One of them was the Anglo-Dutch Treaty of 1824. This particular treaty effectively delineated the border of future British Malaya and Dutch East Indies. In 1901 the Dutch adopted what they called the Ethical Policy, which included somewhat increased investment in indigenous education, and modest political reforms. Under governor-general J.B. van Heutsz the government extended more direct colonial rule throughout the Dutch East Indies, thereby laying the foundations of today's Indonesian state.

The emergence of Indonesia

Indonesian National Revival

In 1908 the first nationalist movement was formed, Budi Utomo, followed in 1912 by the first nationalist mass movement, Sarekat Islam. The Dutch responded after the First World War with repressive measures. The nationalist leaders came from a small group of young professionals and students, some of whom had been educated in the Netherlands. Many, including Indonesia's first president, Sukarno (1901-70), were imprisoned for political activities.

In 1914 exiled Dutch socialist Henk Sneevliet founded the Indies Social Democratic Association. Initially a small forum of Dutch socialists, it would later evolve into the Communist Party of Indonesia.

Japanese Occupation

The Japanese invasion and subsequent occupation during WWII ended Dutch rule, and encouraged the previously suppressed Indonesian independence movement. In

May 1940, early in World War II, the Netherlands was occupied by Nazi Germany. The Dutch East Indies declared a state of siege and in July redirected exports for Japan to the US and Britain. Negotiations with the Japanese aimed at securing supplies of aviation fuel collapsed in June 1941, and the Japanese started their conquest of Southeast Asia in December of that year. That same month, factions from Sumatra sought Japanese assistance for a revolt against the Dutch wartime government. The last Dutch forces were defeated by Japan in March 1942.

In July 1942, Sukarno accepted Japan's offer to rally the public in support of the Japanese war effort. Sukarno and Mohammad Hatta were decorated by the Emperor of Japan in 1943. However, experience of the Japanese occupation of Indonesia varied considerably, depending upon where one lived and one's social position. Many who lived in areas considered important to the war effort experienced torture, sex slavery, arbitrary arrest and execution, and other war crimes. Thousands taken away from Indonesia as war labourers (romusha) suffered or died as a result of ill-treatment and starvation. People of Dutch and mixed Dutch-Indonesian descent were particular targets of the Japanese occupation.

In March 1945 Japan organized an Indonesian committee (BPUPKI) on independence. At its first meeting in May, Supomo spoke of national integration and against personal individualism; while Muhammad Yamin suggested that the new nation should claim Sarawak, Sabah, Malaya, Portuguese Timor, and all the pre-war territories of the Dutch East Indies. The committee drafted the 1945 Constitution, which remains in force, though now much amended. On 9 August 1945 Sukarno, Hatta, and Radjiman Wediodiningrat were flown to meet Marshal Hisaichi Terauchi in Vietnam. They were told that Japan intended to announce Indonesian independence on 24 August. After the Japanese surrender however, Sukarno unilaterally proclaimed Indonesian independence on 17 August.

Indonesian National Revolution

Under pressure from radical and politicised *pemuda* ('youth') groups, Sukarno and Hatta proclaimed Indonesian independence, on 17 August 1945, two days after the Japanese Emperor's surrender in the Pacific. The following day, the Central Indonesian National Committee (KNIP) declared Sukarno President, and Hatta Vice President. Word of the proclamation spread by shortwave and fliers while the Indonesian war-time military (PETA), youths, and others rallied in support of the new republic, often moving to take over government offices from the Japanese.

The Netherlands, initially backed by the British tried to re-establish their rule, and a bitter armed and diplomatic struggle ended in December 1949, when in the face of international pressure, the Dutch formally recognised Indonesian independence. Dutch efforts to re-establish complete control met resistance. At the end of World War II, a power vacuum arose, and the nationalists often succeeded in seizing the arms of the demoralised Japanese. A period of unrest with city guerrilla warfare called the Bersiap period ensued. Groups of Indonesian nationalists armed with improvised weapons (like bamboo spears) but also firearms attacked returning Allied troops. 3500 Europeans were killed and 20000 were missing, meaning more European deaths in Indonesia after the war than during the war.

After returning to Java, Dutch forces quickly re-occupied the colonial capital of Batavia (now Jakarta), so the city of Yogyakarta in central Java became the capital of the nationalist forces. Negotiations with the nationalists led to two major truce agreements, but disputes about their implementation, and much mutual provocation, led each time to renewed conflict. Within four years the Dutch had recaptured almost the whole of Indonesia, but guerrilla resistance, led on Java by commander Nasution persisted. On 27 December 1949, after four years of sporadic warfare and fierce criticism of the Dutch by the United Nations, the Netherlands officially recognised Indonesian sovereignty under the federal structure of the United States of Indonesia (RUSI). On 17 August 1950, exactly five years after the proclamation of independence, the last of the federal states were dissolved and Sukarno proclaimed a single unitary Republic of Indonesia.

Sukarno's Presidency

Democratic Experiment

With the unifying struggle to secure Indonesia's independence over, divisions in Indonesian society began to appear. These included regional differences in customs, religion, the impact of Christianity and Marxism, and fears of Javanese political domination. Following colonial rule, Japanese occupation, and war against the Dutch, the new country suffered from severe poverty, a ruinous economy, low educational and skills levels, and authoritarian traditions. Challenges to the authority of the Republic included the militant *Darul Islam* who waged a guerrilla struggle against the Republic from 1948 to 1962; the declaration of an independent Republic of South Maluku by Ambonese formerly of the Royal Dutch Indies Army; and rebellions in Sumatra and Sulawesi between 1955 and 1961.

In contrast to the 1945 Constitution, the 1950 constitution mandated a parliamentary system of government, an executive responsible to the parliament, and stipulated at length constitutional guarantees for human rights, drawing heavily on the 1948 United Nations Universal Declaration of Human Rights. A proliferation of political parties dealing for shares of cabinet seats resulted in a rapid turnover of coalition governments including 17 cabinets between 1945 and 1958. The long-postponed parliamentary elections were held in 1955; the Indonesian National Party (PNI)—considered Sukarno's party—topped the poll, and the Communist Party of Indonesia (PKI) received strong support, but no party garnered more than a quarter of the votes, which resulted in short-lived coalitions.

Guided Democracy

By 1956, Sukarno was openly criticising parliamentary democracy, stating that it was "based upon inherent conflict" which ran counter to Indonesian notions of harmony as being the natural state human relationships. Instead, he sought a system based on the traditional village system of discussion and consensus, under the guidance of village elders. He proposed a threefold blend of *nasionalisme* ('nationalism'), *agama* ('religion'), and *komunisme* ('communism') into a co-operative 'Nas-A-Kom' government. This was intended to appease the three main factions in Indonesian politics–the army, Islamic groups, and the communists. With the support of the military, he proclaimed in February 1957, 'Guided Democracy', and proposed a cabinet of representing all the political parties of importance (including the PKI).

Sukarno abrogated the 1950 Constitution on 9 July 1959 by a decree dissolving the Constitutional Assembly and restoring the 1945 Constitution. The elected parliament was replaced by one appointed by, and subject to the will of, the President. Another non-elected body, the Supreme Advisory Council, was the main policy development body, while the National Front was set up in September 1960 and presided over by the president to "mobilise the revolutionary forces of the people". Western-style parliamentary democracy was thus finished in Indonesia until the 1999 elections of the *Reformasi* era.

Sukarno's revolution and nationalism

Charismatic Sukarno spoke as a romantic revolutionary, and under his increasingly authoritarian rule, Indonesia moved on a course of stormy nationalism. Sukarno was popularly referred to as *bung* ("older brother"), and he painted himself as a man of the people carrying the aspirations of Indonesia and one who dared take on the West. He instigated a number of large, ideologically-driven infrastructure projects and monuments celebrating Indonesia's identity, which were criticised as substitutes for real development in a deteriorating economy.

Western New Guinea had been part of the Dutch East Indies, and Indonesian nationalists had thus claimed it on this basis. Indonesian was able to instigate a diplomatic and military confrontation with the Dutch over the territory following an Indonesian-Soviet arms agreement in 1960. It was, however, United States pressure on the

Netherlands that led to an Indonesian takeover in 1963. Also in 1963, Indonesia commenced *Konfrontasi* with the new state of Malaysia. The northern states of Borneo, formerly British Sarawak and Sabah, had wavered in joining Malaysia, whilst Indonesia saw itself as the rightful rulers of the Malay race and supported an unsuccessful revolution attempt in Brunei. Reviving the glories of the Indonesian National Revolution, Sukarno rallied against notions of British imperialism mounting military offensives along the Indonesia-Malaysia border in Borneo. As the PKI rallied in Jakarta streets in support, the West became increasingly alarmed at Indonesian foreign policy and the United States withdrew its aid to Indonesia.

Indonesia's economic position continued to deteriorate; by the mid-1960s, the cash-strapped government had to scrap critical public sector subsidies, inflation was at 1,000%, export revenues were shrinking, infrastructure crumbling, and factories were operating at minimal capacity with negligible investment. Severe poverty and hunger was widespread.

The New Order

Transition to the New Order

Described as the great *dalang* ("puppet master"), Sukarno's position depended on balancing the opposing and increasingly hostile forces of the army and PKI. Sukarno's anti-imperial ideology saw Indonesia increasingly dependent on Soviet and then communist China. By 1965, the PKI was the largest communist party in the world outside the Soviet Union or China, and penetrated all levels of government extensively. It increasingly gained influence at the expense of the army. By late 1965, the Indonesian Army was divided between a left-wing allied with the Communist Party of Indonesia (PKI), and a right-wing that were being courted from abroad by the United States.

On September 30, 1965 six of the most senior generals within the military and other officers were executed in an attempted coup. Led by Colonel Untung of the palace guards and backed by elements of the armed forces, the insurgents took up positions and later seized the national radio station. They claimed they were acting against a plot organised by the generals to overthrow Sukarno. Within a few hours, Major General Suharto, commander of the Army Strategic Reserve (Kostrad), mobilised counteraction, and by the evening of 1 October, it was clear the coup, which had little coordination and was largely limited to Jakarta, had failed.

Complicated and partisan theories continue to this day over the identity of the coup attempt organisers and their aims. According to the Indonesian army, the PKI were behind the coup and used disgruntled army officers to carry it out. This would become the official account of Suharto's subsequent New Order's administration. Other theories suggest it was largely an internal army affair led by younger officers against the older leadership. Other theories suggest that Sukarno himself was behind the coup, and others that suggest that Suharto was involved. Most historians agree that the coup was not lead by a single mastermind controlling all events and that the full truth will never likely be known.

While the PKI's role in the events of the night of 30 September-1 October remains debated, the effects on it were devastating. Anti-communists, initially following the army's lead, and encouraged by Western embassies, went on a violent anti-communist purge through villages, during which the PKI was blamed for the coup and effectively destroyed. The most widely accepted estimates are between 500,000 and one million people killed. The violence was especially brutal in Java and Bali. The party was outlawed and possibly more than 1 million of its leaders and affiliates were imprisoned.

Throughout the 1965-66 period, President Sukarno attempted to restore his political position and shift the country back to its pre-October 1965 position. Although he remained president, the weakened Sukarno was out-manoeuvred and forced to transfer key political and military powers to General Suharto, who by that time had become head of the armed forces. In March 1967, the Provisional People's Consultative Assembly (MPRS) named General Suharto acting president. Suharto was formally appointed president in March 1968. Sukarno ceased to be a political force and lived under virtual house arrest until his death in 1970.

Entrenchment of the New Order

In the aftermath of Suharto's rise, hundreds of thousands of people were killed or imprisoned by the military and religious groups in a backlash against alleged communist supporters. Suharto's administration is commonly called the *New Order* era. Suharto invited major foreign investment, which produced substantial, if uneven, economic growth. However, Suharto enriched himself and his family through widespread corruption and was forced to step down amid massive popular demonstrations and a faltering economy by the Indonesian Revolution of 1998. On May 21, 1998, President Suharto announced his resignation and ask Indonesian Vice President DR BJ Habibie to become the new Indonesian President. From 1998 to 2005, the country had four presidents: Bacharuddin Jusuf (BJ) Habibie (1998 to 1999), Abdurrahman Wahid (1999 to 2001), Megawati Sukarnoputri (2001 to 2004) and Susilo Bambang Yudhoyono (2004 to Current).

Annexation of West Irian

At the time of independence, the Dutch retained control over the western half of New Guinea, and permitted steps toward their own self-government and declaration of independence December 1, 1961. After negotiations with the Dutch on the incorporation of the territory into Indonesia failed, an Indonesian paratroop invasion December 18 preceded armed clashes between Indonesian and Dutch troops in 1961 and 1962. In 1962 the United States pressured the Netherlands into secret talks with Indonesia which in August 1962 produced the New York Agreement, and Indonesia assumed administrative responsibility for West Irian on May 1, 1963.

Rejecting United Nations supervision, the Indonesian government under Suharto decided to settle the question of West Irian, the former Dutch New Guinea, in their favor. Rather than a referendum of all residents of West Irian as had been agreed under Sukarno, an "Act of Free Choice" was conducted 1969 in which 1,025 Papuan representatives of local councils were selected by the Indonesians. After training in Indonesian language they were warned to vote in favor of Indonesian integration with the group unanimously voting for integration with Indonesia. A subsequent UN General Assembly resolution confirmed the transfer of sovereignty to Indonesia.

West Irian was renamed Irian Jaya ('glorious Irian') in 1973. Opposition to Indonesian administration of Irian Jaya (later known as Papua) gave rise to small-scale guerrilla activity in the years following Jakarta's assumption of control.

Annexation of East Timor

In 1975, the Carnation Revolution in Portugal caused authorities there to announce plans for decolonisation of Portuguese Timor, the eastern half of the island of Timor whose western half was a part of the Indonesian province of East Nusa Tenggara. In the elections held in 1975, Fretilin, a left-leaning party and UDT, aligned with the local elite, emerged as the largest parties, having previously formed an alliance to campaign for independence from Portugal. Apodeti, a party advocating integration with Indonesia, enjoyed little popular support.

Indonesia alleged that Fretilin was communist, and feared that an independent East Timor would influence separatism in the archipelago. Indonesian military intelligence influenced the break-up of the alliance between Fretilin and UDT, which led to a coup by the UDT on August 11, 1975, and a month-long civil war. During this time, the Portuguese government effectively abandoned the territory, and did not resume the decolonisation process. On November 28, Fretilin unilaterally declared independence, and proclaimed the 'Democratic Republic of East Timor'. Nine days later, on December 7, Indonesia invaded East Timor, eventually annexing the tiny country of (then) 680,000 people. Indonesia was supported materially and diplomatically by the United States, Australia and the United Kingdom who regarded Indonesia as an anti-communist ally.

Following the 1998 resignation of Suharto, on August 30, 1999, the people of East Timor voted overwhelmingly for independence in a UN-sponsored referendum. About 99% of the eligible population participated; more than three quarters chose independence despite months of attacks by the Indonesian military and its militia. After the result was announced, elements of the Indonesian military and its militia retaliated by killing approximately 2,000 East Timorese, displacing two-thirds of the population, raping hundreds of women and girls, and destroying much of the country's infrastructure. In October 1999, the Indonesian parliament (MPR) revoked the decree that annexed East Timor, and the United Nations Transitional Administration in East Timor (UNTAET) assumed responsibility for governing East Timor until it officially became an independent state in May 2002.

Transmigration

The Transmigration program (*Transmigrasi*) was a National Government initiative to move landless people from densely populated areas of Indonesia (such as Java and Bali) to less populous areas of the country including Papua, Kalimantan, Sumatra, and Sulawesi. The stated purpose of this program was to reduce the considerable poverty and overpopulation on Java, to provide opportunities for hard-working poor people, and to provide a workforce to better utilise the natural resource of the outer islands. The program, however, has been controversial with critics accusing the Indonesian Government of trying to use these migrants to reduce the proportion of native populations in receiving areas, thus weakening separatist movements. The program has often been cited as a major and ongoing factor in controversies and even conflict and violence between settlers and indigenous populations.

Forcing out Suharto

Pro-democracy Movement

In 1996 Suharto undertook efforts to pre-empt a challenge to the New Order government. The Indonesian Democratic Party (PDI), a legal party that had traditionally propped up the regime had changed direction, and began to assert its independence. Suharto fostered a split over the leadership of PDI, backing a co-opted faction loyal to deputy speaker of Parliament Suryadi against a faction loyal to Megawati Sukarnoputri, the daughter of Sukarno and PDI's proper chairperson.

After the Suryadi faction announced a party congress to sack Megawati would be held in Medan June 20–22, Megawati proclaimed that her supporters would hold demonstrations in protest. The Suryadi faction went through with its sacking of Megawati, and the demonstrations manifested themselves throughout Indonesia. This lead to several confrontations on the streets between protesters and security forces, and recriminations over the violence. The protests culminated in the military allowing Megawati's supporters to take over PDI headquarters in Jakarta, with a pledge of no further demonstrations.

Suharto allowed the occupation of PDI headquarters to go on for almost a month, as attentions were also on Jakarta due to a set of high-profile ASEAN meetings scheduled to take place there. Capitalizing on this, Megawati supporters organized "democracy forums" with several speakers at the site. On July 26, officers of the military, Suryadi, and Suharto openly aired their disgust with the forums. (Aspinall 1996)

On July 27, police, soldiers, and persons claiming to be Suryadi supporters stormed the headquarters. Several Megawati supporters were killed, and over two-hundred arrested and tried under the Anti-Subversion and Hate-spreading laws. The day would become known as "Black Saturday" and mark the beginning of a renewed crackdown by the New Order government against supporters of democracy, now called the "Reformasi" or Reformation. (Amnesty International 1996)

Economic Crisis and Suharto's Resignation

In 1997 and 1998, Indonesia was the country hardest hit by the East Asian Financial Crisis, which had dire consequences for the Indonesian economy and society, and Suharto's regime. The rupiah, the Indonesian currency, took a sharp dive in value. Suharto came under scrutiny from international lending institutions, chiefly the World Bank, International Monetary Fund (IMF) and the United States, over longtime embezzlement of funds and some protectionist policies. In December, Suharto's government signed a letter of intent to the IMF, pledging to enact austerity measures, including cuts to public services and removal of subsidies, in return for receiving the aid of the IMF and other donors. Prices for goods such as kerosene and rice, and fees for public services including education rose dramatically. The effects were exacerbated by widespread corruption. The austerity measures approved by Suharto had started to erode domestic confidence with the New Order and led to popular protests.

Suharto stood for re-election by parliament for the seventh time in March 1998, justifying it on the grounds of the necessity of his leadership during the crisis. The parliament approved a new term. This sparked protests and riots throughout the country, now termed the Indonesian 1998 Revolution. Dissent within the ranks of his own Golkar party and military finally weakened Suharto, and on May 21 he stood down from power. He was replaced by his deputy Jusuf Habibie.

President Habibie quickly assembled a cabinet. One of its main tasks was to re-establish International Monetary Fund and donor community support for an economic stabilization program. He moved quickly to release political prisoners and lift some controls on freedom of speech and association. Elections for the national, provincial, and sub-provincial parliaments were held on June 7, 1999. For the national parliament, Indonesian Democratic Party-Struggle (PDI-P, led by Sukarno's daughter Megawati Sukarnoputri) won 34% of the vote; Golkar (Suharto's party; formerly the only legal party of government) 22%; United Development Party (PPP, led by Hamzah Haz) 12%; and National Awakening Party (PKB, led by Abdurrahman Wahid) 10%.

Anarcho-Democracy

In October 1999, the People's Consultative Assembly (MPR), which consists of the 500-member Parliament plus 200 appointed members, elected Abdurrahman Wahid (commonly referred to as "Gus Dur") as President, and Megawati Sukarnoputri as Vice President, for 5-year terms. Wahid named his first Cabinet in early November 1999 and a reshuffled, second Cabinet in August 2000. President Wahid's government continued to pursue democratization and to encourage renewed economic growth under challenging conditions. In addition to continuing economic malaise, his government faced regional, interethnic, and interreligious conflict, particularly in Aceh, Maluku Islands, and Irian Jaya. In West Timor, the problems of displaced East Timorese and violence by pro-Indonesian East Timorese militias caused considerable humanitarian and social problems. An increasingly assertive Parliament frequently challenged President Wahid's policies and prerogatives, contributing to a lively and sometimes rancorous national political debate.

During the People's Consultative Assembly's first annual session in August 2000, President Wahid gave an account of his government's performance. On January 29, 2001 thousands of student protesters stormed parliament grounds and demanded that President Abdurrahman Wahid resign due to alleged involvement in corruption scandals. Under pressure from the Assembly to improve management and coordination within the government, he issued a presidential decree giving Vice President Megawati control over the day-to-day administration of government. Soon after, Megawati Sukarnoputri assumed the presidency on July 23. In 2004, the largest one-day election in the world and Indonesia's first direct Presidential election was held and was won by Susilo Bambang Yudhoyono, commonly referred by his initials SBY.

Tsunami Disaster and Aceh Peace Deal

On 26 December 2004, a massive earthquake and tsunami devastated parts of northern Sumatra, particularly Aceh. Partly as a result of the need for cooperation and peace during the recovery from the tsunami in Aceh, peace talks between the Indonesian government and the Free Aceh Movement (GAM) were restarted. Accords signed in Helsinki created a framework for military de-escalation in which the government has reduced its military presence, as members of GAM's armed wing decommission their weapons and apply for amnesty. The agreement also allows for Acehnese nationalist forces to form their own party, and other autonomy measures.

HISTORY OF LAOS

The earliest Lao legal document (and the earliest sociological evidence about the existence of the Lao people) is known as "the laws of Khun Borom" (also spelled "Khun Bulom"), still preserved in manuscript form.

This set of memoriter laws is written in a type of indigenous blank verse, and reflects the state of proto-Lao society as early as the 9th century, possibly prior to their adoption of Theravada Buddhism, and prior to (or coeval with) their southward migration into the territory now comprising modern Laos (from North-Western Vietnam).

While most Lao people regard Borom/Bulom as a subject of myth only, Western scholars regard him as an historical figure, albeit there is very little factually known about him aside from the fact of his bare existence and the description of a very primitive kingdom in his laws.

In general terms, these ancient laws describe an agrarian society in which life revolves around subsistence agriculture with domesticated water-buffaloes (the gayal). The strict punishments set down for stealing or killing a neighbor's elephant reflect that these were (evidently) an expensive and important possession of the time.

The official History of Laos as introduced in government textbooks, is conventionally traced to the establishment of the kingdom of Lan Xang by Fa Ngum in 1353. This is a relatively conservative date to begin the history of the nation, providing a contrast to the course taken by Thai historiography (which reaches back implausibly far into proto-history). By the 14th century, when this "official history" begins, the speakers of early Lao-related languages ("Tai-Kadai")had probably developed a reasonable base of population among the prior inhabitants of (what is now) Laos over the prior century or two.

The earlier inhabitation of the land by peoples such as the Mon kingdom of Dvaravati and Proto-Khmer peoples was given a great deal of emphasis in the histories of Laos written during the French colonial period. However, post-colonial historiography has instead sought to represent all peoples of Laos as equally "indigenous", relating the early history in terms of a complex interaction with the (admittedly more ancient) Cambodian kingdoms to the south, and praising the Proto-Khmer as Lao nationalists for their heroism and modern struggles against the French and Americans.

Both French colonial history and post-colonial (Communist) history sought to reverse the obvious racism of earlier, popular accounts that when the Lao migrated into the country, they simply conquered and enslaved the native inhabitants (viz., primarily Proto-Khmer people, described in such a context with the derogatory term "Kha-That"). This traditional view has almost no factual basis, but remains a commonly heard pseudo-history, and a special concern for teachers to address (or redress) in the classroom. Vatthana Pholsena provides a survey of the historiography on this point in *Post-War Laos*, 2006, Silkworm Books.

It is generally assumed that, as late as the 16th century, King Photisarath helped establish Theravada Buddhism as the predominant religion of the country. However, this aspect of official history may now have to change given recent archaeological discoveries in Cambodia and Vietnam, showing intact Pali inscriptions as early as the 9th century.

While there can be no doubt that animism and fragments of Shiva-worship were popular in ancient Laos, evidence increasingly indicates a long, gradual process leading to the ascendancy of Buddhism (rather than a single king converting the country). The reverse also did occur, as with the historical layers of statuary and inscriptions at Wat Phu Champassak; the oldest are in Sanskrit, and worship Shiva, while the later evidence is Buddhist, subsequently reverting to animism (with the most recent statues simply depicting giant elephants and lizards, with no references to the organized religions of India, and neither Sanskrit nor Pali text).

It is significant to note that all of these official histories exclude the (possible and actual) influence of Chinese religion in the region. In fact, the ancient Lao calendar and Thai calendar are both of Chinese origin (adapted from the "Heavenly Stem Branch Calendar"), and do not reflect Indian cosmology. These calendars were both part of the royal religion (preserved in epigraphy) and, apparently, part of popular religion (fortune telling) for centuries.

Before Full Independence in 1954

In the 17th century Lan Xang entered a period of decline and the late 18th century Siam (now Thailand) established control over much of what is now Laos. The region was divided into three dependent states centered on Luang Prabang in the north, Vientiane in the center, and Champassak in the south. The Vientiane Lao rebelled in 1828 but were defeated, and the area was incorporated into Siam. Following its occupation of Vietnam, France absorbed Laos into French Indochina via treaties with Siam in 1893 and 1904.

During World War II, the Japanese occupied French Indochina. When Japan surrendered, Lao nationalists declared Laos independent, but by early 1946, French troops had reoccupied the country and conferred limited autonomy on Laos. During the First Indochina War, the Indochinese Communist Party formed the Pathet Lao resistance organization committed to Lao independence. Laos gained full independence following the French defeat by the Vietnamese communists and the subsequent Geneva peace conference in 1954.

The Period of the Kingdom of Laos

Elections were held in 1955, and the first coalition government, led by Prince Souvanna Phouma, was formed in 1957. The coalition government collapsed in 1958 under pressure from the United States. In 1960 Captain Kong Lae staged a coup when the cabinet was away at the royal capital of Luang Prabang and demanded reformation of a neutralist government. The second coalition government, once again led by Souvanna Phouma, was not successful in holding power. Rightist forces under General Phoumi Nosavan drove out the neutralist government from power later that same year.

A second Geneva conference, held in 1961-62, provided for the independence and neutrality of Laos, but the agreement was subverted by both the United States and North Vietnam and the war soon resumed. The government and army of Laos were generally neutral during the conflict. The United States and North Vietnam subverted the agreement by forming private proxy armies. Growing American and North Vietnamese military presence in the country increasingly drew Laos into the Second Indochina War (1954-1975). For nearly a decade, eastern Laos was subjected to the heaviest bombing in the history of warfare, as the U.S. sought to destroy the Ho Chi Minh Trail that passed through Laos. The country was also repeatedly invaded by Vietnam.

Shortly after the Paris Peace Accords led to the withdrawal of U.S. forces from Vietnam, a ceasefire between the Pathet Lao and the government led to a new coalition government. However, North Vietnam never really withdrew from Laos and the Pathet Lao remained little more than a proxy army for Vietnamese interests. After the fall of South Vietnam to communist forces in April 1975, the Pathet Lao with the backing of North Vietnam were able to take total power with little resistance. On December 2, 1975, the king was forced to abdicate his throne and the Lao People's Democratic Republic was established.

The Period of the Communist Government/Contemporary Period

The new communist government led by Kaysone Phomvihane imposed centralized economic decision-making and incarcerated many members of the previous government and military in "re-education camps" which also included the Hmongs. While nominally independent, the communist government was for many years effectively little more than a puppet regime run from Vietnam. The government's policies prompted about

10 percent of the Lao population to leave the country. Laos depended heavily on Soviet aid channeled through Vietnam up until the Soviet collapse in 1991. In the 1990s the communist party gave up centralised management of the economy but still has a monopoly of political power.

From 1975 to Present

On December 2, 1975, the king abdicated his throne and the communist Lao People's Democratic Republic (LPDR) was established. The new communist government imposed centralized economic decision-making and broad security measures, including control of the media and the arrest and incarceration of many members of the previous government and military in "re-education camps." These draconian policies and deteriorating economic conditions, along with government efforts to enforce political control, prompted an exodus of lowland Lao and ethnic Hmong from Laos. About 10% of the Lao population sought refugee status after 1975, many of whom resettled in third countries, including the United States. From 1975 to 1996, the U.S. resettled some 250,000 Lao refugees from Thailand, including 130,000 Hmong. The last major resettlement to the United States of about 15,000 Hmong from the Wat Tham Krabok camp was in 2004.

Over time, the Lao Government closed the re-education camps and released most political prisoners. By the end of 1999, more than 28,900 Hmong and lowland Lao had voluntarily repatriated to Laos—3,500 from China and the rest from Thailand. The Office of the United Nations High Commissioner for Refugees (UNHCR) monitored returnees for a number of years and reported no evidence of systemic persecution or discrimination against returnees per se. UNHCR closed its Laos office at the end of 2001.

Establishment of the Lao People's Democratic Republic

The National Congress of People's Representatives, recreating the mise-en-scène of 1945, met in the auditorium of the former United States community school on December 1, 1975. Sisana Sisan delivered the opening speech on behalf of the preliminary committee for convening the National Congress of People's Representatives. So far only the LPF and other front organizations and delegations from the various provinces were listed as attending among the 264 delegates. The preliminary committee thereupon dissolved itself.

Prince Souphanouvong, named to the presidium of the National Congress, said in his speech that the congress would "study" the king's abdication, the dissolution of the PGNU and the National Political Consultative Council, and the political report on abolishing the monarchy and establishing a people's democratic republic. This last item was read by Kaysone, who was also on the congress presidium. For most of the world, it was the first look at the man who, for thirty years, had led the revolution in Laos from behind the scenes in Vietnam and in the caves of Houaphan. Kaysone presided at the December 2 session. He began by reading a motion to establish the Lao People's Democratic Republic, which was passed by acclamation. Kaysone then nominated Souphanouvong to be president of the country. Again, the vote was unanimous. Next, Nouhak took the podium to say it was necessary to elect a Supreme People's Assembly. He proposed Souphanouvong as president of the Supreme People's Assembly and then read a list of forty-four names. This vote was also unanimous.

Officially, the party—which had been renamed the Lao People's Revolutionary Party at its Second Party Congress in 1972—played no role in the National Congress. But it began making its public appearance immediately thereafter in indirect ways; for example, banners carrying revolutionary slogans and messages of congratulations from North Vietnamese, Soviet, and Chinese leaders began to appear. With power firmly in its grasp, the LPRP no longer had any reason to hide its identity. For the first time, the party publicly identified the seven members of its Political Bureau (Politburo). From this point, the party alone made decisions in the Lao People's Democratic Republic. Gone were the "democratic freedoms" that had been extolled in the National Political Consultative Council's eighteen points. The Neutralist Party and other noncommunist parties disappeared, leaving a oneparty regime. Those who objected could leave. Some 350,000 availed themselves of this opportunity over the next few years, leaving behind their homes and belongings, and, in many cases, even their loved ones.

"Seminar Camps" and the Death of King Savang Vatthana

"Seminar camps," also called reeducation centers, were the centerpiece of the new regime's policy toward the enemies it had defeated. The LPRP's Marxist-Leninist dogma allowed no respite in the class struggle, and those identified as its former enemies were the presumed saboteurs and subversives of the socialist phase of the revolution that was just getting under way. After its victory, the regime made people judged unfit to participate in the new society in their present frame of mind construct a series of camps, known only by their numbers. They included Camp 01 at Sop Hao; Camp 03 near Na Kai, newly given the Pali name Viangxai, meaning "Victorious Town"; Camp 05 near Muang Xamteu; and Camps 04 and 06 near Muang Et, all in Houaphan. A camp was also built at Muang Khoua on the Nam Ou, and others were built in the center and south. There are no official figures on the numbers of people sent for reeducation, because the camp network was kept a secret from the outside world. The only information was brought out by former inmates and their families. Various published estimates have put the number of inmates at 30,000, at 37,600, and at 50,000.

Even before the communist takeover, the first groups of highlevel officials, including provincial governors and district chiefs, had been transported to the camps, arriving in full dress uniform. They had received letters signed by Souvanna Phouma ordering them to attend an important meeting in Vientiane. After an overnight stay in Vientiane, the group was flown to the Plain of Jars, where a festive atmosphere prevailed. The officials, about seventy in all, were feted with food and a movie, and North Vietnamese advisers were present. They were then flown to Houaphan, separated into small groups, and organized into work parties.

In August and September 1977, a group of twenty-six "reactionary" high-ranking officials and military officers in Camp 05 were accused of plotting a coup and arrested. These persons were taken away to Camp 01. They included Pheng Phongsavan, the minister who had signed the Vientiane Agreement; Touby Lyfoung, the Hmong leader; Soukhan Vilaysan, another of Souvanna Phouma's ministers who had been with him in the Lao Issara and had risen to become secretary general of the Neutralists; and Generals Bounphone Maekthepharak and Ouan Ratikoun. All died in Camp 01. Thus, those who played roles in the modern history of Laos were relegated by the regime to the status of nonpersons and their fate placed in the hands of their prison guards. Others, like Tiao Sisoumang Sisaleumsak, a minister in Souvanna Phouma's 1960 government, General Sengsouvanh Souvannarath, commander of the Neutralist forces, Khamchan Pradith, an intellectual and diplomat, and even Sing Chanthakoummane, a lieutenant in the Second Paratroop Battalion in 1960, were held in seminar camps for fifteen years or more before being released. Souvanna Phouma was allowed to live quietly in Vientiane until his death in January 1984.

The new regime feared that ex-King Savang Vatthana, who until March 1977 had lived quietly in the royal palace as a private citizen with the meaningless title of adviser to President Souphanouvong, would become a symbol of popular resistance. As a result, he was suddenly spirited away by helicopter to Houaphan along with Queen Khamboui and Crown Prince Say Vongsavang. Imprisoned in Camp 01, the crown prince died on May 2, 1978, and the king eleven days later of starvation. The queen died on December 12, 1981. According to an eyewitness, all were buried in unmarked graves outside the camp's perimeter. No official announcement was made. More than a decade later, during a visit to France in December 1989, Kaysone confirmed reports of the king's death in an innocuous aside that attributed it to old age.

The party did not dare abolish the Buddhist community of monks and novices, the clergy (sangha), of which the king had been the supreme patron. It did, however, attempt to reshape the sangha into an instrument of control. In March 1979, the Venerable Thammayano, the eighty-seven-year-old Sangha-raja of Laos, the country's highest-ranking abbott, fled by floating across the Mekong on a raft of inflated car tubes. His secretary, who engineered the escape, reported that the Sangha-raja had been confined to his monastery in Louangphrabang and was forbidden to preach. Ordinary monks were not forbidden to preach, but their sermons were commonly tape recorded and monitored for signs of dissidence. As a result of these pressures, the number of monks in Laos decreased sharply after 1975.

Developments in the Lao People's Democratic Republic

In spite of the regime's revolutionary rhetoric about selfreliance on the march to socialism, Western aid was simply replaced over the 1970s and 1980s by aid from "fraternal countries" of the Soviet bloc. Living standards declined further. Nongovernmental organizations, including some from the United States, in cooperation with local officials, established a few small-scale aid projects that reached out to real needs in the areas of health, education, and economic development.

Kaysone and his colleagues, following the well-known examples of Soviet and East European party leaders, led carefully protected lives behind the walls of their guarded compounds in the capital, secluded from public scrutiny and shielded from any manifestation of hostility, their movements kept secret. The minister of interior, Somseun Khamphithoun, whose ministry was responsible for the operation of the seminar camps, was never seen publicly in Vientiane. Corruption, widespread in the years of the United States civilian and military aid programs, resumed with the new opportunities presented by the "economic opening" beginning in 1986.

The first Supreme People's Assembly, appointed by the National Congress on December 2, 1975, rapidly faded into obscurity, although its twice-yearly meetings were reported in the controlled press. In 1988, perhaps because the regime wished to give itself some semblance of popular underpinning, it suddenly announced that elections would be held for a new Supreme People's Assembly. Elections were held on June 26, 1988, for 2,410 seats on districtlevel people's councils and on November 20, 1988, for 651 seats on province-level people's councils. On March 26, 1989, elections were held for seventy-nine seats on the Supreme People's Assembly. Candidates in all elections were screened by the party. Sixty-five of the seventy-nine members of the assembly were party members.

In the area of foreign relations, Laos joined the ranks of the "socialist camp" on December 2, 1975. Gone was any pretense of neutrality. In the new state of affairs where "peace" had at long last been achieved and no one paid attention to the presence of "fraternal" foreign troops on Laotian soil, the delegations of the ICC in Laos returned to their respective countries, leaving behind piles of unpaid bills.

In accordance with the organic links between the Vietnamese and Laotian parties that have been acclaimed by the highest party leaders, Laos has been tied more closely to Vietnam than to any other country. The term special relations (in Lao, khan phoua phan yang phiset) to describe the linkage between the two parties and governments had come into use as early as November 1973 when Le Duan, first secretary of the Vietnamese party, visited Viangxai. Thereafter, special relations was the term increasingly emphasized in joint statements. In July 1977, Laos and Vietnam signed the twenty-five-year Treaty of Friendship and Cooperation. They also agreed to redefine their common border, which was demarcated in 1986. In early 1989, the Vietnamese troops that had been stationed in Laos continuously since 1961 were reported to have been withdrawn.

Despite some incidents along their common border, Thailand took an accommodating stand toward the country. Opening the border to trade and eliminating the "sanctuary" problem were affirmed as goals in a 1979 joint communiqué between Kaysone and the Thai prime minister, Kriangsak Chomanand, which was subsequently cited by Laotians as the touchstone of their relations with Thailand. Following a series of shooting incidents in 1984 involving rival claims to three border villages, a major dispute arose in December 1987 over territory claimed by Laos as part of Botèn District in Xaignabouri and by Thailand as part of Chat Trakan District in Phitsanulok Province. The fighting that ensued claimed more than 1,000 lives before a cease-fire was declared on February 19, 1988. The origin of the dispute was the ambiguity of the topographic nomenclature used in the 1907 FrancoSiamese border treaty over the area of the Nam Heung, up which Fa Ngum's army had traveled in the fourteenth century. After 1975 the sanctuary problem also defied solution for a decade, with the Hmong and communist rebels occupying some of the old Lao Issara resistance bases in Thailand. However, a series of working-level meetings between the two sides were arranged that served to defuse the conflict, and relations improved markedly in the late 1980s.

Although official relations between Laos and China were strained by the Sino-Vietnamese War of 1979, the two countries maintained diplomatic relations, and local trade continued across their common border. The ending of the brief war saw a rapid and steady improvement in mutual ties and exchanges of visits at all levels. Kaysone visited Beijing, and a border demarcation commission completed its work to mutual satisfaction.

Laos seemed at last to have achieved stable relations with its neighbors. Centuries-old conflicts that had repeatedly seen foreign invaders trampling Laotian soil with their elephants or tanks, Laotians conscripted by this or that pretender to the throne, pagodas built and then destroyed, and the countryside laid waste, had receded. Peace brought the prospect of a better life, if not yet participation in a multiparty democracy. It was as if after so much suffering Laotians had turned inward, seeking the fulfillment that had always come from their families, their villages, their sangha, and their pride in the moments of glory in their country's long history.

HISTORY OF MALAYSIA

History of Malaysia is the written past of a country in South East Asia whose strategic sea-lane position brought trade and foreign influences that fundamentally influenced its history. Hindu India, the Islamic Middle East and Christian Europe to its west, and China and Japan to the north-east were major influences brought by shipping routes passing through the region. Malaysian history is also intertwined with that of neighbouring Indonesia, Singapore, Philippines, Brunei and Thailand. This trade and foreign cultures brought the area great wealth and diversity, but has also domination and colonialism. The history of Malaysia is one of successive phases of outside influence, followed by the mid-twentieth century establishment of independence from foreign colonial powers.

Hindu and Buddhist cultures imported from India dominated early Malaysian history. They reached their peak in the Sumatran-based Srivijaya civilisation, whose influence extended through Sumatra, Java, the Malay Peninsula and much of Borneo from the 7th to the 14th centuries. Although Muslims had passed through Malaysia as early as the tenth century, it was not until the 14th and 15th centuries that Islam first established itself on the Malayan Peninsular. The adoption of Islam by the fifteenth century saw the rise of number sultanates, the most prominent of which was the Melaka (Malacca). Islamic culture has had a profound influence on the Malay people, but has also been influenced by them. The Portuguese were the first European colonial powers to establish themselves in Malaysia, capturing Malacca in 1511, followed by the Dutch. However, it was the British, who after initially establishing bases at Jesselton, Kuching, Penang and Singapore, ultimately secured their hegemony across the territory that is now Malaysia. The Anglo-Dutch Treaty of 1824 defined the boundaries between British Malaya and the Netherlands East Indies (which became Indonesia). A fourth phase of foreign influence was immigration of Chinese and Indian workers to meet the needs of the colonial economy created by the British in the Malay Peninsula and Borneo.

Japanese invasion in World War II ended British domination in Malaysia. The subsequent occupation from 1942 to 1945 unleashed nationalism in Malaya and Borneo. In the Peninsula, the Malayan Communist Party took up arms against the British. A tough military response was needed to end the insurgency and bring about the establishment of an independent, multi-racial Federation of Malaya in 1957. On 31 August 1963, the British territories in North Borneo and Singapore were granted independence and formed Malaysia with the Peninsular states on 16 September 1963. Approximately two years later, Singapore was expelled from the Federation. A confrontation with Indonesia occurred in the early-1960s. Race riots in 1969 led to the imposition of emergency rule, and a curtailment of political life and civil liberties which has never been fully reversed. Since 1970 the "National Front coalition" headed by United Malays National Organisation (UMNO) has governed Malaysia. Economic growth dramatically increased living standards by the 1990s. This growing prosperity helped minimise political discontent. Successive UMNO-dominated governments have promoted the use of the Malay language and carried out systematic positive discrimination in favour of Muslims, measures which cause great resentment.

Indian influence in the region dates back to at least the 3rd century BCE. Indian traders came to the archipelago for abundant forest and marine products, and to trade with merchants from China. Both Hinduism and Buddhism were well established in the Malay Peninsula by the beginning of the 1st century AD, and from there spread across the archipelago. Chinese chronicles of the 5th century CE speak of a great port in the south called Guantoli, which is thought to have been in the Straits of Malacca. In the 7th century, a new port called Shilifoshi is mentioned, and this is believed to be a Chinese rendering of Srivijaya.

The site of Srivijaya's centre is thought be at a river mouth in eastern Sumatra, possibly near Palembang. For 700 years the Maharajahs of Srivijaya ruled a loose-knit maritime empire that controlled the coasts of Sumatra, Peninsular Malaya, and Borneo. Sometimes they also ruled parts of Java, but Javanese states resisted Srivijayan hegemony. Srivijaya was based on trade, welcoming annual trading fleets from China and India, and further afield, including Japanese, Iranians and Arabs. Its greatest enemies were the Siamese in the north. To secure a powerful ally against these enemies, the maharajahs paid tribute to the Chinese Emperors, but they were never under Chinese control.

The power of Srivijaya declined from the 10th century CE. Never a centralised state, it was apparently weakened by a series of wars with the Javanese, which disrupted trade. In the 11th century CE a rival power centre arose at Melayu, a port possibly located further up the Sumatran coast at what is now the Indonesian Jambi province. Melayu's influence is shown by the fact that the name is the origin of the word "Malay." The power of the Hindu Maharajahs was further undermined by the spread of Islam. Areas which were converted to Islam early, such as Aceh, broke away from Srivijaya's control. By the late 13th century, the Siamese kings of Sukhothai had brought most of Malaya under their rule. But the great wealth of the Srivijayan sphere, with its rich resources of aromatic timber, sea products, gold, tin, spices, wax and resins – all highly prized both in China and in the west – kept Srivijaya prosperous until it faded away in the 14th century.

There were numerous Malay kingdoms in the 2nd and 3rd century CE—as many as 30 according to Chinese sources. Kedah—known as Kedaram or Kataha, in ancient Pallava or Sanskrit—was in the direct route of invasions of Indian traders and kings. Rajendra Chola, Tamil Emperor who is now thought to have laid Kota Gelanggi to waste, put Kedah to heel in 1025 but his successor, Vir Rajendra Chola, had to put down a Kedah rebellion to overthrow the invaders. The coming of the Chola reduced the majesty of Srivijaya which had exerted influence over Kedah and Pattani and even as far as Ligor.

The Buddhist kingdom of Ligor took control of Kedah, and its King Chandrabhanu used it as a base to attack Sri Lanka in the 11th century, an event noted in a stone inscription in Nagapattinum in Tamil Nadu and in the Sri Lankan chronicles, *Mahavamsa*. During the first millennium, the people of the Malay peninsula adopted Hinduism and Buddhism and the use of Sanskrit until their later conversion to Islam.

Melaka and Islamic Malaya

The port of Melaka ("Malacca") on the west coast of the Malay Peninsula was founded around 1400 by Parameswara, a rebel prince of the Srivijaya royal line, who was claimed in the Sejarah Melayu to be a descendant of Alexander the Great. Expelled from Sumatra for killing the ruler of Temasek (modern day Singapore), Parameswara established himself in Melaka. The kingdom rapidly assumed the place previously held by Srivijaya, establishing independent relations with China, and exploiting its position dominating the Straits to control the China-India maritime trade, which became increasingly important when the Mongol conquests closed the overland route between China and the west. Within a few years of its establishment, Melaka officially adopted Islam, and the Raja became a Sultan.

The political power of the Malaccan Sultanate helped Islam's rapid spread through the archipelago, reaching as far as modern day Philippines, while leaving Bali as an isolated outpost of Hinduism. Islam came to the Malay Archipelago via India, and unlike Middle Eastern Islam it was influenced by the mystical traditions of Sufism, and also absorbed some elements of Malay animist and Hindu traditions. Because Islam was introduced by traders and not military conquest, there was no imposition of the Arabic language or Arab political customs. Since most ethnic Malays could not read the Arabic Qur'an, the local version of Islam was much less rigorous than in the Arabic world. And since the indigenous Malay rulers retained their power, the Islamic clergy did not gain the political influence it enjoyed in other parts of the Islamic world.

Melaka's reign lasted little more than a century, but it came to be seen as a golden age of Malay self-rule, and the Sultans of Melaka became the models for all subsequent Malay rulers. Melaka became a cultural centre, creating the matrix of the modern

Malay culture: a blend of indigenous Malay and imported Indian, Chinese and Islamic elements. Melaka's fashions in literature, art, music, dance and dress, and the ornate titles of its royal court, came to be seen as the standard for all ethnic Malays. The court of Melaka also gave great prestige to the Malay language, which had originally evolved in Sumatra and been brought to Melaka at the time of its foundation. In time Malay came to be the official language of all the Malaysian states, although local languages survived in many places.

Struggles for Hegemony

The closing of the overland route from Asia to Europe by the Ottoman Empire and the claim towards trade monopoly with India and south-east Asia by Arab traders, led European powers to look for a maritime route. In 1498 Vasco da Gama, sent by King John II of Portugal, found the route around the Cape of Good Hope to India, and in 1511 Afonso de Albuquerque led an expedition to Malaya which seized Melaka following a month-long siege and made it the centre of Portugal's eastern activity. The son of the last Sultan of Melaka fled to the island of Bintan off the southern tip of Malaya, where he founded a state that which became the Sultanate of Johore. By the late sixteenth century the tin mines of northern Malaya had been discovered by European traders, and Perak grew wealthy on the proceeds of tin exports. The European colonial expanded further into the region. The Portuguese gained control over the trade from the spice-rich Maluku islands, and in 1571 the Spanish captured Manila.

In the early sixteenth century, the Dutch established Dutch East India Company (VOC), initially based trade and Maluku, and their post Batavia in west Java. From there they expanded across the archipelago, forming an alliance with Johore against their main enemies, the Portuguese at Melaka and the powerful Sultan of Aceh. In 1641, after several attempts, the VOC-Johore alliance captured Melaka, breaking Portuguese power in Malaya for good – Portugal was left with only Portuguese Timor. Backed by the Dutch, Johore established a loose hegemony over the Malay states, except Perak, which was able to play off Johore against the Siamese to the north and retain its independence.

The weakness of the Malay states in this period allowed other people to migrate into the Malay homelands. The most significant migrants being the Bugis, seafarers from eastern Indonesia, who regularly raided the Malay coasts. They seized control of Johore following the assassination of the last Sultan of the old Melaka royal line in 1699 and other Bugis took control of Selangor. The Minangkabau from northern Sumatra migrated into Malaya, and eventually established their own state in Negeri Sembilan. The fall of Johore left a power vacuum on the Malay Peninsula which was partly filled by the Siamese kings of Ayutthaya kingdom, who made the five northern Malay states

– Kedah, Kelantan, Patani, Perlis and Terengganu – their vassals. Johore's eclipse also left Perak as the unrivalled leader of the Malay states.

The economic importance of Malaya to Europe grew rapidly during the 18th century. The fast-growing tea trade between China and Britain increased the demand for high-quality Malayan tin, which was used to line tea-chests. Malayan pepper also had a high reputation in Europe, while Kelantan and Pahang had gold mines. The growth of tin and gold mining and associated service industries led to the first influx of foreign settlers into the Malay world – initially Arabs and Indians, later Chinese – who colonised the towns and soon dominated economic activities. This established a pattern which characterised Malayan society for the next 200 years – a rural Malay population increasingly under the domination of wealthy urban immigrant communities, whose power the Sultans were unable to resist.

English traders had been present in Malay waters since the 17th century, but it was not until the mid 18th century that the British East India Company, based in British India, developed a serious interest in Malayan affairs. The growth of the China trade in British ships increased the Company's desire for bases in the region. Various islands were used for this purpose, but the first permanent acquisition was Penang, leased from the Sultan of Kedah in 1786. This was followed soon after by the leasing of a block of territory on the mainland opposite Penang (known as Province Wellesley). In 1795, during the Napoleonic Wars, the British occupied Dutch Melaka to forestall possible French interest in the area. When Melaka was handed back to the Dutch in 1815, the British governor, Stamford Raffles, looked for an alternative base, and in 1819 he acquired Singapore from the Sultan of Johore. The twin bases of Penang and Singapore, together with the decline of the Netherlands as a naval power, made Britain the dominant force in Malayan affairs. British influence was increased by Malayan fears of Siamese expansionism, to which Britain made a useful counterweight. During the 19th century the Malay Sultans became loyal allies of the British Empire.

British Influence

In 1824 British hegemony in Malaya was formalised by the Anglo-Dutch Treaty, the decisive event in the formation of modern Malaysia. The Dutch evacuated Melaka and renounced all interest in Malaya, while the British recognised Dutch rule over the rest of the East Indies. Penang, Melaka and Singapore were united as the Straits Settlements, ruled by a British Governor in Singapore. During the 19th century, the British concluded treaties with the Malay states, installing "residents" who advised the Sultans and soon became the effective rulers of their states. The wealth of Perak's tin mines made political stability there a priority for British investors, and Perak was thus the first Malay state to agree to the supervision of a British resident. Johore alone resisted, holding out until 1914. In 1909 the weakened Siamese kingdom was compelled to cede Kedah, Kelantan, Perlis and Terengganu to the British. (Siam retained the Sultanate of Patani, leaving a Muslim minority in southern Thailand which has been a source of much trouble for successive Thai governments.)

During the late 19th century the British also gained control of the north coast of Borneo, where Dutch rule had never been established. The eastern part of this region (now Sabah) was under the nominal control of the Sultan of Sulu, a vassal of the Spanish Philippines. The rest was the territory of the Sultanate of Brunei. In 1841, a British adventurer, James Brooke, leased Kuching from the Sultan and made himself the "White Raja" of Sarawak, steadily expanding his territory at Brunei's expense. North-eastern Borneo was colonised by British traders, and in 1881 the British North Borneo Company was granted control of the territory under the distant supervision of the governor in Singapore. The Spanish Philippines never recognised this loss of the Sultan of Sulu's territory, laying the basis of the subsequent Filipino claim to Sabah. In 1888 what was left of Brunei was made a British protectorate, and in 1891 another Anglo-Dutch treaty formalised the border between British and Dutch Borneo. Thus the borders of modern Malaysia were formed, in complete disregard of ethnic and linguistic factors, by the colonial powers.

By 1910 the pattern of British rule in the Malay lands was established. The Straits Settlements were a Crown Colony, ruled by a governor under the supervision of the Colonial Office in London. Their population was about half Chinese, but all residents, regardless of race, were British subjects. The first four states to accept British residents, Perak, Selangor, Negeri Sembilan and Pahang, were termed the Federated Malay States: while technically independent, they were placed under a Resident-General in 1895, making them British colonies in all but name. The Unfederated Malay States (Johore, Kedah, Kelantan, Perlis and Terengganu) had a slightly larger degree of independence, although they were unable to resist the wishes of their British Residents for long. Johore, as Britain's closest ally in Malay affairs, had the privilege of a written constitution, which gave the Sultan the right to appoint his own Cabinet, but he was generally careful to consult the British first.

Multi-racial Influence

Unlike some colonial powers, the British always saw their empire as primarily an economic concern, and its colonies were expected to turn a profit for British shareholders. Malaya's obvious attractions were its tin and gold mines, but British planters soon began to experiment with tropical plantation crops – tapioca, gambier, pepper and coffee. But in 1877 the rubber plant was introduced from Brazil, and rubber soon became Malaya's staple export, stimulated by booming demand from European industry.

Rubber was later joined by palm oil as an export earner. All these industries required a large and disciplined labour force, and the British did not regard the Malays as reliable workers. The solution was the importation of plantation workers from India, mainly Tamil-speakers from South India. The mines, mills and docks also attracted a flood of immigrant workers from southern China. Soon towns like Singapore, Penang and Ipoh were majority Chinese, as was Kuala Lumpur, founded as a tin-mining centre in 1857. By 1891, when Malaya's first census was taken, Perak and Selangor, the main tin-mining states, had Chinese majorities.

The Chinese mostly arrived poor, but their industrious habits and tight-knit networks of mutual aid (run by secret societies or Triads) soon made many of them rich. In the 1890s Yap Ah Loy, who held the title of Kapitan China of Kuala Lumpur, was the richest man in Malaya, owning a chain of mines, plantations and shops. Malaya's banking and insurance industries were run by the Chinese from the start, and Chinese businesses, usually in partnership with London firms, soon had a stranglehold on the economy. Since the Malay Sultans tended to spend well beyond their incomes, they were soon in debt to Chinese bankers, and this gave the Chinese political as well as economic power. At first the Chinese immigrants were nearly all men, and most intended to return home when they had made their fortunes. Many did go home, but many more stayed. At first they married Malay women, producing a community of Sino-Malayans or baba people, but soon they began importing Chinese brides, establishing permanent communities and building schools and temples.

The Indians were initially less successful, since unlike the Chinese they came mainly as indentured labourers to work in the rubber plantations, and had few of the economic opportunities that the Chinese had. They were also a less united community, since they were divided between Hindus and Muslims and along lines of language and caste. An Indian commercial and professional class emerged during the early 20th century, but the majority of Indians remained poor and uneducated in rural ghettos in the rubber-growing areas.

Traditional Malay society had great difficulty coping with both the loss of political sovereignty to the British and of economic sovereignty to the Chinese. By the early 20th century it seemed possible that the Malays would become a minority in their own country. The Sultans, who were seen as collaborators with both the British and the Chinese, lost some of their traditional prestige, particularly among the increasing number of Malays with a western education, but the mass of rural Malays continued to revere the Sultans and their prestige was thus an important prop for colonial rule. A small class of Malay nationalist intellectuals began to emerge during the early 20th century, and there was also a revival of Islam in response to the perceived threat of other imported religions, particularly Christianity. In fact few Malays converted to Christianity, although many Chinese did. The northern regions, which were less influenced by western ideas, became strongholds of Islamic conservatism, as they have remained.

The one consolation to Malay pride was that the British allowed them a virtual monopoly of positions in the police and local military units, as well as a majority of those administrative positions open to non-Europeans. While the Chinese mostly built and paid for their own schools and colleges, importing teachers from China, the colonial government fostered education for Malays, opening Malay College in 1905 and creating the Malay Administrative Service in 1910. (The college was dubbed "Bab ud-Darajat" – the Gateway to High Rank.) A Malay Teachers College followed in 1922, and a Malay Women's Training College in 1935. All this reflected the official British policy that Malaya belonged to the Malays, and that the other races were but temporary residents. This view was increasingly out of line with reality, and contained the seeds of much future trouble.

In the years before World War II, the British neglected constitutional development in Malaya. Following their usual policy of indirect rule, they were concerned to prop up the authority of the Sultans and to discourage any talk of Malaya as a united or self-governing country. There were no moves to give Malaya a unitary government, and in fact in 1935 the position of Resident-General of the Federated States was abolished, and its powers decentralised to the individual states. With their usual tendency to racial stereotyping, the British regarded the Malays as amiable but unsophisticated and rather lazy, incapable of self-government, although making good soldiers under British officers. They regarded the Chinese as clever but dangerous – and indeed during the 1920s and '30s, reflecting events in China, the Chinese Nationalist Party (the Kuomintang) and the Communist Party of China built rival clandestine organisations in Malaya, leading to regular disturbances in the Chinese towns. The British saw no way that Malaya's disparate collection of states and races could become a nation, let alone an independent one.

War and Emergency

The outbreak of war in the Pacific in December 1941 found the British in Malaya completely unprepared. During the 1930s, anticipating the rising threat of Japanese naval power, they had built a great naval base at Singapore, but never anticipated an invasion of Malaya from the north. Because of the demands of the war in Europe, there was virtually no British air capacity in the Far East. The Japanese were thus able to attack from their bases in French Indo-China with impunity, and despite stubborn resistance from British, Australian and Indian forces, they overran Malaya in two months. Singapore, with no landward defences, no air cover and no water supply, was forced to surrender in February 1942, doing irreparable damage to British prestige. British North Borneo and Brunei were also occupied.

The Japanese had a racial policy just as the British did. They regarded the Malays as a colonial people liberated from British imperialist rule, and fostered a limited form of Malay nationalism, which gained them some degree of collaboration from the Malay civil service and intellectuals. (Most of the Sultans also collaborated with the Japanese, although they maintained later that they had done so unwillingly.) The occupiers regarded the Chinese, however, as enemy aliens, and treated them with great harshness: during the so-called *sook ching* (purification through suffering), up to 40,000 Chinese in Malaya and Singapore were killed. Chinese businesses were expropriated and Chinese schools closed. Not surprisingly the Chinese, led by the Malayan Communist Party (MCP), became the backbone of the Malayan People's Anti-Japanese Army (MPAJA), which with British assistance became the most effective resistance force in the occupied Asian countries. But the Japanese also offended Malay nationalism by allowing their ally Thailand to re-annex the four northern states, Kedah, Perlis, Kelantan and Terengganu that had been surrendered to British in 1909. The loss of Malaya's export markets soon produced mass unemployment which affected all races and made the Japanese increasingly unpopular.

The Malayans were thus on the whole glad to see the British back in 1945, but things could not remain as they were before the war. Britain was bankrupt and the new Labour government was keen to withdraw its forces from the East as soon as possible. Colonial self-rule and eventual independence were now British policy. The tide of colonial nationalism sweeping through Asia soon reached Malaya. But most Malays were more concerned with defending themselves against the Malayan Communist Party (MCP) which was mostly made up of Chinese, than with demanding independence from the British – indeed their immediate concern was that the British not leave and abandon the Malays to the armed Communists of the MPAJA, which was the largest armed force in the country. During the last year of the war there had been armed clashes between Chinese and Malays and many Malays were killed by the armed Chinese communists members of the MPAJA and the returning British found a country on the brink of civil war.

In 1946 the British announced plans for a Malayan Union, which would turn the Federated and Unfederated Malay States, plus Penang and Malacca (but not Singapore), into a unitary state, with a view to independence within a few years. There would be a common Malayan citizenship regardless of race. The Malays were horrified at this recognition that the Chinese and Indians were now to be a permanent and equal part of Malaya's future, and vowed their opposition to the plan. The Sultans, who had initially supported it, backed down and placed themselves at the head of the resistance. In 1946 the United Malays National Organisation (UMNO) was founded by Malay nationalists led by Dato Onn bin Jaafar, the Chief Minister of Johore. UMNO favoured independence for Malaya, but only if the new state was run exclusively by the Malays. Faced with implacable Malay opposition, the British dropped the plan.

Meanwhile the Communists were moving towards open insurrection. The MPAJA had been disbanded in December 1945, and the MCP organised as a legal political party, but the MPAJA's arms were carefully stored for future use. The MCP policy was for immediate independence with full equality for all races. This meant it recruited very few Malays. The Party's strength was in the Chinese-dominated trade unions, particularly in Singapore, and in the Chinese schools, where the teachers, mostly born in China, saw the Communist Party of China as the leader of China's national revival. In March 1947, reflecting the international Communist movement's "turn to left" as the Cold War set in, the MCP leader Lai Tek was purged and replaced by the veteran MPAJA guerrilla leader Chin Peng, who turned the party increasingly to direct action. In July, following a string of assassinations of plantation managers, the colonial government struck back, declaring a State of Emergency, banning the MCP and arresting hundreds of its militants. The Party retreated to the jungle and formed the Malayan Peoples' Liberation Army, with about 3,000 men under arms, almost all Chinese.

The Malayan Emergency involved six years of bitter fighting across the Malayan Peninsula. The British strategy, which proved ultimately successful, was to isolate the MCP from its support base by a combination of economic and political concessions to the Chinese and the resettlement of Chinese squatters into "New Villages" in "white areas" free of MCP influence. The effective mobilisation of the Malays against the MCP was also an important part the British strategy. From 1949 the MCP campaign lost momentum and the number of recruits fell sharply. Although the MCP succeeded in assassinating the British High Commissioner, Sir Henry Gurney, in October 1951, this turn to "terrorist" tactics alienated many moderate Chinese from the Party. The arrival of Lt-Gen Sir Gerald Templer as British commander in 1952 was the beginning of the end of the Emergency. Templer invented the techniques of counter-insurgency warfare in Malaya and applied them ruthlessly.

Towards Malaysia

Chinese reaction against the MCP was shown by the formation of the Malayan Chinese Association (MCA) in 1949 as a vehicle for moderate Chinese political opinion. Its leader, Tan Cheng Lock, favoured a policy of collaboration with UMNO to win Malayan independence on a policy of equal citizenship, but with sufficient concessions to Malay sensitivities to ease nationalist fears. Tan formed a close collaboration with Tunku (Prince) Abdul Rahman, the Chief Minister of Kedah and from 1951 successor to Datuk Onn as leader of UMNO. Since the British had announced in 1949 that Malaya would soon become independent whether the Malayans liked it or not, both leaders were determined to forge an agreement their communities could live with as a basis for a stable independent state. The UMNO-MCA Alliance (which was later joined by the Malayan Indian Congress (MIC)), won convincing victories in local and state elections in both Malay and Chinese areas between 1952 and 1955.

The introduction of elected local government was another important step in defeating the Communists. After Joseph Stalin's death in 1953, there was a split in the MCP leadership over the wisdom of continuing the armed struggle. Many MCP militants lost heart and went home, and by the time Templer left Malaya in 1954 the Emergency was over, although Chin Peng led a diehard group that lurked in the inaccessible country along the Thai border for many years. The Emergency left a lasting legacy of bitterness between Malays and Chinese.

During 1955 and 1956 UMNO, the MCA and the British hammered out a constitutional settlement for anciple of equal citizenship for all races. In exchange, the MCA agreed that Malaya's head of state would be drawn from the ranks of the Malay Sultans, that Malay would be the official language, and that Malay education and economic development would be promoted and subsidised. In effect this meant that Malaya would be run by the Malays, particularly since they continued to dominate the civil service, the army and the police, but that the Chinese and Indians would have proportionate representation in the Cabinet and the parliament, would run those states where they were the majority, and would have their economic position protected. The difficult issue of who would control the education system was deferred until after independence. This came on August 31, 1957, when Tunku Abdul Rahman became the first Prime Minister of independent Malaya.

This left the unfinished business of the other British-ruled territories in the region. After the Japanese surrender the Brooke family and the British North Borneo Company gave up their control of Sarawak and Sabah respectively, and these became British Crown Colonies. They were much less economically developed than Malaya, and their local political leaderships were too weak to demand independence. Singapore, with its large Chinese majority, achieved autonomy in 1955, and in 1959 the young socialist leader Lee Kuan Yew became Chief Minister. The Sultan of Brunei remained as a British client in his oil-rich enclave. Between 1959 and 1962 the British government orchestrated complex negotiations between these local leaders and the Malayan government.

In 1961, Abdul Rahman mooted the idea of forming "Malaysia", which would consist of Brunei, Malaya, Sabah, Sarawak and Singapore, all of which had been British colonies. The reasoning behind this was that this would allow the central government to control and combat communist activities, especially in Singapore. It was also feared that if Singapore achieved independence, it would become a base for Chinese chauvinists to threaten Malayan sovereignty. To balance out the ethnic composition of the new nation, the other states, whose Malay and indigenous populations would cancel out the Singaporean Chinese majority, were also included.

Although Lee Kuan Yew supported the proposal, his opponents from the Singaporean Socialist Front resisted, arguing that this was a ploy for the British to continue controlling the region. Most political parties in Sarawak were also against the merger, and in Sabah, where there were no political parties, community representatives also stated their opposition. Although the Sultan of Brunei supported the merger, the Parti Rakyat Brunei opposed it as well. At the Commonwealth Heads of Government Meeting in 1961, Abdul Rahman explained his proposal further to its opponents. In October, he obtained agreement from the British government to the plan, provided that feedback be obtained from the communities involved in the merger. The Cobbold Commission, named after its head, Lord Cobbold, conducted a study in the Borneo territories and approved a merger with Sabah and Sarawak; however, it was found that a substantial number of Bruneians opposed merger. A referendum was conducted in Singapore to gauge opinion, and 70% supported merger with substantial autonomy given to the state government.

After reviewing the Cobbold Commission's findings, the British government appointed the Landsdowne Commission to draft a constitution for Malaysia. The eventual constitution was essentially the same as the 1957 constitution, albeit with some rewording. For instance, giving recognition to the special position of the natives of the Borneo States. Sabah, Sarawak and Singapore were also granted some autonomy unavailable to the states of Malaya. After negotiations in July 1963, it was agreed that Malaysia would come into being on 31 August 1963, consisting of Malaya, Sabah, Sarawak and Singapore. Brunei pulled out after Parti Rakyat Brunei staged an armed revolt, which, though it was put down, was viewed as potentially destabilising to the new nation.

The Philippines and Indonesia strenuously objected to this development, with Indonesia claiming Malaysia represented a form of "neocolonialism" and the Philippines claiming Sabah as its territory. Indonesian President Sukarno, backed by the powerful Communist Party of Indonesia (PKI), chose to regard Malaysia as a "neocolonialist" plot against his country, and backed a Communist insurgency in Sarawak, mainly involving elements of the local Chinese community. Indonesian irregular forces were infiltrated into Sarawak, where they were contained by Malaysian and Commonwealth of Nations forces. This period of *Konfrontasi* lasted until the downfall of Sukarno in 1965/66. Under Sukarno's successor, Suharto, Indonesian-Malaysian relations improved. At the same time Filipino President Diosdado Macapagal revived the long-dormant

Filipino claim to Sabah, once part of the Sultanate of Sulu. In 1966 the new president, Ferdinand Marcos, dropped the claim, although it is still a point of contention marring Philippine-Malaysian relations. Malaysia formally came into being on 16 September 1963, consisting of Malaya, Sabah, Sarawak and Singapore.

Problems of Independence

The Depression of the 1930s, followed by the outbreak of the Sino-Japanese War, had the effect of ending Chinese emigration to Malaya. This stabilised the demographic situation and ended the prospect of the Malays becoming a minority in their own country. At the time of independence in 1957, the Malays were 55% of the population, the Chinese 35% and the Indians 10%. Since the Malays have until recently had a higher birth rate, the proportion of Malays has increased since independence – by 2000 it was over 60%.

This equation was upset by the inclusion of Singapore, which increased the Chinese proportion to close to 40%. Both UMNO and the MCA were nervous about the possible appeal of Lee's People's Action Party (then seen as a radical socialist party) to voters in Malaya, and tried to organise a party in Singapore to challenge Lee's position there. Lee in turn threatened to run PAP candidates in Malaya at the 1964 federal elections, despite an earlier agreement that he would not do so. This provoked Tunku Abdul Rahman to demand that Singapore withdraw from Malaysia, which it did in August 1965.

The most vexed issues of independent Malaysia were education and the disparity of economic power among the ethnic communities. Since there was no effective opposition party, these issues were contested mainly within the coalition government, which won all but one seat in the first post-independence Malayan Parliament. The two issues were related, since the Chinese advantage in education played a large part in maintaining their control of the economy, which the UMNO leaders were determined to end. The MCA leaders were torn between the need to defend their own community's interests and the need to maintain good relations with UMNO. This produced a crisis in the MCA in 1959, in which a more assertive leadership under Lim Chong Eu defied UMNO over the education issue, only to be forced to back down when Tunku Abdul Rahman threatened to break up the coalition.

The Education Act of 1961 put UMNO's victory on the education issue into legislative form. Henceforward Malay and English would be the only teaching languages in secondary schools, and state primary schools would teach in Malay only. Although the Chinese and Indian communities could maintain their own Mandarin and Tamil-language primary schools, all their students were required to learn Malay, and to study an agreed "Malayan curriculum." Most importantly, the entry exam to the University of

Malaya (which moved from Singapore to Kuala Lumpur in 1963) would be conducted in Malay, even though most teaching at the university was in English until the 1970s. This had the effect of excluding many Chinese students. At the same time Malay schools were heavily subsidised, and Malays were given preferential treatment. This obvious defeat for the MCA greatly weakened its support in the Chinese community.

At the time of independence Malaya had great economic advantages. It was among the world's leading producers of three valuable commodities, rubber, tin and palm oil, and also a significant iron ore producer. These export industries gave the Malayan government a healthy surplus to invest in industrial development and infrastructure projects. Like other developing nations in the 1950s and '60s, Malaya (and later Malaysia) placed great stress on state planning, although UMNO was never a socialist party. The First and Second Malayan Plans (1956-60 and 1961-65 respectively) stimulated economic growth through state investment in industry and repairing infrastructure such as roads and ports, which had been damaged and neglected during the war and the Emergency. The government was keen to reduce Malaya's dependence on commodity exports, which put the country at the mercy of fluctuating prices. The government was also aware that demand for natural rubber was bound to fall as the production and use of synthetic rubber expanded. Since a third of the Malay workforce worked in the rubber industry it was important to develop alternative sources of employment. Competition for Malaya's rubber markets meant that the profitability of the rubber industry increasingly depended on keeping wages low, which perpetuated rural Malay poverty.

As in education, the UMNO government's unspoken agenda in the field of economic development was to shift economic power away from the Chinese and towards the Malays. The two Malayan Plans, and the First Malaysian Plan (1966-70), directed resources heavily into developments which would benefit the rural Malay community, such as village schools, rural roads, clinics and irrigation projects. Several agencies were set up to enable Malay smallholders to upgrade their production and increase their incomes. The Federal Land Development Authority (FELDA) helped many Malays buy farms or upgrade ones they already owned. The state also provided a range of incentives and low-interest loans to help Malays start businesses, and government tendering systematically favoured Malay companies, leading many Chinese-owned businesses to "Malayanise" their management. All this certainly tended to reduce to gap between Chinese and Malay standards of living, although some argued that this would have happened anyway as Malaysia's trade and general prosperity increased.

The Crisis of 1969

The collaboration of the MCA and the MIC in these policies weakened their hold on the Chinese and Indian electorates. At the same time, the effects of the government's affirmative action policies of the 1950s and '60s had been to create a discontented class of educated but underemployed Malays. This was a dangerous combination, and led to the formation of a new party, the Malaysian People's Movement (Gerakan Rakyat Malaysia) in 1968. Gerakan was a deliberately non-communal party, bringing in Malay trade unionists and intellectuals as well as Chinese and Indian leaders. At the same time, an Islamist party, the Islamic Party of Malaysia (PAS) and a Chinese socialist party, the Democratic Action Party (DAP), gained increasing support, at the expense of UMNO and the MCA respectively.

At the May 1969 federal elections, the UMNO-MCA-MIC Alliance polled only 48 percent of the vote, although it retained a majority in the legislature. The MCA lost most of the Chinese-majority seats to Gerakan or DAP candidates. The result was anti-government demonstrations by Chinese in Kuala Lumpur, provoking a Malay backlash and leading rapidly to riots and inter-communal violence in which about 6,000 Chinese homes and businesses were burned and at least 184 people were killed. The government declared a state of emergency, and a National Operations Council, headed by the Deputy Prime Minister, Tun Abdul Razak, took power from the government of Tunku Abdul Rahman, who in September 1970 was forced to retire in favour of Abdul Razak.

Using the Emergency-era Internal Security Act (Malaysia) (ISA), the new government suspended Parliament and political parties, imposed press censorship and placed severe restrictions on political activity. The ISA gave the government power to intern any person indefinitely without trial. These powers were widely used to silence the government's critics, and have never been repealed. The Constitution was changed to make illegal any criticism, even in Parliament, of the Malaysian monarchy, the special position of Malays in the country, or the status of Malay as the national language.

In 1971 Parliament reconvened, and a new government coalition, the National Front (Barisan Nasional), took office. This included UMNO, the MCA, the MIC, the much weakened Gerakan, and regional parties in Sabah and Sarawak. The DAP was left outside as the only significant opposition party. The PAS also joined the Front but was expelled in 1977. Abdul Razak held office until his death in 1976. He was succeeded by Datuk Hussein Onn, the son of UMNO's founder Onn Jaafar, and then by Tun Dr Mahathir bin Mohamad, who had been Education Minister since 1971, and who held power for 22 years. During these years policies were put in place which led to the rapid transformation of Malaysia's economy and society.

Modern Malaysia

In 1970, 75 percent of Malaysians living below the poverty line were Malays, the majority of Malays were still rural workers, and Malays were still largely excluded from the modern economy. The government's response was the New Economic Policy of 1971, which was to be implemented through a series of four five-year plans from 1971 to 1990. The plan had two objectives: the elimination of poverty, particularly rural poverty, and the elimination of the identification between race and economic function. This latter policy was understood to mean a decisive shift in economic power from the Chinese to the Malays.

Poverty was tackled through an agricultural policy which resettled 250,000 Malays on newly cleared farmland, more investment in rural infrastructure, and the creation of free trade zones in rural areas to create new manufacturing jobs. During the 1970s and '80s rural poverty did decline, particularly in the Malayan Peninsula, but critics of the government's policy contend that this was mainly due to the growth of overall national prosperity (due in large part to the discovery of important oil and gas reserves) and migration of rural people to the cities rather than to state intervention. Little was done to improve the living standards of the low-paid workers in plantation agriculture, although this group steadily declined as a proportion of the workforce. By 1990 the poorest parts of Malaysia were rural Sabah and Sarawak, which lagged significantly behind the rest of the country. These years saw rapid growth in Malaysian cities, particularly Kuala Lumpur, which became a magnet for immigration both from rural Malaya and from poorer neighbours such as Indonesia, Bangladesh, Thailand and the Philippines. Urban poverty became a problem for the first time, with shanty towns growing up around the cities.

The second arm of government policy, driven mainly by Mahathir first as Education Minister and then as Prime Minister, was the transfer of economic power to the Malays. Mahathir greatly expanded the number of secondary schools and universities throughout the country, and enforced the policy of teaching in Malay rather than English. This had the effect of creating a large new Malay professional class. It also created an unofficial barrier against Chinese access to higher education, since few Chinese are sufficiently fluent in Malay to study at Malay-language universities. Chinese families therefore sent their children to universities in Singapore, Australia, Britain or the United States – by 2000, for example, 60,000 Malaysians held degrees from Australian universities. This had the unintended consequence of exposing large numbers of Malaysians to life in Western countries, creating a new source of discontent. Mahathir also greatly expanded educational opportunities for Malay women – by 2000 half of all university students were women.

To find jobs for all these new Malay graduates, the government created several agencies for intervention in the economy. The most important of these were PERNAS (National Corporation Ltd), PETRONAS (National Petroleum Ltd), and HICOM (Heavy Industry Corporation of Malaysia), which not only directly employed many Malays but also invested in growing areas of the economy to create new technical and administrative jobs which were preferentially allocated to Malays. As a result, the share of Malay equity in the economy rose from 1.5 percent in 1969 to 20.3 percent in 1990, the percentage of businesses of all kinds owned by Malays rose from 39 percent to 68 percent. This latter figure was deceptive because many businesses that appeared to be Malay-owned were still indirectly controlled by Chinese, but there is no doubt that the Malay share of the economy considerably increased. The Chinese remained disproportionately powerful in Malaysian economic life, but by 2000 the distinction between Chinese and Malay business was fading as many new corporations, particularly in growth sectors such as information technology, were owned and managed by people from both ethnic groups.

Malaysia's rapid economic progress since 1970, which was only temporarily disrupted by the Asian financial crisis of 1997, has not been matched by change in Malaysian politics. The repressive measures passed in 1970 remain in place. Malaysia has had regular elections since 1974, and although campaigning is reasonably free at election time, it is in effect a one-party state, with the UMNO-controlled National Front usually winning nearly all the seats, while the DAP wins some Chinese urban seats and the PAS some rural Malay ones. Since the DAP and the PAS have diametrically opposed policies, they have been unable to form an effective opposition coalition. There is almost no criticism of the government in the media and public protest remains severely restricted. The ISA continues to be used to silence dissidents, and the members of the UMNO youth movement are deployed to physically intimidate opponents.

Mahathir Administration

Under Mahathir's long Prime Ministership (1981-2003), Malaysia's political culture became increasingly authoritarian, culminating in the dismissal and imprisonment on unsubstantiated charges of the Deputy Prime Minister, Anwar Ibrahim, in 1997 after an internal dispute within the government. The complicity of the judiciary in this piece of persecution was seen as a particularly clear sign of the decline of Malaysian democracy. The Anwar affair led to the formation of a new party, the People's Justice Party, or Keadilan, led by Anwar's wife, Dr Wan Azizah Wan Ismail. At the 1999 elections Keadilan formed a coalition with the DAP and the PAS known as the Alternative Front (Barisan Alternatif). The result of this was that the PAS won a number of Malay seats from UMNO, but many Chinese voters disapproved of this unnatural alliance with the Islamist PAS, causing the DAP to lose many of its seats to the MCA, including that of its veteran leader, Lim Kit Siang. Wan Azizah won her husband's former constituency in Penang but otherwise Keadilan made little impact.

Badawi Administration

Mahathir retired in 2003, and his successor, Dato Seri Abdullah Ahmad Badawi, freed Anwar and allowed him to go abroad, which was seen as a portent of a mild liberalisation. At the 2004 election, the National Front led by Abdullah had a massive victory, virtually wiping out the PAS and Keadilan, although the DAP recovered the seats it had lost in 1999. This victory was seen as the result mainly of Abdullah's personal popularity and the strong recovery of Malaysia's economy, which has lifted the living standards of most Malaysians to almost first world standards, coupled with an ineffective opposition. The government's objective is for Malaysia to become a fully developed country by 2020 as expressed in *Wawasan 2020*. It leaves unanswered, however, the question of when and how Malaysia will acquire a first world political system (a multi-party democracy, a free press, an independent judiciary and the restoration of civil and political liberties) to go with its new economic maturity.

In November 2007, Malaysia was rocked by two anti-government rallies. The 2007 Bersih Rally which was attended by 40,000 people was held in Kuala Lumpur, Malaysia, on November 10 to campaign for electoral reform. It was precipitated by allegations of corruption and discrepancies in the Malaysian election system that heavily favor the ruling political party, Barisan Nasional, which has been in power since Malaysia achieved its independence in 1957. The 2007 HINDRAF rally was a rally held in Kuala Lumpur, Malaysia, on November 25. The rally organizer, the Hindu Rights Action Force, had called the protest over alleged discriminatory policies which favour ethnic Malays. The crowd was estimated to be between 5,000 to 30,000. In both cases the government and police were heavy handed and tried to prevent the gatherings from taking place.

The issues of high inflation, rising crime rates, ethnic tensions in the multicultural nation, and many other issues came back to haunt Prime Minister Abdullah Ahmad Badawi in the next general elections in 2008. The Opposition coalition of DAP, PAS and PKR won 82 seats in Malaysia's parliament, denying the government its two-thirds majority. The Opposition also took the 4 states of Penang, Kedah, Perak and Selangor, while retaining the opposition stronghold of Kelantan. Still Barisan Nasional, with a simple majority of 140 seats in Parliament, were able to form the next government. Malaysia's Prime Minister Abdullah Ahmad Badawi was sworn in for a second term on 10 March 2008, defying calls to quit after presiding over the ruling coalition's worst ever election performance.

HISTORY OF MYANMAR

The History of Burma, now officially Myanmar, is long and complicated. Several ethnic groups have lived in the region, the oldest of which are probably the Mon or the Pyu. In the 9th century the Bamar (Burman) people migrated from the then China-Tibet border region into the valley of the Ayeyarwady, and now form the governing majority.

The history of the region comprises complexities not only within the country but also with its neighbouring countries, China, India, Bangladesh, Viet Nam, Laos and Thailand.

Humans lived in the region that is now Myanmar as early as 11,000 years ago, but archeological evidence dates the first settlements at about 2500 BC with cattle rearing and the production of bronze. By about 1500 BC, ironworks were in existence in the Irrawaddy Valley but cities, and the emergence of city states, probably did not occur till the early years of the Christian era when advances in irrigation systems and the building of canals allowed for year long agriculture and the consolidation of settlements.

Little is known about life in early Burma but there is evidence that land and sea traders from China and India passed by and left their mark on the region and the local people traded ivory, precious stones, gold and silver, rhinoceros horns, and horses with these traders. Roman envoys from Alexandria also passed through the Irrawaddy valley in A.D. 79 en-route to China. Second century Burmese sea-farers, trading with Southern India across the Bay of Bengal, are thought to have brought Buddhism to Burma in the 2nd Century C.E. and by the 4th Century, much of the Irrawaddy Valley was Buddhist including the then dominant city-state, Prome (modern Pyay).

Oral Traditions

While little is known about the early people of Burma, the Mon were the first of the modern ethnic groups to migrate into the region, starting around 1500 BC. Oral tradition suggests that they had contact with Buddhism via seafaring as early as the 3rd century BC, though definitely by the 2nd century BC when they received an envoy of monks from Ashoka. Much of the Mon's written records have been destroyed through wars. The Mons blended Indian and Mon cultures together in a hybrid of the two civilisations. By the mid-9th century, they had come to dominate all of southern Myanmar. From that time, Northern Burma was a group of city-states in a loose coalition. The 'King' of each city-state would change allegiance as he saw fit, so throughout history, much of the Shan-Tai north has been part of the Tai countries of Nan Zhao (now Yunnan and GuangXi, China), SipSong Panna, Lanna (Chiangmai in Thailand–Siam), Ayuttaya (old capital of Siam) and even affiliated with Laos.

Pyu

The Pyu arrived in Burma in the 1st century BC and established city kingdoms at Binnaka, Mongamo, Sri Ksetra, Peikthanomyo, and Halingyi. During this period, Burma was part of an overland trade route from China to India. Chinese sources state that the Pyu controlled 18 kingdoms and describe them as a humane and peaceful people. War was virtually unknown amongst the Pyu, and disputes were often solved through duels by champions or building competitions. They even wore silk cotton instead of actual silk so they would not have to kill silk worms. Crime was punished by whippings and jails were unknown, though serious crimes could result in the death penalty. The

Pyu practiced Theravada Buddhism, and all children were educated as novices in the temples from the age of seven until the age of 20.

The Pyu city-states never unified into a Pyu kingdom, but the more powerful cities often dominated and called for tribute from the lesser cities. The most powerful city by far was Sri Ksetra, which archaeological evidence indicates was the largest city that has ever been built in Burma. The exact date of its founding is not known, though likely to be prior to a dynastic change in A.D. 94 that Pyu chronicles speak of. Sri Ksetra was apparently abandoned around A.D. 656 in favour of a more northerly capital, though the exact site is not known. Some historians believe it was Halingyi. Wherever the new capital was located, it was sacked by the kingdom of Nanzhao in the mid-9th century, ending the Pyu's period of dominance.

Mon

The 6th century Mon kingdom of Dvaravati in the lower Chao Phraya valley in present day Thailand extended its frontiers to the Tenasserim Yoma (mountains). With subjugation by the Khmer Empire from Angkor in the 11th century the Mon shifted further west deeper into present day Burma. Oral tradition suggests that they had contact with Buddhism via seafaring as early as the 3rd century BC and had received an envoy of monks from Ashoka in the 2nd century BC.

The Mons adopted Indian culture together with Theravada Buddhism and are thought to have founded kingdoms in Lower Burma including Thaton in the 6th or 7th century and Bago (Pegu) in 825 with the kingdom of Raman'n'adesa (or Ramanna which is believed to be Thaton) referenced by Arab geographers in 844–8. The lack of archaeological evidence for this may in part be due to the focus of excavation work predominantly being in Upper Burma.

Pagan Kingdom

To the north another group of people, the Bamar (Mranma / Myanma), also began to settle in the area. By 849, they had founded a powerful kingdom centred on the city of Pagan (spelled Bagan today) filling the void left by the Pyu.

Bamar tradition maintains that the Bamar were originally of three tribes: the Pyu; the Thet; and the Kanyan. Indeed, Pyu as a language and as a people simply disappeared soon after the Myazedi Inscription of 1113. The word Mranma, in both Mon and Myanmar inscriptions, came into being only at about the same time, lending support to this claim that the Pyu were an earlier vanguard of southward Tibeto-Burman migration who were entirely absorbed into a newly formed identity by later waves of similar people.

The Pagan Kingdom grew in relative isolation until the reign of Anawrahta (1044-77) who successfully unified all of Burma by defeating the Mon city of Thaton in 1057. Consolidation was accomplished under his successors Kyanzittha (1084–1112) and Alaungsithu (1112-67), so that by the mid-12th century, most of continental Southeast Asia was under the control of either the Pagan Kingdom or the Khmer Empire. The Pagan kingdom went into decline as more land and resources fell into the hands of the powerful Sangha (monkhood) and the Mongols threatened from the north. The last true ruler of Pagan, Narathihapate (1254-87) felt confident in his ability to resist the Mongols and advanced into Yunnan in 1277 to make war upon them. He was thoroughly crushed at the Battle of Ngasaunggyan, and Pagan resistance virtually collapsed. The king was assassinated by his own son in 1287, precipitating a Mongol invasion in the Battle of Pagan; the Mongols successfully captured most of the empire, including its capital, and ended the dynasty in 1289 when they installed a puppet ruler in Burma.

Ava and Pegu (c. 1364–1555)

After the collapse of Pagan authority, Burma was divided. A Burman Ava Dynasty (1364–527) was eventually established at the city of Ava by 1364. Pagan culture was revived and a great age of Burmese literature ensued. The kingdom lacked easily defendable borders, however, and was overrun by the Shan in 1527.

To the south in Lower Burma, a Mon dynasty established itself first at Martaban and then at Pegu. During the reign of king Rajadhirat (1383–1421) Ava and Pegu were involved in continuous warfare. The peaceful reign of Queen Baña Thau (Burmese: Shin Saw Bu;1453-72) came to an end when she chose the Buddhist monk Dhammazedi (1472-92) to succeed her. Under·Dhammazedi Pegu became a centre of commerce and Theravada Buddhism.

The Kingdom of Ava was involved in continuous warfare with Tai (Shan) saophas to the north on the frontier with Yunnan. There were repeated Tai raids on the capital of Ava and Ava sent military northwards to attack Tai fiefdoms such as Mong Mao. The Ming dynasty that ruled China from the late fourteenth century often tried unsuccessfully to put an end to this warfare through traditional Chinese diplomacy. Ava occasionally became involved in the warfare between the Ming and Tai in Yunnan such as in the Luchuan-Pingmian Campaigns (1436-49).

Toungoo Dynasties

King Mingyinyo founded the First Toungoo Dynasty (1486–1599) at Toungoo, south of Ava, towards the end of the Ava dynasty. After the conquest of Ava by the

Shan invaders in 1527 many Burmans migrated to Toungoo which became a new center for Burmese rule.

• Mingyinyo's son king Tabinshwehti (1531-50) unified most of Burma. By this time, the geopolitical situation in Southeast Asia had changed dramatically. The Shan gained power in a new kingdom in the North, Ayutthaya (Siam), while the Portuguese had arrived in the south and conquered Malacca. With the coming of European traders, Burma was once again an important trading centre, and Tabinshwehti moved his capital to Pegu due to its strategic position for commerce. Tabinshwehti was able to gain control of Lower Burma up to Prome, but the campaigns he led to the Arakan, Ayutthaya, and Ava in Upper Burma were unsuccessful.

When Bayinnaung (1551-81), Tabinshwehti's brother-in-law, succeeded to the throne he launched a campaign of conquest invading several states, including Manipur (1560) and Ayutthaya (1569). His wars stretched Burma to the limits of its resources, however, and both Manipur and Ayutthaya were soon independent once again.

Faced with rebellion by several cities and renewed Portuguese incursions, the Toungoo rulers withdrew from southern Burma and founded a second dynasty at Ava, the Restored Toungoo Dynasty (1597–1752). Bayinnaung's grandson, Anaukpetlun, once again reunited Burma in 1613 and decisively defeated Portuguese attempts to take over Burma. His successor Thalun reestablished the principles of the old Pagan kingdom, but concentrated his efforts on religious merit and paid little attention to the southern part of his kingdom. Encouraged by the French in India, Pegu finally rebelled against Ava, further weakening the state, which fell in 1752.

Konbaung Dynasty

It did not take long for a new dynasty, the Konbaung Dynasty, to arise and bring Burma to its greatest power yet. A popular Burmese leader named Alaungpaya drove the Pegu forces out of northern Burma by 1753, and by 1759 he had once again conquered Pegu, resulting in total subjugation of the Mon people, and southern Burma, while also regaining control of Manipur. He established his capital briefly at Dagon, renaming it Yangon (End of Strife). In 1760, he briefly conquered Tenasserim. He also marched on Ayutthaya, but became seriously ill and was forced to withdraw, ending the invasion, and he died on the journey back. His second son Hsinbyushin (1763-76) returned to Ayutthaya (Siam) in 1766 and had conquered it before the end of the next year. Even China began to fear expansion of Burmese power in the East and sent armies to Burma, but Hsinbyushin successfully repulsed four Chinese invasions between 1766 and 1769 stretching its limits within Chinese borders. Another of Alaungpaya's sons, Bodawpaya (1781–1819), lost control of Ayutthaya, but added Arakan (1784) and Tenasserim (1793) to the kingdom. In January 1824, during the reign of King Bagyidaw (1819-37), a

Burmese general Maha Bandula succeeded in conquering Assam, bringing Burma face to face with British interests in India.

War with Britain and the Fall of Burma

The expansion of Burma had consequences along its frontiers. As those frontiers moved ever closer to British India, there were problems both with refugees and military operations spilling over ill-defined borders. In response to the continued expansion and even direct attacks by Burma, the British and the Siamese joined forces against it in 1824. The First Anglo-Burmese War (1824-26) ended in a British victory, and by the Treaty of Yandabo, Burma lost territory previously conquered in Assam, Manipur and Arakan. The British also took possession of Tenasserim with the intention to use it as a bargaining chip in future negotiations with either Burma or Siam. As the century wore on, the British in India began to covet the resources and main port of Burma during an era of great territorial expansion. In 1852, Commodore Lambert was despatched to Burma by Lord Dalhousie over a number of minor issues related to the previous treaty.

The Burmese immediately made concessions including the removal of a governor whom the British had made their casus belli. Lambert eventually provoked a naval confrontation in extremely questionable circumstances and thus started the Second Anglo-Burmese War in 1852, which ended in the British annexation of Pegu province, renamed Lower Burma. The war resulted in a palace revolution in Burma, with King Pagan Min (1846–52) being replaced by his half brother, Mindon Min (1853-78). King Mindon tried to modernise the Burmese state and economy to resist British encroachments, and he established a new capital at Mandalay, which he proceeded to fortify. This was not enough to stop the British, however, who claimed that Mindon's son Thibaw Min (ruled 1878–85) was a tyrant intending to side with the French, that he had lost control of the country, thus allowing for disorder at the frontiers, and that he was reneging on a treaty signed by his father. Taking advantage of France's recent defeat of China, and confident that China would not intervene to defend its tributary, the British declared war once again in 1885, conquering the remainder of the country in the Third Anglo-Burmese War resulting in total annexation of Burma.

British Rule

Britain made Burma a province of India in 1886 with the capital at Rangoon. Traditional Burmese society was drastically altered by the demise of the monarchy and the separation of religion and state. Though war officially ended after only a couple of weeks, resistance continued in northern Burma until 1890, with the British finally resorting to a systematic destruction of villages and appointment of new officials to finally halt all guerrilla activity. The economic nature of society also changed dramatically. After the opening of the Suez Canal, the demand for Burmese rice grew and vast tracts of land were opened up for cultivation. However, in order to prepare the new land for cultivation, farmers were forced to borrow money from Indian moneylenders called chettiars at high interest rates and were often foreclosed on and evicted losing land and livestock. Most of the jobs also went to indentured Indian labourers, and whole villages became outlawed as they resorted to 'dacoity' (armed robbery). While the Burmese economy grew, all the power and wealth remained in the hands of several British firms and migrants from India. The civil service was largely staffed by Indians, and Burmese were excluded almost entirely from military service. Though the country prospered, the Burmese people failed to reap the rewards.

By the turn of the century, a nationalist movement began to take shape in the form of Young Men's Buddhist Associations (YMBA), modelled on the YMCA, as religious associations were allowed by the colonial authorities. They were later superseded by the General Council of Burmese Associations (GCBA) which was linked with *Wunthanu athin* or National Associations that sprang up in villages throughout Burma Proper. A new generation of Burmese leaders arose in the early twentieth century from amongst the educated classes that were permitted to go to London to study law. They came away from this experience with the belief that the Burmese situation could be improved through reform. Progressive constitutional reform in the early 1920s led to a legislature with limited powers, a university and more autonomy for Burma within the administration of India. Efforts were also undertaken to increase the representation of Burmese in the civil service. Some people began to feel that the rate of change was not fast enough and the reforms not expansive enough.

In 1920 the first university students strike in history broke out in protest against the new University Act which the students believed would only benefit the elite and perpetuate colonial rule. 'National Schools' sprang up across the country in protest against the colonial education system, and the strike came to be commemorated as 'National Day'. There were further strikes and anti-tax protests in the later 1920s led by the *Wunthanu athins*. Prominent among the political activists were Buddhist monks (*pongyi*), such as U Ottama and U Seinda in the Arakan who subsequently led an armed rebellion against the British and later the nationalist government after independence, and U Wisara, the first martyr of the movement to die after a protracted hunger strike in prison. (One of the main thoroughfares in Yangon is named after U Wisara.) In December 1930, a local tax protest by Saya San in Tharrawaddy quickly grew into first a regional and then a national insurrection against the government. Lasting for two years, the *Galon* rebellion, named after the mythical bird Garuda — enemy of the Nagas i.e. the British — emblazoned on the pennants the rebels carried, required thousands of British troops to suppress along with promises of further political reform. The eventual trial of Saya San, who was executed, allowed several future national leaders, including Dr Ba Maw and U Saw, who participated in his defence, to rise to prominence.

May 1930 saw the founding of the *Dobama Asiayone* (We Burmans Association) whose members called themselves *Thakin* (an ironic name as *thakin* means "master" in the Burmese language—rather like the Indian 'sahib'— proclaiming that they were the true masters of the country entitled to the term usurped by the colonial masters). The second university students strike in 1936 was triggered by the expulsion of Aung San and Ko Nu, leaders of the Rangoon University Students Union (RUSU), for refusing to reveal the name of the author who had written an article in their university magazine, making a scathing attack on one of the senior university officials. It spread to Mandalay leading to the formation of the All Burma Students Union (ABSU). Aung San and Nu subsequently joined the Thakin movement progressing from student to national politics. The British separated Burma from India in 1937 and granted the colony a new constitution calling for a fully elected assembly, but this proved to be a divisive issue as some Burmese felt that this was a ploy to exclude them from any further Indian reforms whereas other Burmese saw any action that removed Burma from the control of India to be a positive step. Ba Maw served as the first prime minister of Burma, but he was succeeded by U Saw in 1939, who served as prime minister from 1940 until he was arrested on January 19, 1942 by the British for communicating with the Japanese.

A wave of strikes and protests that started from the oilfields of central Burma in 1938 became a general strike with far-reaching consequences. In Rangoon student protesters, after successfully picketing the Secretariat, the seat of the colonial government, were charged by the British mounted police wielding batons and killing a Rangoon University student called Aung Kyaw. In Mandalay, the police shot into a crowd of protesters led by Buddhist monks killing 17 people. The movement became known as *Htaung thoun ya byei ayeidawbon* (the '1300 Revolution' named after the Burmese calendar year), and December 20, the day the first martyr Aung Kyaw fell, commemorated by students as 'Bo Aung Kyaw Day'.

World War II and Japan

Some Burmese nationalists saw the outbreak of World War II as an opportunity to extort concessions from the British in exchange for support in the war effort. Other Burmese, such as the Thakin movement, opposed Burma's participation in the war under any circumstances. Aung San co-founded the Communist Party of Burma (CPB) with other Thakins in August 1939. Marxist literature as well as tracts from the Sinn Féin movement in Ireland had been widely circulated and read among political activists. Aung San also co-founded the People's Revolutionary Party (PRP), renamed the Socialist Party after the World War II. He was also instrumental in founding the *Bama htwet yat gaing* (Freedom Bloc) by forging an alliance of the Dobama, ABSU, politically active monks and Ba Maw's *Sinyètha* (Poor Man's) Party.

After the Dobama organization called for a national uprising, an arrest warrant was issued for many of the organization's leaders including Aung San, who escaped to China. Aung San's intention was to make contact with the Chinese Communists but he was detected by the Japanese authorities who offered him support by forming a secret intelligence unit called the *Minami Kikan* headed by Colonel Suzuki with the objective of closing the Burma Road and supporting a national uprising. Aung San briefly returned to Burma to enlist twenty-nine young men who went to Japan with him in order to receive military training on Hainan Island, China, and they came to be known as the "Thirty Comrades". When the Japanese occupied Bangkok in December 1941, Aung San announced the formation of the Burma Independence Army (BIA) in anticipation of the Japanese invasion of Burma in 1942.

The BIA formed a provisional government in some areas of the country in the spring of 1942, but there were differences within the Japanese leadership over the future of Burma. While Colonel Suzuki encouraged the Thirty Comrades to form a provisional government, the Japanese Military leadership had never formally accepted such a plan. Eventually the Japanese Army turned to Ba Maw to form a government. During the war in 1942, the BIA had grown in an uncontrolled manner, and in many districts officials and even criminals appointed themselves to the BIA. It was reorganised as the Burma Defence Army (BDA) under the Japanese but still headed by Aung San. While the BIA had been an irregular force, the BDA was recruited by selection and trained as a conventional army by Japanese instructors. Ba Maw was afterwards declared head of state, and his cabinet included both Aung San as War Minister and the Communist leader Thakin Than Tun as Minister of Land and Agriculture as well as the Socialist leaders Thakins Nu and Mya. When the Japanese declared Burma, in theory, independent in 1943, the Burma Defence Army (BDA) was renamed the Burma National Army (BNA).

It soon became apparent that Japanese promises of independence were merely a sham and that Ba Maw was deceived. As the war turned against the Japanese, they declared Burma a fully sovereign state on August 1, 1943, but this was just another facade. Disillusioned, Aung San began negotiations with Communist leaders Thakin Than Tun and Thakin Soe, and Socialist leaders Ba Swe and Kyaw Nyein which led to the formation of the Anti-Fascist Organisation (AFO) in August 1944 at a secret meeting of the CPB,the PRP and the BNA in Pegu. The AFO was later renamed the Anti-Fascist People's Freedom League(AFPFL). Thakins Than Tun and Soe, while in Insein prison in July 1941, had co-authored the *Insein Manifesto* which, against the prevailing opinion in the Dobama movement, identified world fascism as the main enemy in the coming war and called for temporary cooperation with the British in a broad allied coalition which should include the Soviet Union. Soe had already gone underground to organise resistance against the Japanese occupation, and Than Tun was able to pass on Japanese intelligence to Soe, while other Communist leaders Thakins Thein Pe and Tin Shwe made contact with the exiled colonial government in Simla, India.

There were informal contacts between the AFO and the Allies in 1944 and 1945 through the British organisation Force 136. On March 27, 1945 the Burma National Army rose up in a countrywide rebellion against the Japanese. March 27 had been celebrated as 'Resistance Day' until the military renamed it 'Tatmadaw (Armed Forces) Day'. Aung San and others subsequently began negotiations with Lord Mountbatten and officially joined the Allies as the Patriotic Burmese Forces (PBF). At the first meeting, the AFO represented itself to the British as the provisional government of Burma with Thakin Soe as Chairman and Aung San as a member of its ruling committee. The Japanese were routed from most of Burma by May 1945. Negotiations then began with the British over the disarming of the AFO and the participation of its troops in a post-war Burma Army. Some veterans had been formed into a paramilitary force under Aung San, called the *Pyithu yèbaw tat* or People's Volunteer Organisation (PVO), and were openly drilling in uniform. The absorption of the PBF was concluded successfully at the Kandy conference in Ceylon in September 1945.

From the Japanese Surrender to Aung San's Assassination

The surrender of the Japanese brought a military administration to Burma and demands to try Aung San for his involvement in a murder during military operations in 1942. Lord Mountbatten realized that this was an impossibility considering Aung San's popular appeal. After the war ended, the British Governor, Sir Reginald Dorman-Smith returned. The restored government established a political program that focused on physical reconstruction of the country and delayed discussion of independence. The AFPFL opposed the government, leading to political instability in the country. A rift had also developed in the AFPFL between the Communists and Aung San together with the Socialists over strategy, which led to Than Tun being forced to resign as general secretary in July 1946 and the expulsion of the CPB from the AFPFL the following October. Dorman-Smith was replaced by Sir Hubert Rance as the new governor, and almost immediately after his appointment the Rangoon Police went on strike.

The strike, starting in September 1946, then spread from the police to government employees and came close to becoming a general strike. Rance calmed the situation by meeting with Aung San and convincing him to join the Governor's Executive Council along with other members of the AFPFL. The new executive council, which now had increased credibility in the country, began negotiations for Burmese independence, which were concluded successfully in London as the Aung San-Atlee Agreement on January 27, 1947. The agreement left parts of the communist and conservative branches of the AFPFL dissatisfied, however, sending the Red Flag Communists led by Thakin Soe underground and the conservatives into opposition. Aung San also succeeded in concluding an agreement with ethnic minorities for a unified Burma at the Panglong Conference on February 12, celebrated since as 'Union Day'. Shortly after, rebellion broke out in the Arakan led by the veteran monk U Seinda, and it began to spread to other districts. The popularity of the AFPFL, now dominated by Aung San and the Socialists, was eventually confirmed when it won an overwhelming victory in the April 1947 constituent assembly elections.

Then a momentous event stunned the nation on July 19, 1947. U Saw, a conservative pre-war Prime Minister of Burma, engineered the assassination of Aung San and several members of his cabinet including his eldest brother Ba Win, the father of today's National League for Democracy exile-government leader Dr Sein Win, while meeting in the Secretariat. July 19 has been commemorated since as Martyrs' Day. Thakin Nu, the Socialist leader, was now asked to form a new cabinet, and he presided over Burmese independence on January 4, 1948. The popular sentiment to part with the British was so strong at the time that Burma opted not to join the British Commonwealth, unlike India or Pakistan.

Independent Burma

The first years of Burmese independence were marked by successive insurgencies by the Red Flag Communists led by Thakin Soe, the White Flag Communists led by Thakin Than Tun, the *Yèbaw Hpyu* (White-band PVO) led by Bo La Yaung, a member of the Thirty Comrades, army rebels calling themselves the Revolutionary Burma Army (RBA) led by Communist officers Bo Zeya, Bo Yan Aung and Bo Yè Htut — all three of them members of the Thirty Comrades, Arakanese Muslims or the Mujahid, and the Karen National Union (KNU). Remote areas of Northern Burma were for many years controlled by an army of Kuomintang (KMT) forces after the Communist victory in China in 1949. Burma accepted foreign assistance in rebuilding the country in these early years, but continued American support for the Chinese Nationalist military presence in Burma finally resulted in the country rejecting most foreign aid, refusing to join the South-East Asia Treaty Organization (SEATO) and supporting the Bandung Conference of 1955. Burma generally strove to be impartial in world affairs and was one of the first countries in the world to recognize Israel and the People's Republic of China.

By 1958, the country was largely beginning to recover economically, but was beginning to fall apart politically due to a split in the AFPFL into two factions, one led by Thakins Nu and Tin, the other by Ba Swe and Kyaw Nyein. And this despite the unexpected success of U Nu's 'Arms for Democracy' offer taken up by U Seinda in the Arakan, the Pa-O, some Mon and Shan groups, but more significantly by the PVO surrendering their arms. The situation however became very unstable in parliament, with U Nu surviving a no-confidence vote only with the support of the opposition National United Front (NUF), believed to have 'crypto-communists' amongst them. Army hardliners now saw the 'threat' of the CPB coming to an agreement with U Nu through the NUF, and in the end U Nu 'invited' Army Chief of Staff General Ne Win to take over the country. Over 400 'communist sympathisers' were arrested, of which 153 were deported to the Coco Island in the Andaman Sea. Among them was the NUF leader Aung Than, older brother of Aung San. The *Botahtaung, Kyemon* and *Rangoon Daily* were also closed down.

Ne Win's caretaker government successfully established the situation and paved the way for new general elections in 1960 that returned U Nu's Union Party with a large majority. The situation did not remain stable for long, when the Shan Federal Movement, started by Nyaung Shwe Sawbwa Sao Shwe Thaik (the first President of independent Burma 1948-52) and aspiring to a 'loose' federation, was seen as a separatist movement insisting on the government honouring the right to secession in 10 years provided for by the 1947 Constitution. Ne Win had already succeeded in stripping the Shan Sawbwas of their feudal powers in exchange for comfortable pensions for life in 1959. He staged a coup d'etat on March 2, 1962, arrested U Nu, Sao Shwe Thaik and several others, and declared a 'socialist state' run by a 'Revolutionary Council' of senior military officers. Sao Shwe Thaik's son, Sao Mye Thaik, was shot dead in what was generally described as a 'bloodless' coup. Thibaw Sawbwa Sao Kya Seng also disappeared mysteriously after being stopped at a checkpoint near Taunggyi.

Military Era

Soon after seizing power, a peaceful student protest on Rangoon University campus was suppressed by the military, killing over 100 students on July 7, 1962. The next day, the army blew up the Students Union building. Peace talks were convened between the RC and various armed insurgent groups in 1963, but without any breakthrough, and during the talks as well as in the aftermath of its failure, hundreds were arrested in Rangoon and elsewhere from both the right and the left of the political spectrum. All opposition parties were banned on March 28, 1964. The Kachin insurgency by the Kachin Independence Organisation (KIO) had begun earlier in 1961 triggered by U Nu's declaration of Buddhism as the state religion, and the Shan State Army (SSA), led by Sao Shwe Thaik's wife Mahadevi and son Chao Tzang Yaunghwe, launched a rebellion in 1964 as a direct consequence of the 1962 military coup.

Ne Win quickly took steps to transform Burma into his vision of a 'socialist state' and to isolate the country from contact with the rest of the world. A one-party system was established with his newly formed Burma Socialist Programme Party (BSPP) in complete control. Commerce and industry were nationalized across the board, but the economy did not grow at first as the government put too much emphasis on industrial development at the expense of agriculture. In April 1972, General Ne Win and the rest of the Revolutionary Council retired from the military, but now as U Ne Win, he continued to run the country through the BSPP. A new constitution was promulgated in January 1974 that resulted in the creation of a People's Assembly (*Pyithu Hluttaw*) that held supreme legislative, executive, and judicial authority, and local People's Councils. Ne Win became the president of the new government.

Beginning in May 1974, a wave of strikes hit Rangoon and elsewhere in the country against a backdrop of corruption, inflation and food shortages, especially rice. In Rangoon workers were arrested at the Insein railway yard, and troops opened fire on workers at the Thamaing textile mill and Simmalaik dockyard. In December 1974, the biggest anti-government demonstrations to date broke out over the funeral of former UN Secretary-General U Thant. U Thant had been former prime minister U Nu's closest advisor in the 1950s and was seen as a symbol of opposition to the military regime. The Burmese people felt that U Thant was denied a state funeral that he deserved as a statesman of international stature because of his association with U Nu.

On March 23 1976, over 100 students were arrested for holding a peaceful ceremony (*Hmaing yabyei*) to mark the centenary of the birth of Thakin Kodaw Hmaing who was the greatest Burmese poet and writer and nationalist leader of the 20th century history of Burma. He had inspired a whole generation of Burmese nationalists and writers by his work mainly written in verse, fostering immense pride in their history, language and culture, and urging them to take direct action such as strikes by students and workers. It was Hmaing as leader of the mainstream Dobama who sent the Thirty Comrades abroad for military training, and after independence devoted his life to internal peace and national reconciliation until he died at the age of 88 in 1964. Hmaing lies buried in a mausoleum at the foot of the Shwedagon Pagoda.

In 1978, a military operation was conducted against the Rohingya Muslims in Arakan, called the King Dragon operation, causing 250,000 refugees to flee to neighboring Bangladesh.

U Nu, after his release from prison in October 1966, had left Burma in April 1969, and formed the Parliamentary Democracy Party (PDP) the following August in Bangkok,Thailand with the former Thirty Comrades, Bo Let Ya, co-founder of the CPB and former Minister of Defence and deputy prime minister, Bo Yan Naing, and U Thwin, ex-BIA and former Minister of Trade. Another member of the Thirty Comrades,

Bohmu Aung, former Minister of Defence, joined later. The fourth, Bo Setkya, who had gone underground after the 1962 coup, died in Bangkok shortly before U Nu arrived. The PDP launched an armed rebellion across the Thai border from 1972 till 1978 when Bo Let Ya was killed in an attack by the Karen National Union (KNU). U Nu, Bohmu Aung and Bo Yan Naing returned to Rangoon after the 1980 amnesty. Ne Win also secretly held peace talks later in 1980 with the KIO and the CPB, again ending in a deadlock as before.

Crisis and 1988 Uprising

In the 1980s, the economy began to grow as the government relaxed restrictions on foreign aid, but by the late 1980s falling commodity prices and rising debt led to an economic crisis. This led to economic reforms in 1987-88 that relaxed socialist controls and encouraged foreign investment. This was not enough, however, to stop growing turmoil in the country, compounded by periodic 'demonetization' of certain bank notes in the currency, the last of which was decreed in September 1987 wiping out the savings of the vast majority of people. Burma's admittance to Least Developed Country status by the UN the following December highlighted its economic bankruptcy. Ne Win retired as president in 1981, but remained in power as Chairman of the BSPP until his sudden unexpected announcement to step down on July 23, 1988.

Triggered by brutal police repression of student-led protests causing the death of over a hundred students and civilians in March and June 1988, widespread protests and demonstrations broke out on August 8 throughout the country. The military responded by firing into the crowds, alleging Communist infiltration. Violence, chaos and anarchy reigned. Civil administration had ceased to exist, and by September of that year, the country was on the verge of a revolution. The armed forces, under the nominal command of General Saw Maung staged a coup on September 18 to restore order. During the 8888 Uprising, as it became known, the military killed thousands. The military swept aside the Constitution of 1974 in favor of martial law under the State Law and Order Restoration Council (SLORC) with Saw Maung as chairman and prime minister.

At a special six-hour press conference on August 5, 1989, Brig. Gen. Khin Nyunt, the SLORC Secretary 1 and chief of Military Intelligence Service (MIS), claimed that the uprising had been orchestrated by the Communist Party of Burma through its underground organisation. Although there had inevitably been some underground CPB presence as well as that of ethnic insurgent groups, there was no evidence of their being in charge to any extent. In fact, in March 1989, the CPB leadership was overthrown by a rebellion by the Kokang and Wa troops that it had come to depend on after losing its former strongholds in central Burma and re-establishing bases in the northeast in the late 1960s; the Communist leaders were soon forced into exile across the Chinese border.

Military Era II

The military government announced a change of name for the country in English from Burma to Myanmar in 1989. It also continued the economic reforms started by the old regime and called for a Constituent Assembly to revise the 1974 Constitution. This led to multiparty elections in May 1990 in which the National League for Democracy (NLD) won a landslide victory over the National Unity Party (NUP, the successor to the BSPP) and about a dozen smaller parties. The military, however, would not let the assembly convene, and continued to hold the two leaders of the NLD, U Tin U and Aung San Suu Kyi, daughter of Aung San, under house arrest imposed on them the previous year. Burma came under increasing international pressure to convene the elected assembly, particularly after Aung San Suu Kyi was awarded the Nobel Peace Prize in 1991, and also faced economic sanctions. In April 1992 the military replaced Saw Maung with General Than Shwe.

Than Shwe released U Nu from prison and relaxed some of the restrictions on Aung San Suu Kyi's house arrest, finally releasing her in 1995, although she was forbidden to leave Rangoon. Than Shwe also finally allowed a National Convention to meet in January 1993, but insisted that the assembly preserve a major role for the military in any future government, and suspended the convention from time to time. The NLD, fed up with the interference, walked out in late 1995, and the assembly was finally dismissed in March 1996 without producing a constitution.

During the 1990s, the military regime had also had to deal with several insurgencies by tribal minorities along its borders. General Khin Nyunt was able to negotiate cease-fire agreements that ended the fighting with the Kokang, hill tribes such as the Wa, and the Kachin, but the Karen would not negotiate. The military finally captured the main Karen base at Manerplaw in spring 1995, but there has still been no final peace settlement. Khun Sa, a major opium warlord who nominally controlled parts of Shan State, made a deal with the government in December 1995 after U.S. pressure.

After the failure of the National Convention to create a new constitution, tensions between the government and the NLD mounted, resulting in two major crackdowns on the NLD in 1996 and 1997. The SLORC was abolished in November 1997 and replaced by the State Peace and Development Council (SPDC), but it was merely a cosmetic change. Continuing reports of human rights violations in Burma led the United States to intensify sanctions in 1997, and the European Union followed suit in 2000. The military placed Aung San Suu Kyi under house arrest again in September 2000 until May 2002, when her travel restrictions outside of Rangoon were also lifted. Reconciliation talks were held with the government, but these came to a stalemate and Suu Kyi was once again taken into custody in May 2003 after an ambush on her motorcade reportedly by a pro-military mob. She remains under house arrest today. The government also carried out another large-scale crackdown on the NLD, arresting many of its leaders and closing down most of its offices. The situation in Burma remains tense to this day.

In August 2003, Kyin Nyunt announced a seven-step "roadmap to democracy", which the government claims it is in the process of implementing. There is no timetable associated with the government's plan, or any conditionality or independent mechanism for verifying that it is moving forward. For these reasons, most Western governments and Burma's neighbors have been skeptical and critical of the roadmap.

On February 17, 2005, the government reconvened the National Convention, for the first time since 1993, in an attempt to rewrite the Constitution. However, major pro-democracy organisations and parties, including the National League for Democracy, were barred from participating, the military allowing only selected smaller parties. It was adjourned once again in January 2006.

In November 2005, the military junta started moving the government away from Yangon to an unnamed location near Kyatpyay just outside Pyinmana, to a newly designated capital city. This public action follows a long term unofficial policy of moving critical military and government infrastructure away from Yangon to avoid a repetition of the events of 1988. On Armed Forces Day (March 27, 2006), the capital was officially named Naypyidaw Myodaw (lit. Royal City of the Seat of Kings).

HISTORY OF PHILIPPINES

The history of the Philippines is believed to have begun with the arrival of the first humans via land bridges at least 30,000 years ago. The first recorded visit from the West is the arrival of Ferdinand Magellan on Homonhon Island, southeast of Samar on March 16, 1521.

Spanish colonization began with the arrival of Miguel López de Legazpi's expedition and permanent settlement in the island of Cebu, and more settlements continued northward with the colonizers reaching the bay of Manila on the island of Luzon. In Manila, they established a new town and thus began an era of Spanish colonization that lasted for more than three centuries.

Spanish rule brought political unification to an archipelago of previously independent islands and communities that later became the Philippines, and introduced elements of western civilization such as the code of law, printing and the calendar. The Philippines was ruled as a territory of New Spain from 1565 to 1821, and then administered directly from Madrid. During the Spanish period numerous towns were founded, infrastructures built, new crops and livestock introduced, and trade flourished. Spanish missionaries converted most of the population to Christianity and founded schools, universities and hospitals across the islands.

The Philippine Revolution against Spain began in April 1896, culminating two years later with a proclamation of independence and the establishment of the First Philippine Republic. However, the Treaty of Paris, at the end of the Spanish-American War, transferred control of the Philippines to the United States. This agreement was not recognized by the Philippine Government which, on June 2, 1899, proclaimed a Declaration of War against the U.S. The Philippine-American War which ensued resulted in massive Filipino casualties. Filipino leader Emilio Aguinaldo was captured in 1901 and the U.S. government declared the conflict officially over in 1902. The Filipino leaders, for the most part, accepted that the Americans had won, but hostilities continued until 1913. U.S. colonial rule of the Philippines started in 1905 with very limited local rule. Partial autonomy (commonwealth status) was granted in 1935, preparatory to a planned full independence from the United States in 1946. Preparation for a fully sovereign state was interrupted by the Japanese occupation of the islands during World War II.

With a promising economy in the 1950s and 1960s (even being second to Japan), the Philippines in the late 1960s and early 1970s saw a rise of student activism and civil unrest against the corrupt dictatorship of President Ferdinand Marcos who declared martial law in 1972. Because of close ties between United States and President Marcos, the U.S. government continued to support Marcos even though his administration was well-known for massive corruption and extensive human rights abuse. The peaceful and bloodless People Power Revolution of 1986, however, brought about the ousting of Marcos (who fled Manila on board a U.S. military helicopter, eventually arriving in Hawaii where he was exiled until his death) and a return to democracy for the country. The period since then, however, has been marked by political instability and hampered economic productivity.

Human fossil records indicate that the Philippines may have been inhabited for thousands of years. According to earlier archaeological findings, the first man in the Philippines came from the islands around Asia which Professor H. Otley Beyer, eminent American authority on Philippine archeology and anthropology, dubbed the "Dawn Man". Yet the oldest human fossil found in the Philippines thus far is the 22,000-year-old skull cap of a "Stone-Age Filipino" discovered by Dr. Robert B. Fox, an American anthropologist of the National Museum, inside Lucy Cave, Palawan, on May 28, 1962 and dubbed the "Tabon Man". The Tabon caves of Palawan indicate settlement for at least 30,500 years; these hunter-gatherers used stone flake tools. After these early settlers, the Negrito arrived, whose ancestors include the Ati and the Aeta.

The Austronesian-speaking peoples originated from Proto-Austronesian peoples in South China, coastal Southeast Asia, and island Southeast Asia. The two best known hypotheses are that the Austronesian languages developed either in Taiwan about 7,000 years ago or in island Southeast Asia. The Malayo-Polynesian-speaking peoples, an Austronesian branch, settled in the Philippines about 3,000 BC, and spread eastward to the Pacific Islands, and westward to Madagascar.

The Philippines had trade relations with China and Japan and strong cultural ties with India through neighboring present-day Malaysia and Indonesia as early as the 9th to the 12th century. The social and political organization of the population, in the widely scattered islands, evolved into a generally common pattern. Only the permanent-field rice farmers of northern Luzon had any concept of territoriality. The basic unit of settlement was the barangay, originally a kinship group headed by a datu (chief). Within the barangay, the broad social divisions consisted of the *maharlika* (nobles), including the datu; *timawa* (freemen); and a group described before the Spanish period as dependents. Dependents included several categories with differing status: landless agricultural workers; those who had lost freeman status because of indebtedness or punishment for crime; and *alipin* (slaves), most of whom appear to have been war captives.

Islam was brought to the Philippines by traders and proselytizers from Malaysia and Indonesia. Islamization of the Philippines is due to the strength of Muslim India. By the 13th century, Islam was established in the Sulu Archipelago and spread from there to Mindanao; it had reached the Manila area by 1565. Although Islam spread to Luzon, Animism, syncretized with Hinduism and Vajrayana Buddhism, was still the religion of the majority of the Philippine islands. Muslim immigrants introduced a political concept of territorial states ruled by rajas or sultans who exercised suzerainty over the datu. Neither the political state concept of the Muslim rulers nor the limited territorial concept of the sedentary rice farmers of Luzon, however, spread beyond the areas where they originated. When the Spanish arrived in the 16th century, the majority of the estimated 500,000 people in the islands lived in barangay settlements.

Spanish Rule (1565–1898)

Early Spanish Expeditions

The Philippine islands first came to the attention of Europeans with the Spanish expedition around the world led by Portuguese explorer Ferdinand Magellan in 1521. Magellan landed on the island called Homonhon, claiming the archipelago for Spain and naming them *Islas de San Lazaro*. He established friendly relations with some of the local chieftains and converted some of them to Roman Catholicism.In the island they explored many islands including the island of Mactan. However, Magellan was killed in a dispute with indigenous tribal groups led by a chieftain named Lapu-Lapu.

Over the next several decades, other Spanish expeditions were dispatched to the islands. In 1543, Ruy López de Villalobos led an expedition to the islands and gave the name *Las Islas Filipinas* (after Philip II of Spain) to the islands of Samar and Leyte. The name would later be given to the entire archipelago.

Spanish Colonization

Permanent Spanish settlement was not established until 1565 when an expedition led by the Conquistador, Miguel López de Legazpi, arrived in Cebu from Mexico (New Spain). Six years later, following the defeat of the local Muslim ruler, Rajah Solayman, Legazpi established a capital at Manila, a location that offered the excellent harbor of Manila Bay, a large population, and proximity to the ample food supplies of the central Luzon rice lands. Manila became the center of Spanish government, including military, religious, and commercial activities in the islands. Despite the opposition of the Portuguese, who desired to maintain their monopoly on East Indies trade, the Spanish had secured a foothold in the Philippines, which became their outpost as the Spanish East Indies. Spanish leadership was soon established over a large archipelago, including many independent communities that previously had known no central rule. The Philippines was administered as a province of New Spain until Mexican independence (1821).

Occupation of the islands was accomplished with relatively little bloodshed, partly because most of the population (except the Muslims) offered little armed resistance initially. A significant problem the Spanish faced was the subjugation of the Muslims of western Mindanao and the Sulu Archipelago. The Muslims, in response to attacks on them from the Spanish and their native allies, raided areas of Luzon and the Visayas that were under Spanish colonial control. The Spanish conducted intermittent military campaigns against the Muslims, but without conclusive results until after the middle of the 19th century.

The Philippines would have had a similar battle standard, with the coat of arms of Manila in place of the one of Mexico City. Church and state were inseparably linked in Spanish policy, with the state assuming responsibility for religious establishments. One of Spain's objectives in colonizing the Philippines was the conversion of the local population to Roman Catholicism. The work of conversion was facilitated by the absence of other organized religions, except for Islam, which predominated in the southwest. The pageantry of the church had a wide appeal, reinforced by the incorporation of Filipino social customs into religious observances. The eventual outcome was a new

Roman Catholic majority of the main Austronesian lowland population, from which the Muslims of western Mindanao and the upland tribal peoples of Luzon remained detached and alienated (such as the Ifugaos of the Cordillera region and the Mangyans of Mindoro).

At the lower levels of administration, the Spanish built on traditional village organization by co-opting local leaders. This system of indirect rule helped create a Filipino upper class, called the *principalia,* who had local wealth, high status, and other privileges. This perpetuated an oligarchic system of local control. Among the most significant changes under Spanish rule was that the Filipino idea of communal use and ownership of land was replaced with the concept of private ownership and the conferring of titles on members of the principalia.

The Philippines was not profitable as a colony, and a long war with the Dutch in the 17th century and intermittent conflict with the Muslims nearly bankrupted the colonial treasury. Colonial income derived mainly from entrepôt trade: The *Manila Galleons* sailing from Acapulco on the west coast of New Spain brought shipments of silver bullion and minted coin that were exchanged for return cargoes of Chinese goods. There was no direct trade with Spain.

Decline of Spanish Rule

Spanish rule on the Philippines was briefly interrupted in 1762, when British troops occupied Manila as a result of Spain's entry into the Seven Years' War. The Treaty of Paris of 1763 restored Spanish rule and in 1764 the British left the country fearing another costly war with Spain. The brief British occupation weakened Spain's grip on power and sparked rebellions and demands for independence.

In 1781, Governor-General José Basco y Vargas established the Economic Society of the Friends of the Country. The Philippines by this time was administered directly from Spain. Developments in and out of the country helped to bring new ideas to the Philippines. The opening of the Suez Canal in 1869 cut travel time to Spain. This prompted the rise of the *ilustrados,* an enlightened Filipino upper class, since many young Filipinos were able to study in Europe.

Enlightened by the Propaganda Movement to the injustices of the Spanish colonial government and the "frailocracy", the *ilustrados* originally clamored for adequate representation to the Spanish Cortes and later for independence. José Rizal, the most celebrated intellectual and radical *illustrado* of the era, wrote the novels *Noli Me Tangere* and *El Filibusterismo,* which greatly inspired the movement for independence. The Katipunan, a secret society whose primary purpose was that of overthrowing Spanish rule in the Philippines, was founded by Andrés Bonifacio who became its Supremo (leader).

The Philippine Revolution began in 1896. Rizal was implicated in the outbreak of the revolution and executed for treason in 1896. The Katipunan in Cavite split into two groups, *Magdiwang*, led by Mariano Alvarez (a relative of Bonifacio's by marriage), and *Magdalo*, led by Emilio Aguinaldo. Leadership conflicts between Bonifacio and Aguinaldo culminated in the execution or assassination of the former by the latter's soldiers. Aguinaldo agreed to a truce with the Pact of Biak-na-Bato and Aguinaldo and his fellow revolutionaries were exiled to Hong Kong. Not all the revolutionary generals complied with the agreement. One, General Francisco Makabulos, established a Central Executive Committee to serve as the interim government until a more suitable one was created. Armed conflicts resumed, this time coming from almost every province in Spanish-governed Philippines.

In 1898, as conflicts continued in the Philippines, the USS *Maine*, having been sent to Cuba because of U.S. concerns for the safety of its citizens during an ongoing Cuban revolution, exploded and sank in Havana harbor. This event precipitated the Spanish-American war. After Commodore George Dewey defeated the Spanish squadron at Manila, the U.S. invited Aguinaldo to return to the Philippines, which he did on May 19, 1898, in the hope he would rally Filipinos against the Spanish colonial government. By the time U.S. land forces had arrived, the Filipinos had taken control of the entire island of Luzon, except for the walled city of Intramuros. On June 12, 1898, Aguinaldo declared the independence of the Philippines in Kawit, Cavite, establishing the First Philippine Republic under Asia's first democratic constitution.

Simultaneously, a German squadron arrived in Manila and declared that if the United States did not seize the Philippines as a colonial possession, Germany would. In the Battle of Manila, the United States captured the city from the Spanish. This battle marked an end of Filipino-American collaboration, as Filipino forces were prevented from entering the captured city of Manila, an action deeply resented by the Filipinos. Spain and the United States sent commissioners to Paris to draw up the terms of the Treaty of Paris which ended the Spanish-American War. The Filipino representative, Felipe Agoncillo, was excluded from sessions as the revolutionary government was not recognized by the family of nations. Although there was substantial domestic opposition, the United States decided neither to return the Philippines to Spain, nor to allow Germany to annex the Philippines. In addition to Guam and Puerto Rico, Spain was forced in the negotiations to hand over the Philippines to the U.S. in exchange for US$20,000,000.00, which the U.S. later claimed to be a "gift" from Spain. The first Philippine Republic rebelled against the U.S. occupation, resulting in the Philippine-American War (1899–1913).

American Territorial Period (1898–1946)

Filipinos initially saw their relationship with the United States as that of two nations joined in a common struggle against Spain. As allies, Filipinos had provided the American forces with valuable intelligence and military support. However, the United States later distanced itself from the interests of the Filipino insurgents. Aguinaldo was unhappy that the United States would not commit to paper a statement of support for Philippine independence. Relations deteriorated and tensions heightened as it became clear that the Americans were in the islands to stay.

Philippine-American War

Hostilities broke out on February 4, 1899, after two American privates on patrol killed three Filipino soldiers in San Juan, a Manila suburb. This incident sparked the Philippine-American War, which would cost far more money and took far more lives than the Spanish-American War. Some 126,000 American soldiers would be committed to the conflict; 4,234 Americans died, as did 16,000 Filipino soldiers who were part of a nationwide guerrilla movement of indeterminate numbers. Estimates on civilian deaths during the war range between 250,000 and 1,000,000, largely because of famine and disease. Atrocities were committed by both sides.

The poorly-equipped Filipino troops were easily overpowered by American troops in open combat, but they were formidable opponents in guerrilla warfare. Malolos, the revolutionary capital, was captured on March 31, 1899. Aguinaldo and his government escaped however, establishing a new capital at San Isidro, Nueva Ecija. Antonio Luna, Aguinaldo's most capable military commander, Gregorio del Pilar, was killed in June at Tirad Pass. With his best commander dead and his troops suffering continued defeats as American forces pushed into northern Luzon, Aguinaldo dissolved the regular army in November 1899 and ordered the establishment of decentralized guerrilla commands in each of several military zones. The general population, caught between Americans and rebels, suffered significantly.

Aguinaldo was captured at Palanan, Isabela on March 23, 1901 and was brought to Manila. Convinced of the futility of further resistance, he swore allegiance to the United States and issued a proclamation calling on his compatriots to lay down their arms, officially bringing an end to the war. However, sporadic insurgent resistance continued in various parts of the Philippines, especially in the Muslim south, until 1913.

In *The Specter of Genocide: Mass Murder in Historical Perspective* (2003), Prof. Gavan McCormack argues that during the Philippine-American War the outright counter-guerilla operations launched by the U.S. against the Filipinos, an integral part of its violent pacification program, which claimed the lives of over a million Filipinos, constitutes genocide.

United States Territory

The United States defined its territorial mission as one of tutelage, preparing the Philippines for eventual independence. Civil government was established by the United

States in 1901, with William Howard Taft as the first American Governor-General of the Philippines, replacing the military governor, Arthur MacArthur, Jr. The governor-general acted as head of the Philippine Commission, a body appointed by the U.S. president with legislative and limited executive powers. The commission passed laws to set up the fundamentals of the new government, including a judicial system, civil service, and local government. A Philippine Constabulary was organized to deal with the remnants of the insurgent movement and gradually assume the responsibilities of the United States Army. The elected Philippine Assembly was inaugurated in 1907, becoming a lower house of a bicameral legislature, with the appointed Philippine Commission as upper house.

Frank Murphy was the last Governor-General of the Philippines (1933-35), and the first U.S. High Commissioner of the Philippines (1935-36). The change in form was more than symbolic: it was intended as a manifestation of the transition to independence.

United States policies towards the Philippines shifted with changing administrations. During the early years of territorial administration, the Americans were reluctant to delegate authority to the Filipinos. However, when Woodrow Wilson became U.S. President in 1913, a new policy was adopted to put into motion a process that would gradually lead to Philippine independence. The Jones Act, passed by the U.S. Congress in 1916 to serve as the new organic law in the Philippines, promised eventual independence and instituted an elected Philippine senate.

The 1920s saw alternating periods of cooperation and confrontation with American governors-general, depending on how intent the incumbent was on exercising his powers vis-à-vis the Philippine legislature. Members to the elected legislature lobbied for immediate and complete independence from the United States. Several independence missions were sent to Washington, D.C. A civil service was formed and was gradually taken over by Filipinos, who had effectively gained control by 1918.

Philippine politics during the American territorial era was dominated by the Nacionalista Party, which was founded in 1907. Although the party's platform called for "immediate independence", their policy toward the Americans was highly accommodating. Within the political establishment, the call for independence was spearheaded by Manuel L. Quezon, who served continuously as Senate president from 1916 until 1935.

Commonwealth

In 1933, the United States Congress passed the Hare-Hawes-Cutting Act as a Philippine Independence Act over President Herbert Hoover's veto. Though the bill had been drafted with the aid of a commission from the Philippines, it was opposed by

Philippine Senate President Manuel L. Quezon, partially because of provisions leaving the United States in control of naval bases. Under his influence, the Philippine legislature rejected the bill. The following year, a revised act known as the Tydings-McDuffie Act was finally passed. The act provided for the establishment of the Commonwealth of the Philippines with a ten-year period of peaceful transition to full independence. The commonwealth would have its own constitution and be self-governing, though foreign policy would be the responsibility of the United States, and certain legislation required approval of the United States president.

A constitution was framed and approved by Franklin D. Roosevelt in March 1935. On May 14, 1935, and a Filipino government was formed on the basis of principles similar to the U.S. Constitution. The commonwealth was established in 1935, electing Manuel Quezon as the president and featuring a very strong executive, a unicameral National Assembly, and a Supreme Court composed entirely of Filipinos for the first time since 1901.

World War II and Japanese Occupation

Japan launched a surprise attack on the Clark Air Base in Pampanga, Philippines on December 8, 1941, just ten hours after the attack on Pearl Harbor. Aerial bombardment was followed by landings of ground troops on Luzon. The defending Philippine and United States troops were under the command of General Douglas MacArthur. Under the pressure of superior numbers, the defending forces withdrew to the Bataan Peninsula and to the island of Corregidor at the entrance to Manila Bay.

On January 2, 1942, General MacArthur declared the capital city, Manila, an open city to prevent its destruction, The Philippine defense continued until the final surrender of United States-Philippine forces on the Bataan Peninsula in April 1942 and on Corregidor in May of the same year. Most of the 80,000 prisoners of war captured by the Japanese at Bataan were forced to undertake the infamous Bataan Death March to a prison camp 105 kilometers to the north. It is estimated that about 10,000 Filipinos and 1,200 Americans died before reaching their destination.

President Quezon and Osmeña had accompanied the troops to Corregidor and later left for the United States, where they set up a government in exile. MacArthur was ordered to Australia, where he started to plan for a return to the Philippines. The Japanese military authorities immediately began organizing a new government structure in the Philippines and established the Philippine Executive Commission. They initially organized a Council of State, through which they directed civil affairs until October 1943, when they declared the Philippines an independent republic. The Japanese-sponsored republic headed by President José P. Laurel proved to be unpopular.

Japanese occupation of the Philippines was opposed by large-scale underground and guerrilla activity. The Philippine Army continued to fight the Japanese in a guerrilla war and was considered an auxiliary unit of the United States Army. Their effectiveness was such that by the end of the war, Japan controlled only twelve of the forty-eight provinces. The major element of resistance in the Central Luzon area was furnished by the Hukbalahap (Filipino: "Hukbong Bayan Laban sa mga Hapon") ("People's Army Against the Japanese"), which armed some 30,000 people and extended their control over much of Luzon.

MacArthur's Sixth United States Army landed on Leyte on October 20, 1944. Landings in other parts of the country followed, and the Allies with the Philippine Commonwealth troops pushed toward Manila. Fighting continued until Japan's formal surrender on September 2, 1945. The Philippines suffered great loss of life and tremendous physical destruction by the time the war was over. The Japanese committed widespread abuse of the Filipino people, including murder, rape, theft, forced labor, and punishment for having been under US rule. An estimated 1 million Filipinos had been killed, and Manila was extensively damaged as the Japanese did not declare it an open city as the Americans had done in 1942.

Independent Philippines and the Third Republic (1946–1972)

Elections were held in April 1946, with Manuel Roxas becoming the first president of the independent Republic of the Philippines. The United States ceded its sovereignty over the Philippines on July 4, 1946, as scheduled. However, the Philippine economy remained highly dependent on United States markets– more dependent, according to United States high commissioner Paul McNutt, than any single U.S. state was dependent on the rest of the country. The Philippine Trade Act, passed as a precondition for receiving war rehabilitation grants from the United States, exacerbated the dependency with provisions further tying the economies of the two countries. A military assistance pact was signed in 1947 granting the United States a 99-year lease on designated military bases in the country (the lease was later reduced to 25 years beginning 1967).

The Roxas administration granted general amnesty to those who had collaborated with the Japanese in World War II, except for those who had committed violent crimes. Roxas died suddenly of a heart attack in April 1948, and the vice president, Elpidio Quirino, was elevated to the presidency. He ran for president in his own right in 1949, defeating Jose P. Laurel and winning a four-year term.

World War II had left the Philippines demoralized and severely damaged. The task of reconstruction was complicated by the activities of the Communist-supported Hukbalahap guerrillas (known as "Huks"), who had evolved into a violent resistance force against the new Philippine government. Government policy towards the Huks alternated between gestures of negotiation and harsh suppression. Secretary of Defense Ramon Magsaysay initiated a campaign to defeat the insurgents militarily and at the same time win popular support for the government. The Huk movement had waned in the early 1950s, finally ending with the unconditional surrender of Huk leader Luis Taruc in May 1954.

Supported by the United States, Magsaysay was elected president in 1953 on a populist platform. He promised sweeping economic reform, and made progress in land reform by promoting the resettlement of poor people in the Catholic north into traditionally Muslim areas. Though this relieved population pressure in the north, it heightened religious hostilities. Nevertheless, he was extremely popular with the common people, and his death in an airplane crash in March 1957 dealt a serious blow to national morale.

Carlos P. Garcia succeeded to the presidency after Magsaysay's death, and was elected to a four-year term in the election of November that same year. His administration emphasized the nationalist theme of "Filipino first", arguing that the Filipino people should be given the chances to improve the country's economy. Garcia successfully negotiated for the United States' relinquishment of large military land reservations. However, his administration lost popularity on issues of government corruption as his term advanced.

Diosdado Macapagal was elected president in the 1961 election, defeating Garcia's re-election bid. Macapagal's foreign policy sought closer relations with neighboring Asian nations, particularly Malaya (later Malaysia) and Indonesia. Negotiations with the United States over base rights led to anti-American sentiment. Notably, the celebration of Independence Day was changed from July 4 to June 12, to honor the day that Emilio Aguinaldo declared independence from Spain in 1898.

Marcos Era and Martial Law (1965–1986)

Macapagal ran for re-election in 1965, but was defeated by his former party-mate, Senate President Ferdinand Marcos, who had switched to the Nacionalista Party. Early in his presidency, Marcos initiated ambitious public works projects and intensified tax collection which brought the country economic prosperity throughout the 1970s. His administration built more roads (including a substantial portion of the Pan-Philippine Highway) than all his predecessors combined, and more schools than any previous administration. Marcos was re-elected president in 1969, becoming the first president of the independent Philippines to achieve a second term.

The Philippine Legislature was corrupt and impotent. Opponents of Marcos blocked the necessary legislation to implement his ambitious plans. Because of this, optimism faded early in his second term and economic growth slowed. Crime and civil disobedience increased. The Communist Party of the Philippines formed the New People's Army. The Moro National Liberation Front continued to fight for an independent Muslim nation in Mindanao. An explosion during the proclamation rally of the senatorial slate of the Liberal Party on August 21, 1971 prompted Marcos to suspend the writ of habeas corpus, which he restored on January 11, 1972 after public protests.

Martial Law

Amidst the rising wave of lawlessness and the threat of a Communist insurgency, Marcos declared martial law on September 21, 1972 by virtue of Proclamation No. 1081. Marcos, ruling by decree, curtailed press freedom and other civil liberties, closed down Congress and media establishments, and ordered the arrest of opposition leaders and militant activists, including his staunchest critics senators Benigno Aquino, Jr., Jovito Salonga and Jose Diokno. The declaration of martial law was initially well received, given the social turmoil the Philippines was experiencing. Crime rates plunged dramatically after a curfew was implemented. Many political opponents were forced to go into exile.

A constitutional convention, which had been called for in 1970 to replace the colonial 1935 Constitution, continued the work of framing a new constitution after the declaration of martial law. The new constitution went into effect in early 1973, changing the form of government from presidential to parliamentary and allowing Marcos to stay in power beyond 1973.

Marcos claimed that martial law was the prelude to creating a "New Society" based on new social and political values. The economy during the 1970s was robust, with budgetary and trade surpluses. The Gross National Product rose from P55 billion in 1972 to P193 billion in 1980. Tourism rose, contributing to the economy's growth. However, Marcos, his cronies and his wife, Imelda Romualdez-Marcos, wilfully engaged in rampant corruption.

Fourth Republic

Appeasing the Roman Catholic Church before the visit of Pope John Paul II, Marcos officially lifted martial law on January 17, 1981. However, he retained much of the government's power for arrest and detention. Corruption and nepotism as well as civil unrest contributed to a serious decline in economic growth and development under Marcos, whose health declined due to lupus.

The political opposition boycotted the 1981 presidential elections, which pitted Marcos against retired general Alejo Santos. Marcos won by a margin of over 16 million votes, which constitutionally allowed him to have another six-year term. Finance Minister Cesar Virata was elected as Prime Minister by the Batasang Pambansa.

In 1983, opposition leader Benigno Aquino, Jr. was assassinated at the Manila International Airport upon his return to the Philippines after a long period of exile. This coalesced popular dissatisfaction with Marcos and began a succession of events, including pressure from the United States, that culminated in a snap presidential election in February 1986. The opposition united under Aquino's widow, Corazon Aquino.

The official election canvasser, the Commission on Elections (Comelec), declared Marcos the winner of the election. However, there was a large discrepancy between the Comelec results and that of Namfrel, an accredited poll watcher. The allegedly fraudulent result was rejected by Corazon Aquino and her supporters. International observers, including a U.S. delegation, denounced the official results. Gen. Fidel Ramos and Defense Minister Juan Ponce Enrile withdrew their support for Marcos. A peaceful civilian-military uprising, now popularly called the People Power Revolution, forced Marcos into exile and installed Corazon Aquino as president on February 25, 1986.

Fifth Republic (1986–present)

Corazon Aquino immediately formed a revolutionary government to normalize the situation, and provided for a transitional "Freedom Constitution". A new permanent constitution was ratified and enacted in February 1987. The constitution crippled presidential power to declare martial law, proposed the creation of autonomous regions in the Cordilleras and Muslim Mindanao, and restored the presidential form of government and the bicameral Congress. Progress was made in revitalizing democratic institutions and respect for civil liberties, but Aquino's administration was also viewed as weak and fractious, and a return to full political stability and economic development was hampered by several attempted coups staged by disaffected members of the Philippine military. Economic growth was additionally hampered by a series of natural disasters, including the 1991 eruption of Mount Pinatubo that left 700 dead and 200,000 homeless.

In 1991, the Philippine Senate rejected a treaty that would have allowed a 10-year extension of the U.S. military bases in the country. The United States turned over Clark Air Base in Pampanga to the government in November, and Subic Bay Naval Base in Zambales in December 1992, ending almost a century of U.S. military presence in the Philippines.

In the 1992 elections, Defense Secretary Fidel V. Ramos, endorsed by Aquino, won the presidency with just 23.6% of the vote in a field of seven candidates. Early in his administration, Ramos declared "national reconciliation" his highest priority and worked at building a coalition to overcome the divisiveness of the Aquino years. He legalized the Communist Party and laid the groundwork for talks with communist insurgents, Muslim separatists, and military rebels, attempting to convince them to cease their armed activities against the government. In June 1994, Ramos signed into law a general conditional amnesty covering all rebel groups, and Philippine military and police personnel accused of crimes committed while fighting the insurgents. In October 1995, the government signed an agreement bringing the military insurgency to an end. A peace agreement with the Moro National Liberation Front (MNLF), a major separatist group fighting for an independent homeland in Mindanao, was signed in 1996, ending the 24-year old struggle. However, an MNLF splinter group, the Moro Islamic Liberation Front continued the armed struggle for an Islamic state. Efforts by Ramos supporters to gain passage of an amendment that would allow him to run for a second term were met with large-scale protests, leading Ramos to declare he would not seek re-election.

Joseph Estrada, a former movie actor who had served as Ramos' vice president, was elected president by a landslide victory in 1998. His election campaign pledged to help the poor and develop the country's agricultural sector. He enjoyed widespread popularity, particularly among the poor. Under the cloud of the Asian financial crisis which began in 1997, Estrada's wayward governance took a heavy toll on the economy. Unemployment worsened, the budget deficit grew, and the currency plunged. Eventually, the country's economy recovered but at a much slower pace than that of its Asian neighbors.

Within a year of his election, Estrada's popularity declined sharply amid allegations of cronyism and corruption, and failure to remedy the problems of poverty. In October 2000, Estrada was accused of having accepted millions of pesos in payoffs from illegal gambling businesses. He was impeached by the House of Representatives, but his impeachment trial in the Senate broke down when the senate voted to block examination of the president's bank records. In response, massive street protests erupted demanding Estrada's resignation. Faced with street protests, cabinet resignations, and a withdrawal of support from the armed forces, Estrada was forced from office on January 20, 2001.

Vice President Gloria Macapagal-Arroyo (the daughter of the late President Diosdado Macapagal) was sworn in as Estrada's successor on the day of his departure. Her accession to power was further legitimated by the mid-term congressional and local elections held four months later, when her coalition won an overwhelming victory. Arroyo's initial term in office was marked by fractious coalition politics as well as a military mutiny in Manila in July 2003 that led her to declare a month-long nationwide state of rebellion.

Arroyo had declared in December 2002 that she would not run in the May 2004 presidential election, but she reversed herself in October 2003 and decided to join the race. She was re-elected and sworn in for her own six-year term as president on June 30, 2004. In 2005, a tape of a wiretapped conversation surfaced bearing the voice of Arroyo apparently asking an election official if her margin of victory could be maintained. The tape sparked protests calling for Arroyo's resignation. Arroyo admitted to inappropriately speaking to an election official, but denied allegations of fraud and refused to step down. Attempts to impeach the president failed later that year.

Arroyo currently spearheads a controversial plan for an overhaul of the constitution to transform the present presidential-bicameral republic into a federal parliamentary-unicameral form of government.

HISTORY OF THAILAND

The history of Thailand begins with the migration of the Thais from their ancestral home in southern China into mainland southeast Asia around the 10th century AD. Prior to this Mon, Khmer and Malay kingdoms ruled the region. The Thais established their own states starting with Sukhothai and then Ayutthaya kingdom. These states fought each other and were under constant threat from the Khmers, Burma and Vietnam. Much later, the European colonial powers threatened in the 19th and early 20th centuries, but Thailand survived as the only Southeast Asian state to avoid colonial rule. After the end of the absolute monarchy in 1932, Thailand endured sixty years of almost permanent military rule before the establishment of a democratic system.

Prior to the southwards migration of the Tai people from Yunnan in the 10 century, the Indochina peninsula had been a home to various indigenous animistic communities for as far back as 500,000 years ago. The recent discovery of Homo erectus fossils such as Lampang man is but one example. The remains were first discovered during excavations in Lampang province, Thailand. The finds have been dated from roughly 1,000,000–500,000 years ago in the Pleistocene. Historians agree that the diverse Austro-Asiatic groups that inhabited the Indochina peninsula are related to the people which today inhabit the islands of the Pacific. As these peoples dispersed along the Gulf of Thailand, Malay Peninsula and Malay Archipelago, they inhabited the coastal areas of the archipelago as well as other remote islands. The seafarers possessed advanced navigation skills, sailing as far as New Zealand, Hawaii and Madagascar.

The most well known pre-historic settlement in Thailand is often associated to the major archaeological site at Ban Chiang; dating of artifacts from this site is a consensus that at least by 1500 BC, the inhabitants had developed bronze tools and also the grew rice. There are myriad sites in Thailand dating to the Bronze (1500 BC-500 BC) and Iron Ages (500 BC-500 AD). The most thoroughly researched of these sites are located in the country's Northeast, especially in the Mun and Chi River valleys. The Mun River in particular is home to many 'moated' sites which comprise mounds surrounded by ditches and ramparts. The mounds contain evidence of prehistoric occupation. Around the first century of the Christian era, according to Funan epigraphy and the records of Chinese historians(Coedes), a number of trading settlements of the South, appears to have been organized into several Indianised states, among the earliest of which are believed to be Langkasuka and Tambralinga.

Dvaravati

Dvaravati first came to the attention of modern scholars during the 19th century through the translation of Chinese texts. These texts mentioned To-lo-po-ti, Tu-ho-po-ti and Tu-ho- lo-po-ti, names that were translated into Sanskrit- Dvaravati. We know that this polity had an international presence, as it sent a number of missions to the Chinese court, but it is difficult to reconstruct what kind of polity is represented and scholarly opinion is split. Clearly the issue cannot be resolved until further research is undertaken but the current evidence appears to favour an interpretation of Dvaravati as a loosely organized political entity at a pre-state level. The situation is confused further by the use of the term Dvaravati to describe a school of art and a culture. It is best to consider Dvaravati as a broad term, encompassing all of these things, a culture, comprised mostly of Mon speakers who produced predominantly religious art and lived in large towns concentrated in the Chao Phraya Valley whose influence extended into other parts of Thailand.

Sukhothai Kingdom

The Sukhothai kingdom was an early kingdom in the area around the city Sukhothai, in north central Thailand. It existed from 1238 till 1438. The old capital, now 12 km outside of New Sukhothai in Tambon Mueang Kao, is in ruins and is a historical park.

Chiang Saen was established in the early 700s and Mueang Sua (Luang Prabang) around AD 728 making them the first kingdoms established by the Tai-speaking people in southeast Asia, prior to the migration and expansion of the Tai-speaking people into northern Thailand, Laos, and eventually into central Thailand and central Laos.

The city of Sukhotai was part of the Khmer empire until 1238, when two Thai chieftains, Pho Khun Pha Muang and Pho Khun Bang Klang Hao, declared their independence and established a Thai-ruled kingdom. Pho Khun Bang Klang Hao later became the first king of Sukhotai, calling himself Pho Khun Si Indrathit (or Intradit). This event traditionally marks the founding of the modern Thai nation, although other less well-known Thai kingdoms, such as Lanna, Phayao and Chiang Saen, were established around the same time.

Sukhotai expanded by forming alliances with the other Thai kingdoms, adopting Theravada Buddhism as the state religion with the help of Ceylonese monks. Intradit was succeeded by his son Pho Khun Ban Muang, who was followed in 1278 by his brother, Pho Khun Ramkhamhaeng. Under King Ramkhamhaeng the Great, as he is now known, Suriyothai enjoyed a golden age of prosperity. Ramkhamhaeng is credited with designing the Thai alphabet (traditionally dated from 1283, on the evidence of the controversial Ramkhamhaeng stele, an inscribed stone allegedly bearing the earliest known Thai writing). At its peak, supposedly stretching from Martaban (now in Burma) to Luang Prabang (now in Laos) and down the Malay Peninsula as far south as Nakhon Sri Thammarat, the kingdom's sphere of influence was larger than that of modern Thailand, although the degree of control exercised over outlying areas was variable.

After Ramkhamhaeng's death, he was succeeded by his son Loethai. The vassal kingdoms, first Uttaradit in the north, then soon after the Laotian kingdoms of Luang Prabang and Vientiane (Wiangchan), liberated themselves from their overlord. In 1319 the Mon state to the west broke away, and in 1321 Lanna placed Tak, one of the oldest towns under the control of Suriyothai, under its control. To the south the powerful city of Suphanburi also broke free early in the reign of Loethai. Thus the kingdom was quickly reduced to its former local importance only. Meanwhile, Ayutthaya rose in strength, and finally in 1378 King Thammaracha II had to submit to this new power.

The Silajaruek Sukhotai are hundreds of stone inscriptions that form a historical record of the period. Among the most important inscriptions are Silajaruek Pho Khun Ramkamhaeng (Stone Inscription of King Ramkamhaeng), Silajaruek Wat Srichum (an account on history of the region itself and of Srilanka), and Silajaruek Wat Pamamuang (a Politico-Religious record of King Loethai).

Sukhotai became a tributary state of Ayutthaya between 1365 and 1378. In 1412 Ayutthaya installed a chief resident, and King Thammaracha IV was installed on the throne by Ayutthaya. Around 1430 Thammaracha moved his capital to Phitsanulok, and after his death in 1438 the kingdom was reduced in status to a mere province of Ayutthaya.

The Kings of Sukkhothai

- King Pho Khun Sri Indraditya (1249- 1257)
- King Pho Khun Ban Muang (1257–1277)
- King Pho Khun Ramkhamhaeng (Ramkhamhaeng the Great) (ruled 1277–1298 or 1317) (called Rammaraj in the Ayutthaya chronicles)
- King Pu Saisongkhram: After Ramkhamheang's death, ruled temporarily in absence of Loethai who was on trip to China. He was not styled Pho Khun.
- King Pho Khun Loethai (1298–1347)
- King Pho Khun Nguanamthom (1347)
- King Phya Lithai or Thammaracha I (1347–1368/1374)
- King Thammaracha II or Phya Sai Leu Thai (1368/1374–1399)
- King Thammaracha III or Phya Sai Luthai (1399–1419)
- King Thammaracha IV (1419–1438)

Lanna Kingdom

Lanna was a kingdom in the north of Thailand around the city of Chiang Mai. The kingdom was founded in 1296 by King Mangrai the Great, when he succeeded his father as the leader of the Ngoen Yang city state. In 1262 he founded the city Chiang Rai as his capital, naming it after himself. The kingdom quickly grew by unifying the many local Tai rulers of the area under his leadership, as well as by enlarging to the south by annexing the Mon kingdom of Hariphunchai in 1292–the area around the modern-day city Lamphun. In 1296 he founded the city of Chiang Mai as the new capital of the kingdom with help from allies Ngam Muang of Phayao and Ramkhamhaeng of Sukhothai.

The golden age of Lanna was in the 15th century during the reign of Tilokkarat or Tilokaraja. In 1477 the 8th of the Buddhist councils was held near Chiang Mai, which worked on improving the Buddhist scriptures. The previously independent city state Nan, capital of a Tai Lue people, was added to the kingdom in 1449. Wars with Ayutthaya Kingdom, another Thai kingdom, also broke out.

Initial decline of the kingdom began in the early 16th century, and worsened after the death of King Kaeo in 1526. A war of succession ensued among the royal factions, kings were assassinated; or others had to abdicate. This political instability invited an invasion from the neighboring Burmese kingdom, and in 1558 Lanna had to surrender and thus became a vassal of Burma. When the dynasty of Mangrai became extinct in 1578, the Burmese sent their own princes to serve as rulers of Lanna.

The kings of Ayutthaya tried to capture Lanna several times, as the Burmese posed a threat to their kingdom as well. Even though around 1600 King Naresuan, and later in 1662 King Narai as well, succeeded in occupying Chiang Mai, they were repulsed by the Burmese after a short time.

In the early 1700s the Burmese divided the kingdom into a northern part, ruled from Chiang Saen, and a southern part, ruled from Chiang Mai. The northern part was for all practical purposes annexed by Burma, while the southern continued to be a vassal state.

After the Burmese destroyed Ayutthaya, King Taksin drove the Burmese out of Siam or Central Thailand. In Lanna, King Taksin helped Phraya Chaban (Bunma) of Chiang Mai and Prince Kawila of Lampang to successfully drive out the Burmese. On the night of February 14, 1774 Chiang Mai fell to the Siamese. Phraya Chaban (Bunma) ruled Chiang Mai as the first Duke of Chiang Mai and Prince Kawila became the first Duke of Lampang under Siamese rulership. King Rama I after ascending to the throne, awarded Kawila with more power, Kawila become the second Duke of Chiang Mai who ruled 57 cities. The two families became closer. Not only Princess Sri Anocha,

Duke Kawila's sister, married to Vice King Boonma, King Rama I's only brother, but Princess Dararasmi, Duke Inthawichayanon's daughter also become King Rama V's Princess Consort. In 1877 a Viceroy from Bangkok was sent to help the duke. In 1899 Lanna was formally annexed by Siam, and administrated as the Monthon Phayap. The last of the Chiang Mai duke, Kaeo Nawarat, never held any true administrative power. Upon his death in 1939, no successor was named to replace him.

Ayutthaya Kingdom

The kingdom of Ayutthaya was a Thai kingdom that existed from 1351 to 1767. Ayutthaya was friendly towards foreign traders, including the Chinese, Vietnamese (Annam), Indians, Japanese and Persians, and later the Portuguese, Spanish, Dutch and French, permitting them to set up villages outside the city walls. In the sixteenth century, it was described by foreign traders as one of the biggest and wealthiest city in the East. The court of King Narai (1656-1688) had strong links with that of King Louis XIV of France, whose ambassadors compared the city in size and wealth to Paris. Before Ayutthaya fell to Burmese attack in 1767, its vassals included the Northern Shan states of present- day Myanmar, Lanna (Chiang Mai, Yunnan & Shan Sri (China), Lan Xang (Laos), Cambodian Kingdom, and some city- states in the Malay Peninsula.

The Siamese state based at Ayutthaya in the valley of the Chao Phraya River grew from the earlier kingdom of Lavo, which it absorbed, and its rise continued the steady shift southwards of the centre of gravity of the Tai-speaking peoples as other kingdoms in this area such as the kingdom of Supannaphum (Dvaravati) or, the kingdom of Sukhothai. In 1351, to escape the threat of an epidemic, King U Thong moved his court south into the rich floodplain of the Chao Phraya. On an island in the river which is the seaport city of Ayothaya was settled before, and he founded a new capital, which he called Ayutthaya, after the Hindu holy city Ayodhya in northern India, the birth city of the Hindu god Rama who is the hero in the Hindu epic Ramayana. U Thong assumed the royal name of Ramathibodi in 1351.

Ramathibodi tried to unify his kingdom. In 1360 he declared Theravada Buddhism the official religion of Ayutthaya and brought members of a sangha, a Buddhist monastic community, from Ceylon to establish new religious orders and spread the faith among his subjects. He also compiled a legal code, based on the Indian Dharmashastra (a Hindu legal text) and Thai custom, which became the basis of royal legislation. Composed in Pali — an Indo-Aryan language closely related to Sanskrit and the language of the Theravada Buddhist scriptures — it had the force of divine injunction. Supplemented by royal decrees, Ramathibodi's legal code remained generally in force until the late nineteenth century.

Conquests

By the end of the fourteenth century, Ayutthaya was regarded as the strongest power in Indochina, but it lacked the manpower to dominate the region. In the last year of his reign, Ramathibodi had seized Angkor during what was to be the first of many successful Thai assaults on the Khmer capital. The policy was aimed at securing Ayutthaya's eastern frontier by preempting Vietnamese designs on Khmer territory. The weakened Khmer periodically submitted to Ayutthaya's suzerainty, but efforts to maintain control over Angkor were repeatedly frustrated. However Angkor eventually fell. Thai troops were frequently diverted to suppress rebellions in Sukhothai or to campaign against Chiang Mai, where Ayutthaya's expansion was tenaciously resisted. Eventually Ayutthaya subdued the territory that had belonged to Sukhothai, and the year after Ramathibodi died, his kingdom was recognized by the emperor of China's newly established Ming Dynasty as Sukhothai's rightful successor.

The Thai kingdom was not a single, unified state but rather a patchwork of self-governing principalities and tributary provinces owing allegiance to the king of Ayutthaya under the mandala system. These countries were ruled by members of the royal family of Ayutthaya who had their own armies and warred among themselves, as well as self governing but subservient Malay states in the south. The king had to be vigilant to prevent royal princes from combining against him or allying with Ayutthaya's enemies. Due to the lack of succession law and strong concept of merit, whenever the succession was in dispute, princely governors or powerful dignitaries gathered their forces and moved on the capital to press their claims.

During much of the fifteenth century Ayutthaya's energies were directed toward the Malay Peninsula, where the great trading port of Malacca contested its claims to sovereignty. Ayutthaya's conquests were unsuccessful, however, due to the military support of Ming China, who backed the Sultanate diplomatically and economically. The Ming Admiral Zheng He had established one of his bases of operation in the port city, so the Chinese could not afford to loose such a strategic position to the Siamese. Under this umbrella of protection, Malacca flourished into one of Ayutthaya's great rivals, until its conquest in 1511 by the Portuguese.

Malacca and other Malay states south of Tambralinga had become Muslim early in the century, and thereafter Islam served as a symbol of Malay solidarity against the Thais. As it failed to make a vassal state of Malacca, Ayutthayan control of the strait was gradually displaced by Malay and Chinese.

However in the mid sixteenth century, Burmese Kingdom of Tounggoo became stronger, it then began the 'imperial expansion'. Its kings Tabinshwehti and Bayinnaung attacked Ayutthaya. In 1569 Ayutthaya eventually fell and became Toungoo's vassal.

The royal princes and high officials were taken back to Tounggoo. One of those princes was Prince Naret or widely known later as King Naresuan.

Ayutthaya became great power again after Prince Naret or Naresuan returned to Ayutthaya. He started gathering troops to resist the Burmese. King Naresuan finally defeated Burmese force in famous elephant battle with Toungoo's heir apparent, who was killed in the battle. Since then Ayutthaya became one of the most powerful kingdom in the region. It began expand towards the northern region, Sukhothai and Lanna area, the maritime, southern peninsula and Cambodia due to interest in foreign contact. Foreign trade brought her not only luxury items but also new arms and weapons. In the mid- seventeenth century, in the King Narai's reign, Ayutthaya became very prosperous.

Fall

The eighteenth century brought Ayutthaya's decline. Due to rifts among royal princes and high dignitaries, the kingdom started shattering. Outlying cities and its vassals became more independent; tributes and incomes became more rare. Orders from the capital were ignored. The sign of its 'total collapse' started with the Burmese invasion. Ayutthayan vassals and satellite towns were defeated rapidly. Ayutthaya eventually became helpless. In 1767 Burma attacked Ayutthaya after months of besiege. The city- state was totally destroyed.

Some of its officials had to flee and gather force. After months of striking back. Praya Tak, former Ayutthaya's general, founded Thon Buri, near present day Bangkok, as the new capital. It was the last of many Burmese invasions of Ayutthaya.

Thai Kingship

Thai rulers were absolute monarchs whose office was partly religious in nature. They derived their authority from the ideal qualities they were believed to possess. The king was the moral model, who personified the virtue of his people, and his country lived at peace and prospered because of his meritorious actions. In Sukhothai kingdom, according to the Inscription No-1 found in Sukhothai, Ramkhamhaeng was said to hear the petition of any subject who rang the bell at the palace gate to summon him, the king was revered as a father by his people. But the paternal aspects of kingship disappeared at Ayutthaya. The king was considered chakkraphat, the Sanskrit-Pali term for the chakravartin who through his adherence to the law made all the world revolve around him. As the Hindu god Shiva was "lord of the universe". However, according the codes, the king had ultimate duty as the protector of the people and the annihilator of evil guys, as the duties of the Gods Shiva and Vishnu.

The Thai king also became by analogy "lord of the land," (Pra Cao Phaendin) distinguished in his appearance and bearing from his subjects. According to the elaborate court etiquette, even a special language, Rachasap, was used to communicate with or about royalty. In Ayutthaya, the King was said to grant land to his subjects, from nobles to commoners, even monks and beggars, according to the rule of Sakna or Sakdina.

As *devaraja* (Sanskrit for "divine king"), the king ultimately came to be recognized as the earthly incarnation of Shiva and,or Vishnu, and became the sacred object of a politico-religious cult officiated over by a corps of royal Brahmans who were part of the Buddhist court retinue. In the Buddhist context, the *devaraja* was a bodhisattva (an enlightened being who, out of compassion, foregoes nirvana in order to aid others). The belief in divine kingship prevailed into the eighteenth century, although by that time its religious implications had limited impact. The French Abbe de Choisy, who came to Ayutthaya in 1685, wrote that, "the king has absolute power. He is truly the god of the Siamese: no-one dares to utter his name." Another 17th century writer, the Dutchman Van Vliet, remarked that the King of Siam was "honoured and worshipped by his subjects more than a god." Law and orders were issued by the King. For sometimes the King himself was also the highest judge who judged and punished important criminals such as ones who were traitors or rebels.

One of the numerous institutional innovations of King Trailokanat (1448-88) was to adopt the position of uparaja, translated as "viceroy" or "underking", usually held by the king's senior son or full brother, in an attempt to regularize the succession to the throne — a particularly difficult feat for a polygamous dynasty. In practice, there was inherent conflict between king and uparaja and frequent disputed successions.

Social and Political Development

The king stood at the apex of a highly stratified social and political hierarchy that extended throughout the society. In Ayutthayan society the basic unit of social organization was the village community composed of extended family households. Generally the elected headmen provided leadership for communal projects. Title to land resided with the headman, who held it in the name of the community, although peasant proprietors enjoyed the use of land as long as they cultivated it.

With ample reserves of land available for cultivation, the viability of the state depended on the acquisition and control of adequate manpower for farm labor and defense. The dramatic rise of Ayutthaya had entailed constant warfare and, as none of the parties in the region possessed a technological advantage, the outcome of battles was usually determined by the size of the armies. After each victorious campaign, Ayutthaya carried away a number of conquered people to its own territory, where they were assimilated and added to the labor force.

Every freeman had to be registered as a servant, or phrai, with the local lord, or nai, for military service and corvee labor on public works and on the land of the official to whom he was assigned. The phrai could also meet his labor obligation by paying a tax. If he found the forced labor under his nai repugnant, he could sell himself into slavery to a more attractive nai, who then paid a fee to the government in compensation for the loss of corvee labor. As much as one-third of the manpower supply into the nineteenth century was composed of phrai.

Wealth, status, and political influence were interrelated. The king allotted rice fields to governors, military commanders, and court officials in payment for their services to the crown, according to the 'sakdi na' system. The size of each official's allotment was determined by the number of persons he could command to work it. The amount of manpower a particular nai could command determined his status relative to others in the hierarchy and his wealth. At the apex of the hierarchy, the king, who was symbolically the realm's largest landholder, also commanded the services of the largest number of phrai, called phrai luang (royal servants), who paid taxes, served in the royal army, and worked on the crown lands. King Trailok established definite allotments of land and phrai for the royal officials at each rung in the hierarchy, thus determining the country's social structure until the introduction of salaries for government officials in the nineteenth century.

Outside this system to some extent were the Buddhist monkhood, or *sangha*, which all classes of Siamese men could join, and the Chinese. Buddhist monasteries (wats) became the centres of Siamese education and culture, while during this period the Chinese first began to settle in Siam, and soon began to establish control over the country's economic life: another long-standing social problem. The Chinese were not obliged to register for corvee duty, so they were free to move about the kingdom at will and engage in commerce. By the sixteenth century, the Chinese controlled Ayutthaya's internal trade and had found important places in the civil and military service. Most of these men took Thai wives because few women left China to accompany the men.

Ramathibodi I was responsible for the compilation of the Dharmashastra, a legal code based on Hindu sources and traditional Thai custom. The Dharmashastra remained a tool of Thai law until late in the 19th century. A bureaucracy based on a hierarchy of ranked and titled officials was introduced, and society was organised in a manner reminiscent of, though not as strict as, the Indian caste system.

The sixteenth century witnessed the rise of Burma, which, under an aggressive dynasty, had overrun Chiang Mai and Laos and made war on the Thai. In 1569 Burmese forces, joined by Thai rebels mostly royal family members of Siam, captured the city of Ayutthaya and carried off the whole royal family to Burma. Dhammaraja (1569-90), a Thai governor who had aided the Burmese, was installed as vassal king at

Ayutthaya. Thai independence was restored by his son, King Naresuan (1590- 1605), who turned on the Burmese and by 1600 had driven them from the country.

Determined to prevent another treason like his father's, Naresuan set about unifying the country's administration directly under the royal court at Ayutthaya. He ended the practice of nominating royal princes to govern Ayutthaya's provinces, assigning instead court officials who were expected to execute policies handed down by the king. Thereafter royal princes were confined to the capital. Their power struggles continued, but at court under the king's watchful eye.

In order to ensure his control over the new class of governors, Naresuan decreed that all freemen subject to phrai service had become phrai luang, bound directly to the king, who distributed the use of their services to his officials. This measure gave the king a theoretical monopoly on all manpower, and the idea developed that since the king owned the services of all the people, he also possessed all the land. Ministerial offices and governorships—and the sakdi na that went with them—were usually inherited positions dominated by a few families often connected to the king by marriage. Indeed, marriage was frequently used by Thai kings to cement alliances between themselves and powerful families, a custom prevailing through the nineteenth century. As a result of this policy, the king's wives usually numbered in the dozens.

Even with Naresuan's reforms, the effectiveness of the royal government over the next 150 years should not be overestimated. Royal power outside the crown lands—although in theory absolute- -was in practice limited by the looseness of the civil administration. The influence of central government ministers was not extensive beyond the capital until the late nineteenth century.

Economic Development

The Thais never lacked a rich food supply. Peasants planted rice for their own consumption and to pay taxes. Whatever remained was used to support religious institutions. From the thirteenth to the fifteenth century, however, a remarkable transformation took place in Thai rice cultivation. In the highlands, where rainfall had to be supplemented by a system of irrigation that controlled the water level in flooded paddies, the Thais sowed the glutinous rice that is still the staple in the geographical regions of the North and Northeast. But in the floodplain of the Chao Phraya, farmers turned to a different variety of rice—the so-called floating rice, a slender, nonglutinous grain introduced from Bengal—that would grow fast enough to keep pace with the rise of the water level in the lowland fields.

The new strain grew easily and abundantly, producing a surplus that could be sold cheaply abroad. Ayutthaya, situated at the southern extremity of the floodplain, thus became the hub of economic activity. Under royal patronage, corvee labor dug canals on which rice was brought from the fields to the king's ships for export to China. In the process, the Chao Phraya Delta—mud flats between the sea and firm land hitherto considered unsuitable for habitation—was reclaimed and placed under cultivation.

Contacts with the West

In 1511 Ayutthaya received a diplomatic mission from the Portuguese, who earlier that year had conquered Malacca. These were probably the first Europeans to visit the country. Five years after that initial contact, Ayutthaya and Portugal concluded a treaty granting the Portuguese permission to trade in the kingdom. A similar treaty in 1592 gave the Dutch a privileged position in the rice trade.

Foreigners were cordially welcomed at the court of Narai (1657–1688), a ruler with a cosmopolitan outlook who was nonetheless wary of outside influence. Important commercial ties were forged with Japan. Dutch and English trading companies were allowed to establish factories, and Thai diplomatic missions were sent to Paris and The Hague. By maintaining all these ties, the Thai court skillfully played off the Dutch against the English and the French, avoiding the excessive influence of a single power.

In 1664, however, the Dutch used force to exact a treaty granting them extraterritorial rights as well as freer access to trade. At the urging of his foreign minister, the Greek adventurer Constantine Phaulkon, Narai turned to France for assistance. French engineers constructed fortifications for the Thai and built a new palace at Lopburi for Narai. In addition, French missionaries engaged in education and medicine and brought the first printing press into the country. Louis XIV's personal interest was aroused by reports from missionaries suggesting that Narai might be converted to Christianity.

The French presence encouraged by Phaulkon, however, stirred the resentment and suspicions of the Thai nobles and Buddhist clergy. When word spread that Narai was dying, a general, Phetracha, killed the designated heir, a Christian, and had Phaulkon put to death along with a number of missionaries. The arrival of English warships provoked a massacre of more Europeans. Phetracha (reigned 1688-93) seized the throne, expelled the remaining foreigners. Some studies said Ayutthaya began the period of alienation from the western traders, while welcoming more Chinese merchants. But some recent studies argue that, due to wars and conflicts in Europe in the mid-eighteenth century, European merchants reduced their activities in the East. However it was apparent that the Dutch East Indies Company or VOC was still running business in Ayutthaya despite political difficulty.

During the early 20th Century, Thailand, after learning lessons from Burma–a militarily stronger neighbour that failed to protect itself from western powerhouse

Britain in 1885–mostly used flexible and significantly compromising approach towards its counterparts including numerous western nations and Japan.

The Final Phase V

After a bloody period of dynastic struggle, Ayutthaya entered into what has been called its golden age, a relatively peaceful episode in the second quarter of the eighteenth century when art, literature, and learning flourished. There were foreign wars. The Ayutthaya fought with Nguyen Lords (Vietnamese rulers of South Vietnam) for control of Cambodia starting around 1715. But a greater threat came from Burma, where the new Alaungpaya dynasty had subdued the Shan states.

In 1765 Thai territory was invaded by two Burmese armies that converged on Ayutthaya. The only notable example of successful resistance to these forces was found at the village of Bang Rajan. After a lengthy siege, the city capitulated and was burned in 1767. Ayutthaya's art treasures, the libraries containing its literature, and the archives housing its historic records were almost totally destroyed, and Burmese brought the Ayutthaya Kingdom to ruin.

The country was reduced to chaos. Provinces were proclaimed independent states under military leaders, rogue monks, and cadet members of the royal family. The Thais were saved from Burmese subjugation, however, by an opportune Chinese invasion of Burma and by the leadership of a Thai military commander, Phraya Taksin.

All that remains of the old city are some impressive ruins of the royal palace. King Taksin established a capital at Thonburi, across the Chao Phraya from the present capital, Bangkok. The ruins of the historic city of Ayutthaya and "associated historic towns" in the Ayutthaya historical park have been listed by the UNESCO as World Heritage Sites. The city of Ayutthaya was refounded near the old city, and is now capital of the Ayutthaya province.

History from 1768 to 1932

From 1768 to 1932 the area of modern Thailand was dominated by Siam, an absolute monarchy with capitals briefly at Thonburi and later at Rattanakosin, both in modern-day Bangkok. The first half of this period was a time of consolidation of the kingdom's power, and was punctuated by periodic conflicts with Burma, Vietnam and Laos. The later period was one of engagement with the colonial powers of Britain and France, in which Siam managed to be the only southeast Asian country not to be colonised by a European country. Internally the kingdom developed into a centralised nation state with borders defined by its interaction with the Western powers. Significant economic and social progress was made, with an increase in foreign trade, the abolition of slavery and the expansion of education to the emerging middle class. However, there was no substantial political reform until the monarchy was overthrown in a military coup in 1932.

Thonburi Period

In 1767, after dominating southeast Asia for almost 400 years, the Ayutthaya kingdom was brought down by invading Burmese armies, its capital burned, and its territory occupied by the invaders.

Despite its complete defeat and occupation by Burma, Siam made a rapid recovery. The resistance to Burmese rule was led by a noble of Chinese descent, Taksin, a capable military leader. Initially based at Chanthaburi in the south-east, within a year he had defeated the Burmese occupation army and re-established a Siamese state with its capital at Thonburi on the west bank of the Chao Phraya, 20 km from the sea. In 1768 he was crowned as King Taksin (now officially known as Taksin the Great). He rapidly re-united the central Thai heartlands under his rule, and in 1769 he also occupied western Cambodia. He then marched south and re-established Siamese rule over the Malay Peninsula as far south as Penang and Terengganu. Having secured his base in Siam, Taksin attacked the Burmese in the north in 1774 and captured Chiang Mai in 1776, permanently uniting Siam and Lanna. Taksin's leading general in this campaign was Thong Duang, known by the title Chaophraya Chakri. In 1778 Chakri led a Siamese army which captured Vientiane and re-established Siamese domination over Laos.

Despite these successes, by 1779 Taksin was in political trouble at home. He seems to have developed a religious mania, alienating the powerful Buddhist monkhood by claiming to be a *sotapanna* or divine figure. He also attacked the Chinese merchant class, and foreign observers began to speculate that he would soon be overthrown. In 1782 Taksin sent his armies under Chakri to invade Cambodia, but while they were away a rebellion broke out in the area around the capital. The rebels, who had wide popular support, offered the throne to Chakri. Chakri marched back from Cambodia and deposed Taksin, who was secretly executed shortly after. Chakri ruled under the name Ramathibodi (he was posthumously given the name Phutthayotfa Chulalok), but is now generally known as King Rama I, first king of the Chakri dynasty. One of his first decisions was to move the capital across the river to the village of Bang Makok (meaning "place of olive plums"), which soon became the city of Bangkok. The new capital was located on the island of Rattanakosin, protected from attack by the river to the west and by a series of canals to the north, east and south. Siam thus acquired both its current dynasty and its current capital.

Bangkok Period

Rama I

Rama I restored most of the social and political system of the Ayutthaya kingdom, promulgating new law codes, reinstating court ceremonies and imposing discipline on the Buddhist monkhood. His government was carried out by six great ministries headed by royal princes. Four of these administered particular territories: the Kalahom the south; the Mahatthai the north and east; the Phrakhlang the area immediately south of the capital; and the Krommueang the area around Bangkok. The other two were the ministry of lands (Krom Na) and the ministry of the royal court (Krom Wang). The army was controlled by the King's deputy and brother, the Uparat. The Burmese, seeing the disorder accompanying the overthrow of Taksin, invaded Siam again in 1785. Rama allowed them to occupy both the north and the south, but the Uparat led the Siamese army into western Siam and defeated the Burmese in a battle near Kanchanaburi. This was the last major Burmese invasion of Siam, although as late as 1802 Burmese forces had to be driven out of Lanna. In 1792 the Siamese occupied Luang Prabang and brought most of Laos under indirect Siamese rule. Cambodia was also effectively ruled by Siam. By the time of his death in 1809 Rama I had created a Siamese Empire dominating an area considerably larger than modern Thailand.

Invasion of Vietnam

In 1776 when Tay-Son rebel forces captured Gia Dinh they executed the entire Nguyen royal family and much of the local population. Nguyen Anh, the only member of the Nguyen family still alive, managed to escape across the river to Siam. While in exile Nguyen Anh wished to retake Gia Dinh and push the Tay-Son rebels out. He convinced the neutral King Buddha Yodfa Chulaloke of Siam to provide him with support troops and a small invasion force.

In mid-1784 Nguyen Anh, with 50,000 Siamese troops and 300 ships, moved through Cambodia, then East of Tonle Sap (Toh Lay Sap in Thai) and penetrated the recently annexed provinces of Annam. 20,000 Siamese troops reached Kien Giang and another 30,000 landed in Chap Lap, as the Siamese advanced towards Can Tho. Later that year the Siamese captured the former Cambodian province of Gia Dinh where, it was claimed, they committed atrocities against the population of Viet settlers.

NguyÅn HuÇ anticipating a move from the Siamese, had secretly positioned his infantry along the Mekong River (Mae Nam Khong), and on some islands in the middle, facing other troops on the northern banks with naval reinforcements on both sides of the infantry positions.

On the morning of January 19 Nguyen Hue sent a small naval force, under a banner of truce, to lure the Siamese into his trap. After so many victories, the Siamese army and naval forces were confident of a surrender. So, they went to the parley, unaware of the trap. Nguyen Hue's troops dashed into the Siamese formation, slaughtered the unarmed emissaries and turned on the unprepared troops. The battle ended with a near annihilation of the Siamese force. All the ships of the Siamese navy were destroyed and only 1,000 of the original expedition survived to escape back across the river into Siam.

Rama II

The reign of Rama I's son Phuttaloetla Naphalai (now known as King Rama II) was relatively uneventful. The Chakri family now controlled all branches of Siamese government — since Rama I had 42 children, his brother the Uparat had 43 and Rama II had 73, there was no shortage of royal princes to staff the bureaucracy, the army, the senior monkhood and the provincial governments. (Most of these were the children of concubines and thus not eligible to inherit the throne.) There was a confrontation with Vietnam, now becoming a major power in the region, over control of Cambodia in 1813, ending with the *status quo* restored. But during Rama II's reign western influences again began to be felt in Siam. In 1785 the British occupied Penang, and in 1819 they founded Singapore. Soon the British displaced the Dutch and Portuguese as the main western economic and political influence in Siam. The British objected to the Siamese economic system, in which trading monopolies were held by royal princes and businesses were subject to arbitrary taxation. In 1821 the government of British India sent a mission to demand that Siam lift restrictions on free trade — the first sign of an issue which was to dominate 19th century Siamese politics.

Rama III

Rama II died in 1824, and was peacefully succeeded by his son Chetsadabodin, who reigned as King Nangklao, now known as Rama III. Rama II's younger son, Mongkut, was ordered to become a monk to remove him from politics.

In 1825 the British sent another mission to Bangkok. They had by now annexed southern Burma and were thus Siam's neighbours to the west, and they were also extending their control over Malaya. The King was reluctant to give in to British demands, but his advisors warned him that Siam would meet the same fate as Burma unless the British were accommodated. In 1826, therefore, Siam concluded its first commercial treaty with a western power. Under the treaty, Siam agreed to establish a uniform taxation system, to reduce taxes on foreign trade and to abolish some of the royal monopolies. As a result, Siam's trade increased rapidly, many more foreigners settled in Bangkok, and western cultural influences began to spread. The kingdom became wealthier and its army better armed.

A Lao rebellion led by Anouvong was defeated in 1827, following which Siam destroyed Vientiane, carried out massive forced population transfers from Laos to the more securely held area of Isan, and divided the Lao mueang into smaller units to prevent another uprising. In 1842–1845 Siam waged a successful war with Vietnam, which tightened Siamese rule over Cambodia. Rama III's most visible legacy in Bangkok is the Wat Pho temple complex, which he enlarged and endowed with new temples.

Rama III regarded his brother Mongkut as his heir, although as a monk Mongkut could not openly assume this role. He used his long sojourn as a monk to acquire a western education from French and American missionaries, one of the first Siamese to do so. He learned English and Latin, and studied science and mathematics. The missionaries no doubt hoped to convert him to Christianity, but in fact he was a strict Buddhist and a Siamese nationalist. He intended using this western knowledge to strengthen and modernise Siam when he came to the throne, which he did in 1851. By the 1840s it was obvious that Siamese independence was in danger from the colonial powers: this was shown dramatically by the British Opium Wars with China in 1839–1842. In 1850 the British and Americans sent missions to Bangkok demanding the end of all restrictions on trade, the establishment of a western-style government and immunity for their citizens from Siamese law (extraterritoriality). Rama III's government refused these demands, leaving his successor with a dangerous situation. Rama III reportedly said on his deathbed: "We will have no more wars with Burma and Vietnam. We will have them only with the West."

Mongkut

Mongkut came to the throne as Rama IV in 1851, determined to save Siam from colonial domination by forcing modernisation on his reluctant subjects. But although he was in theory an absolute monarch, his power was limited. Having been a monk for 27 years, he lacked a base among the powerful royal princes, and did not have a modern state apparatus to carry out his wishes. His first attempts at reform, to establish a modern system of administration and to improve the status of debt-slaves and women, were frustrated. Rama IV thus came to welcome western pressure on Siam. This came in 1855 in the form of a mission led by the Governor of Hong Kong, Sir John Bowring, who arrived in Bangkok with demands for immediate changes, backed by the threat of force. The King readily agreed to his demand for a new treaty, called the Bowring Treaty, which restricted import duties to 3%, abolished royal trade monopolies, and granted extraterritoriality to British subjects. Other western powers soon demanded and got similar concessions.

The king soon came to consider that the real threat to Siam came from the French, not the British. The British were interested in commercial advantage, the French in building a colonial empire. They occupied Saigon in 1859, and 1867 established a protectorate over southern Vietnam and eastern Cambodia. Rama IV hoped that the British would defend Siam if he gave them the economic concessions they demanded. In the next reign this would prove to be an illusion, but it is true that the British saw Siam as a useful buffer state between British Burma and French Indochina.

Chulalongkorn

Rama IV died in 1868, and was succeeded by his 15-year-old son Chulalongkorn, who reigned as Rama V and is now known as Rama the Great. Rama V was the first Siamese king to have a full western education, having been taught by a British governess, Anna Leonowens–whose place in Siamese history has been fictionalised as *The King and I*. At first Rama V's reign was dominated by the conservative regent, Chaophraya Si Suriyawongse, but when the king came of age in 1873 he soon took control. He created a Privy Council and a Council of State, a formal court system and budget office. He announced that slavery would be gradually abolished and debt-bondage restricted.

At first the princes and other conservatives successfully resisted the king's reform agenda, but as the older generation was replaced by younger and western-educated princes, resistance faded. The king could always argue that the only alternative was foreign rule. He found powerful allies in his brothers Prince Chakkraphat, whom he made finance minister, Prince Damrong, who organized interior government and education, and his brother-in-law Prince Devrawongse, foreign minister for 38 years. In 1887 Devrawonge visited Europe to study government systems. On his recommendation the king established Cabinet government, an audit office and an education department. The semi-autonomous status of Chiang Mai was ended and the army was reorganised and modernised.

In 1893 the French authorities in Indochina used a minor border dispute to provoke a crisis. French gunboats appeared at Bangkok, and demanded the cession of Lao territories east of the Mekong. The King appealed to the British, but the British minister told the King to settle on whatever terms he could get, and he had no choice but to comply. Britain's only gesture was an agreement with France guaranteeing the integrity of the rest of Siam. In exchange, Siam had to give up its claim to the Tai-speaking Shan region of north-eastern Burma to the British.

The French, however, continued to pressure Siam, and in 1906–1907 they manufactured another crisis. This time Siam had to concede French control of territory on the west bank of the Mekong opposite Luang Prabang and around Champasak in southern Laos, as well as western Cambodia. The British interceded to prevent more French bullying of Siam, but their price, in 1909 was the acceptance of British sovereignty over of Kedah, Kelantan, Perlis and Terengganu under Anglo-Siamese Treaty of 1909. All of these "lost territories" were on the fringes of the Siamese sphere of influence and had never been securely under their control, but being compelled to abandon all claim to them was a substantial humiliation to both king and country (historian David K. Wyatt describes Chulalongkorn as "broken in spirit and health" following the 1893 crisis). In the early 20th century these crises were adopted by the increasingly nationalist government as symbols of the need for the country to assert itself against the West and its neighbours.

Meanwhile, reform continued apace transforming an absolute monarchy based on relationships of power into a modern, centralised nation state. The process was increasingly under the control of Rama V's sons, who were all educated in Europe. Railways and telegraph lines united the previously remote and semi-autonomous provinces. The currency was tied to the gold standard and a modern system of taxation replaced the arbitrary exactions and labour service of the past. The biggest problem was the shortage of trained civil servants, and many foreigners had to be employed until new schools could be built and Siamese graduates produced. By 1910, when the King died, Siam had become at least a semi-modern country, and continued to escape colonial rule.

Vajiravudh and the Ascent of Elite Nationalism

One of Rama V's reforms was to introduce a western-style law of royal succession, so in 1910 he was peacefully succeeded by his son Vajiravudh, who reigned as Rama VI. He had been educated at Sandhurst military academy and at Oxford, and was a thoroughly anglicised Edwardian gentleman. Indeed one of Siam's problems was the widening gap between the westernised royal family and upper aristocracy and the rest of the country. It took another 20 years for western education to extend to the rest of the bureaucracy and the army: a potential source of conflict.

There had been no political reform under Rama V: the king was still an absolute monarch, who acted as his own prime minister and staffed all the agencies of the state with his own relatives. Vajiravudh, with his British education, knew that the rest of the nation could not be excluded from government for ever, but he was no democrat. He applied his observation of the success of the British monarchy, appearing more in public and instituting more royal ceremonies. But he also carried on his father's modernisation programme. Polygamy was abolished, primary education made compulsory, and in 1916 higher education came to Siam with the founding of Chulalongkorn University, which in time became the seedbed of a new Siamese intelligentsia.

Another solution he found was to establish the Wild Tiger Corps, a paramilitary organisation of Siamese citizens of good character united to further the nation's cause. The King spent much time on the development of the movement as he saw it as an opportunity to create a bond between himself and loyal citizens; a volunteer corps willing to make sacrifices for the king and the nation.

At first the Wild Tigers were drawn from the king's personal entourage (it is likely that many joined in order to gain favour with Vajiravhud), but a genuine widespread enthusiasm rapidly arose.

Of the movement, a German observer wrote in September 1911:

This is a troop of volunteers in black uniform, drilled in a more or less military fashion, but without weapons. The British Scouts are apparently the paradigm for the Tiger Corps. In the whole country, at the most far-away places, units of this corps are being set up. One would hardly recognise the quiet and phlegmatic Siamese.

Vajiravudh's style of government differed greatly from that of his father. In the beginning of the sixth reign, the king continued to use his father's team and there was no sudden break in the daily routine of government. Much of the running of daily affairs was therefore in the hands of experienced and competent men. To them and their staff Siam owed many progressive steps, such as the development of a national plan for the education of the whole populance, the setting up of clinics where free vaccination was given against smallpox, and the continuing expansion of railways.

However, senior posts were gradually filled with one of the King's coterie when a vacancy occurred through death, retirement, or resignation. By 1915, half the cabinet consisted of new faces. Most notable was Prince Damrong's absence. He resigned from his post as Minister of the Interior officially because of ill health, but in actuality because of friction between himself and the king.

In 1917 Siam declared war on Germany, mainly to gain favour with the British and the French. Siam's token participation in World War I gained it a seat at the Versailles Peace Conference, and Foreign Minister Devrawongse used this opportunity to argue for the repeal of the 19th century treaties and the restoration of full Siamese sovereignty. The United States obliged in 1920, while France and Britain delayed until 1925. This victory gained the king some popularity, but it was soon undercut by discontent over other issues, such as his extravagance, which became more noticeable when a sharp postwar recession hit Siam in 1919. There was also the fact that the king had no son; he obviously preferred the company of men to women (a matter which of itself did not much concern Siamese opinion, but which did undermine the stability of the monarchy).

Thus when Rama VI died suddenly in 1925, aged only 44, the monarchy was already in a weakened state. He was succeeded by his younger brother Prajadhipok.

Prajadhipok

Unprepared for his new responsibilities, all Prajadhipok had in his favour was a lively intelligence, a certain diplomacy in his dealings with others, a modesty and industrious willingness to learn, and the somewhat tarnished, but still potent, magic of the crown.

Unlike his predecessor, the king diligently read virtually all state papers that came his way, from ministerial submissions to petitions by citizens. Within half a year only three of Vajiravhud's twelve ministers stayed on, the rest having been replaced by members of the royal family. On the one hand, these appointments brought back men of talent and experience, on the other, it signalled a return to royal oligarchy. The King obviously wanted to demonstrate a clear break with the discredited sixth reign, and the choice of men to fill the top positions appeared to be guided largely be a wish to restore a Chulalongkorn-type government.

The initial legacy that Prajadhipok received from his elder brother were problems of the sort that had become chronic in the Sixth Reign. The most urgent of these was the economy: the finances of the state were in chaos, the budget heavily in deficit, and the royal accounts an accountant's nightmare of debts and questionable transactions. That the rest of the world was in deep economic depression following World War I did not help the situation either.

Virtually the first act of Prajadipok as king entailed an institutional innovation intended to restore confidence in the monarchy and government, the creation of the Supreme Council of the State. This privy council was made up of a number of experienced and extremely competent members of the royal family, including the long time Minister of the Interior (and Chulalongkorn's right hand man) Prince Damrong. Gradually these princes arrogated increasing power by monopolising all the main ministerial positions. Many of them felt it their duty to make amends for the mistakes of the previous reign, but it was not generally appreciated.

With the help of this council, the king managed to restore stability to the economy, although at a price of making a significant amount of the civil servants redundant and cutting the salary of those that remained. This was obviously unpopular among the officials, and was one of the trigger events for the coup of 1932.

Prajadhipok then turned his attention to the question of future politics in Siam. Inspired by the British example, the King wanted to allow the common people to have a say in the country's affair by the creation of a parliament. A proposed constitution was ordered to be drafted, but the King's wishes were rejected, perhaps wisely, by his advisers, who felt that the population was not yet ready for democracy.

In 1932, with the country deep in depression, the Supreme Council opted to introduce cuts in official spending, including the military budget. The King foresaw that these policies might create discontent, especially in the army, and he therefore convened a special meeting of officials to explain why the cuts were necessary. In his addressed he stated the following:

I myself know nothing at all about finances, and all I can do is listen to the opinions of others and choose the best... If I have made a mistake, I really deserve to be excused by the people of Siam.

No previous monarch of Siam had ever spoken in such terms. Many interpreted the speech not as Prajadhipok apparently intended, namely as a frank appeal for understanding and cooperation. They saw it as a sign of his weakness and evidence that a system which perpetuated the rule of fallible autocrats should be abolished. Serious political disturbances were threatened in the capital, and in April the king agreed to introduce a constitution under which he would share power with a prime minister. This was not enough for the radical elements in the army, however. On June 24, 1932, while the king was holidaying at the seaside, the Bangkok garrison mutinied and seized power, led by a group of 49 officers known as "the Promoters." Thus ended 150 years of Siamese absolute monarchy.

Military Rule

The Siamese coup d'état of 1932 transformed the Government of Thailand from an absolute to a constitutional monarchy. King Prajadhipok initially accepted this change but later surrendered the throne to his ten year old nephew, Ananda Mahidol. Upon his abdication, King Prajadhipok said that the duty of a ruler was to reign for the good of the whole people, not for a select few. King Ananda Mahidol (Rama VIII) died in 1946 under somewhat mysterious circumstances, the official explanation being that he shot himself by accident while cleaning his gun. He was succeeded by his brother Bhumibol Adulyadej, the longest reigning king of Thailand, and very popular with the Thais. Although nominally a constitutional monarchy, Thailand was ruled by a series of military governments, most prominently led by Luang Phibunsongkhram and Sarit Dhanarajata, interspersed with brief periods of democracy.

In early January 1941, Thailand invaded French Indochina, beginning the French-Thai War. The Thais, better equipped and outnumbering the French forces, easily reclaiming Laos. The French decisively won the naval Battle of Koh Chang.

The Japanese mediated the conflict, and a general armistice was declared on January

28. On May 9 a peace treaty was signed in Tokyo, with the French being coerced by the Japanese into relinquishing its hold on the disputed territories.

On December 8, 1941, a few hours after the attack on Pearl Harbor, Japan demanded the right to move troops across Thailand to the Malayan frontier. Japan invaded the country and engaged the Thai army for six to eight hours before Phibunsongkhram ordered an armistice. Shortly thereafter Japan was granted free passage, and on December 21, 1941, Thailand and Japan signed a military alliance with a secret protocol wherein Tokyo agreed to help Thailand regain territories lost to the British and French (i.e. the Shan States of Burma, Malaya, Singapore, & part of Yunnan, plus Laos & Cambodia) Subsequently, Thailand undertook to 'assist' Japan in her war against the Allies. NOTE: Japan's distrust of Thailand extended to the point of rearming their 'Allies' with controlled munitions, including the famous Siamese Mauser, which was manufactured in an unusual caliber. It should be remembered that the Seri Thai operated freely, often with support from members of the Royal family (Prince Chula Chakrabongse) and members of the government and that the Thai Army was considered untrustworthy by the Japanese.

After the end of World War II, Prime Minister Pridi Phanomyong agreed to return the captured territories to France, as a condition for admission to the newly created United Nations.

After Japan's defeat in 1945, with the help of a group of Thais known as Seri Thai who were supported by the United States, Thailand was treated as a defeated country by the British and French, although American support mitigated the Allied terms. Thailand was not occupied by the Allies, but it was forced to return the territory it had regained to the British and the French. In the postwar period Thailand enjoyed close relations with the United States, which it saw as a protector from the communist revolutions in neighboring countries.

Communist guerillas existed in country from early 60's up to 1987, but never posed a serious threat to the state, but at the peak of movement they counted almost 12,000 full-time fighters.

Recently, Thailand also has been an active member in the regional Association of Southeast Asian Nations (ASEAN), especially after democratic rule was restored in 1992.

Democracy

Post-1973 has been marked by a struggle to define the political contours of the state. It was won by the King and General Prem Tinsulanonda, who favored a democratic constitutional order.

The post-1973 years have seen a difficult and sometimes bloody transition from military to civilian rule, with several reversals along the way. The revolution of 1973 inaugurated a brief, unstable period of democracy, with military rule being reimposed after the 6 October 1976 Massacre. For most of the 1980s, Thailand was ruled by Prem, a democratically-inclined strongman who restored parliamentary politics. Thereafter the country remained a democracy apart from a brief period of military rule from 1991 to 1992. The populist Thai Rak Thai party, led by prime minister Thaksin Shinawatra, came to power in 2001.

On September 19, 2006, with the prime minister in New York for a meeting of the UN, Army Commander-in-Chief Lieutenant General Sonthi Boonyaratglin launched a successful **coup d'état**. A general election on 23 December 2007 restored a civilian government, lead by Samak Sundaravej of the People Power Party.

HISTORY OF SINGAPORE

Singapore rose in importance during the 14th century under the rule of Srivijayan prince Parameswara and became an important port until it was destroyed by Portuguese raiders in 1613. The modern history of Singapore began in 1819 when Englishman Sir Thomas Stamford Raffles established a British port on the island. Under British colonial rule, it grew in importance as a centre for both the India-China trade and the entrepôt trade in Southeast Asia, rapidly becoming a major port city.

During World War II, Singapore was conquered and occupied by the Japanese Empire from 1942 to 1945. When the war ended, Singapore reverted to British control, with increasing levels of self-government being granted, culminating in Singapore's merger with the Federation of Malaya to form Malaysia in 1963. However, social unrest and disputes between Singapore's ruling People's Action Party and Malaysia's Alliance Party resulted in Singapore's expulsion from Malaysia. Singapore became an independent republic on 9 August 1965.

Facing severe unemployment and a housing crisis, Singapore embarked on a modernisation programme that focused on establishing a manufacturing industry, developing large public housing estates and investing heavily on public education. Since independence, Singapore's economy has grown by an average of nine percent each year. By the 1990s, the country has become one of the world's most prosperous nations, with a highly-developed free market economy, strong international trading links, and the highest per capita gross domestic product in Asia outside of Japan.

The earliest written record of Singapore was a Chinese account from the third century, describing the island of *Pu Luo Chung*. This itself is transliterated from the Malay name *"Pulau Ujong"*, or "island at the end" (of the Malay peninsula). The quasi-mythological Sejarah Melayu (*Malay Annals*) contains a tale of a prince of Srivijaya, Sri Tri Buana (also known as Sang Nila Utama), who landed on the island during the 13th century. When he saw a lion, the prince took this as an auspicious sign and founded a settlement called Singapura, which means "Lion City" in Sanskrit.

In 1320, the Mongol Empire sent a trade mission to a place called *Long Ya Men* (or *Dragon's Tooth Strait*), which is believed to be Keppel Harbour, at the southern part of the island. The Chinese traveler Wang Dayuan, visiting the island around 1330, described a small settlement called Dan Ma Xi with Malay and Chinese residents. The Nagarakretagama, a Javanese epic poem written in 1365, also referred to a settlement on the island called Temasek (*Sea Town*). Recent excavations in Fort Canning found evidences indicating that Singapore was an important port in the 14th century.

In the 1390s, Srivijayan prince Parameswara fled to Temasek after being deposed by the Majapahit Empire. He ruled the island for several years, before being forced to Melaka where he founded the Sultanate of Malacca. Singapore became an important trading port of the Malacca Sultanate and later the Sultanate of Johor. In 1613, Portuguese raiders burnt down the settlement at the mouth of Singapore River and the island sank into obscurity.

Founding of Modern Singapore (1819)

Between the 16th and 19th centuries, the Malay archipelago was gradually taken over by the European colonial powers, beginning with the arrival of the Portuguese at Malacca in 1509. The early dominance of the Portuguese was challenged during the 17th century by the Dutch, who came to control most of the ports in the region. The Dutch established a monopoly over trade within the archipelago, particularly in spices, then the region's most important product. Other colonial powers, including the British, were limited to a relatively minor presence.

In 1818, Sir Thomas Stamford Raffles was appointed as the Lieutenant Governor of the British colony at Bencoolen. He was determined that British should replace the Dutch as the dominant power in the archipelago, since the trade route between China and British India, which had become vitally important with the institution of the opium trade with China, passed through the archipelago. The Dutch had been stifling British trade in the region by prohibiting the British from operating in Dutch-controlled ports or by subjecting them with high tariff. Raffles hoped to challenge the Dutch by establishing a new port along the Straits of Malacca, the main ship passageway for the India-China trade. He convinced Lord Hastings, the Governor-General of India and his superior at the British East India Company, to fund an expedition to seek a new British base in the region.

Raffles arrived in Singapore on 29 January 1819 and soon recognised the island as a natural choice for the new port. It lay at the southern tip of the Malay peninsula, near the Straits of Malacca, and possessed a natural deep harbour, fresh water supplies, and timber for repairing ships. Raffles found a small Malay settlement, with a population of a few hundreds, at the mouth of the Singapore River, headed by Temenggong Abdu'r Rahman. The island was nominally ruled by the Sultan of Johor, Tengku Rahman, who was controlled by the Dutch and the Bugis. However, the Sultanate was weakened by factional division and Temenggong Abdu'r Rahman and his officials were loyal to Tengku Rahman's elder brother Tengku Hussein (or Tengku Long) who was living in exile in Riau. With the Temenggong's help, Raffles managed to smuggle Hussein back into Singapore. He offered to recognise Hussein as the rightful Sultan of Johor and provide him with a yearly payment; in return, Hussein would grant the British the right to establish a trading post on Singapore. A formal treaty was signed on 6 February 1819 and modern Singapore was born.

Early Growth (1819–1826)

Raffles returned to Bencoolen soon after the signing of the treaty and left Major William Farquhar in charge of the new settlement, with some artillery and a small regiment of Indian soldiers. Establishing a trading port from scratch was a daunting endeavour. Farquhar's administration was fairly funded and was prohibited from collecting port duties to raise revenue as Raffles had decided that Singapore would be a free port. Despite these difficulties, the new colony grew rapidly. As news of the free port spread across the archipelago, Bugis, Peranakan Chinese, and Arab traders flocked to the island, seeking to circumvent the Dutch trade restrictions. During the starting year of operation, $400,000 (Spanish dollars) worth of trade passed through Singapore. By 1821, the island's population had gone up to around 5,000, and the trade volume was $8 million. The population reached the 10,000 mark in 1825, and with a trade volume of $22 million, Singapore surpassed the long-established port of Penang.

Raffles returned to Singapore in 1822 and became critical of many of Farquhar's decisions, despite Farquhar's success in leading the settlement through its difficult early years. In order to generate much-needed revenue, Farquhar had resorted to selling licenses for gambling and the sale of opium, which Raffles saw as social evils. Shocked at the disarray of the colony, Raffles set about drafting a set of new policies for the settlement. He also organised Singapore into functional and ethnic subdivisions under the *Raffles Plan of Singapore*. Today, remnants of this organisation can still be found in the ethnic neighbourhoods.

On 7 June 1823, Raffles signed a second treaty with the Sultan and Temenggong, which extended British possession to most of the island. The Sultan and Temenggong traded most of their administrative rights of the island, including the collection of port taxes for lifelong monthly payments of $1500 and $800 respectively. This agreement brought the island under the British law, with the provision that it would take into account Malay customs, traditions and religion. Raffles replaced Farquhar with John Crawfurd, an efficient and frugal administrator, as the new governor. In October 1823, Raffles departed for Britain and would never return to Singapore as he died in 1826, at the age of 44.

The Straits Settlements (1826–1867)

The establishment of a British outpost in Singapore was initially in doubt as the Dutch government soon protested to Britain for violating their sphere of influence. But as Singapore rapidly emerged as an important trading post, Britain consolidated its claim on the island. The status of Singapore as a British possession was cemented by the Anglo-Dutch Treaty of 1824, which carved up the Malay archipelago between the two colonial powers with the area north of the Straits of Malacca, including Singapore, falling under Britain's sphere of influence. In 1826, Singapore was grouped together with Penang and Malacca to form the Straits Settlements, administrated by the British East India Company. In 1830, the Straits Settlements became a *residency*, or subdivision, of the Presidency of Bengal in British India.

During the subsequent decades, Singapore grew to become an important port in the region. Its success was due to several reasons including the opening of market in China, the advent of ocean-going steamships, and the production of rubber and tin in Malaya. Its status as a free port provided crucial advantage over other colonial port cities in Batavia (Jakarta) and Manila where tariffs were levied, and it drew many Chinese, Malay, Indian, and Arab traders operating in South-East Asia to Singapore. The later opening of the Suez Canal in 1869 would further boost trade in Singapore. By 1880, over 1.5 million tons of goods were passing through Singapore each year, with around 80% of the cargo transported by steamships. The main commercial activity was entrepôt trade which flourished under no taxation and little restriction. Many merchant houses were set up in Singapore mainly by European trading firms, but also by Jewish, Chinese, Arab, Armenian, American and Indian merchants. There were also many Chinese middlemen who handled most of the trade between the European and Asian merchants.

By 1827, the Chinese became the largest ethnic group in Singapore. They consisted of Peranakans, who were descendants of early Chinese settlers, and Chinese coolies who flocked to Singapore to escape the economic hardship in southern China due to the Opium Wars. Many arrived in Singapore as impoverished indentured labourers and they were predominantly males. The Malays were the second largest ethnic group until the 1860s and they worked as fishermen, craftsmen, or as wage earners while continued to live mostly in kampungs. By 1860, the Indians became the second largest ethnic group. They consisted of unskilled labourers, traders, and convicts who were sent to carry out public works projects such as clearing jungles and laying out roads. There were also Indian Sepoy troops garrisoned at Singapore by the British.

Despite Singapore's growing importance, the administration governing the island was understaffed, ineffectual and were unconcerned with the welfare of the populace. Administrators were usually posted from India and were unfamiliar with local culture and languages. While the population had quadrupled during 1830 to 1867, the size of the civil service in Singapore had remained unchanged. Most people had no access to public health services and diseases such as cholera and smallpox caused severe health problem, especially in overcrowded working-class areas. As a result of the administration's ineffectiveness and the predominantly male, transient, and uneducated nature of the population, the society was lawless and chaotic. In 1850 there were only twelve police officers in the city of nearly 60,000 people. Prostitution, gambling, and drug abuse (particularly of opium) were widespread. Chinese criminal secret societies (analogous to modern-day triads) were extremely powerful, and some had tens of thousands of members. Turf wars between rival societies occasionally led to hundreds of deaths and attempts to suppress them had limited success.

Crown Colony (1867–1942)

As Singapore continued to grow, the deficiencies in the Straits Settlements administration became serious and Singapore's merchant community began agitating against British Indian rule. The British government agreed to establish the Straits Settlements as a separate Crown Colony on 1 April 1867. This new colony was ruled by a governor under the supervision of the Colonial Office in London. The governor was assisted by an executive council and a legislative council. Although members of the councils were not elected, more representatives for the local population were gradually included over the years.

The colonial government embarked on several measures to address the serious social problems facing Singapore. A Chinese Protectorate under Pickering was established in 1877 to address the needs of the Chinese community, especially in controlling the worst abuses of the coolie trade and protecting Chinese women from forced prostitution. In 1889 Governor Sir Cecil Clementi Smith banned secret societies, driving them underground. Nevertheless, many social problems persisted up through the post-war era, including an acute housing shortage and poor health and living standards. In 1906, the Tongmenghui, a revolutionary Chinese organisation dedicated to the overthrow of the Qing Dynasty and led by Sun Yat-Sen, founded its Nanyang branch in Singapore, which served as the organisation's headquarters in Southeast Asia. The immigrant Chinese population in Singapore donated generously to Tongmenghui, which organised the 1911 Xinhai Revolution that led to the establishment of the Republic of China.

Singapore was not much affected by World War I (1914–18), as the conflict did not spread to Southeast Asia. The only significant event during the war was a 1915 mutiny by the British Muslim Indian sepoys garrisoned in Singapore. After hearing rumours that they were to be sent off to fight the Ottoman Empire, the soldiers revolted, killing their officers and several British civilians before being suppressed by troops arriving from Johor and Burma. After the war, the British government devoted significant resources into building a naval base in Singapore, as a deterrent to the increasingly ambitious Japanese Empire. Completed in 1939 at a staggering cost of $500 million, the naval base boasted what was then the largest dry dock in the world, the third-largest floating dock, and having enough fuel tanks to support the entire British navy for six months. It was defended by heavy 15-inch naval guns and by Royal Air Force squadrons stationed at Tengah Air Base. Winston Churchill touted it as the "Gibraltar of the East." Unfortunately, it was a base without a fleet. The British Home Fleet was stationed in Europe and the plan was for it to sail quickly to Singapore when needed. However, after World War II broke out in 1939, the Fleet was fully occupied with defending Britain.

The Battle of Singapore and the Japanese Occupation (1942–1945)

On 7 December 1941, Japan attacked Pearl Harbor and the Pacific War began in earnest. One of Japan's objectives was to capture Southeast Asia and secure the rich supply of natural resources to feed its military and industry needs. Singapore, the main Allied base in the region, was an obvious military target. The British military commanders in Singapore had believed that the Japanese attack would come by sea from the south, since the dense Malayan jungle in the north would serve as a natural barrier against invasion. Although the British had drawn up a plan for dealing with an attack on northern Malaya, preparations were never completed. The military was confident that "Fortress Singapore" would withstand any Japanese attack and this confidence was further reinforced by the arrival of Force Z, a squadron of British warships dispatched to the defense of Singapore, including the battleship *HMS Prince of Wales*, and cruiser *HMS Repulse*. The squadron was to have been accompanied by a third capital ship, the aircraft carrier *HMS Indomitable*, but it ran aground en route, leaving the squadron without air cover.

On 8 December 1941, Japanese forces landed at Kota Bahru in northern Malaya. Just two days after the start of the invasion of Malaya, *Prince of Wales* and *Repulse* were sunk 50 miles off the coast of Kuantan in Pahang, by a force of Japanese bombers and torpedo bomber aircraft, in the worst British naval defeat of World War II. Allied air support did not arrive in time to protect the two capital ships. After this incident, Singapore and Malaya suffered daily air raids, including those targeting civilian structures such as hospitals or shophouses with casualties ranging from the tens to the hundreds each time.

The Japanese army advanced swiftly southward through the Malay Peninsula, crushing or bypassing Allied resistance. The Allied forces did not have tanks, which they considered as unsuitable in the tropical rainforest, and their infantry proved powerless against the Japanese light tanks. As their resistance failed against the Japanese advance, the Allied forces were forced to retreat southwards towards Singapore. By 31 January 1942, a mere 55 days after the start of the invasion, the Japanese had conquered the entire Malay peninsula and were poised to attack Singapore.

The causeway linking Johar and Singapore was blown up by the Allied forces in an effort to stop the Japanese army. However, the Japanese managed to cross the Straits of Johor in inflatable boats days after. Several heroic fights by the Allied forces and volunteers of Singapore's population against the advancing Japanese, such as the Battle of Pasir Panjang, took place during this period. However, with most of the defences shattered and supplies exhausted, Lieutenant-General Arthur Percival surrendered the Allied forces in Singapore to General Tomoyuki Yamashita of the Imperial Japanese Army on Chinese New Year, 15 February 1942. About 130,000 Indian, Australian and British troops became prisoners of war, many of whom would later be transported to Burma, Japan, Korea, or Manchuria for use as slave labour via prisoner transports known as "hell ships." The fall of Singapore was the largest surrender of British-led forces in history.

Singapore, renamed Syonan-to ("Light of the South Island" in Japanese), was occupied by the Japanese from 1942 to 1945. The Japanese Occupation is the darkest period of Singaporean history as the Japanese army imposed harsh measures against the local population. Numerous atrocities were committed by Japanese troops, particularly by the Kempeitai, the Japanese military police. They were the enforcers of the Sook Ching Massacre of Chinese civilians, to retaliate against them for their support of the war effort in China. The mass executions claimed between 25,000 and 50,000 lives in Malaya and Singapore. The rest of the population suffered severe hardship throughout the three and a half years of Japanese occupation.

Post-war Period (1945–1955)

After the Japanese surrender to the Allies on 15 August 1945, Singapore fell into a brief state of anomie and looting and revenge-killing were widespread. British troops led by Lord Louis Mountbatten, Supreme Allied Commander for Southeast Asia Command, returned to Singapore to receive formal surrender of the Japanese forces in the region from General Itagaki Seishiro on behalf of General Hisaichi Terauchi on September 12, 1945 and a British Military Administration was formed to govern the island until March 1946. Much of the infrastructure had been destroyed during the war, including electricity and water supply systems, telephone services, as well as the harbour facilities at the Port of Singapore. There was also a shortage of food leading to malnutrition, diseases and rampant crimes and violence. High food prices, unemployment, and workers' discontent culminated into a series of strikes in 1947 causing massive stoppages in public transport and other services. By late 1947, the economy began to recover, facilitated by a growing demand for tin and rubber around the world, but it would take several more years before the economy returned to pre-war levels.

The failure of Britain to defend Singapore had destroyed its credibility as infallible ruler in the eyes of Singaporeans. The decades after the war saw a political awakening amongst the local populace and the rise of anti-colonial and nationalist sentiments, epitomised by the slogan *Merdeka*, or "independence" in the Malay language. The British, on their part, were prepared to gradually increase self-governance for Singapore and Malaya. On 1 April 1946, the Straits Settlements was dissolved and Singapore became a separate Crown Colony with a civil administration headed by a Governor. In July 1947, separate Executive and Legislative Councils were established and the election of six members of the Legislative Council was scheduled in the following year.

First Legislative Council (1948-1951)

The first Singaporean elections, held in March 1948, were limited as only six of the twenty-five seats on the Legislative Council were to be elected. Only British subjects had the rights to vote, and only 23,000 or about 10% of those eligible registered to vote. Other members of the Council were chosen either by the Governor or by the chambers of commerce. Three of the elected seats were won by a newly-formed Singapore Progressive Party (SPP), a conservative party whose leaders were businessmen and professionals and were disinclined to press for immediate self-rule. The other three seats were won by independents.

Three months after the elections, an armed insurgency by communist groups in Malaya — the Malayan Emergency — broke out. The British imposed tough measures to control left-wing groups in both Singapore and Malaya and introduced the controversial Internal Security Act, which allowed indefinite detention without trial for persons suspected of being "threats to security". Since the left-wing groups were the strongest critics of the colonial system, progress on self-government was stalled for several years.

Second Legislative Council (1951-1955)

A second Legislative Council election was held in 1951 with the number of elected seats increased to nine. This election was again dominated by the SPP which won six seats. While this contributed to the formation of a distinct local government of Singapore, the colonial administration was still dominant. In 1953, with the communists in Malaya suppressed and the worst of the Emergency over, a British Commission, headed by Sir George Rendel, proposed a limited form of self-government for Singapore. A new Legislative Assembly with twenty-five out of thirty-two seats chosen by popular election would replace the Legislative Council, from which a Chief Minister as head of government and Council of Ministers as a cabinet would be picked under a parliamentary system. The British would retain control over areas such as internal security and foreign affairs, as well as veto power over legislation.

The election for the Legislative Assembly held on 2 April 1955 was a lively and closely-fought affair, with several new political parties joining the fray. Unlike previous elections, voters were automatically registered, expanding the electorate to around 300,000. The SPP was soundly defeated in the election, winning only four seats. The newly-formed, left-leaning Labour Front was the biggest winner with ten seats and it formed a coalition government with the UMNO-MCA Alliance, which won three seats. Another new party, the leftist People's Action Party (PAP), won three seats.

Self-government (1955–1963)

David Marshall, leader of the Labour Front, became the first Chief Minister of Singapore. He presided over a shaky government, receiving little cooperation from either the colonial government or the other local parties. Social unrest was on the rise, and in May 1955, the Hock Lee Bus Riots broke out, killing four people and seriously discrediting Marshall's government. In 1956, the Chinese Middle School riots broke out among students in The Chinese High School and other schools, further increasing the tension between the local government and the Chinese students and unionists who were regarded of having communist sympathies.

In April 1956, Marshall led a delegation to London to negotiate for complete self-rule in the Merdeka Talks, but the talks failed when the British were reluctant to give up control over Singapore's internal security. The British were concerned about communist influence and labour strikes which were undermining Singapore's economic stability, and felt that the local government was ineffective in handling earlier riots. Marshall resigned following the failure of the talk.

The new Chief Minister, Lim Yew Hock, launched a crackdown on communist and leftist groups, imprisoning many trade union leaders and several pro-communist members of the PAP under the Internal Security Act. The British government approved of Lim's tough stance against communist agitators, and when a new round of talks was held beginning in March 1957, they agreed to grant complete internal self-government. A State of Singapore would be created, with its own citizenship. The Legislative Assembly would be expanded to fifty-one members, entirely chosen by popular election, and the Prime Minister and cabinet would control all aspects of government except defence and foreign affairs. The governorship was replaced by a *Yang di-Pertuan Negara* or head of state.

Full Internal Self-government (1959-1963)

Elections for the new Legislative Assembly were held in May 1959. The People's Action Party (PAP) swept the election, winning forty-three of the fifty-one seats. They accomplished this by courting the Chinese-speaking majority, particularly those in the labour unions and radical student organisations. Its leader Lee Kuan Yew, a young Cambridge-educated lawyer, became the first Prime Minister of Singapore.

The PAP's victory was viewed with dismay by foreign and local business leaders because some party's members were pro-communists. Many businesses promptly shifted their headquarters from Singapore to Kuala Lumpur. Despite these ill omens, the PAP government embarked on a vigorous program to address Singapore's various economic and social problems. Economic development was overseen by the new Minister of Finance Goh Keng Swee, whose strategy was to encourage foreign and local investment with measures ranging from tax incentives to the establishment of a large industrial estate in Jurong. The education system was revamped to train a skilled workforce and the English language was promoted over the Chinese language as the language of instruction. To eliminate labour unrest, existing labour unions were consolidated, sometimes forcibly, into a single umbrella organisation, called the National Trades Union Congress (NTUC) with strong oversight from the government. On the social front, an aggressive and well-funded public housing program was launched to solve the long-standing housing problem. More than 25,000 high-rise, low-cost apartments were constructed during the first two years of the program.

Campaign for Merger

Despite their successes in governing Singapore, the PAP leaders, including Lee and Goh, believed that Singapore's future lay with Malaya. They felt that the historical and economic ties between Singapore and Malaya were too strong for them to continue as separate nations, and they campaigned vigorously for a merger. On the other hand, the sizeable pro-communist wing of the PAP were strongly opposed to the merger, fearing a loss of influence as the ruling party of Malaya, United Malays National Organisation, was staunchly anti-communist and would support the non-communist faction of PAP against them. The UMNO leaders were also skeptical of the merger idea due to their distrust of the PAP government and concerns that the large Chinese population in Singapore would alter the racial balance on which their political power base depended. The issue came to a head in 1961 when pro-communist PAP minister Ong Eng Guan defected from the party and beat a PAP candidate in a subsequent by-election, a move that threatened to bring down Lee's government.

Faced with the prospect of a takeover by the pro-communists, UMNO did an about-face on the merger. On 27 May, Malaya's Prime Minister, Tunku Abdul Rahman, mooted the idea of a Federation of Malaysia, comprised of the existing Federation of Malaya, Singapore, Brunei and the British Borneo territories of Sabah and Sarawak. The UMNO leaders believed that the additional Malay population in the Borneo territories would offset Singapore's Chinese population.

The Malaysia proposal ignited the long-brewing conflict between the moderates and pro-communists within the PAP. The pro-communists, led by Lim Chin Siong, left the PAP to form a new opposition party, the Barisan Sosialis (Socialist Front), to campaign against entry into Malaysia under the PAP's plan. In response, Lee called for a referendum on the merger and campaigned vigorously for his proposal, aided by the government's strong influence over the media. In the referendum, held on 1 September 1962, 70% of the votes supported the PAP's proposal for merger.

On 9 July 1963, the leaders of Singapore, Malaya, Sabah and Sarawak signed the Malaysia Agreement to establish the Federation of Malaysia.

Singapore in Malaysia (1963–1965)

Mèrger

On 16 September 1963, Malaya, Singapore, Sabah and Sarawak were formally merged and Malaysia was formed. For Singapore, the merger was thought to benefit the economy by creating a common free market, eliminating trade tariffs, and solving unemployment woes. The British government approved the merger, convinced that Singapore's security would be safeguarded within the much larger Malaysia.

The union was rocky from the start. During the 1963 Singapore state elections, a local branch of UMNO took part in the election despite an earlier UMNO's agreement with the PAP not to participate in the state's politics during Malaysia's formative years. Although UMNO lost all its bids, relations between PAP and UMNO worsened as the PAP, in a tit-for-tat, challenged UMNO candidates in the 1964 federal election as part of the Malaysian Solidarity Convention, winning one seat in Malaysian Parliament.

Racial Tension

Racial tensions increased dramatically within a year and were fueled by Barisan Sosialis's tactics of stirring up communal sentiment to discredit the government of Singapore and the federal government of Malaysia. In particular, the Chinese in Singapore disdained being discriminated against by the federal policies of affirmative action, which granted special privileges to the Malays guaranteed under Article 153 of the Constitution of Malaysia. There were also other financial and economic benefits that were preferentially given to Malays. Lee Kuan Yew and other political leaders began advocating for the fair and equal treatment of all races in Malaysia, with a rallying cry of *"Malaysian Malaysia!"*.

Meanwhile, the Malays in Singapore were being increasingly incited by the federal government's accusations that the PAP was mistreating the Malays. The external political situation was also tense when Indonesian President Sukarno declared a state of *Konfrontasi* (Confrontation) against Malaysia and initiated military and other actions against the new nation, including the bombing of MacDonald House in Singapore in March 1965 by Indonesian commandos, killing three people. Indonesia also conducted sedition activities to provoke the Malays against the Chinese. Numerous racial riots resulted and curfews were frequently imposed to restore order. The most notorious riots were the 1964 Race Riots that first took place on Prophet Muhammad's birthday on 21 July with twenty three people killed and hundreds injured. During the unrest, the price of food skyrocketed when transport system was disrupted, causing further hardship for the people.

The state and federal governments also had conflicts on the economic front. UMNO leaders feared that the economic dominance of Singapore would inevitably shift political power away from Kuala Lumpur. Despite earlier agreement to establish a common market, Singapore continued to face restrictions when trading with the rest of Malaysia. In retaliation, Singapore refused to provide Sabah and Sarawak the full extent of the loans previously agreed to for the economic development of the two eastern states. The situation escalated to such intensity that talks soon broke down and abusive speeches and writings became rife on both sides. UMNO extremists called for the arrest of Lee Kuan Yew.

Separation

Seeing no other alternative to avoid further bloodshed, the Malaysian Prime Minister Tunku Abdul Rahman decided to expel Singapore from the federation. The Parliament of Malaysia voted 126-0 in favour of the expulsion on 9 August 1965. On that day, a tearful Lee Kuan Yew announced on a televised press conference that Singapore was a sovereign, independent nation. In a widely remembered quote, he uttered that: *"For me, it is a moment of anguish. All my life, my whole adult life, I have believed in merger and unity of the two territories."* The new state became the Republic of Singapore and Yusof bin Ishak was appointed the first President.

Republic of Singapore (1965–present)

After gaining independence abruptly, the future of Singapore was filled with uncertainties. The Konfrontasi was on-going and conservative UMNO faction strongly opposed the separation; Singapore faced the danger of being attacked by Indonesian military or forcibly re-absorbed into the Malaysia Federation in unfavourable terms. Singapore immediately sought international recognition of its sovereignty. Singapore joined the United Nations on 21 September 1965 and the Commonwealth in October that year. Foreign minister Sinnathamby Rajaratnam headed a new foreign service and helped asserting Singapore's independence and establishing diplomatic relations with other countries. Singapore later co-founded the Association of Southeast Asian Nations on 8 August 1967 and was admitted into the Non-Aligned Movement in 1970.

As a small island nation, Singapore was seen as inadequate to be a viable country and much of the international media was skeptical of prospects for Singapore's survival. Besides the issue of sovereignty, the pressing problems were unemployment, housing, education, and the lack of natural resources and land. Unemployment rate was ranging between 10-12% threatening to trigger civil unrest.

The Economic Development Board was set up in 1961 to formulate and implement national economic strategies, focusing on promoting Singapore's manufacturing sector. Industrial estates were set up, especially in Jurong, and foreign investment was attracted to the country with tax incentives. The industrialisation transformed the manufacturing sector to one that produced higher value-added goods and achieved greater revenue. The service industry also grew at this time, driven by demand for services by ships calling at the port and increasing commerce. These progresses helped to alleviate the unemployment crisis. Singapore also attracted big oil companies like Shell and Esso to establish oil refineries in Singapore which, by the mid 1970s, became the third largest oil-refining centre in the world. The government invested heavily in an education system that adopted English as the language of instruction and emphasised on practical training to develop a competent workforce well suited for the industry.

The lack of good public housing, poor sanitation, and high unemployment led to social problems from crime to health issues. The proliferation of squatter settlements resulted in safety hazards and caused the Bukit Ho Swee Squatter Fire in 1961 that killed four people and left 16,000 others homeless. The Housing Development Board set up before independence continued to be largely successful and huge building projects sprung up to provide affordable public housing to resettle the squatters. Within a decade, the majority of the population had been housed in these apartments. The Central Provident Fund (CPF) Housing Scheme, introduced in 1968, allows residents to use their compulsory savings account to purchase HDB flats and gradually increases home ownership in Singapore.

British troops had remained in Singapore following its independence, but in 1968, London announced its decision to withdraw the forces by 1971. Singapore set out to build its military, called the Singapore Armed Forces, and a national service programme was introduced in 1967.

The 1980s and 1990s

Further economic success continued through the 1980s onwards, with the unemployment rate falling to 3% and real GDP growth averaging at about 8% during this time until 1999. During the 1980s, Singapore began to upgrade its industries to higher-technology industries, such as the wafer fabrication sector, in order to compete with its neighbours which now have cheaper labour forces. Singapore Changi Airport was opened in 1981 and Singapore Airlines was developed to become a major airline in the world. The Port of Singapore became one of the world's busiest ports and the service and tourism industry also grew immensely during this period. Singapore emerged as an important transportation hub and a major tourist destination.

The Housing Development Board continued to promote public housing with new towns, such as in Ang Mo Kio, were designed and built. These new residential estates have larger and higher-standard apartments and are served with better amenities. Today, 80-90% of the population lives in HDB apartments. In 1987, the first Mass Rapid Transit (MRT) line began operation, connecting most of these housing estates and the city centre.

The political situation in Singapore was stable and dominated by the People's Action Party which had a 15-year monopoly in parliament during 1966 to 1981, winning all seats in elections during that period. The PAP rule is termed authoritarian by some activists and opposition politicians who see the strict regulation of political and media activities by the government as an infringement on political rights. The conviction of opposition politician Chee Soon Juan for illegal protests and the defamation lawsuits against J. B. Jeyaretnam have been cited by the opposition parties as examples of such authoritarianism. The lack of separation of powers between the court system and the government led to further accusations by the opposition parties of miscarriage of justice.

The government of Singapore underwent several significant changes. Non-Constituency Members of Parliament were introduced in 1984 to allow up to three losing opposition parties candidates be appointed as MPs. Group Representation Constituencies (GRCs) was introduced in 1988 to create multi-seat electoral divisions, intended to ensure minority representation in parliament. Nominated Members of Parliament was introduced in 1990 to allow non-elected non-partisan MPs. The Constitution was amended in 1991 to provide for an Elected President who has veto power in the use of national reserves and appointments to public office. The opposition parties have complained that the GRC system has made it difficult for them to gain a foothold in parliamentary elections in Singapore, and the plurality voting system tends to exclude minority parties.

In 1990, Lee Kuan Yew passed the leadership rein to successor Goh Chok Tong who became the second prime minister of Singapore. Goh presented a more open and consultative style of leadership as the country continued to modernise. In 1997, Singapore experienced the effect of the Asian financial crisis and tough measures, such as cuts in the CPF contribution, were implemented.

2000–present

In the early 2000s, Singapore went through some post-independence crises, including the SARS outbreak in 2003 and the threat of terrorism. In December 2001, a plot to bomb embassies and other infrastructure in Singapore was uncovered and as many as 36 members of the Jemaah Islamiyah group were arrested under the Internal Security Act. Major counter-terrorism measures were put in place to detect and prevent potential terrorism acts and to minimise damages should they occur.

In 2004, Lee Hsien Loong, the eldest son of Lee Kuan Yew, became the third prime minister of Singapore. He introduced several policy changes, including the reduction of national service duration from two and a half years to two years, and the legalisation of casino gambling. The general election of 2006 was a landmark election because of the prominent use of the internet and blogging to cover and comment on the election, circumventing the official media. The PAP returned to power, winning 82 of the 84 parliamentary seats and 66% of the votes.

HISTORY OF BRUNEI

The Sultanate of **Brunei** was very powerful from the fourteenth to the sixteenth century CE. Its realm covered the northern part of Borneo and the southwestern Philippines. European influence gradually brought an end to this regional power. Later, there was a brief war with Spain, in which Brunei was victorious. The decline of the Bruneian Empire culminated in the nineteenth century when Brunei lost much of its territory to the White Rajahs of Sarawak, resulting in its current small landmass and separation into two parts. Brunei was a British protectorate from 1888 to 1984.

Before the Sultanate

Historians believe that there was a forerunner to the present day Brunei Sultanate. One possible predecessor state was called Vijayapura, which possibly existed in northwest Borneo in the seventh century A.D. It was probably a subject state of the powerful Srivijaya empire based in Sumatra. Another possible predecessor state was called Po-ni. Chinese and Arabic records indicate that this trading kingdom existed at the mouth of the Brunei River as early as the seventh or eighth century A.D. By the tenth century

Po-ni had a close mercantile relationship with first the Song and later the Ming Dynasty and at some point even entered into a tributary relationship with China.

By the fourteenth century Po-ni also fell under the influence of the Javanese Majapahit Empire. The book of Nagarakertagama canto 14 written by Prapanca in 1365 mentioned *Berune* as a vassal state of Majapahit. However this may have been nothing more than a symbolic relationship, as one account of the annual tribute owed each year to Majapahit was a jar of areca juice obtained from the young green nuts of the areca palm. The relationship with mainland China nevertheless continued, culminating in 1408, when the Po-ni ruler Abdul Majid Hassan visited China and died there. Around the same time, the Chinese admiral Zheng He visited the region and found a large trading port with numerous Chinese traders carrying on business with the mainland. In 1424, the Hongxi Emperor ended China's maritime program, and the mainland's relationship with Po-ni effectively ended.

Song historians and archaeological evidence suggest that Po-ni was heavily influenced by Hindu civilization, as transmitted by Hindu culture in Java and Sumatra, and not directly from India. The system of writing used was a Hindu script, and discovered artifacts include elephants, bulls, and yonis. There was also a heavy Chinese influence, with Chinese coins dating from as early as the seventh century being found in present-day Brunei.

Conversion to Islam and "Golden Age"

The later history of Po-ni, or Brunei, remains somewhat obscure. By the middle of the fifteenth century the state had entered into a close relationship with the Muslim kingdom of Malacca. This era also saw the origin of the ruling dynasty, which continues to this day. According to *the Syuir Awang Semaun* (also spelled Simawn), Brunei's national epic poem, the present-day sultanate originated when Dewa Emas Kayangan descended to earth from heav.en in an egg. He had children with a number of aboriginal maidens, and one of these children converted to Islam and became the first sultan. However, the state continued to be multicultural. The second sultan was either Chinese or married a Chinese woman. The third sultan was said to be part Arab, who are seen in South and Southeast Asia as the descendents of Muhammed.

The sultanate oversaw a gradual expansion of the state's influence and borders. This was accelerated with the conquest of Malacca by the Portuguese in 1511. Brunei benefited from the scattering of Muslim merchants and traders who were forced to use other ports. These merchants probably also helped to speed the conversion of the general population to Islam.

The sultanate was a thalassocracy, a realm based more on controlling trade than land. Situated in a strategic location between China and the trading networks of southeast Asia, the state served as an entrepot and collected tolls on water traffic. The society was hierarchical, with the sultan serving as despot. His powers were limited, however, by a council of princes of royal blood. One of the council's duties was to arrange for royal succession.

The reign of the fifth sultan, Bolkiah (1485-1521), is often marked as Brunei's "golden age". The sultanate's control extended over the coastal regions of modern-day Sarawak and Sabah, the Sulu archipelago, and the islands off the northwest tip of Borneo. The sultanate's influence also spread north into the Philippines, where colonies were planted in Manila Bay. The sultan also visited Java and Malacca. At the end of Bolkiah's reign, in 1521, the first Europeans visited Brunei when Ferdinand Magellan's expedition arrived at the port. Antonio Pigafetta, a navigator on the trip, described an amazing city. The Europeans rode to visit the sultan on top of *"elephants, caparisoned in silk-cloth"*. The inhabitants of the palace *"had their loins covered with gold-embroidered cloth and silk, wore poniards with golden hilts, ornamented with pearls and precious stones, and had many rings on their fingers"*. The visitors were fed meals on porcelain plateware.

Pigafetta described a city of 25 000 families living in wooden houses built on stilts to raise them above the water. During high tides women would ride in boats selling merchandise. The sultan's palace was surrounded by brick ramparts and protected by numerous brass and iron cannons.

This prosperous era continued through the reign of the ninth sultan, Hassan, who is credited with developing an elaborate Royal Court structure, elements of which remain today.

Relations with Europeans

Brunei's relations varied with the different European powers in the region. The Portuguese, for the most part, were more interested in economic and trading relations with the regional powers and did little to interfere with Brunei's development. This does not mean that relations were always cordial, such as in 1536 when the Portuguese attacked the Muslims in the Moluccas and the ambassador to the Brunei court had to leave because of the sultan's hostility. The Portuguese also noted that the sultanate was heavily involved in the region's politics and wars, and that Brunei merchants could be found in Ligor and Siam.

Relations with the Spanish were far more hostile. From 1565 on, Spanish and Brunei forces engaged in a number of naval skirmishes, and in 1571 the Spanish succeeded in capturing Manila from the Brunei aristocracy that had been established there. Brunei raised several large fleets with the intention of recapturing the city, but the campaigns, for various reasons, never launched. In 1578, the Spanish took Sulu and late in the year attacked and captured Brunei itself, after demanding that the sultan cease sending missionaries to the Philippines and, in turn, allow Christian missionaries to visit his kingdom. The invaders were forced to withdraw. The short term damage to the sultanate was minimal, as Sulu was recaptured soon after.

The long term effects of regional changes could not be avoided. After Sultan Hassan, Brunei entered a period of decline, due to internal battles over royal succession as well as the rising influences of European colonial powers in the region, that, among other things, disrupted traditional trading patterns, destroying the economic base of Brunei and many other Southeast Asian sultanates.

In 1839, the English adventurer James Brooke arrived in Borneo and helped the Sultan put down a rebellion. As a reward, he became governor and later "White Rajah" of Sarawak in northwest Borneo and gradually expanded the territory under his control. Brooke never gained control of Brunei; though he did attempt to. He asked the British to check whether or not it would be acceptable for him to claim Brunei as his own, however, they came back with bad news; although Brunei was poorly run, it had a definite sense of national identity and could therefore not be absorbed by Brooke.

Modern History

Brunei was occupied by Japan from 1941 to 1945 during World War II; Britain did not defend Brunei in spite of an Agreement to do so.

In 1959, a new constitution was written declaring Brunei a self-governing state, while its foreign affairs, security, and defence remained the responsibility of the United Kingdom, now represented by a High Commissioner. An attempt in 1962 to introduce a partially elected legislative body with limited powers was abandoned after the opposition political party, Parti Rakyat Brunei, launched an armed uprising, which the government put down with the help of British forces. In the late 1950s and early 1960s, the government also resisted pressures to join neighbouring Sabah and Sarawak in the newly formed Malaysia. The Sultan eventually decided that Brunei would remain a separate state.

In 1967, Omar Ali Saifuddin abdicated in favour of his eldest son, Hassanal Bolkiah, who became the 29th ruler. The former Sultan remained as Defence Minister and assumed the royal title Seri Begawan. In 1970, the national capital, Brunei Town, was renamed Bandar Seri Begawan in his honour. The Seri Begawan died in 1986.

On January 4, 1979, Brunei and the United Kingdom signed a new treaty of friendship and cooperation. On January 1, 1984, Brunei Darussalam became a fully independent state.

HISTORY OF EAST TIMOR

East Timor is a small country in Southeast Asia. It comprises the eastern half of the island of Timor, the nearby islands of Atauro and Jaco. The first people's are thought to be descendant of Australoid and Melanesian peoples. The Portuguese began to trade with the island of Timor in the early 16th century and colonized it in mid-century. Skirmishing with the Dutch in the region eventually resulted in an 1859 treaty in which Portugal ceded the western portion of the island. Imperial Japan occupied East Timor from 1942 to 1945, but Portugal resumed colonial authority after the Japanese defeat in World War II.

East Timor declared itself independent from Portugal on 28 November 1975 and was invaded and occupied by Indonesian forces nine days later. It was incorporated into Indonesia in July 1976 as the province of East Timor. During the subsequent 24-year occupation a campaign of pacification ensued. Between 1974 and 1999, there were an estimated 102,800 conflict-related deaths (approximately 18,600 killings and 84,200 'excess' deaths from hunger and illness), the majority of which occurred during the Indonesian occupation.

On 30 August 1999, in a UN-sponsored referendum, an overwhelming majority of East Timor voted for independence from Indonesia. Immediately following the referendum, anti-independence Timorese militias – organised and supported by the Indonesian military – commenced a punitive scorched-earth campaign. The militias killed approximately 1,400 Timorese and forcibly pushed 300,000 people into West Timor as refugees. The majority of the country's infrastructure was destroyed. On 20 September 1999 the International Force for East Timor (INTERFET) was deployed to the country and brought the violence to an end. Following a United Nations-administer transition period, East Timor was internationally recognised as an independent state in 2002.

Pre-colonial History

The island of Timor was populated as part of the human migrations that have shaped Australasia more generally. It is believed that survivors from three waves of migration still live in the country. The first is described by anthropologists as people of the Vedo-Australoid type, who arrived from the north and west approximately 40,000 to 20,000 years BC. Others of this type include the Wanniyala-Aetto (*Veddas*) of Sri Lanka. Around 3000 BC, a second migration brought Melanesians. The earlier Vedo-Australoid peoples withdrew at this time to the mountainous interior. Finally, proto-Malays arrived from south China and north Indochina. Hakka traders are among those descended from this final group. Timorese origin myths tell of ancestors that sailed around the eastern end of Timor arriving on land in the south. Some stories recount Timorese ancestors journeying from Malay Peninsula or the Minangkabau Highlands of Sumatra.

The Timorese were not seafarers, rather they were land focussed peoples who did not make contact with other islands and peoples by sea. Timor was part of a region of small islands with small populations of similarly land-focussed peoples that now make up eastern Indonesia. Contact with the outside world was via networks of foreign seafaring traders from as far as China and India that served the archipelago. Outside products brought to the region included metal goods, rice, fine textiles, and coins exchanged for local spices, sandalwood, deer horn, bees' wax, and slaves.

Early European explorers report that the island had a number of small chiefdoms or princedoms in the early 16th century. One of the most significant is the Wehali kingdom in central Timor, to which the Tetum, Bunaq and Kemak ethnic groups were aligned.

Portuguese Rule

The first Europeans to arrive in the area were the Portuguese, who landed near modern Pante Macassar. In 1556 a group of Dominican friars established their missionary work in the area. By the seventeenth century the village of Lifau became the centre of Portuguese activities. In 1702 the territory officially became a Portuguese colony, known as Portuguese Timor, when Lisbon sent its first governor, with Lifau as its capital. Portuguese control over the territory was tenuous particularly in the mountainous interior. Dominican friars, the occasional Dutch raid, and the Timorese themselves provided opposition to the Portuguese. The control of colonial administrators, largely restricted to Dili, had to rely on traditional tribal chieftains for control and influence.

For the Portuguese, East Timor remained little more than a neglected trading post until the late nineteenth century. Investment in infrastructure, health, and education was minimal. Sandalwood remained the main export crop with coffee exports becoming significant in the mid-nineteenth century. In places where Portuguese rule was asserted, it tended to be brutal and exploitative. At the beginning of the twentieth century, a faltering home economy prompted the Portuguese to extract greater wealth from its colonies.

The capital was moved from Lifau to Dili in 1769, due to attacks from the Topasses, an independent-minded Eurasian group. Meanwhile, the Dutch were colonizing the rest of the island and the surrounding archipelago that is now Indonesia. The border between Portuguese Timor and the Dutch East Indies was formally decided in 1859 with the Treaty of Lisbon. The definitive border was drawn by the Hague in 1916, and it remains the international boundary between the modern states of East Timor and Indonesia.

Although Portugal was neutral during World War II, in December 1941, Portuguese Timor was occupied by Australian and Dutch forces, which were expecting a Japanese invasion. When the Japanese did occupy Timor, in February 1942, a 400-strong Dutch-Australian force and large numbers of Timorese volunteers engaged them in a one-year guerilla campaign. After the allied evacuation in February 1943 the East Timorese continued fighting the Japanese, with comparatively little collaboration with the enemy taking place. This assistance cost the civilian population dearly: Japanese forces burned many villages and seized food supplies. The Japanese occupation resulted in the deaths of 40,000–70,000 Timorese.

Portuguese Timor was handed back to Portugal after the war, but Portugal continued to neglect the colony. Very little investment was made in infrastructure, education and healthcare. The colony was declared an 'Overseas Province' of the Portuguese Republic in 1955. Locally, authority rested with the Portuguese Governor and the Legislative Council, as well as local chiefs or *liurai*. Only a small minority of Timorese were educated, and even fewer went on to university in Portugal (there were no universities in the territory until 2000).

During this time, Indonesia did not express any interest in Portuguese Timor, despite the anti-colonial rhetoric of President Sukarno. This was partly as Indonesia was preoccupied with gaining control of West Irian, now called Papua, which had been retained by the Netherlands after Indonesian independence. In fact, at the United Nations, Indonesian diplomats stressed that their country did not seek control over any territory outside the former Netherlands East Indies, explicitly mentioning Portuguese Timor.

Decolonisation, Coup, and Independence

After the fall of the Portuguese regime in 1974, independence was encouraged by the new, democratic Portuguese government. One of the first acts of the new government in Lisbon was to appoint a new Governor for the colony on November 18, 1974, in the form of Mário Lemos Pires, who would ultimately be, as events were to prove, the last Governor of Portuguese Timor.

One of his first decrees made upon his arrival in Dili was to legalise political parties in preparation for elections to a Constituent Assembly in 1976. Three main political parties were formed:

- The *União Democrática Timorense* (Timorese Democratic Union or UDT), was supported by the traditional elites, initially argued for a continued association with Lisbon, or as they put it in Tetum, *mate bandera hum* — 'in the shadow of the [Portuguese] flag', but later adopted a 'gradualist' approach to independence. One of its leaders, Mário Viegas Carrascalão, one of the few Timorese to have been educated at university in Portugal, later became Indonesian Governor of East Timor during the 1980s and early 1990s, although with the demise of Indonesian rule, he would change to supporting independence.

- The *Associação Social Democrática Timorense* (Timorese Social Democratic Association ASDT) supported a rapid movement to independence. It later changed its name to *Frente Revolucionária de Timor-Leste Independente* (Revolutionary Front of Independent East Timor or Fretilin). Fretilin was criticised by many in Australia and Indonesia as being Marxist, its name sounding reminiscent of FRELIMO in Mozambique but it was more influenced by African nationalists like Amílcar Cabral in Portuguese Guinea (now Guinea-Bissau) and Cape Verde.
- The *Associação Popular Democrática Timorense* (Timorese Popular Democratic Association or Apodeti) supported integration with Indonesia, as an autonomous province, but had very little grassroots support. One of its leaders, Abílio Osório Soares, later served as the last Indonesian-appointed Governor of East Timor. Apodeti drew support from a few *liurai* in the border region, some of whom had collaborated with the Japanese during the Second World War. It also had some support in the small Muslim minority, although Marí Alkatiri, a Muslim, was a prominent Fretilin leader, and became Prime Minister in 2002.

Other smaller parties included *Klibur Oan Timur Asuwain* or KOTA whose name translated from the Tetum language as 'Sons of the Mountain Warriors', which sought to create a form of monarchy involving the local *liurai*, and the *Partido Trabalhista* or Labour Party, but neither had any significant support. They would, however, collaborate with Indonesia. The *Associação Democrática para a Integração de Timor-Leste na Austrália* (ADITLA), advocated integration with Australia, but folded after the Australian government emphatically ruled out the idea.

Parties Compete, Foreign Powers Take Interest

Developments in Portuguese Timor during 1974 and 1975 were watched closely by Indonesia and Australia. Suharto's "New Order", which had effectively eliminated Indonesia's Communist Party PKI in 1965, was alarmed by what it saw as the increasingly left-leaning Fretilin, and by the prospect of a small state in the midst of the sprawling archipelago serving as an inspiration to independence-minded provinces of the Republic such as Aceh, West Irian and the Moluccas.

Australia's Labor Prime Minister, Gough Whitlam, had developed a close working relationship with the Indonesian leader, and also followed events with concern. At a meeting in the Javanese town of Wonosobo in 1974, he told Suharto that an independent Portuguese Timor would be 'an unviable state, and a potential threat to the stability of the region'. While recognising the need for an act of self-determination, he considered integration with Indonesia to be in Portuguese Timor's best interests.

In local elections on 13 March 1975, Fretilin and UDT emerged as the largest parties, having previously formed an alliance to campaign for independence.

Indonesian military intelligence, known as BAKIN, began attempting to cause divisions between the pro-independence parties, and promote the support of Apodeti. This was known as *Operasi Komodo* or 'Operation Komodo' after the giant Komodo lizard found in the eastern Indonesian island of the same name. Many Indonesian military figures held meetings with UDT leaders, who made it plain that Jakarta would not tolerate a Fretilin-led administration in an independent East Timor. The coalition between Fretilin and UDT later broke up.

During the course of 1975, Portugal became increasingly detached from political developments in its colony, becoming embroiled in civil unrest and political crises, and more concerned with decolonisation in its African colonies of Angola and Mozambique than with Portuguese Timor. Many local leaders saw independence as unrealistic, and were open to discussions with Jakarta over Portuguese Timor's incorporation into the Indonesian state.

The United States had also expressed concerns over Portuguese Timor in the wake of the war in Vietnam. Having gained Indonesia as an ally, Washington did not want to see the vast archipelago destabilised by a left-wing regime in its midst.

The Coup

On August 11, 1975, the UDT mounted a coup, in a bid to halt the increasing popularity of Fretilin. Governor Pires fled to the offshore island of Atauro, north of the capital, Dili, from where he later attempted to broker an agreement between the two sides. He was urged by Fretilin to return and resume the decolonisation process, but he insisted that he was awaiting instructions from the government in Lisbon, now increasingly uninterested.

Indonesia sought to portray the conflict as a civil war, which had plunged Portuguese Timor into chaos, but after only a month, aid and relief agencies from Australia and elsewhere visited the territory, and reported that the situation was stable. Nevertheless, many UDT supporters had fled across the border into Indonesian Timor, where they were coerced into supporting integration with Indonesia. In October 1975, in the border town of Balibo, two Australian television crews (the "Balibo Five") reporting on the conflict were killed by Indonesian forces, after they witnessed Indonesian incursions into Portuguese Timor.

Break from Portugal

While Fretilin had sought the return of the Portuguese Governor, pointedly flying the Portuguese flag from government offices, the deteriorating situation meant that it had to make an appeal to the world for international support, independently of Portugal.

On November 28, 1975, Fretilin made a unilateral declaration of independence of the *Democratic Republic of East Timor* (Republica Democrática de Timor-Leste in Portuguese). This was not recognised by either Portugal, Indonesia, or Australia; however, the new state received formal diplomatic recognition from six countries, namely Albania, Cape Verde, Guinea, Guinea-Bissau, Mozambique, and São Tomé and Príncipe. Fretilin's Francisco Xavier do Amaral became the first President, while Fretilin leader Nicolau dos Reis Lobato was Prime Minister.

Indonesia's response was to have UDT, Apodeti, KOTA and Trabalhista leaders sign a declaration calling for integration with Indonesia called the *Balibo Declaration,* although it was drafted by Indonesian intelligence and signed in Bali, Indonesia not Balibo, Portuguese Timor. Xanana Gusmão, now the country's President, described this as the 'Balibohong Declaration', a pun on the Indonesian word for 'lie'.

East Timor Solidarity Movement

An international *East Timor solidarity movement* arose in response to the 1975 invasion of East Timor by Indonesia and the occupation that followed. The movement was supported by churches, human rights groups, and peace campaigners, but developed its own organizations and infrastructure in many countries. Many demonstrations and vigils backed legislative actions to cut off military supplies to Indonesia. The movement was most extensive in neighboring Australia, in Portugal, and the former Portuguese colonies in Africa, but had significant force in the United States, Canada and Europe.

José Ramos-Horta, current President of East Timor, stated in a 2007 interview that the solidarity movement "was instrumental. They were like our peaceful foot soldiers, and fought many battles for us."

Indonesian Invasion and Annexation

The Indonesian invasion of East Timor began on December 7 1975. Indonesian forces launched a massive air and sea invasion, known as *Operasi Seroja,* or 'Operation Komodo', almost entirely using US-supplied equipment. Reported death tolls from the 24-year occupation range from 60,000 to 200,000. A detailed statistical report prepared for the Commission for Reception, Truth and Reconciliation in East Timor cited a lower range of 102,800 conflict-related deaths in the period 1974-1999, namely, approximately 18,600 killings and 84,200 'excess' deaths from hunger and illness.

A puppet "Provisional Government of East Timor" was installed in mid-December, consisting of Apodeti and UDT leaders. Attempts by the United Nations Secretary General's Special Representative, Vittorio Winspeare Guicciardi to visit Fretilin-held areas from Darwin, Australia were obstructed by the Indonesian military, which blockaded East Timor. On May 31, 1976, a 'People's Assembly' in Dili, selected by Indonesian intelligence, unanimously endorsed an 'Act of Integration', and on July 17, East Timor officially became the 27th province of the Republic of Indonesia. Although the United Nations had not responded to the Indonesian annexation of West Irian some years previously, the occupation of East Timor remained a public issue in many nations, Portugal in particular, and the UN never recognised either the regime installed by the Indonesians or the subsequent annexation.

Towards Independence

Timorese groups fought a campaign of resistance against Indonesian forces for the independence of East Timor, during which many atrocities and human rights violations by the Indonesian army were reported. The Indonesian army is reported to have trained and supplied militias imported from Indonesia to terrorise the population. Foreign powers such as the Australian government worked to prevent the push for independence, and assisted the Indonesian government in obscuring and discouraging media reporting on atrocities committed by Indonesian militias.

Effects of the Dili Massacre

The Dili Massacre on 12 November 1991 was a turning point for sympathy for pro-independence East Timorese. A burgeoning East Timor solidarity movement grew in Portugal, Australia, and the United States. After the Santa Cruz massacre, the US Congress voted to cut off funding for IMET training of Indonesian military personnel. However, arms sales continued from the US to TNI. President Clinton cut off all US military ties with the Indonesian military in 1999. The Australian government promoted a strong connection with the Indonesian military at the time of the massacre, but also cut off ties in 1999.

The Massacre had a profound effect on public opinion in Portugal, especially after television footage showing East Timorese praying in Portuguese, and independence leader Xanana Gusmão gained widespread respect, being awarded the Portugal's highest honour in 1993, after he had been captured and imprisoned by the Indonesians.

In Australia, there was also widespread public outrage, and criticism of Canberra's close relationship with the Suharto regime and recognition of Jakarta's sovereignty over East Timor. This caused the Australian government embarrassment, but Foreign Minister Gareth Evans played down the killings, describing them as 'an aberration, not an act of state policy'. Gareth Evans and Prime Minister Keating, along with subsequent Prime Minister John Howard and Foreign Affairs minister Alexander Downer, sought to maintain close relations with Indonesia. Neither Liberal nor Labor ministers challenged the persecution of the East Timorese until the Australian Labor Party member Laurie Brereton spoke out in 1999, and he was quickly discredited by both the Howard Government and Kevin Rudd.

International Lobbying

Portugal started to apply international pressure unsuccessfully, constantly raising the issue with its fellow European Union members in their dealings with Indonesia. However, other EU countries like the UK had close economic relations with Indonesia, including arms sales, and saw no advantage in forcefully raising the issue.

In 1996, Bishop Carlos Filipe Ximenes Belo and José Ramos-Horta, two leading East Timorese activists for peace and independence, received the Nobel Peace Prize. In the mid-1990s, the pro-democracy People's Democratic Party (PRD) in Indonesia called for withdrawal from East Timor. The party's leadership was arrested in July 1996.

In July 1997, visiting South African President Nelson Mandela visited Suharto as well as the imprisoned Xanana Gusmão. He urged the freeing of all East Timorese leaders in a note reading, "We can never normalize the situation in East Timor unless all political leaders, including Mr. Gusmão, are freed. They are the ones who must bring about a solution." Indonesia's government refused but did announce that it would take three months off Gusmão's 20-year sentence.

In 1998, following the resignation of Suharto and his replacement by President Habibie, Jakarta moved towards offering East Timor autonomy within the Indonesian state, although ruled out independence, and stated that Portugal and the UN must recognise Indonesian sovereignty.

Referendum for Independence, Violence

However in 1999, the Indonesian government decided, under strong international pressure, to hold a referendum on the future of East Timor. Portugal had started to gain some political allies firstly in the EU, and after that in other places of the world to pressure Indonesia. The referendum, held on August 30, gave a clear majority (78.5%) in favour of independence, rejecting the alternative offer of being an autonomous province within Indonesia, to be known as the Special Autonomous Region of East Timor (SARET).

Directly after this, Indonesian military-supported East Timorese pro-integration militia and Indonesian soldiers carried out a campaign of violence and terrorism in retaliation. Approximately 1,400 Timorese were killed and 300,000 and forcibly pushed into West Timor as refugees. The majority of the country's infrastructure, including homes, irrigation systems, water supply systems, and schools, and nearly 100% of the country's electrical grid were destroyed. According to Noam Chomsky, "In one month, this massive military operation murdered some 2,000 people, raped hundreds of women and girls, displaced three-quarters of the population, and demolished 75 percent of the country's infrastructure" (*Radical Priorities*, 72).

On 20 September 1999 the Australian-led peacekeeping troops of the International Force for East Timor (INTERFET) deployed to the country and brought the violence to an end. Activists in Portugal, Australia, the United States, and elsewhere pressured their governments to take action, with US President Bill Clinton eventually threatening Indonesia, in dire economic straits already, with the withdrawal of IMF loans. The Indonesian government consented to withdraw its troops and allow a multinational force into Timor to stabilize the area. It was clear that the UN did not have sufficient resources to combat the paramilitary forces directly. Instead, the UN authorised the creation of a multinational military force known as INTERFET (International Force for East Timor), with Security Council Resolution 1264. Troops were contributed by 17 nations, about 9,900 in total. 4,400 came from Australia, the remainder mostly from South-East Asia. The force was led by Major-General (now General) Peter Cosgrove. Troops landed in East Timor on September 20, 1999.

The Independent Republic

The administration of East Timor was taken over by the UN through the United Nations Transitional Administration in East Timor (UNTAET), established on October 25, 1999. The INTERFET deployment ended on February 14, 2000 with the transfer of military command to the UN. Elections were held in late 2001 for a constituent assembly to draft a constitution, a task finished in February 2002. East Timor became formally independent on May 20, 2002. Xanana Gusmão was sworn in as the country's President. East Timor became a member of the UN on September 27, 2002.

On December 4, 2002, after a student had been arrested the previous day, rioting students set fire to the house of the Prime Minister Marí Alkatiri and advanced on the police station. The police opened fire and one student was killed, whose body the students carried to the National Parliament building. There they fought the police, set a supermarket on fire and plundered shops. The police opened fire again and four more students were killed. Alkatiri called an inquiry and blamed foreign influence for the violence.

Relations with Australia have been strained by disputes over the maritime boundary between the two countries. Canberra claims petroleum and natural gas fields in an area known as the 'Timor Gap', which East Timor regards as lying within its maritime boundaries.

2006 Crisis

Unrest started in the country in April 2006 following the riots in Dili. A rally in support of 600 East Timorese soldiers, who were dismissed for deserting their barracks, turned into rioting where five people were killed and over 20,000 fled their homes. Fierce fighting between pro-government troops and disaffected Falintil troops broke out in May 2006. While unclear, the motives behind the fighting appears to be the distribution of oil funds and the poor organization of the Timorese army and police, which includes former Indonesian-trained police and former Timorese rebels. Prime Minister Mari Alkatiri has called the violence a "coup" and has welcomed offers of foreign military assistance from several nations.. As of May 25, 2006, Australia, Portugal, New Zealand, and Malaysia have sent troops to Timor, attempting to quell the violence. At least 23 deaths occurred as a result of the violence.

On June 21, 2006, President Xanana Gusmao formally requested Prime Minister Minister Alkatiri step down. A majority of Fretilin party members demanded the prime minister's resignation, accusing him of lying about distributing weapons to civilians. On June 26, 2006 Prime Minister Mari Alkatiri resigned stating, "I declare I am ready to resign my position as prime minister of the government... so as to avoid the resignation of His Excellency the President of the Republic". In August, rebel leader Alfredo Reinado escaped from Becora Prison, in Dili. Tensions were later raised after armed clashes between youth gangs forced the closure of Presidente Nicolau Lobato International Airport in late October.

3

CAMBODIA

The Kingdom of Cambodia is a country in South East Asia with a population of over 14 million people. The kingdom's capital and largest city is Phnom Penh. Cambodia is the successor state of the once powerful Hindu and Buddhist Khmer Empire, which ruled most of the Indochinese Peninsula between the eleventh and fourteenth centuries.

A citizen of Cambodia is usually identified as "Cambodian" or "Khmer," though the latter strictly refers to ethnic Khmers. Most Cambodians are Theravada Buddhists of Khmer extraction, but the country also has a substantial number of predominantly Muslim Cham, as well as ethnic Chinese, Vietnamese and small animist hill tribes.

The country borders Thailand to its west and northwest, Laos to its northeast, and Vietnam to its east and southeast. In the south it faces the Gulf of Thailand. The geography of Cambodia is dominated by the Mekong river (colloquial Khmer: *Tonle Thom* or "the great river") and the Tonlé Sap ("the fresh water lake"), an important source of fish.

Cambodia's main industries are garments, tourism, and construction. In 2007, foreign visitors to Angkor Wat alone almost hit the 4 million mark. In 2005, oil and natural gas deposits were found beneath Cambodia's territorial water, and once commercial extraction begins in 2011, the oil revenues could profoundly affect Cambodia's economy.

GEOGRAPHY OF CAMBODIA

Cambodia is a country in Southeastern Asia, bordering the Gulf of Thailand, between Thailand, Vietnam, and Laos. Its approximate geographical coordinates are 13° N 105° E. Its 2,572 km border is split among Vietnam (1,228 km), Thailand (803 km) and Laos (541 km), as well as 443 km of coastline. Cambodia covers 181,040 square kilometres in the southwestern part of the Indochina peninsula. It lies completely within the tropics; its southernmost points are only slightly more than 10° above the equator. Roughly square in shape, the country is bounded on the north by Thailand and by Laos, on the east and southeast by Vietnam, and on the west by the Gulf of

Thailand and by Thailand. Much of the country's area consists of rolling plains. Dominant features are the large, almost centrally located, Tonle Sap (Great Lake) and the Mekong River, which traverses the country from north to south.

The climate is monsoonal and has marked wet and dry seasons of relatively equal length. Both temperature and humidity generally are high throughout the year. Forest covers about two-thirds of the country, but it has been somewhat degraded in the more readily accessible areas by burning (a method called slash-and-burn agriculture), and by shifting agriculture.

The Mekong river and Tonale Sap Lake join. Mekong river basically runs through Asia except for some countries.

Total area 181,040 square kilometers, about the size of the U.S. state Missouri; country shares 803-kilometer border with Thailand on north and west, 541-kilometer border with Laos on northeast, 1,228-kilometer border with Vietnam on east and southeast, for a total of 2,572 kilometers of land borders; coastline along Gulf of Thailand about 443 hores.

Topography

Cambodia falls within several well-defined geographic regions. The largest part of the country, about 75 percent, consists of the Tonle Sap Basin and the Mekong Lowlands. To the southeast of this great basin is the Mekong Delta, which extends through Vietnam to the South China Sea. The basin and delta regions are rimmed with mountain ranges to the southwest by the Cardamom Mountains and the Elephant Rangeand to the north by the Dangrek Mountains. Higher land to the northeast and to the east merges into the Central Highlands of southern Vietnam.

The Tonle Sap Basin-Mekong Lowlands region consists chiefly of plains with elevations generally of less than 100 meters. As the elevation increases, the terrain becomes more rolling and dissected.

The Cardamom Mountains in the southwest, oriented generally in a northwest-southeast direction, rise to more than 1,500 meters. The highest mountain in Cambodia—Phnom Aural, at 1,771 meters—is in the eastern part of this range. The Elephant Range, an extension running toward the south and the southeast from the Cardamom Mountains, rises to elevations of between 500 and 1,000 meters. These two ranges are bordered on the west by a narrow coastal plain that contains Kampong Saom Bay, which faces the Gulf of Thailand. This area was largely isolated until the opening of the port of Kampong Saom (formerly called Sihanoukville) and the construction of a road and railroad connecting Kampong Saom, Kampot, Takev, and Phnom Penh in the 1960s.

The Dangrek Mountains at the northern rim of the Tonle Sap Basin consist of a steep escarpment with an average elevation of about 500 meters, the highest points of which reach more than 700 meters. The escarpment faces southward and is the southern edge of the Korat Plateau in Thailand. The watershed along the escarpment marks the boundary between Thailand and Cambodia. The main road through a pass in the Dangrek Mountains at O Smach connects northwestern Cambodia with Thailand. Despite this road and those running through a few other passes, in general the escarpment impedes easy communication between the two countries. Between the western part of the Dangrek and the northern part of the Cardamom ranges, however, lies an extension of the Tonle Sap Basin that merges into lowlands in Thailand, which allows easy access from the border to Bangkok.

The Mekong Valley, which offers a communication route between Cambodia and Laos, separates the eastern end of the Dangrek Mountains and the northeastern highlands. To the southeast, the basin joins the Mekong Delta, which, extending into Vietnam, provides both water and land communications between the two countries.

Climate

Cambodia's climate—like that of the rest of Southeast Asia—is dominated by the monsoons, which are known as tropical wet and dry because of the distinctly marked seasonal differences. The monsoonal airflows are caused by annual alternating high pressure and low pressure over the Central Asian landmass. In summer, moisture-laden air—the southwest monsoon—is drawn landward from the Indian Ocean. The flow is reversed during the winter, and the northeast monsoon sends back dry air. The southwest monsoon brings the rainy season from mid-May to mid-September or to early October, and the northeast monsoon flow of drier and cooler air lasts from early November to March. The southern third of the country has a two-month dry season; the northern two-thirds, a four-month one. Short transitional periods, which are marked by some difference in humidity but by little change in temperature, intervene between the alternating seasons. Temperatures are fairly uniform throughout the Tonle Sap Basin area, with only small variations from the average annual mean of around 25°C. The maximum mean is about 28°C; the minimum mean, about 22°C. Maximum temperatures of higher than 32°C, however, are common and, just before the start of the rainy season, they may rise to more than 38°C. Minimum temperatures rarely fall below 10°C. January is the coldest month, and April is the warmest. Typhoons—tropical cyclones—that often devastate coastal Vietnam rarely cause damage in Cambodia.

The total annual rainfall average is between 100 and 150 centimeters, and the heaviest amounts fall in the southeast. Rainfall from April to September in the Tonle

Sap Basin-Mekong Lowlands area averages 130 to 190 centimeters annually, but the amount varies considerably from year to year. Rainfall around the basin increases with elevation. It is heaviest in the mountains along the coast in the southwest, which receive from 250 to more than 500 centimeters of precipitation annually as the southwest monsoon reaches the coast. This area of greatest rainfall, however, drains mostly to the sea; only a small quantity goes into the rivers flowing into the basin. The relative humidity is high at night throughout the year; usually it exceeds 90 percent. During the daytime in the dry season, humidity averages about 50 percent or slightly lower, but it may remain about 60 percent in the rainy period.

Drainage

Except for the smaller rivers in the southeast, most of the major rivers and river systems in Cambodia drain into the Tonle Sap or into the Mekong River. The Cardamom Mountains and Elephant Range form a separate drainage divide. To the east the rivers flow into the Tonle Sap, while on the west they flow into the Gulf of Thailand. Toward the southern end of the Elephant Mountains, however, because of the topography, some small rivers flow southward on the eastern side of the divide.

The Mekong River in Cambodia flows southward from the Cambodia-Laos border to a point below Kracheh city, where it turns west for about 50 kilometers and then turns southwest to Phnom Penh. Extensive rapids run above Kracheh city. From Kampong Cham the gradient slopes very gently, and inundation of areas along the river occurs at flood stage—June through November—through breaks in the natural levees that have built up along its course. At Phnom Penh four major water courses meet at a point called the Chattomukh (Four Faces). The Mekong River flows in from the northeast and the Tonle Sab—a river emanating from the Tonle Sap—flows in from the northwest. They divide into two parallel channels, the Mekong River proper and the Basak River, and flow independently through the delta areas of Cambodia and Vietnam to the South China Sea.

The flow of water into the Tonle Sap is seasonal. In September or in October, the flow of the Mekong River, fed by monsoon rains, increases to a point where its outlets through the delta cannot handle the enormous volume of water. At this point, the water pushes northward up the Tonle Sab and empties into the Tonle Sap, thereby increasing the size of the lake from about 2,590 square kilometers to about 24,605 square kilometers at the height of the flooding. After the Mekong's waters crest—when its downstream channels can handle the volume of water—the flow reverses, and water flows out of the engorged lake.

As the level of the Tonle Sap retreats, it deposits a new layer of sediment. The annual flooding, combined with poor drainage immediately around the lake, transforms the surrounding area into marshlands unusable for agricultural purposes during the dry season. The sediment deposited into the lake during the Mekong's flood stage appears to be greater than the quantity carried away later by the Tonle Sap River. Gradual silting of the lake would seem to be occurring; during low-water level, it is only about 1.5 meters deep, while at flood stage it is between 10 and 15 meters deep.

Regional Divisions

Cambodia's boundaries were for the most part based upon those recognized by France and by neighboring countries during the colonial period. The 800-kilometre boundary with Thailand, coincides with a natural feature, the watershed of the Dangrek Mountains, only in its northern sector. The 541-kilometer border with Laos and the 1,228-kilometer border with Vietnam result largely from French administrative decisions and do not follow major natural features. Border disputes have broken out in the past between Cambodia and Thailand as well as between Cambodia and Vietnam.

DEMOGRAPHY OF CAMBODIA

More than 90% of its population is of Khmer origin and speaks the Khmer language, the country's official language. The remainder include Chinese, Vietnamese, Cham, Khmer Loeu and Indians.

The Khmer language is a member of the Mon-Khmer subfamily of the Austroasiatic language group. French, once the lingua franca of Indochina and still spoken by some, mostly older Cambodians as a second language, remains the language of instruction in various schools and universities that are often funded by the government of France. Cambodian French, a remnant of the country's colonial past, is a dialect found in Cambodia and is frequently used in government. However, in recent decades, many younger Cambodians and those in the business-class have favoured learning English. In the major cities and tourist centers, English is widely spoken and taught at a large number of schools due to the overwhelming number of tourists from English-speaking countries. Even in the most rural outposts, however, most young people speak at least some English, as it is often taught by monks at the local pagodas where many children are educated.

The dominant religion, a form of Theravada Buddhism (95%), was suppressed by the Khmer Rouge but has since experienced a revival. Islam (3%) and Christianity (2%) are also practiced.

Civil war and its aftermath have had a marked effect on the Cambodian population. The median age is 20.6 years, with more than 50% of the population younger than 25. At 0.95 males/female, Cambodia has the most female-biased sex ratio in the Greater

Mekong Subregion. In the Cambodian population over 65, the female to male ratio is 1.6:1. UNICEF has designated Cambodia the third most mined country in the world, attributing over 60,000 civilian deaths and thousands more maimed or injured since 1970 to the unexploded land mines left behind in rural areas. The majority of the victims are children herding animals or playing in the fields. Adults that survive landmines often require amputation of one or more limbs and have to resort to begging for survival. In 2006, the number of landmines casualties in Cambodia took a sharp decrease of more than 50% compared to 2005, with the number of landmines victims down from 800 in 2005 to less than 400 in 2006. The reduced casualty rate continued in 2007, with 208 casualties (38 killed and 170 injured)."

CULTURE OF CAMBODIA

The culture of Cambodia has had a rich and varied history dating back many centuries, and has been heavily influenced by India. In turn, Cambodia greatly influenced Thailand, Laos and vice versa. Throughout Cambodia's long history, a major source of inspiration was from religion. Throughout nearly two millennium, Cambodians developed a unique Khmer belief from the syncreticism of indigenous animistic beliefs and the Indian religions of Buddhism and Hinduism. Indian culture and civilization, including its language and arts reached mainland Southeast Asia around the 1st century A.D. Its is generally believed that seafaring merchants brought Indian customs and culture to ports along the gulf of Thailand and the Pacific while trading with China. The first state to benefit from this was Funan. At various times, Cambodia culture also absorbed elements from Thai, Lao, Chinese, and Javanese cultures.

The majority of Cambodians (nearly 90%) are of Khmer heritage, and an even greater proportion speak Khmer the official language of Cambodia. Other languages spoken include French, Chinese, Vietnamese and English (which has become increasingly common).

The golden age of Cambodia was between the 9th and 14th century, during the Angkor period, during which it was a powerful and prosperous empire that flourished and dominated almost all of inland south east Asia. However, Angkor would eventually collapse after much in-fighting between royalty and constant warring with its increasingly powerful neighbors, notably Siam and Dai Viet. Many temples from this period however, like Bayon and Angkor Wat still remain today, scattered throughout Thailand, Cambodian, Laos, and Vietnam as a reminder of the grandeur of Khmer arts and culture. Cambodia's unparalleled achievements in art, architectures, music, and dance during this period have had a great influence on many neighboring kingdoms, namely

Thailand and Laos. The affect of Angkorian culture can still be seen today in those countries, as they share many close characteristics with current-day Cambodia.

Architecture and Housing

The Angkorian architects and sculptors created temples that mapped the cosmic world in stone. Khmer decorations drew inspiration from religion, and mythical creatures from Hinduism and Buddhism were carved on walls. Temples were built in accordance to the rule of ancient Khmer architecture that dictated that a basic temple layout include a central shrine, a courtyard, an enclosing wall, and a moat. Khmer motifs use many creatures from Buddhist and Hindu mythology, like the Royal Palace in Phnom Penh, use motifs such as the garuda, a mythical bird in the Hinduism. The architecture of Cambodia developed in stages under the Khmer empire from 9th to the 15th century, preserved in many buildings of the Angkor temple. The remains of secular architecture from this time are rare, as only religious buildings were made of stone. The architecture of the Angkor period used specific structural features and styles, which are one of the main methods used to date the temples, along with inscriptions.

In modern rural Cambodia, the nuclear family typically lives in a rectangular house that may vary in size from four by six meters to six by ten meters. It is constructed of a wooden frame with gabled thatch roof and walls of woven bamboo. Khmer houses typically are raised on stilts as much as three meters for protection from annual floods. Two ladders or wooden staircases provide access to the house. The steep thatch roof overhanging the house walls protects the interior from rain. Typically a house contains three rooms separated by partitions of woven bamboo. The front room serves as a living room used to receive visitors, the next room is the parents' bedroom, and the third is for unmarried daughters. Sons sleep anywhere they can find space. Family members and neighbors work together to build the house, and a house-raising ceremony is held upon its completion. The houses of poorer persons may contain only a single large room. Food is prepared in a separate kitchen located near the house but usually behind it. Toilet facilities consist of simple pits in the ground, located away from the house, that are covered up when filled. Any livestock is kept below the house. Chinese and Vietnamese houses in Cambodian town and villages typically are built directly on the ground and have earthen, cement, or tile floors, depending upon the economic status of the owner. Urban housing and commercial buildings may be of brick, masonry, or wood.

Religion

Cambodia is predominantly Buddhist with 95% of the population being Theravada Buddhist, and the majority of the remaining population follow Islam, atheism, or animism.

Ways of life

Birth and Death Rituals

The birth of a child is a happy event for the family. According to traditional beliefs, however, confinement and childbirth expose the family, and especially the mother and the child to harm from the spirit world. A woman who dies in childbirth—crosses the river (chhlong tonle) in Khmer is believed to become an evil spirit. In traditional Khmer society, a pregnant woman respects a number of food taboos and avoids certain situations. These traditions remain in practice in rural Cambodia, but they have become weakened in urban areas.

Death is not viewed with the great outpouring of grief common to Western society; it is viewed as the end of one life and as the beginning of another life that one hopes will be better. Buddhist Khmer usually are cremated, and their ashes are deposited in a stupa in the temple compound. A corpse is washed, dressed, and placed in a coffin, which may be decorated with flowers and with a photograph of the deceased. White pennant-shaped flags, called "white crocodile flags," outside a house indicate that someone in that household has died. A funeral procession consisting of an achar, Buddhist monks, members of the family, and other mourners accompanies the coffin to the crematorium. The spouse and the children show mourning by shaving their heads and by wearing white clothing. Relics such as teeth or pieces of bone are prized by the survivors, and they are often worn on gold chains as amulets.

Childhood and Adolescence

A Cambodian child may be nursed until he or she is between two and four years of age. Up to the age of three or four, the child is given considerable physical affection and freedom. Children around five years of age also may be expected to help look after younger siblings. Children's games emphasize socialization or skill rather than winning and losing.

Most children begin school when they are seven or eight. By the time they reach this age, they are familiar with the society's norms of politeness, obedience, and respect toward their elders and toward Buddhist monks. The father at this time begins his permanent retreat into a relatively remote, authoritarian role. By age ten, a girl is expected to help her mother in basic household tasks; a boy knows how to care for the family's livestock and can do farm work under the supervision of older males. Adolescent children usually play with members of the same sex. During his teens, a boy may become a temple servant and go on to serve a time as a novice monk, which is a great honor for the parents.

In precommunist days, parents exerted complete authority over their children until the children were married, and the parents continued to maintain some control well into the marriage. Age difference is strictly recognized with polite vocabulary and special generational terms for "you".

Courtship, Marriage, and Divorce

In Cambodia, premarital sex is deplored. The choice of a spouse is a complex one for the young male, and it may involve not only his parents and his friends, as well as those of the young woman, but also a matchmaker. In theory, a girl may veto the spouse her parents have chosen. Courtship patterns differ between rural and urban Khmer; romantic love is a notion that exists to a much greater extent in larger cities. A man usually marries between the ages of nineteen and twenty-five, a girl between the ages of sixteen and twenty-two. After a spouse has been selected, each family investigates the other to make sure its child is marrying into a good family. In rural areas, there is a form of bride-service; that is, the young man may take a vow to serve his prospective father-in-law for a period of time.

The traditional wedding is a long and colorful affair. Formerly it lasted three days, but in the 1980s it more commonly lasted a day and a half. Buddhist priests offer a short sermon and recite prayers of blessing. Parts of the ceremony involve ritual hair cutting, tying cotton threads soaked in holy water around the bride's and groom's wrists, and passing a candle around a circle of happily married and respected couples to bless the union. After the wedding, a banquet is held. Newlyweds traditionally move in with the wife's parents and may live with them up to a year, until they can build a new house nearby.

Divorce is legal and relatively easy to obtain, but not common. Divorced persons are viewed with some disapproval. Each spouse retains whatever property he or she brought into the marriage, and jointly-acquired property is divided equally. Divorced persons may remarry, but the woman must wait ten months. Custody of minor children is usually given to the mother, and both parents continue to have an obligation to contribute financially toward the rearing and education of the child.

Social Organization

Khmer culture is very hierarchical. The greater a person's age, the greater the level of respect that must be granted to them. Cambodians are addressed with a hierarchical title corresponding to their seniority before the name. When a married couple become too old to support themselves, they may invite the youngest child's family to move in and to take over running the household. At this stage in their lives, they enjoy a position of high status.

The individual Khmer is surrounded by a small inner circle of family and friends who constitute his or her closest associates, those he would approach first for help. The nuclear family, consisting of a husband and a wife and their unmarried children, is the most important kin group. Within this unit are the strongest emotional ties, the assurance of aid in the event of trouble, economic cooperation in labor, sharing of produce and income, and contribution as a unit to ceremonial obligations. In rural communities, neighbors—who are often also kin—may be important, too. Fictive child-parent, sibling, and close friend relationships Cambodia transcend kinship boundaries and serve to strengthen interpersonal and interfamily ties. Beyond this close circle are more distant relatives and casual friends. In rural Cambodia, the strongest ties a Khmer may develop—besides those to the nuclear family and to close friends—are those to other members of the local community. A strong feeling of pride—for the village, for the district, and province—usually characterizes Cambodian community life.

Legally, the husband is the head of the Khmer family, but the wife has considerable authority, especially in family economics. The husband is responsible for providing shelter and food for his family; the wife is generally in charge of the family budget, and she serves as the major ethical and religious model for the children, especially the daughters. Both husbands and wives are responsible for domestic economic tasks.

Customs

In Khmer culture a person's head is believed to contain the persons soul—therefore making it taboo to touch or point your feet at it. It is also considered to be extremely disrespectful to point or sleep with your feet pointing at a person, as the feet are the lowest part of the body and are considered to be impure.

When greeting people or to show respect in Cambodia people do the "sampeah" gesture, identical to the Thai wai and similar to the Indian namaste.

Customary Cambodian teachings include: that if a person does not wake up before sunrise he is lazy; you have to tell your parents or elders where you are going and what time you are coming back home; close doors gently, otherwise you have a bad temper; sit with your legs straight down and not crossed (crossing your legs shows that you are an impolite person); and always let other people talk more than you.

Clothing

Cambodians traditionally wear a checkered scarf called a "Krama". The "krama" is what distinctly separates the Khmer (Cambodians) from their neighbors the Thai, the

Vietnamese, and the Laotians. The scarf is used for many purposes including for style, protection from the sun, an aid (for your feet) when climbing trees, a hammock for infants, a towel, or as a "sarong". A "krama" can also be easily shaped into a small child's doll for play. Under the Khmer Rouge, all Khmer were forced to wear a red checkered "krama".

Some Khmer men and women wear a Buddha pendant in a necklace fashion. There are different pendants for different uses; some are meant for protection from evil spirits, some are meant to bring good luck. However, women are only allowed to wear a Buddha pendant if she remains "pure," or a virgin. It is considered a sin for non-virgin Khmer Buddhist women to wear the pendant.

Cuisine

Khmer cuisine is similar to that of its Southeast Asian neighbors. It is relatively unknown to the world compared to its neighbors but has been described as somewhat similar to Thai cuisine but less spicy. Many of the Khmers who knew how to cook authentic Khmer cuisine before the civil war were killed during the Khmer Rouge Regime. Cambodian cuisine also uses fish sauce widely in soups, stir-fried cuisine, and as dippings. Curry dishes known as *kari* shows it's ties with Indian cuisine. Influences from Chinese cuisine can be noted in the use of many variations of rice noodles. Beef noodle soup known simply as *Kuyteav* is a popular dish brought to Cambodia by its Chinese settlers. Also, *Banh Chiao* is the Khmer version of the Vietnamese *Bánh xèo.*

Khmer cuisine is noted for the use of prahok, a type of fermented fish paste, in many dishes as a distinctive flavoring. When prahok is not used, it is likely to be *kapÐ* instead, a kind of fermented shrimp paste. Coconut milk is the main ingredient of many Khmer curries and desserts. In Cambodia there is regular aromatic rice and glutinous or sticky rice. The latter is used more in dessert dishes with fruits such as durian. Almost every meal is eaten with a bowl of rice.

Typically, Cambodians eat their meals with at least three or four separate dishes. Each individual dish will usually be one of either sweet, sour, salty or bitter. Chili is usually left up to the individual to add themselves. In this way Cambodians ensure that they get a bit of every flavor to satisfy their palates.

Arts

Visual Art

The history of visual arts in Cambodia stretches back centuries to ancient crafts; Khmer art reached its peak during the Angkor period. Traditional Cambodian arts and crafts include textiles, non-textile weaving, silversmithing, stone carving, lacquerware, ceramics, wat murals, and kite-making. Beginning in the mid-20th century, a tradition of modern art began in Cambodia, though in the later 20th century both traditional and modern arts declined for several reasons, including the killing of artists by the Khmer Rouge. The country has experienced a recent artistic revival due to increased support from governments, NGOs, and foreign tourists.

Music

Especially in the 60s and 70s, the 'big two' duet of Sinn Sisamouth and Ros Sereysothea had been a large hit in the country. However after their deaths, new music stars have tried to bring back the music. Cambodian music has undergone heavy westernization.

The Cambodian pinpeat ensemble is traditionally heard on feast days in the pagodas. It is also a court ensemble used to accompany classical dance for ritual occasions or theatrical events. The pinpeat is primarily made up of percussion instruments: the roneat ek (lead xylophone), roneat thung (low bamboo xylophone), kong vong touch and kong vong thom (small and large sets of tuned gongs), sampho (two-sided drum), skor thom (two large drums), and sralai (quadruple-reed instrument).

Dance

Cambodian Dance can be divided into three main categories: classical dance, folk dances, and vernacular dances.

Khmer classical dance is a form of Cambodian dance originally performed only for royalty. The dances have many elements in common with Thai classical dance. During the mid-20th century, it was introduced to the public where it now remains a celebrated icon of Khmer culture, often being performed during public events, holidays, and for tourists visiting Cambodia.

Khmer folk dances, which are performed for audiences, are fast-paced. The movements and gestures are not as stylized as Khmer classical dance. Folk dancers wear clothes of the people they are portraying such as Chams, hill tribes, farmers, and peasants. The folk dance music is played by a mahori orchestra.

Cambodian vernacular dances (or social dances) are those danced at social gatherings. Such dances include *ram vong, ram kbach, ram saravan,* and *lam leav*. Some of these dances have much influence from the traditional dances of Laos. But *rom kbach,* for example, take heavily from the classical dance of the royal court. Other social dances from around the world have had an impact on Cambodian social culture include the Cha-cha, Bolero, and the Madison.

Film

Cinema in Cambodia began in the 1950s, and many films were being screened in theaters throughout the country by the 1960s, which are regarded as the "golden age". After a decline during the Khmer Rouge regime, competition from video and television has meant that the Cambodian film industry is relatively weak today.

GOVERNMENT AND POLITICS OF CAMBODIA

The politics of Cambodia formally takes place according to the nation's constitution (enacted in 1993) in a framework of a parliamentary representative democratic monarchy, whereby the Prime Minister of Cambodia is the head of government, and of a multi-party system. Executive power is exercised by the government. Legislative power is vested in both the government and the two chambers of parliament, the National Assembly of Cambodia and the Senate

The Prime Minister of Cambodia is a representative from the ruling party of the National Assembly. He or she is appointed by the King on the recommendation of the President and Vice Presidents of the National Assembly. In order for a person to become Prime Minister, he or she must first be given a vote of confidence by the National Assembly.

The Prime Minister is officially the Head of Government in Cambodia. Upon entry into office, he appoints a Council of Ministers who are responsible to the Prime Minister. Officially, the Prime Minister's duties include chairing meetings of the Council of Ministers (Cambodia's version of a Cabinet) and appointing and leading a government. The Prime Minister and his government make up Cambodia's executive branch of government.

The current Cambodian Prime Minister is Cambodian's People Party (CPP) member, staged a bloody coup in Phnom Penh to overthrow elected Prime Minister Prince Norodom Ranariddh, president of the FUNCINPEC party.

Legislative Branch

The legislative branch of the Cambodian government is made up of a bicameral parliament.

- The National Assembly of Cambodia (*Radhsaphea ney Preah Reacheanachak Kampuchea*) has 123 members, elected for a five-year term by proportional representation.
- The Senate (*Sénat*) has 61 members. Two of these members are appointed by the King, two are elected by the lower house of the government, and the remaining fifty-seven are elected popularly by "functional constituencies." Members in this house serve a five-year term.

The official duty of the Parliament is to legislate and make laws. Bills passed by the Parliament are given to the King who gives the proposed bills Royal Assent. The King does not have veto power over bills passed by the National Assembly (the lower house) and, thus, cannot withhold Royal Assent. The National Assembly also has the power to dismiss the Prime Minister and his government by a two-thirds vote of no confidence.

Senate

The upper house of the Cambodian legislature is called the *Senate*. It consists of sixty-one members. Two of these members are appointed by the King, two are elected by the lower house of the government, and the remaining fifty-seven are elected popularly by "functional constituencies." Members in this house serve six year terms.

Elections were last held for the Senate in 1999. New elections were supposed to have occurred in 2004, but these elections were initially postponed. On January 22, 2006, 11,352 possible voters went to the poll and chose their candidates. This election was criticized by local monitoring non-governmental organizations as being undemocratic.

As of 2006, the Cambodian People's Party holds forty-three seats in the Senate, constituting a significant majority. The two other major parties holding seats in the Senate are the Funcinpec party (holding twelve seats) and the Sam Rainsy Party (holding two seats).

National Assembly

The lower house of the legislature is called the *National Assembly*. It is made up of 123 members, elected by popular vote to serve a five-year term. Elections were last held for the National Assembly in 2003, with the next elections scheduled for July 2008.

In order to vote in legislative elections, one must be at least eighteen years of age. However, in order to be elected to the Legislature, one must be at least twenty-five years of age.

The National Assembly is led by a President and two Vice Presidents who are selected by Assembly members prior to each session.

As of 2005, the Cambodian People's Party holds a majority of the seats in the National Assembly, controlling seventy-three out of the 123 seats. The Funcinpec party holds twenty-six seats, while the Sam Rainsy Party holds the remaining twenty-four seats.

Judicial Branch

The judicial branch is independent from the rest of the government, as specified by the Cambodian Constitution. The highest court of judicial branch is the Supreme

Council of the Magistracy. Other, lower courts also exist. Until 1997, Cambodia didn't have a judicial branch of government despite the nation's Constitution requiring one.

The main duties of the judiciary are to prosecute criminals, settle lawsuits, and, most importantly, protect the freedoms and rights of Cambodian citizens. However, in reality, the judicial branch in Cambodia is highly corrupt and often serves as a tool of the executive branch to silence civil society and its leaders.

Monarchy

Cambodia is a constitutional monarchy, i.e. the King reigns but does not rule, in similar fashion to Queen Elizabeth II of the United Kingdom. The King is officially the Head of State and is the symbol of unity and "eternity" of the nation, as defined by Cambodia's constitution.

From September 24, 1993 through October 7, 2004, Norodom Sihanouk reigned as King. Under the Constitution, the King has no political power, but as Norodom Sihanouk was revered in the country, his word often carried much influence in the government. For example, in February 2004, he issued a proclamation stating that since Cambodia is a "liberal democracy," the Kingdom should allow gay marriage. While such views aren't prevalent in Cambodia, his word was respected by his subjects. The King, often irritated over the conflicts in his government, several times threatened to abdicate unless the political factions in the government got along. This put pressure on the government to solve their differences. This influence of the King was often used to help mediate differences in government.

After the abdication of King Norodom Sihanouk in 2004, he was succeeded by his son Norodom Sihamoni. While the retired King is highly revered in his country for dedicating his lifetime to Cambodia, the current King has spent most of his life abroad in France. Thus, it remains to be seen whether the new king's views will be as highly respected as his father's.

Although in the Khmer language there are many words meaning "king", the word officially used in Khmer (as found in the 1993 Cambodian Constitution) is *preahmâhaksat,* which literally means: *preah-* ("sacred", cognate of the Indian word Brahmin) *-mâha-* (from Sanskrit, meaning "great", cognate with "maha-" in maharaja) *-ksat* ("warrior, ruler", cognate of the Indian word Kshatriya).

On the occasion of HM King Norodom Sihanouk's retirement in September 2004, the Cambodian National Assembly coined a new word for the retired king: *preahmâhaviraksat,* where *vira* comes from Sanskrit *vîra,* meaning "brave or eminent man, hero, chief", cognate of Latin *vir, viris,* English *virile. Preahmâhaviraksat* is translated in English as "King-Father", although the word "father" does not appear in the Khmer noun.

As *preahmâhaviraksat*, Norodom Sihanouk retains many of the prerogatives he formerly held as *preahmâhaksat* and is a highly respected and listened-to figure. Thus, in effect, Cambodia can be described as a country with two heads of state: an official one, the *preahmâhaksat* Norodom Sihamoni, and an unofficial one, the *preahmâhaviraksat* Norodom Sihanouk.

Succession to the Throne

Unlike most monarchies, Cambodia's monarchy isn't necessarily hereditary and the King is not allowed to select his own heir. Instead, a new King is chosen by a Royal Council of the Throne, consisting of the president of the National Assembly, the Prime Minister, the Chiefs of the orders of Mohanikay and Thammayut, and the First and Second Vice-President of the Assembly. The Royal Council meets within a week of the King's death or abdication and selects a new King from a pool of candidates with royal blood.

It has been suggested that Cambodia's ability to peacefully appoint a new King shows that Cambodia's government has stabilized incredibly from the situation the country was in during the 1970's

Provincial and Local Governments

Below the central government are 24 provincial and municipal administration. (In rural areas, first-level administrative divisions are called provinces; in urban areas, they are called municipalities.) The administrations are a part of the Ministry of the Interior and their members are appointed by the central government. Provincial and municipal administrations participate in the creation of nation budget; they also issue land titles and license businesses.

Since 2002, commune-level governments (commune councils) have been composed of members directly elected by commune residents every five years.

In practice, the allocation of responsibilities between various levels of government is uncertain. This uncertainty has created additional opportunities for corruption and increased costs for investors.

ECONOMY OF CAMBODIA

The economy of Cambodia has seen rapid progress in the last decade. Per capita income, although rapidly increasing, is low compared with most neighbouring countries. The main domestic activity on which most rural households depend is agriculture and its related sub-sectors. Manufacturing output is varied but is not very extensive and is mostly conducted on a small-scale and informal basis. The service sector is heavily concentrated in trading activities and catering-related services. Reuters has reported that oil and natural gas reserves have been found off-shore. Production of oil could potentially have a great effect on the future of the economy.

During 1995, the government implemented firm stabilization policies under difficult circumstances. Overall, macroeconomic performance was good. Growth in 1995 was estimated at 7% because of improved agricultural production (rice in particular). Strong growth in construction and services continued. Inflation dropped from 26% in 1994 to only 6% in 1995. Imports increased as a result of the availability of external financing. Exports also increased, due to an increase in log exports. With regard to the budget, both the current and overall deficits were lower than originally targeted.

After four years of solid macroeconomic performance, Cambodia's economy slowed dramatically in 1997-98 due to the regional economic crisis, civil violence, and political infighting. Foreign investment and tourism fell off. Also, in 1998 the main harvest was hit by drought. But in 1999, the first full year of peace in 30 years, progress was made on economic reforms and growth resumed at 4%. The long-term development of the economy after decades of war remains a daunting challenge. The population lacks education and productive skills, particularly in the poverty-ridden countryside, which suffers from an almost total lack of basic infrastructure. Recurring political instability and corruption within government discourage foreign investment and delay foreign aid. On the brighter side, the government is addressing these issues with assistance from bilateral and multilateral donors. So long as political stability lasts, the Cambodian economy is likely to grow at a respectable pace.

Foreign Aid

Cambodia's emerging democracy has received strong international support. Under the mandate carried out by the United Nations Transitional Authority in Cambodia (UNTAC), $1.72 billion (1.72 G$) was spent in an effort to bring basic security, stability and democratic rule to the country. Regarding economic assistance, official donors had pledged $880 million at the Ministerial Conference on the Rehabilitation of Cambodia (MCRRC) in Tokyo in June 1992, to which pledges of $119 million were added in September 1993 at the meeting of the International Committee on the Reconstruction of Cambodia (ICORC) in Paris, and $643 million at the March 1994 ICORC meeting in Tokyo. To date, therefore, the total amount pledged for Cambodia's rehabilitation is approximately 1.6 G$.

Recent Developments

In 2007 GDP (or gross monetarised product GMP)grew an estimated 9.6%, in line with the 2000/06 average of 9.5 percent. Foreign direct investment reached US$600 million (7% of GDP), slightly more than was received in foreign aid. Garment exports rose almost 8%, tourist arrivals jumped nearly 35%, and construction activity doubled. With exports decelerating somewhat, the 2007 GDP growth was driven by consumption and investment. Foreign direct investment (FDI) inflows reached US$600 million (7 percent of GDP), slightly more than the country received in official aid. Domestic investment, driven largely by the private sector, accounted for 23.4 percent of GDP. Approximately 2,860 new businesses registered for operation in 2007, a 71 percent increase over 2006.

Although risks have increased, economic prospects for 2008 remain strong. The projected 7.5 percent growth rate for 2008 reflects a mix of growth in services (mainly tourism) and construction combined with a slowdown in garment exports. Export growth, especially to the US, began to slow in late 2007 accompanied by stiffer competition from Vietnam and emerging risks (slowdown in the US economy and lifting of safeguards on China's exports). Although exports of cash crops have grown fast in recent years, developments in the garment industry have a major impact on Cambodia's export performance. On the other hand, Cambodia's exporters might benefit from the depreciation of the dollar. Another risk is uncertainties in the construction sector. However, although the boom driven by real estate could slow, other sources of demand–-tourism and infrastructure—could enable continued growth in construction.

4

INDONESIA

The Republic of Indonesia, is a country in Southeast Asia. Comprising 17,508 islands, it is the world's largest archipelagic state. With a population of 222 million people in 2006, it is the world's fourth most populous country and the most populous Muslim-majority nation, although officially it is not an Islamic state. Indonesia is a republic, with an elected parliament and president. The nation's capital city is Jakarta. The country shares land borders with Papua New Guinea, East Timor and Malaysia. Other neighboring countries include Singapore, the Philippines, Australia, and the Indian territory of the Andaman and Nicobar Islands.

The Indonesian archipelago has been an important trade region since at least the seventh century, when the Srivijaya Kingdom formed trade links with China. Indonesian history has been influenced by foreign powers drawn to its natural resources. Under Indian influence, Hindu and Buddhist kingdoms flourished from the early centuries CE. Muslim traders brought Islam, and European powers fought one another to monopolize trade in the Spice Islands of Maluku during the Age of Discovery. Following three and a half centuries of Dutch colonialism, Indonesia secured its independence after World War II. Indonesia's history has since been turbulent, with challenges posed by natural disasters, corruption, separatism, a democratization process, and periods of rapid economic change.

Across its many islands, Indonesia consists of distinct ethnic, linguistic, and religious groups. The Javanese are the largest and most politically dominant ethnic group. As a unitary state and a nation, Indonesia has developed a shared identity defined by a national language, a majority Muslim population, and a history of colonialism and rebellion against it. Indonesia's national motto, *"Bhinneka tunggal ika"* ("Unity in Diversity" *lit.* "many, yet one"), articulates the diversity that shapes the country. However, sectarian tensions and separatism have led to violent confrontations that have undermined political and economic stability. Despite its large population and densely populated regions, Indonesia has vast areas of wilderness that support the world's second highest level of biodiversity. The country is richly endowed with natural resources, yet poverty is a defining feature of contemporary Indonesia.

GEOGRAPHY OF INDONESIA

Indonesia consists of 17,508 islands, about 6,000 of which are inhabited. These are scattered over both sides of the equator. The five largest islands are Java, Sumatra, Kalimantan (the Indonesian part of Borneo), New Guinea (shared with Papua New Guinea), and Sulawesi. Indonesia shares land borders with Malaysia on the islands of Borneo and Sebatik, Papua New Guinea on the island of New Guinea, and East Timor on the island of Timor. Indonesia also shares borders with Singapore, Malaysia, and the Philippines to the north and Australia to the south across narrow straits of water. The capital, Jakarta, is on Java and is the nation's largest city, followed by Surabaya, Bandung, Medan, and Semarang.

At 1,919,440 square kilometers (741,050 sq mi), Indonesia is the world's 16th-largest country in terms of land area. Its average population density is 134 people per square kilometer (347 per sq mi), 79th in the world, although Java, the world's most populous island, has a population density of 940 people per square kilometer (2,435 per sq mi). At 4,884 meters (16,024 ft), Puncak Jaya in Papua is Indonesia's highest peak, and Lake Toba in Sumatra its largest lake, with an area of 1,145 square kilometers (442 sq mi). The country's largest rivers are in Kalimantan, and include the Mahakam and Barito; such rivers are communication and transport links between the island's river settlements.

Indonesia's location on the edges of the Pacific, Eurasian, and Australian tectonic plates makes it the site of numerous volcanoes and frequent earthquakes. Indonesia has at least 150 active volcanoes, including Krakatoa and Tambora, both famous for their devastating eruptions in the 19th century. The eruption of the Toba supervolcano, approximately 70,000 years ago, was one of the largest eruptions ever, and a global catastrophe. Recent disasters due to seismic activity include the 2004 tsunami that killed an estimated 167,736 in northern Sumatra, and the Yogyakarta earthquake in 2006. However, volcanic ash is a major contributor to the high agricultural fertility that has historically sustained the high population densities of Java and Bali.

Lying along the equator, Indonesia has a tropical climate, with two distinct monsoonal wet and dry seasons. Average annual rainfall in the lowlands varies from 1,780–3,175 millimeters (70–125 in), and up to 6,100 millimeters (240 in) in mountainous regions. Mountainous areas—particularly in the west coast of Sumatra, West Java, Kalimantan,

Sulawesi, and Papua—receive the highest rainfall. Humidity is generally high, averaging about 80%. Temperatures vary little throughout the year; the average daily temperature range of Jakarta is 26–30 °C (79–86 °F).

DEMOGRAPHY OF INDONESIA

The national population from the 2000 national census is 206 million, and the Indonesian Central Statistics Bureau and *Statistics Indonesia* estimate a population of 222 million for 2006. 130 million people live on the island of Java, the world's most populous island. Despite a fairly effective family planning program that has been in place since the 1960s, the population is expected to grow around 315 million by 2035, based on the current estimated annual growth rate of 1.25%.

Most Indonesians are descendant from Austronesian-speaking peoples who originated from Taiwan. The other major grouping are Melanesians, who inhabit eastern Indonesia. There are around 300 distinct native ethnicities in Indonesia, and 742 different languages and dialects. The largest is the Javanese, who comprise 42% of the population, and are politically and culturally dominant. The Sundanese, ethnic Malays, and Madurese are the largest non-Javanese groups. A sense of Indonesian nationhood exists alongside strongly maintained regional identities. Society is largely harmonious, although social, religious and ethnic tensions have triggered horrendous violence. Chinese Indonesians are an influential ethnic minority comprising less than 5% of the population. Much of the country's privately-owned commerce and wealth is Chinese-controlled, which has contributed to considerable resentment, and even anti-Chinese violence.

The official national language, Indonesian, is universally taught in schools, and is spoken by nearly every Indonesian. It is the language of business, politics, national media, education, and academia. It was originally a lingua franca for most of the region, including present-day Malaysia, and is thus closely related to Malay. Indonesian was first promoted by nationalists in the 1920s, and declared the official language on independence in 1945. Most Indonesians speak at least one of the several hundred local languages (*bahasa daerah*), often as their first language. Of these, Javanese is the most widely-spoken as the language of the largest ethnic group. On the other hand, Papua has 500 or more indigenous Papuan and Austronesian languages, in a region of just 2.7 million people. Much of the older population can still speak a level of Dutch.

Although religious freedom is stipulated in the Indonesian constitution, the government officially recognizes only six religions: Islam; Protestantism; Roman Catholicism; Hinduism; Buddhism; and Confucianism. Although it is not an Islamic state, Indonesia is the world's most populous Muslim-majority nation, with almost 86.1% of Indonesians declared Muslim according to the 2000 census. 8.7% of the population is

Christian, 3% are Hindu, and 1.8% Buddhist or other. Most Indonesian Hindus are Balinese, and most Buddhists in modern-day Indonesia are ethnic Chinese. Though now minority religions, Hinduism and Buddhism remain defining influences in Indonesian culture. Islam was first adopted by Indonesians in northern Sumatra in the 13th century, through the influence of traders, and became the country's dominant religion by the 16th century. Roman Catholicism was brought to Indonesia by early Portuguese colonialists and missionaries, and the Protestant denominations are largely a result of Dutch Calvinist and Lutheran missionary efforts during the country's colonial period. A large proportion of Indonesians—such as the Javanese *abangan*, Balinese Hindus, and Dayak Christians—practice a less orthodox, syncretic form of their religion, which draws on local customs and beliefs.

CULTURE OF INDONESIA

Indonesia has around 300 ethnic groups, each with cultural differences developed over centuries, and influenced by Indian, Arabic, Chinese, Malay, and European sources. Traditional Javanese and Balinese dances, for example, contain aspects of Hindu culture and mythology, as do *wayang kulit* (shadow puppet) performances. Textiles such as batik, ikat and songket are created across Indonesia in styles that vary by region. The most dominant influences on Indonesian architecture have traditionally been Indian; however, Chinese, Arab, and European architectural influences have been significant. The most popular sports in Indonesia are badminton and football; Liga Indonesia is the country's premier football club league. Traditional sports include *sepak takraw*, and bull racing in Madura. In areas with a history of tribal warfare, mock fighting contests are held, such as, *caci* in Flores, and *pasola* in Sumba. *Pencak Silat* is an Indonesian martial art. Sports in Indonesia are generally male-orientated and spectator sports are often associated with illegal gambling.

Indonesian cuisine varies by region and is based on Chinese, European, Middle Eastern, and Indian precedents. Rice is the main staple food and is served with side dishes of meat and vegetables. Spices (notably chili), coconut milk, fish and chicken are fundamental ingredients. Indonesian traditional music includes *gamelan* and *keroncong*. *Dangdut* is a popular contemporary genre of pop music that draws influence from Arabic, Indian, and Malay folk music. The Indonesian film industry's popularity peaked in the 1980s and dominated cinemas in Indonesia, although it declined significantly in the early 1990s. Between 2000 and 2005, the number of Indonesian films released each year has steadily increased.

The oldest evidence of writing in Indonesia is a series of Sanskrit inscriptions dated to the 5th century CE. Important figures in modern Indonesian literature include: Dutch author Multatuli, who criticized treatment of the Indonesians under Dutch colonial rule; Sumatrans Muhammad Yamin and Hamka, who were influential pre-independence nationalist writers and politicians; and proletarian writer Pramoedya Ananta Toer, Indonesia's most famous novelist. Many of Indonesia's peoples have strongly-rooted oral traditions, which help to define and preserve their cultural identities. Media freedom in Indonesia increased considerably after the end of President Suharto's rule, during which the now-defunct Ministry of Information monitored and controlled domestic media, and restricted foreign media. The TV market includes ten national commercial networks, and provincial networks that compete with public TVRI. Private radio stations carry their own news bulletins and foreign broadcasters supply programs. At a reported 20 million users in 2007, Internet usage is limited to a minority of the population, approximately 8.5%.

GOVERNMENT AND POLITICS OF INDONESIA

The politics of Indonesia takes place in a framework of a presidential representative democratic republic, whereby the President of Indonesia is both head of state and head of government, and of a multi-party system. Executive power is exercised by the government. Legislative power is vested in both the government and the two People's Representative Councils. The Judiciary is independent of the executive and the legislature. The 1945 constitution provided for a limited separation of executive, legislative, and judicial power. The governmental system has been described as "presidential with parliamentary characteristics." Following the Indonesian 1998 Revolution and the resignation of President Suharto, several political reforms were set in motion.

Reform Process

A constitutional reform process has been underway since 1999, and has already produced several important changes. Among these are term limits of up to two five-year terms for the President and Vice President, and measures to institute checks and balances. The highest state institution is the People's Consultative Assembly (MPR), whose functions included electing the president and vice president (since 2004 the president is elected directly by the people), establishing broad guidelines of state policy, and amending the constitution. The 695-member MPR includes all 550 members of the People's Representative Council (DPR) (the House of Representatives) plus 130 "regional representatives" elected by the twenty-six provincial parliaments and sixty-five appointed members from societal groups.

The DPR, which is the premier legislative institution, originally included 462 members elected through a mixed proportional/district representational system and thirty-eight appointed members of the armed forces (TNI) and police (POLRI). TNI/POLRI representation in the DPR was ended before the general election in 2004 and will end in the MPR in 2009. Societal group representation in the MPR was eliminated in 2004 through further constitutional change. Military domination of regional administration is gradually breaking down, with new regulations prohibiting active-duty officers from holding political office.

Having served as rubberstamp bodies in the past, the DPR and MPR have gained considerable power and are increasingly assertive in oversight of the executive branch. Under constitutional changes in 2004, the MPR became a bicameral legislature, with the creation of the Dewan Perwakilan Daerah (DPD) or Senate, in which each province is represented by four members, although its legislative powers are more limited than those of the DPR. Through his appointed cabinet, the president retains the authority to conduct the administration of the government, but some observers believe the balance of power has shifted too far in the direction of the legislature.

A general election in June 1999 produced the first freely elected national, provincial, and regional parliaments in over forty years. In October 1999 the MPR elected a compromise candidate, Abdurrahman Wahid, as the country's fourth president, and Megawati Sukarnoputri — a daughter of Sukarno, the country's first president — as the vice president. Megawati's PDI-P party had won the largest share of the vote (34%) in the general election, while Golkar, the dominant party during the Soeharto era, came in second (22%). Several other, mostly Islamic parties won shares large enough to be seated in the DPR.

Executive Branch

The president and vice president are selected by vote of the citizens for five-year terms. Prior to 2004, they were chosen by People's Consultative Assembly. The last election was held 20 September 2004. The president heads the United Indonesia Cabinet (Kabinet Indonesia Bersatu) The President of Indonesia is directly-elected for five-year terms, and is the head of state, commander-in-chief of Indonesian armed forces and responsible for domestic governance and policy-making and foreign affairs. The president appoints a council of ministers, who don't have to be elected members of the legislature.

Legislative Branch

The People's Representative Council (*Dewan Perwakilan Rakyat*) has 550 members, elected for a five year term by proportional representation in multi-member constituencies. The other chamber of the People's Consultative Assembly(*Majelis Permusyawaratan Rakyat*) is the Regional Representatives Council (*Dewan Perwakilan Daerah*). Following elections in 2004, the MPR became a bicameral parliament, with the creation of the DPD as its second chamber in an effort to increase regional representation.

ECONOMY OF INDONESIA

Indonesia has a market-based economy in which the government plays a significant role. It owns more than 164 state-owned enterprises and administers prices on several basic goods, including fuel, rice, and electricity. In the aftermath of the financial and economic crisis that began in mid-1997, the government took custody of a significant portion of private sector assets through acquisition of nonperforming bank loans and corporate assets through the debt restructuring process.

Current GDP per capita grew 545% from 1970 to 1980 as a result of the sudden increase in oil export revenues from 1973 to 1979. However, in the 1980s oil glut, the GDP per capita shrank 20% from 1980 to 1990 and by 13% from 1990 to 2000.

During the thirty years of president Suharto's "New Order" government, Indonesia's economy grew from a per capita GDP of $70 to more than $1,000 by 1996. Through prudent monetary and fiscal policies, inflation was held between 5%–10%, the rupiah was stable and predictable, and the government avoided domestic financing of budget deficits. Much of the development budget was financed by concessional foreign aid.

In the mid-1980s, the government began eliminating regulatory obstacles to economic activity. The steps were aimed primarily at the trade and finance sectors and were designed to stimulate employment and growth in the non-oil export sector. Annual real GDP growth averaged nearly 7% from 1987–1997, and most analysts recognized Indonesia as a newly industrialized economy and emerging market.

High levels of economic growth from 1987–1997 masked a number of structural weaknesses in Indonesia's economy. The legal system was very weak, and there was no effective way to enforce contracts, collect debts, or sue for bankruptcy. Banking practices were very unsophisticated, with collateral-based lending the norm and widespread violation of prudential regulations, including limits on connected lending. Non-tariff barriers, rent-seeking by state-owned enterprises, domestic subsidies, barriers to domestic trade and export restrictions all created economic distortions.

The Asian financial crisis began to affect Indonesia 1997 quickly became an economic and political crisis. Indonesia's initial response was to float the rupiah, raise key domestic interest rates, and tighten fiscal policy. In October 1997, Indonesia and the International Monetary Fund (IMF) reached agreement on an economic reform program aimed at macroeconomic stabilization and elimination of some of the country's most damaging economic policies, such as the National Car Program and the clove monopoly, both involving family members of President Suharto. The rupiah failed to stabilize for any significant period of time, however, and President Suharto was forced to resign in May 1998. In August 1998, Indonesia and the IMF agreed on an Extended Fund Facility (EFF) under President B.J Habibie that included significant structural reform targets.

President Abdurrahman Wahid took office in October 1999, and Indonesia and the IMF signed another EFF in January 2000. The new program also has a range of economic, structural reform and governance targets.

The effects of the financial and economic crisis were severe. In 1998 real GDP contracted by 13.7%. The economy reached its low point in mid-1999 and real GDP growth for the year was 0.3%. Inflation reached 77% in 1998 but slowed to 2% in 1999. The rupiah, which had been in the Rp 2,400/USD1 range in 1997 reached Rp 17,000/ USD1 at the height of the 1998 violence, returned to the Rp 6,500–8,000/USD1 range in late 1998. It has traded in the Rp 6,500–9,000/USD1 range ever since, with significant volatility. Although a severe drought in 1997–1998 forced Indonesia to import record amounts of rice, overall imports dropped precipitously in the early stage of the crisis in response to the unfavorable exchange rate, reduced domestic demand, and absence of new investment. Formal sector employment contracted significantly.

In late 2005 Indonesia faced a 'mini-crisis' due to international oil prices rises and imports. The currency reached Rp 12,000/USD1 before stabilizing. The government was forced to cut its massive fuel subsidies, which were planned to cost $14 billion for 2005, in October. This led to a more than doubling in the price of consumer fuels, resulting in double-digit inflation. The situation has stabilized, but the economy continues to struggle with inflation at 17% in 2005. To mitigate consequent economic hardship, the government has offered one-time subsidies to eligible citizens, effectively becoming Indonesia's first significant government-funded social security benefit scheme.

For 2006, Indonesia's economic outlook was more positive. Economic growth accelerated to 5.1% in 2004 and reached 5.6% in 2005. Real per capita income has reached fiscal year 1996/1997 levels. Growth was driven primarily by domestic consumption, which accounts for roughly three-fourths of Indonesia's gross domestic product. The Jakarta Stock Exchange was the best performing market in Asia in 2004 up by 42%. Problems that continue to put a drag on growth include low foreign investment levels, bureaucratic red tape, and very widespread corruption which causes 51.43 trillion Rupiah or 5.6573 billion US Dollar or approximately 1.4% of GDP to be lost on a yearly basis. However, there is very strong optimism with the conclusion of peaceful elections during the year 2004 and the election of the reformist president Susilo Bambang Yudhoyono.

Investment

Since the late 1980s, Indonesia has made significant changes to its regulatory framework to encourage economic growth. This growth was financed largely from private investment, both foreign and domestic. U.S. investors dominated the oil and gas sector and undertook some of Indonesia's largest mining projects. In addition, the presence of US banks, manufacturers, and service providers expanded, especially after the industrial and financial sector reforms of the 1980s. Other major foreign investors included Japan, the United Kingdom, Singapore, the Netherlands, Hong Kong, Taiwan, and South Korea.

The economic crisis made continued private financing imperative but problematic. New foreign investment approvals fell by almost two-thirds between 1997 and 1999. The crisis further highlighted areas where additional reform was needed. Frequently cited areas for improving the investment climate were establishment of a functioning legal and judicial system, adherence to competitive processes, and adoption of internationally acceptable accounting and disclosure standards. Despite improvements in the laws in recent years, Indonesia's intellectual property rights regime remains weak; lack of effective enforcement is a major concern. Under Suharto, Indonesia had moved toward private provision of public infrastructure, including electric power, tollroads, and telecommunications. The financial crisis brought to light serious weaknesses in the process of dispute resolution, however, particularly in the area of private infrastructure projects. Although Indonesia continued to have the advantages of a large labor force, abundant natural resources and modern infrastructure, private investment in new projects largely ceased during the crisis.

The stock market capitalization of listed companies in Indonesia was valued at $81,428 million in 2005 by the World Bank. Even though the Indonesian Investment Coordinating Board likes to project the impression that foreign direct investment is welcome in the country, many of the country's laws and regulations are tilted against foreign investors. For example, potential foreign investors and their executive staff cannot maintain own bank accounts in Indonesia, unless they are tax-paying local residents (paying tax in Indonesia for their worldwide income). Furthermore, foreign investors visiting the country on tourist visas violate local laws and face the danger of exorbitant under-the-table settlement payments or legal prosecution.

Structure of the Economy

Agriculture, Livestock, Forestry and Fishery

Statistics Indonesia provisionally valued *food crop* yields at 213,529,700 million rupiahs in 2006 thus registering over 35% growth since 2003. Badan Pusat Statistik provisionally valued *estate crop* yields at 62,690,900 million rupiahs in 2006 thus registering over 34% growth since 2003. Badan Pusat Statistik provisionally valued livestock and its derivative products at 51,276,400 million rupiahs in 2006 thus registering over 37% growth since 2003. Badan Pusat Statistik provisionally valued forestry at 30,017,000 million rupiahs in 2006 thus registering over 63% growth since

2003. Badan Pusat Statistik provisionally valued fishery at 72,979,900 million rupiahs in 2006 thus registering over 60% growth since 2003.

Mining and Quarrying

Badan Pusat Statistik provisionally valued the oil and gas mining industry at 187,893,200 million rupiahs in 2006 thus registering over 97% growth since 2003.

Indonesia is the only Asian member of the Organization of Petroleum Exporting Countries (OPEC) outside of the Middle East, and is the only OPEC member that is a net oil importer. In early 2005, Indonesian crude oil and condensate output was 1.07 million barrels per day. This is a substantial decline from the 1990s, due primarily to aging oil fields and a lack of investment in oil production equipment. In 1999, Crude and condensate output averaged 1.5 million barrels (240,000 m^3) per day, and in the 1998 calendar year the oil and gas sector, including refining, contributed approximately 9% to GDP. This decline in production since the 1990s has been accompanied by a substantial increase in domestic consumption, about 5.4% per year, leading to an expected US$1.2 billion cost for importing oil in 2005.

The state owns all petroleum and mineral rights. Fôreign firms participate through production-sharing and work contracts. Oil and gas contractors are required to finance all exploration, production, and development costs in their contract areas; they are entitled to recover operating, exploration, and development costs out of the oil and gas produced.

Indonesia's fuel production has declined significantly over the years, owing to aging oil fields and lack of investment in new equipment. As a result, despite being an exporter of crude oil, Indonesia is now a net importer of oil and had previously subsidized fuel prices to keep prices low, costing US$ 7 billion in 2004. The current president has mandated a significant reduction of government subsidy of fuel prices in several stages. In order to alleviate economic hardships, the government has offered one-time subsidies to qualified citizens. The government has stated the cuts in subsidies are aimed at reducing the budget deficit to 1% of gross domestic product (GDP) this year, down from around 1.6% last year.

Non-oil and Gas Mining

Badan Pusat Statistik provisionally valued the non-oil and gas mining industry at 130,861,000 million rupiahs in 2006 thus registering over 145% growth since 2003.

Indonesia is the world's largest tin market. Although mineral production traditionally centered on bauxite, silver, and tin, Indonesia is expanding its copper, nickel, gold, and coal output for export markets. In mid-1993, the *Department of Mines and Energy* reopened the coal sector to foreign investment, with the result that the leading Indonesian coal producer now is a joint venture between UK firms–BP and Rio Tinto. Total coal production reached 74 million metric tons in 1999, including exports of 55 million tons. Two US firms operate three copper/gold mines in Indonesia, with a Canadian and British firm holding significant other investments in nickel and gold, respectively. In 1998, the value of Indonesian gold production was $1 billion and copper, $843 million. Receipts from gold, copper, and coal comprised 84% of the $3 billion. Earned in 1998 by the mineral mining sector.

LAOS

Laos, officially the Lao People's Democratic Republic, is a landlocked country in southeast Asia, bordered by Burma (Myanmar) and China to the northwest, Vietnam to the east, Cambodia to the south, and Thailand to the west. Laos traces its history to the Kingdom of Lan Xang or *Land of a Million Elephants*, which existed from the fourteenth to the eighteenth century.

After a period as a French protectorate, it gained independence in 1949. A long civil war ended officially when the communist Pathet Lao movement came to power in 1975 but the protesting between factions continued for several years.

Private enterprise has increased since the late 1990s when economic reforms including rapid business licensing were introduced. Laos is still ranked among the lowest countries in terms of economic and political freedom. The economy of Laos grew at 7.2% in 2006, 35th fastest in the world. Eighty percent of the employed practice subsistence agriculture. The country's ethnic make-up is diverse, with around 70% belonging to the largest ethnic group, the Lao.

GEOGRAPHY OF LAOS

Laos is a landlocked nation in Southeast Asia, northeast of Thailand, west of Vietnam, that covers 236,800 square kilometers in the center of the Southeast Asian peninsula, is surrounded by Burma (Myanmar), Cambodia, the People's Republic of China, Thailand, and Vietnam. Its location has often made it a buffer between more powerful neighboring states, as well as a crossroads for trade and communication. Migration and international conflict have contributed to the present ethnic composition of the country and to the geographic distribution of its ethnic groups.

Most of the western border of Laos is demarcated by the Mekong River, which is an important artery for transportation. The Dong falls at the southern end of the country prevent access to the sea, but cargo boats travel along the entire length of the Mekong in Laos during most of the year. Smaller power boats and pirogues provide an important means of transportation on many of the tributaries of the Mekong.

The Mekong has thus not been an obstacle but a facilitator for communication, and the similarities between Laos and northeast Thai society—same people, same language—reflect the close contact that has existed across the river for centuries. Also, many Laotians living in the Mekong Valley have relatives and friends in Thailand. Prior to the twentieth century, Laotian kingdoms and principalities encompassed areas on both sides of the Mekong, and Thai control in the late nineteenth century extended to the left bank. Although the Mekong was established as a border by French colonial forces, travel from one side to the other has been significantly limited only since the establishment of the Lao People's Democratic Republic (LPDR, or Laos) in 1975.

The eastern border with Vietnam extends for 2,130 kilometers, mostly along the crest of the Annamite Chain, and serves as a physical barrier between the Chinese-influenced culture of Vietnam and the Indianized states of Laos and Thailand. These mountains are sparsely populated by tribal minorities who traditionally have not acknowledged the border with Vietnam any more than lowland Lao have been constrained by the 1,754-kilometer Mekong River border with Thailand. Thus, ethnic minority populations are found on both the Laotian and Vietnamese sides of the frontier. Because of their relative isolation, contact between these groups and lowland Lao has been mostly confined to trading.

Laos shares its short—only 541 kilometers—southern border with Cambodia, and ancient Khmer ruins at Wat Pho and other southern locations attest to the long history of contact between the Lao and the Khmer. In the north, the country is bounded by a mountainous 423-kilometer border with China and shares the 235-kilometer-long Mekong River border with Burma.

The topography of Laos is largely mountainous, with elevations above 500 meters typically characterized by steep terrain, narrow river valleys, and low agricultural potential. This mountainous landscape extends across most of the north of the country, except for the plain of Vientiane and the Plain of Jars in Xiangkhoang Province. The southern "panhandle" of the country contains large level areas in Savannakhét and Champasak provinces that are well suited for extensive paddy rice cultivation and livestock raising. Much of Khammouan Province and the eastern part of all the southern provinces are mountainous. Together, the alluvial plains and terraces of the Mekong and its tributaries cover only about 20% of the land area.

Only about 4% of the total land area is classified as arable. The forested land area has declined significantly since the 1970s as a result of commercial logging and expanded swidden, or slash-and-burn, farming.

Climate

Laos has a tropical monsoon climate, with a pronounced rainy season from May through October, a cool dry season from November through February, and a hot dry season in March and April. Generally, monsoons occur at the same time across the country, although that time may vary significantly from one year to the next. Rainfall also varies regionally, with the highest amounts— 3,700 millimeters annually—recorded on the Bolovens Plateau in Champasak Province. City rainfall stations have recorded that Savannakhét averages 1,440 millimeters of rain annually; Vientiane receives about 1,700 millimeters, and Louangphrabang (Luang Prabang) receives about 1,360 millimeters. Rainfall is not always adequate for rice cultivation, however, and the relatively high average precipitation conceals years where rainfall may be only half or less of the norm, causing significant declines in rice yields. Such droughts often are regional, leaving production in other parts of the country unaffected. Temperatures range from highs around 40°C along the Mekong in March and April to lows of 5°C or less in the uplands of Xiangkhoang and Phôngsali in January.

GOVERNMENT AND POLITICS OF LAOS

Laos is a single-party socialist republic. The only legal political party is the Lao People's Revolutionary Party (LPRP). The head of state is President Choummaly Sayasone, who also is secretary-general (leader) of the LPRP. The head of government is Prime Minister Bouasone Bouphavanh. Government policies are determined by the party through the all-powerful nine-member Politburo and the 49-member Central Committee. Important government decisions are vetted by the Council of Ministers.

Laos' first, French-written and monarchical constitution was promulgated on May 11, 1947 and declared it to be an independent state within the French Union. The revised constitution of May 11, 1957 omitted reference to the French Union, though close educational, health and technical ties with the former colonial power persisted. The 1957 document was abrogated on December 3, 1975, when a communist People's Republic was proclaimed. A new constitution was adopted in 1991 and enshrined a "leading role" for the LPRP. The following year, elections were held for a new 85-seat National Assembly with members elected by secret ballot to five-year terms. This National Assembly, which essentially acts as a rubber stamp for the LPRP, approves all new laws, although the executive branch retains authority to issue binding decrees. The most recent elections took place in April 2006. The assembly was expanded to 99 members in 1997 and in 2006 elections had 115.

The FY 2000 central government budget plan called for revenue of $180 million and expenditures of $289 million, including capital expenditures of $202 million.

In recent years bomb attacks against the government have occurred, coupled with small exchanges of fire, across Laos. A variety of different groups have claimed responsibility including the Committee for Independence and Democracy in Laos and Lao Citizens Movement for Democracy.

DEMOGRAPHY OF LAOS

About 69% of the country's people are ethnic Lao, the principal lowland inhabitants and the politically and culturally dominant group. The Lao belong to the Tai linguistic group who began migrating southward from China in the first millennium AD. A further 8% belong to other "lowland" groups, which together with the Lao people make up the Lao Loum.

Hill people and minority cultures of Laos such as the Hmong (Miao), Yao (Mien), Tai dumm, Dao, Shan, and several Tibeto-Burman speaking peoples have lived in isolated regions of Laos for many years. Mountain/hill tribes of mixed ethno/cultural-linguistic heritage are found in northern Laos which include the Lua (Lua) and Khmu people who are indigenous to Laos. Today, the Lua people are considered endangered. Collectively, they are known as Lao Soung or highland Laotians. In the central and southern mountains, Mon-Khmer tribes, known as Lao Theung or mid-slope Laotians, predominate. Some Vietnamese and Chinese minorities remain, particularly in the towns, but many left in two waves; after independence in the late 1940s and again after 1975.

The term "Laotian" does not necessarily refer to the ethnic Lao language, ethnic Lao people, language or customs, but is a political term that also includes the non-ethnic Lao groups within Laos and identifies them as "Laotian" because of their political citizenship. In a similar vein, the word "Lao" can also describe the people, cuisine, language and culture of the people of Northeast Thailand (Isan) who are ethnic Lao.

The predominant religion in Laos is Theravada Buddhism which, along with the common Animism practiced among the mountain tribes, coexists peacefully with spirit worship. There also are a small number of Christians, mostly restricted to the Vientiane area, and Muslims, mostly restricted to the Myanmar border region. Christian missionary work is regulated by the government.

The official and dominant language is Lao, a tonal language of the Tai linguistic group. Midslope and highland Lao speak an assortment of tribal languages. French, still common in government and commerce, has declined in usage, while knowledge of English, the language of the Association of Southeast Asian Nations (ASEAN), has increased in recent years.

CULTURE OF LAOS

Theravada Buddhism is a dominant influence in Lao culture. It is reflected throughout the country from language to the temple and in art, literature, performing arts, etc. Many elements of Lao culture predate Buddhism, however. For example, Laotian music is dominated by its national instrument, the khaen, a type of bamboo pipe that has prehistoric origins. The khaen traditionally accompanied the singer in *lam*, the dominant style of folk music. Among the various *lam* styles, the *lam saravane* is probably the most popular.

The country has two World Heritage Sites: Luang Prabang and Vat Phou. The government is seeking the same status for the Plain of Jars.

The People's Republic of China has recently allowed its citizens to travel more freely to Laos. As such, Chinese tourists are expected to account for 25% of the total number of visitors to Laos (up from only a few percent) in 2006. Pressures to modernize tourist infrastructure, particularly to cater to package tourism, are expected to significantly impact Luang Prabang and other culturally important Laotian cities. The people of Laos have a reputation for being very kind and welcoming to all visitors.

Rice is the staple food and has cultural and religious significance. There are many traditions and rituals associated with rice production in different environments, and among many ethnic groups. For example, Khammu farmers in Luang Prabang plant the rice variety Khao Kam in small quantities near the hut in memory of dead parents, or at the edge of the rice field to indicate that parents are still alive.

ECONOMY OF LAOS

Laos is a landlocked country with an inadequate infrastructure and a largely unskilled work force. The country's per capita income in 2004 was estimated to be $1,900 on a purchasing power parity-basis.

Agriculture, mostly subsistence rice farming, dominates the economy, employing an estimated 85% of the population and producing 51% of GDP. Domestic savings are low, forcing Laos to rely heavily on foreign assistance and concessional loans as investment sources for economic development. In FY 1999, for example, foreign grants and loans accounted for more than 20% of GDP and more than 75% of public investment. In 1998, the country's foreign debt was estimated at $1.9 billion.

Following its accession to power in 1975, the communist government imposed a harsh, Soviet-style command economy system, replacing the private sector with state enterprises and cooperatives; centralizing investment, production, trade, and pricing; and creating barriers to internal and foreign trade.

Within a few years, the Lao Government realized these types of economic policies were preventing, rather than stimulating, growth and development. No substantive reform was introduced, however, until 1986 when the government announced its "new economic mechanism" (NEM). Initially timid, the NEM was expanded to include a range of reforms designed to create conditions conducive to private sector activity. Prices set by market forces replaced government-determined prices. Farmers were permitted to own land and sell crops on the open market. State firms were granted increased decisionmaking authority and lost most of their subsidies and pricing advantages. The government set the exchange rate close to real market levels, lifted trade barriers, replaced import barriers with tariffs, and gave private sector firms direct access to imports and credit.

In 1989, the Lao Government reached agreement with the World Bank and the International Monetary Fund on additional reforms. The government agreed to expand fiscal and monetary reform, promote private enterprise and foreign investment, privatize or close state firms, and strengthen banking. In addition, it also agreed to maintain a market exchange rate, reduce tariffs, and eliminate unneeded trade regulations. A liberal foreign investment code was enacted and appears to be slowly making a positive impact in the market. Enforcement of intellectual property rights is governed by two Prime Minister's Decrees dating from 1995 and 2002.

In an attempt to stimulate further international commerce, the Lao Government accepted Australian aid to build a bridge across the Mekong River to Thailand. The "Thai-Lao Friendship Bridge," between Vientiane Prefecture and Nong Khai Province, Thailand, was inaugurated in April 1994. Although the bridge has created additional commerce, the Lao Government does not yet permit a completely free flow of traffic across the span.

These reforms led to economic growth and an increased availability of goods. However, the Asian financial crisis, coupled with the Lao Government's own mismanagement of the economy, resulted in spiraling inflation and a steep depreciation of the kip, which lost 87% of its value from June 1997 to June 1999. Tighter monetary policies brought about greater macroeconomic stability in FY 2000, and monthly inflation, which had averaged about 10% during the first half of FY 1999, dropped to an average 1% over the same period in FY 2000. The economy continues to be dominated by an unproductive agricultural sector operating largely outside the money economy and in which the public sector continues to play a dominant role.

5

MALAYSIA

Malaysia is a country that consists of thirteen states and three federal territories in Southeast Asia with a total landmass of 329,847 square kilometres (127,355 sq mi). The capital city is Kuala Lumpur, while Putrajaya is the seat of the federal government. The population stands at over 25 million. The country is separated into two regions — Peninsular Malaysia and Malaysian Borneo — by the South China Sea. Malaysia borders Thailand, Indonesia, Singapore, Brunei and the Philippines. The country is located near the equator and experiences a tropical climate. Malaysia's head of state is the Yang di-Pertuan Agong (conventionally refered to as 'the King' or 'the Agong') and the government is headed by a Prime Minister. The government is closely modeled after the Westminster parliamentary system.

Malaysia as a unified state did not exist until 1963. Previously, a set of colonies were established by the United Kingdom from the late-18th century, and the western half of modern Malaysia was composed of several separate kingdoms. This group of colonies was known as British Malaya until its dissolution in 1946, when it was reorganised as the Malayan Union. Due to widespread opposition, it was reorganised again as the Federation of Malaya in 1948 and later gained independence on 31 August 1957. Singapore, Sarawak, British North Borneo and the Federation of Malaya joined to form Malaysia on 16 September 1963. The early years of the new union were marred by an armed conflict with Indonesia and the expulsion of Singapore. The Southeast Asian nation experienced an economic boom and underwent rapid development during the late-20th century. With a GDP per capita standing at USD14,400, it has, from time to time, been considered a newly industrialised country. Because Malaysia is one of three countries that control the Strait of Malacca, international trade plays a large role in its economy. At one time, it was the largest producer of tin, rubber and palm oil in the world. Manufacturing has a large influence in the country's economy.

The Malays form the majority of the population. Some Malays are of Arab descent and there are sizable Chinese and Indian communities. Islam is the largest as well as the official religion of the federation. The Malay language is the official language. Malay was originally written in Jawi, based on Arabic script, but nowadays, the Roman alphabet (Rumi) is more often used.

Malaysia is a founding member of the Association of Southeast Asian Nations and participates in many international organisations such as the United Nations. As a former British colony, it is also a member of the Commonwealth of Nations. It is also a member of the Developing 8 Countries.

GEOGRAPHY OF MALAYSIA

The geography of Malaysia deals with the physical and human geography of Malaysia, a country located in Southeast Asia. There are two distinct parts to this country being Peninsular Malaysia to the west and East Malaysia to the east. Peninsular Malaysia is located south of Thailand, north of Singapore and east of the Indonesian island of Sumatra. East Malaysia is located on the island of Borneo and shares borders with Brunei and Indonesia.

Climate

Located near the equator, Malaysia's climate is categorised as equatorial, being hot and humid throughout the year. Annual rainfall exceeds 2000mm a year and the average temperature is 27 degrees Celsius. Malaysia faces two monsoon winds seasons – the Southwest Monsoon from late May to September, and the Northeast Monsoon from November to March. The Northeast Monsoon brings in more rainfall compared to the Southwest Monsoon.

The highest temperature was recorded at Chuping, Perlis on 9 April 1998 at 40.1 degrees Celsius. The lowest temperature was recorded at Cameron Highlands on 1 February 1978 at 7.8 degrees Celsius. The highest rainfall recorded in a day was 608 mm in Kota Bharu, Kelantan on 6 January 1967. The highest rainfall recorded in a year was 5687mm at Sandakan, Sabah in 2006. Meanwhile, the lowest rainfall recorded in a year was 1151 mm at Tawau, Sabah in 1997. The wettest place in Malaysia is Kuching, Sarawak with an average rainfall of 4128mm with 247 days of rain a year. The driest place in Malaysia is in Chuping, Perlis with average rainfall of only 1746mm a year.

Land

The total land area of Malaysia is 329,847 km^2, the 66th largest country in the world in terms of area. Peninsular Malaysia makes up 131,000 km^2 or 39.7%, while

East Malaysia covers 198,847 km^2 or 60.3% of the total land of the country. About half of Peninsular Malaysia is covered by granite and other igneous rocks, a third more is covered by stratified rocks older than the granite, and the remainder is covered by alluvium. The terrain can be characterised as coastal plains which rises towards the hills and mountains.

From the total land area, 1,200 km^2 or 0.37% is made up of water such as lakes, rivers, or other internal waters. Malaysia has a total coastline of 4,675 km, whereby Peninsular Malaysia has 2,068 km, while East Malaysia has 2,607 km of coastline. Malaysia has the 29th longest coastline in the world.

Mountain Ranges

The highest mountain range in Malaysia is the Crocker Range in Sabah. This range houses Mount Kinabalu, the highest mountain in the country, as well as Mount Tambuyukon, the third highest in the country. The Trus Madi Range, also in Sabah, houses Mount Trus Madi, the second highest peak in Malaysia. Bombalai Hill in Sabah is the only active volcano in Malaysia.

The main mountain range in Peninsular Malaysia is the Titiwangsa Mountains. It houses Mount Korbu, the second highest peak in the Peninsular. The highest peak in the Peninsular is Mount Tahan, located on the Tahan Range.

Forests

Malaysian forests can be categorised as tropical rainforest. This can be further divided into dipterocarp, swamps, and mangrove forest. Approximately 58.2% of Malaysian land is covered by forest. Some areas are designated as forest reserves, state parks, or national parks. The management of these reserves as under control of the Department of Wildlife and National Park, the Forest Department of Sarawak, the Sabah Forestry Department, Sabah Foundation, and Sabah Parks. As of 2008, there are two World Heritage Sites under the natural category – Kinabalu National Park and Gunung Mulu National Park.

Human Geography

Peninsular Malaysia is more populated than East Malaysia where 79.2% of the population lives in the Peninsular. In 2002, 59% of Malaysian population lived in urban areas, while the rest live in rural areas. The largest city is Kuala Lumpur with a population of 1.89 million people in the city, and about 7 million in the metropolitan area known as Klang Valley. Other major cities include Georgetown, Johor Bahru, Ipoh, Kuching, and Kota Kinabalu.

GOVERNMENT AND POLITICS OF MALAYSIA

Malaysia is a federal constitutional elective monarchy. The federal head of state of Malaysia is the *Yang di-Pertuan Agong*, commonly referred to as the King of Malaysia. The Yang di-Pertuan Agong is elected to a five-year term among the nine hereditary Sultans of the Malay states; the other four states, which have titular Governors, do not participate in the selection.

The system of government in Malaysia is closely modeled on that of Westminster parliamentary system, a legacy of British colonial rule. In practice however, more power is vested in the executive branch of government than in the legislative, and the judiciary has been weakened by sustained attacks by the government during the Mahathir era. Since independence in 1957, Malaysia has been governed by a multi-party coalition known as the Barisan Nasional (formerly known as the Alliance).

Legislative power is divided between federal and state legislatures. The bicameral parliament consists of the lower house, the House of Representatives or *Dewan Rakyat* (literally the "Chamber of the People") and the upper house, the Senate or *Dewan Negara* (literally the "Chamber of the Nation"). The 222-member House of Representatives are elected from single-member constituencies that are drawn based on population for a maximum term of five years. All 70 Senators sit for three-year terms; 26 are elected by the 13 state assemblies, two representing the federal territory of Kuala Lumpur, one each from federal territories of Labuan and Putrajaya, and 40 are appointed by the king. Besides the Parliament at the federal level, each state has a unicameral state legislative chamber (Malay: *Dewan Undangan Negeri*) whose members are elected from single-member constituencies. Parliamentary elections are held at least once every five years, with the last general election being in March 2008. The cabinet is chosen from among members of both houses of Parliament and is responsible to that body.

State governments are led by Chief Ministers (*Menteri Besar* in Malay states or *Ketua Menteri* in states without hereditary rulers), who is a state assembly member from the majority party in the Dewan Undangan Negeri. In each of the states with a hereditary ruler, the Chief Minister is required to be a Malay Muslim, although this rule is subject the rulers' discretions.

DEMOGRAPHY OF MALAYSIA

Malaysia's population comprises many ethnic groups, with the Malays and other bumiputra groups in Sabah and Sarawak making up the majority, at 65% of the population. By constitutional definition, Malays are Muslims who practice Malay customs (*adat*) and culture. Therefore, technically, a Muslim of any race who practices Malay customs and culture can be considered a Malay and have equal rights when it comes to Malay rights as stated in the constitution. Non-Malay bumiputra groups make up more than half of the state of Sarawak's population (of which 30% are Ibans), and close to 60% of Sabah's population (of which 18% are Kadazan-Dusuns, and 17% are Bajaus). There also exist aboriginal groups in much smaller numbers on the Peninsula, where they are collectively known as Orang Asli.

26% of the population are Malaysians of Chinese descent, while Malaysians of Indian descent comprise 8% of the population. The majority of the Indian community are Tamils but various other groups are also present, including Malayalis, Punjabis and Gujaratis. Other Malaysians also include those whose origin, inter alia, can be traced to the Middle East, Thailand and Indonesia. Europeans and Eurasians include British who settled in Malaysia since colonial times, and a strong Portuguese community in Malacca. A small number of Cambodians and Vietnamese also settled in Malaysia as Vietnam War refugees.

Population distribution is uneven, with some 20 million residents concentrated on the Malay Peninsula, while East Malaysia is relatively less populated. Due to the rise in labour intensive industries, Malaysia has 10 to 20% foreign workers with the uncertainty due in part to the large number of illegal workers, mostly Indonesian. There are a million legal foreign workers and perhaps another million unauthorised foreigners. The state of Sabah alone has nearly 25% of its 2.7 million population listed as illegal foreign workers in the last census. However, this figure of 25% is thought to be less than half the figure speculated by NGOs.

Additionally, according to the *World Refugee Survey 2008*, published by the U.S. Committee for Refugees and Immigrants, Malaysia hosts a population of refugees and asylum seekers numbering approximately 155,700. Of this population, approximately 70,500 refugees and asylum seekers are from the Philippines, 69,700 from Burma, and 21,800 from Indonesia. The U.S. Committee for Refugees and Immigrants named Malaysia as one of the Ten Worst Places for Refugees on account of the country's discriminatory practices toward refugees. Malaysian officials are reported to have turned deportees directly over to human smugglers in 2007, and Malaysia employs the RELA, a volunteer militia, to enforce its immigration law.

MALAYSIAN CULTURE

Malaysia is a multi-ethnic, multi-cultural and multilingual society. The population as of February 2007 is 26.6 million consisting of 62% Malays, 24% Chinese, 8% Indians, with other minorities and indigenous peoples (Dept of Stats. Malaysia). Ethnic tensions have been rising in recent months.

The Malays, who form the largest community, are defined as Muslims in the Constitution of Malaysia. The Malays play a dominant role politically and are included in a grouping identified as bumiputra. Their native language is Malay (*Bahasa Melayu*). Malay is the national language of the country.

In the past, Malays wrote in Sanskrit or using Sanskrit-based alphabets. After the 15th century, Jawi (a script based on Arabic) became popular. Over time, romanised script overtook Sanskrit and Jawi as the dominant script. This was largely due to the influence of the colonial education system, which taught children in romanised writing rather than in Arabic script.

The largest non-Malay indigenous tribe is the Iban of Sarawak, who number over 600,000. Some Iban still live in traditional jungle villages in long houses along the Rajang and Lupar rivers and their tributaries, although many have moved to the cities. The Bidayuhs, numbering around 170,000, are concentrated in the southwestern part of Sarawak. The largest indigenous tribe in Sabah is the Kadazan. They are largely Christian subsistence farmers. The 140,000 Orang Asli, or aboriginal peoples, comprise a number of different ethnic communities living in peninsular Malaysia. Traditionally nomadic hunter/gatherers and agriculturalists, many have been sedentarised and partially absorbed into modern Malaysia.

The Chinese population in Malaysia is mostly Buddhist (of Mahayana sect) or Taoist. Chinese in Malaysia speak a variety of Chinese dialects including Mandarin Chinese, Hokkien, Cantonese, Hakka and Teochew. A large majority of Chinese in Malaysia, especially those from larger cities such as Kuala Lumpur, Petaling Jaya and Penang speak English as well. There has also been an increasing number of the present generation Chinese who consider English as their first language. Chinese have historically been dominant in the Malaysian business community.

The Indians in Malaysia are mainly Hindu Tamils from southern India who native language is Tamil, there are also other Indian communities which is Telugu, Malayalam and Hindi-speaking, living mainly in the larger towns on the west coast of the peninsula. Many middle to upper-middle class Indians in Malaysia also speak English as a first language. A vigorous 200,000-strong Tamil Muslim community also thrives as an independent subcultural group. There are also prevalent Tamil Christian communities in major cities and towns. There is also a sizable Sikh community in Malaysia of over 83,000. Most Indians originally migrated from India as traders, teachers or other skilled workers. A larger number were also part of the forced migrations from India by the British during colonial times to work in the plantation industry.

Eurasians, Cambodians, Vietnamese, and indigenous tribes make up the remaining population. A small number of Eurasians, of mixed Portuguese and Malay descent, speak a Portuguese-based creole, called Papiá Kristang. There are also Eurasians of mixed Filipino and Spanish descent, mostly in Sabah. Descended from immigrants from the Philippines, some speak Chavacano, the only Spanish-based creole language in Asia. Cambodians and Vietnamese are mostly Buddhists (Cambodians of Theravada sect and Vietnamese, Mahayana sect).

Malaysian traditional music is heavily influenced by Chinese and Islamic forms. The music is based largely around the gendang (drum), but includes other percussion instruments (some made of shells); the rebab, a bowed string instrument; the serunai, a double-reed oboe-like instrument; flutes, and trumpets. The country has a strong tradition of dance and dance dramas, some of Thai, Indian and Portuguese origin. Other artistic forms include wayang kulit (shadow puppet theatre), silat (a stylised martial art) and crafts such as batik, weaving, including the ceremonial cloth pua kumbu, and silver and brasswork.

ECONOMY OF MALAYSIA

The Malay Peninsula and indeed Southeast Asia has been a centre of trade for centuries. Various items such as porcelain and spices were actively traded even before Malacca and Singapore rose to prominence.

In the 17th century, they were found in several Malay states. Later, as the British started to take over as administrators of Malaya, rubber and palm oil trees were introduced for commercial purposes. Over time, Malaya became the world's largest major producer of tin, rubber, and palm oil. These three commodities, along with other raw materials, firmly set Malaysia's economic tempo well into the mid-20th century.

Instead of relying on the local Malays as a source of labour, the British brought in Chinese and Indians to work on the mines and plantations. Although many of them returned to their respective home countries after their agreed tenure ended, some remained in Malaysia and settled permanently.

As Malaya moved towards independence, the government began implementing economic five-year plans, beginning with the First Malayan Five Year Plan in 1955. Upon the establishment of Malaysia, the plans were re-titled and renumbered, beginning with the First Malaysia Plan in 1965.

In the 1970s, Malaysia began to imitate the four Asian Tiger economies (Taiwan, South Korea, Hong Kong and Singapore) and committed itself to a transition from being reliant on mining and agriculture to an economy that depends more on manufacturing. With Japanese investment, heavy industries flourished and in a matter of years, Malaysian exports became the country's primary growth engine. Malaysia consistently achieved more than 7% GDP growth along with low inflation in the 1980s and the 1990s.

During the same period, the government tried to eradicate poverty with the controversial New Economic Policy (NEP), after the May 13 Incident of racial rioting in 1969. Its main objective was the elimination of the association of race with economic function, and the first five-year plan to begin implementing the NEP was the Second Malaysia Plan. The success or failure of the NEP is the subject of much debate, although it was officially retired in 1990 and replaced by the National Development Policy (NDP). Recently much debate has surfaced once again with regards to the results and relevance of the NEP. Some have argued that the NEP has indeed successfully created a Middle/Upper Class of Malay businessmen and professionals. Despite some improvement in the economic power of Malays in general, the Malaysian government maintains a policy of discrimination that favours ethnic Malays over other races—including preferential treatment in employment, education, scholarships, business, access to cheaper housing and assisted savings. This special treatment has sparked envy and resentment between non-Malays and Malays.

The Chinese control of the locally-owned sector of the country's economy, meanwhile, has been ceded largely in favour of the Bumiputras/Malays in many essential or strategic industries such as petroleum retailing, transportation, agriculture and etc. The minority of Indian descent has by and large been the most adversely affected by this policy. Indicators point to a higher incidence of crime and gang related activities among the Indians in recent years.

The rapid economic boom led to a variety of supply problems, however. Labour shortages soon resulted in an influx of millions of foreign workers, many illegal. Cash-rich PLCs and consortia of banks eager to benefit from increased and rapid development began large infrastructure projects. This all ended when the Asian Financial Crisis hit in the fall of 1997, delivering a massive shock to Malaysia's economy.

As with other countries affected by the crisis, there was speculative short-selling of the Malaysian currency, the ringgit. Foreign direct investment fell at an alarming rate and, as capital flowed out of the country, the value of the ringgit dropped from MYR 2.50 per USD to, at one point, MYR 4.80 per USD. The Kuala Lumpur Stock Exchange's composite index plummeted from approximately 1300 points to around 400 points in a matter of weeks. After the controversial sacking of finance minister Anwar Ibrahim, a National Economic Action Council was formed to deal with the monetary crisis. Bank Negara imposed capital controls and pegged the Malaysian ringgit at 3.80 to the US dollar. Malaysia refused economic aid packages from the International Monetary Fund (IMF) and the World Bank, however, surprising many analysts.

In March, 2005, the United Nations Conference on Trade and Development (UNCTAD) published a paper on the sources and pace of Malaysia's recovery, written by Jomo K.S. of the applied economics department, University of Malaya, Kuala Lumpur. The paper concluded that the controls imposed by Malaysia's government neither hurt nor helped recovery. The chief factor was an increase in electronics components exports, which was caused by a large increase in the demand for components in the United States, which was caused, in turn, by a fear of the effects of the arrival of the year 2000 (Y2K) upon older computers and other digital devices.

However, the post Y2K slump of 2001 did not affect Malaysia as much as other countries. This may have been clearer evidence that there are other causes and effects that can be more properly attributable for recovery. One possibility is that the currency speculators had run out of finance after failing in their attack on the Hong Kong dollar in August, 1998 and after the Russian ruble collapsed.

Regardless of cause/effect claims, rejuvenation of the economy also coincided with massive government spending and budget deficits in the years that followed the crisis. Later, Malaysia enjoyed faster economic recovery compared to its neighbours. In many ways, however, the country has yet to recover to the levels of the pre-crisis era.

While the pace of development today is not as rapid, it is seen to be more sustainable. Although the controls and economic housekeeping may not have been the principal reason for recovery, there is no doubt that the banking sector has become more resilient to external shocks. The current account has also settled into a structural surplus, providing a cushion to capital flight. Asset prices are now a fraction of their pre-crisis heights.

The fixed exchange rate was abandoned in July 2005 in favour of a managed floating system within an hour of China's announcing of the same move. In the same week, the ringgit strengthened a percent against various major currencies and was expected to appreciate further. As of December 2005, however, expectations of further appreciation were muted as capital flight exceeded USD 10 billion.

In September, 2005, Sir Howard J. Davies, director of the London School of Economics, at a meeting in Kuala Lumpur, cautioned Malaysian officials that if they want a flexible capital market, they will have to lift the ban on short-selling put into effect during the crisis. In March 2006, Malaysia removed the ban on short selling. Currently, Malaysia is considered a newly industrialised country.

6

MYANMAR

Burma, officially the Union of Myanmar, is the largest country by geographical area in mainland Southeast Asia. The country is bordered by the People's Republic of China on the northeast, Laos on the east, Thailand on the southeast, Bangladesh on the west, and India on the northwest, with the Bay of Bengal to the southwest. One-third of Burma's total perimeter, 1,930 kilometers (1,199 mi), forms an uninterrupted coastline.

Burma's diverse population has played a major role in defining its politics, history and demographics in modern times, and the country continues to struggle to mend its ethnic tensions. Its political system remains under the tight control of the SPDC, the military-led government, led since 1992 by Senior General Than Shwe. The military has dominated government since General Ne Win led a coup in 1962 that toppled the civilian government of U Nu. The country's culture, heavily influenced by neighbours, is based on Theravada Buddhism intertwined with local elements.

GEOGRAPHY OF MYANMAR

Burma, which has a total area of 678,500 square kilometers (261,970 sq mi), is the largest country in mainland Southeast Asia, and the 40th-largest in the world.

It is located between Chittagong Division of Bangladesh and Assam, Nagaland and Manipur of India to the northwest. It shares its longest borders with Tibet and Yunnan of China to the northeast for a total of 2,185 km (1,358 mi). It is bounded by Laos and Thailand to the southeast. Burma has 1,930 km (1,199 mi) of contiguous coastline along the Bay of Bengal and Andaman Sea to the southwest and the south, which forms one-third of its total perimeter.

In the north, the Hengduan Shan mountains form the border with China. Hkakabo Razi, located in Kachin State, at an elevation of 5,881 m (19,295 ft), is the highest point in Burma. Three mountain ranges, namely the Rakhine Yoma, the Bago Yoma, and the Shan Plateau exist within Burma, all of which run north-to-south from the Himalayas. The mountain chains divide Burma's three river systems, which are the Ayeyarwady, Salween (Thanlwin), and the Sittang rivers. The Ayeyarwady River, Burma's longest river, nearly 2,170 kilometres (1,348 mi) long, flows into the Gulf of Martaban. Fertile plains exist in the valleys between the mountain chains. The majority of Burma's population lives in the Ayeyarwady valley, which is situated between the Rakhine Yoma and the Shan Plateau.

Much of the country lies between the Tropic of Cancer and the Equator. It lies in the monsoon region of Asia, with its coastal regions receiving over 5,000 mm (200 in) of rain annually. Annual rainfall in the delta region is approximately 2,500 mm (100 in), while average annual rainfall in the Dry Zone, which is located in central Burma, is less than 1,000 mm (40 in). Northern regions of the country are the coolest, with average temperatures of 21 °C (70 °F). Coastal and delta regions have mean temperatures of 32 °C (90 °F).

The country's slow economic growth has contributed to the preservation of much of its environment and ecosystems. Forests, including dense tropical growth and valuable teak in lower Burma, cover over 49% of the country. Other trees indigenous to the region include acacia, bamboo, ironwood, mangrove, michelia champaca coconut and betel palm, and rubber has been introduced. In the highlands of the north, oak, pine and various rhododendrons cover much of the land. The lands along the coast support all varieties of tropical fruits. In the Dry Zone, vegetation is sparse and stunted.

Typical jungle animals, particularly tigers and leopards, are common in Burma. In upper Burma, there are rhinoceros, wild buffalo, wild boars, deer, antelope and elephants, which are also tamed or bred in captivity for use as work animals, particularly in the lumber industry. Smaller mammals are also numerous, ranging from gibbons and monkeys to flying foxes and tapirs. The abundance of birds is notable with over 800 species, including parrots, peafowl, pheasants, crows, herons and paddybirds. Among reptile species there are crocodiles, geckos, cobras, Burmese pythons and turtles. Hundreds of species of freshwater fish are wide-ranging, plentiful and are very important food sources.

GOVERNMENT AND POLITICS OF MYANMAR

Burma is governed by a strict military dictatorship. The current head of state is Senior General Than Shwe, who holds the posts of "Chairman of the State Peace and Development Council" and "Commander in Chief of the Defense Services" as well as the Minister of Defence. General Khin Nyunt was prime minister until 19 October 2004, when he was replaced by General Soe Win, after the purge of Military Intelligence sections within the Burma armed forces. The current Prime Minister is General Thein Sein, who took over upon the death of General Soe Win on October 2nd, 2007. The majority of ministry and cabinet posts are held by military officers, with the exceptions being the Ministry of Health, the Ministry of Education, the Ministry of Labour, and the Ministry of National Planning and Economic Development, posts which are held by civilians.

Elected delegates in the 1990 People's Assembly election formed the National Coalition Government of the Union of Burma (NCGUB), a government-in-exile since December 1990, with the mission of restoring democracy. Dr. Sein Win, a first cousin of Aung San Suu Kyi, has held the position of prime minister of the NCGUB since its inception. The NCGUB has been outlawed by the military government.

Major political parties in the country are the National League for Democracy and the Shan Nationalities League for Democracy, although their activities are heavily regulated and suppressed by the military government. Many other parties, often representing ethnic minorities, exist. The military government allows little room for political organizations and has outlawed many political parties and underground student organizations. The military supported the National Unity Party in the 1990 elections and, more recently, an organization named the Union Solidarity and Development Association.

Several human rights organizations, including Human Rights Watch and Amnesty International, and the American Association for the Advancement of Science have reported on human rights abuses by the military government. They have claimed that there is no independent judiciary in Burma. The military government restricts Internet access through software-based censorship that limits the material citizens can access on-line. Forced labour, human trafficking, and child labour are common. The military is also notorious for rampant use of sexual violence as an instrument of control, including systematic rapes and taking of sex slaves as porters for the military. A strong women's pro-democracy movement has formed in exile, largely along the Thai border and in Chiang Mai. There is a growing international movement to defend women's human rights issues.

In 1988, the army violently repressed protests against economic mismanagement and political oppression. On 8 August 1988, the military opened fire on demonstrators in what is known as 8888 Uprising and imposed martial law. However, the 1988 protests paved way for the 1990 People's Assembly elections. The election results were subsequently annulled by Senior General Saw Maung's government. The National League for Democracy, led by Aung San Suu Kyi, won over 60% of the vote and over 80% of parliamentary seats in the 1990 election, the first held in 30 years. The military-backed National Unity Party won less than 2% of the seats. Aung San Suu Kyi has earned international recognition as an activist for the return of democratic rule, winning the Nobel Peace Prize in 1991.

The ruling regime has repeatedly placed her under house arrest. Despite a direct appeal by former UN Secretary General Kofi Annan to Senior General Than Shwe and pressure by the Association of Southeast Asian Nations (ASEAN), the military junta extended Aung San Suu Kyi's house arrest another year on 27 May 2006 under the 1975 State Protection Act, which grants the government the right to detain any persons on the grounds of protecting peace and stability in the country. The junta faces increasing pressure from the United States and the United Kingdom. Burma's situation was referred to the UN Security Council for the first time in December 2005 for an informal consultation. In September 2006, ten of the United Nations Security Council's 15 members voted to place Myanmar on the council's formal agenda. On Independence Day, 4 January 2007, the government released 40 political prisoners, under a general amnesty, in which 2,831 prisoners were released. On 8 January 2007, UN Secretary-General Ban Ki-moon urged the national government to free all political prisoners, including Aung San Suu Kyi. Three days later, on 11 January, five additional prisoners were released from prison.

ASEAN has also stated its frustration with the Union of Myanmar's government. It has formed the ASEAN Inter-Parliamentary Myanmar Caucus to address the lack of democratisation in the country. Dramatic change in the country's political situation remains unlikely, due to support from major regional powers such as India, Russia, and, in particular, China.

In the annual ASEAN Summit in January 2007, held in Cebu, Philippines, member countries failed to find common ground on the issue of Burma's lack of political reform. During the summit, ASEAN foreign ministers asked Burma to make greater progress on its roadmap toward democracy and national reconciliation. Some member countries contend that Burma's human rights issues are the country's own domestic affairs, while others contend that its poor human rights record is an international issue.

According to Human Rights Defenders and Promoters (HRDP), on April 18, 2007, several of its members (Myint Aye, Maung Maung Lay, Tin Maung Oo and Yin Kyi) were met by approximately a hundred people led by a local official, U Nyunt Oo, and beaten up. Due to the attack, Myint Hlaing and Maung Maung Lay were badly injured and subsequently hospitalized. The HRDP believes that this attack was condoned by the authorities and vows to take legal action. Human Rights Defenders and Promoters was formed in 2002 to raise awareness among the people of Burma about their human rights.

Burma's army-drafted constitution was overwhelmingly approved (by 92.4% of the 22 million voters with alleged voter turnout of 99%) on May 10 in the first phase of a two-stage referendum amid Cyclone Nargis. It was the first national vote since the

1990 election. Multi-party elections in 2010 would end 5 decades of military rule, as the new charter gives the military an automatic 25% of seats in parliament. NLD spokesman Nyan Win, inter alia, criticized the referendum: "This referendum was full of cheating and fraud across the country; In some villages, authorities and polling station officials ticked the ballots themselves and did not let the voters do anything." The constitution would bar Aung San Suu Kyi, from public office. 5 million citizens will vote May 24 in Yangon and the Irrawaddy delta, worst hit by Cyclone Nargis.

DEMOGRAPHY

Burma has a population of about 55 million. Current population figures are rough estimates because the last partial census, conducted by the Ministry of Home and Religious Affairs under the control of the military junta, was taken in 1983. No trustworthy nationwide census has been taken in Burma since 1931. There are over 600,000 registered migrant workers from Burma in Thailand, and millions more work illegally. Burmese migrant workers account for 80% of Thailand's migrant workers. Burma has a population density of 75 inhabitants per square kilometre (194/sq mi), one of the lowest in Southeast Asia. Refugee camps exist along Indian, Bangladeshi and Thai borders while several thousand are in Malaysia. Conservative estimates state that there are over 295,800 refugees from Burma, with the majority being Rohingya, Kayin, and Karenni.

Burma is home to four major linguistic families: Sino-Tibetan, Tai-Kadai, Austro-Asiatic, and Indo-European. Sino-Tibetan languages are most widely spoken. They include Burmese, Karen, Kachin, Chin, and Chinese. The primary Tai-Kadai language is Shan. Mon, Palaung, and Wa are the major Austroasiatic languages spoken in Burma. The two major Indo-European languages are Pali, the liturgical language of Theravada Buddhism, and English.

According to the UNESCO Institute of Statistics, Burma's official literacy rate as of 2000 was 89.9%. Historically, Burma has had high literacy rates. To qualify for least developed country status by the UN in order to receive debt relief, Burma lowered its official literacy rate from 78.6% to 18.7% in 1987.

Burma is ethnically diverse. The government recognizes 135 distinct ethnic groups. While it is extremely difficult to verify this statement, there are at least 108 different ethnolinguistic groups in Burma, consisting mainly of distinct Tibeto-Burman peoples, but with sizable populations of Daic, Hmong-Mien, and Austroasiatic (Mon-Khmer) peoples. The Bamar form an estimated 68% of the population. 10% of the population are Shan. The Kayin make up 7% of the population. The Rakhine people constitute 4% of the population. Overseas Chinese form approximately 3% of the population. Mon, who form 2% of the population, are ethno-linguistically related to the Khmer. Overseas Indians comprise 2%. The remainder are Kachin, Chin, Anglo-Indians and other ethnic minorities. Included in this group are the Anglo-Burmese. Once forming a large and influential community, the Anglo-Burmese left the country in steady streams from 1958 onwards, principally to Australia and the U.K.. Today, it is estimated that only 52,000 Anglo-Burmese remain in the country. 89% of the country's population are Buddhist, according to a report on abc World News Tonight in May 2008.

CULTURE

A diverse range of indigenous cultures exist in Burma, the majority culture is primarily Buddhist and Bamar. Bamar culture has been influenced by the cultures of neighbouring countries. This is manifested in its language, cuisine, music, dance and theatre. The arts, particularly literature, have historically been influenced by the local form of Theravada Buddhism. Considered the national epic of Burma, the *Yama Zatdaw,* an adaptation of *Ramayana,* has been influenced greatly by Thai, Mon, and Indian versions of the play. Buddhism is practiced along with nat worship which involves elaborate rituals to propitiate one from a pantheon of 37 nats.

In a traditional village, the monastery is the centre of cultural life. Monks are venerated and supported by the lay people. A novitiation ceremony called shinbyu is the most important coming of age events for a boy when he enters the monastery for a short period of time. All boys of Buddhist family need to be a novice (beginner for Buddhism) before the age of twenty and to be a monk after the age of twenty. It is compulsory for all boys of Buddhism. The duration can be as little as one week. Girls have ear-piercing ceremonies at the same time. Burmese culture is most evident in villages where local festivals are held throughout the year, the most important being the pagoda festival. Many villages have a guardian nat, and superstition and taboos are commonplace.

British colonial rule also introduced Western elements of culture to Burma. Burma's educational system is modelled after that of the United Kingdom. Colonial architectural influences are most evident in major cities such as Yangon. Many ethnic minorities, particularly the Karen in the southeast, and the Kachin and Chin who populate the north and northwest, practice Christianity.

ECONOMY OF MYANMAR

The country is one of the poorest nations in southeastern Asia, suffering from decades of stagnation, mismanagement and isolation. Burma's GDP grows at an average rate of 2.9% annually – the lowest rate of economic growth in the Greater Mekong Subregion.

Under British administration and until the early 1960s, Burma was the wealthiest country in Southeast Asia. It was once the world's largest exporter of rice. During British administration, Burma supplied oil through the Burmah Oil Company. Burma also had a wealth of natural and labor resources. It produced 75% of the world's teak and had a highly literate population. The country was believed to be on the fast track to development.

After a parliamentary government was formed in 1948, Prime Minister U Nu attempted to make Burma a welfare state. His administration adopted the Two-Year Economic Development Plan, which was a failure. The 1962 coup d'état was followed by an economic scheme called the Burmese Way to Socialism, a plan to nationalize all industries, with the exception of agriculture. In 1989, the government began decentralizing economic control. It has since liberalised certain sectors of the economy. Lucrative industries of gems, oil and forestry remain heavily regulated. They have recently been exploited by foreign corporations and governments which have partnered with the local government to gain access to Burma's natural resources.

Burma was designated a least developed country in 1987. Private enterprises are often co-owned or indirectly owned by the Tatmadaw. In recent years, both China and India have attempted to strengthen ties with the government for economic benefit. Many nations, including the United States and Canada, and the European Union, have imposed investment and trade sanctions on Burma. Foreign investment comes primarily from China, Singapore, South Korea, India, and Thailand.

Modern Economy

Today, the country lacks adequate infrastructure. Goods travel primarily across the Thai border, where most illegal drugs are exported and along the Ayeyarwady River. Railroads are old and rudimentary, with few repairs since their construction in the late nineteenth century. Highways are normally unpaved, except in the major cities. Energy shortages are common throughout the country including in Yangon. Burma is also the world's second largest producer of opium, accounting for 8% of entire world production and is a major source of illegal drugs, including amphetamines. Other industries include agricultural goods, textiles, wood products, construction materials, gems, metals, oil and natural gas.

The major agricultural product is rice which covers about 60% of the country's total cultivated land area. Rice accounts for 97% of total food grain production by weight. Through collaboration with the International Rice Research Institute (IRRI), 52 modern rice varieties were released in the country between 1966 and 1997, helping increase national rice production to 14 million tons in 1987 and to 19 million tons in 1996. By 1988, modern varieties were planted on half of the country's ricelands, including 98 percent of the irrigated areas.

The lack of an educated workforce skilled in modern technology contributes to the growing problems of the economy. Inflation is a serious problem for the economy. In April 2007, the National League for Democracy organized a two-day workshop on the economy. The workshop concluded that skyrocketing inflation was impeding economic growth. "Basic commodity prices have increased from 30 to 60 percent since the military regime promoted a salary increase for government workers in April 2006," said Soe Win, the moderator of the workshop. "Inflation is also correlated with corruption." Myint Thein, an NLD spokesperson, added: "Inflation is the critical source of the current economic crisis." The corruption watchdog organization Transparency International in its 2007 Corruption Perceptions Index released on September 26, 2007 ranked Burma the most corrupt country in the world, tied with Somalia.

Valley of Rubies

The Union of Myanmar's rulers depend on sales of precious stones such as sapphires, pearls and jade to fund their regime. Rubies are the biggest earner; 90% of the world's rubies come from the country, whose red stones are prized for their purity and hue. Thailand buys the majority of the country's gems. Burma's *"Valley of Rubies"*, the mountainous Mogok area, 200 km (125 miles) north of Mandalay, is noted for its rare pigeon's blood rubies and blue sapphires.

Tourism

Since 1992, the government has encouraged tourism in the country. However, fewer than 750,000 tourists enter the country annually. Aung San Suu Kyi has requested that international tourists not visit Burma. The junta's forced labour programmes were focused around tourist destinations which have been heavily criticised for their human rights records.

Tourism has been promoted by a minority of advocacy groups as a method of providing economic benefit to Burmese civilians, and to avoid isolating the country from the rest of the world. "We believe that small-scale, responsible tourism can create more benefits than harm. So long as tourists are fully aware of the situation and take steps to maximise their positive impact and minimise the negatives, we feel their visit can be beneficial overall. Responsible tourists can help Burma primarily by bringing money to local communities and small businesses, and by raising awareness of the situation worldwide," states Voices for Burma, a pro-democracy advocate group.

Humanitarian Aid

In April 2007, the U.S. Government Accountability Office (GAO) identified financial and other restrictions that the military government places on international humanitarian assistance. The GAO report, entitled "Assistance Programs Constrained in Burma", outlined the specific efforts of the government to hinder the humanitarian work of international organizations, including restrictions on the free movement of international staff within the country. The report notes that the regime has tightened its control over assistance work since former Prime Minister Khin Nyunt was purged in October 2004. The military junta passed guidelines in February 2006, which formalized these restrictive policies. According to the report, the guidelines require that programs run by humanitarian groups "enhance and safeguard the national interest" and that international organizations coordinate with state agents and select their Burmese staff from government-prepared lists of individuals. United Nations officials have declared these restrictions unacceptable.

7

PHILIPPINES

The Philippines (officially known as the Republic of the Philippines), is an archipelagic country located in Southeast Asia with Manila as its capital city. The Philippine archipelago comprises 7,107 islands in the western Pacific Ocean, sharing maritime borders with Indonesia, Malaysia, Palau, the Republic of China (Taiwan), and Vietnam. The Philippines is the world's 12th most populous country with a population approaching 90 million people. Its national economy is the 46th largest in the world with an estimated 2008 gross domestic product (GDP) of over US$154.073 billion. There are more than 11 million overseas Filipinos worldwide, the largest diaspora network in the world, about 11% of the total population of the Philippines. Ecologically, Philippines is considered to be among 17 of the most megadiverse countries in the world.

Prior to the arrival of Ferdinand Magellan, the Philippines was already settled by Austronesian peoples, who traded with other Asian peoples such as those from China, India, Japan, and the Malay Archipelago. The Philippines became a Spanish colony in the 16th century, and an American territory at the beginning of the 20th century. In 1896, Katipunan led the Philippine Revolution that won independence from Spain. American occupation of the Philippines during the Spanish-American War led to the outbreak of the Philippine-American War. A Commonwealth-style government was established in 1935, which allowed self-governance as well as the first national elections. The country gained its independence from the United States on July 4, 1946 after the Pacific Theatre of the Second World War. Martial law was declared in 1972 by Ferdinand Marcos, which led to the insurgencies of the New People's Army and the Moro National Liberation Front. Ninoy Aquino's assassination would soon inspire his widow, Corazon Aquino, as well as the country's the-spiritual leader Jaime Cardinal Sin to lead the People Power Revolution of 1986, which would bring the country back to democracy.

Political upheavals and corruption scandals alternated with the peaceful transition of power during the period that followed the restoration of democracy.

Modern Philippines has many affinities with the Western world, derived mainly from the cultures of Spain, Latin America, and the United States. Roman Catholicism is the country's predominant religion, although pre-Hispanic indigenous religious practices still exist; there are also followers of Islam. Spanish was an official language of the Philippines until 1973. Since then, the two official languages are Filipino and English.

GEOGRAPHY OF PHILIPPINES

The Philippines is an archipelago comprising 7,107 islands with a total land area of 300,000 km^2. The 11 largest islands contain 94% of the total land area. The largest of these islands is Luzon at about 105,000 km^2. The next largest island is Mindanao at about 94,600 km^2. The archipelago is around 800 km from the Asian mainland and is located between Taiwan and Borneo.

The islands are divided into three groups: Luzon, Visayas, and Mindanao. The Luzon islands include Luzon itself, Mindoro, Marinduque, Masbate and Batanes Islands,Palawan. The Visayas is the group of islands in the central Philippines, the largest of which are: Panay, Negros, Cebu, Bohol, Leyte and Samar. The Mindanao islands include Mindanao itself, plus the Sulu Archipelago, composed primarily of Basilan, Sulu, and Tawi-Tawi.

Climate

The Philippines has a tropical marine climate dominated by a rainy season and a dry season. The summer monsoon brings heavy rains to most of the archipelago from May to October, whereas the winter monsoon brings cooler and drier air from December to February. Manila and most of the lowland areas are hot and dusty from March to May. Even at this time, however, temperatures rarely rise above 37 °C. Mean annual sea-level temperatures rarely fall below 27 °C. Annual rainfall measures as much as 5,000 millimeters in the mountainous east coast section of the country, but less than 1,000 millimeters in some of the sheltered valleys.

Monsoon rains, although hard and drenching, are not normally associated with high winds and waves. But the Philippines sit astride the typhoon belt, and it suffers an annual onslaught of dangerous storms from July through October. These are especially hazardous for northern and eastern Luzon and the Bicol and Eastern Visayas regions, but Manila gets devastated periodically as well.

In the last decade, the Philippines has been hit severely by natural disasters. In 2005 alone, Central Luzon was hit by both a drought, which sharply curtailed hydroelectric power, and by a typhoon that flooded practically all of low-lying Manila's streets. Still more damaging was the 1990 earthquake that devastated a wide area in Luzon, including Baguio and other northern areas. The city of Cebu and nearby areas were struck by a typhoon that killed more than a hundred people, sank vessels, destroyed part of the sugar crop, and cut off water and electricity for several days. The Philippines is prone to about 18-21 typhoons per year. Of course the 1991 Mount Pinatubo eruption also damaged much of Central Luzon, the lahar burying towns and farmland, and the ashes affecting global temperatures.

Building construction is undertaken with natural disasters in mind. Most rural housing has consisted of nipa huts that are easily damaged but are inexpensive and easy to replace. Most urban buildings are steel and concrete structures designed (not always successfully) to resist both typhoons and earthquakes. Damage is still significant, however, and many people are displaced each year by typhoons, earthquakes, and other natural disasters. In 1987 alone the Department of Social Welfare and Development helped 2.4 million victims of natural disasters.

Terrain

The islands are volcanic in origin, being part of the Pacific Ring of Fire, and are mostly mountainous. The highest point in the country is the peak of Mount Apo in Mindanao, which is 2,954 m above sea level. The second highest point can be found on Luzon at Mount Pulog, a peak 2,842 m above sea level.

Many volcanoes in the country are active, the most recent eruption being that of Mount Pinatubo on Luzon in 1991. Mount Mayon is another of the active volcanoes and has the world's most perfectly-shaped cone. Mayon has a violent history of 47 eruptions since 1616 and another violent eruption is currently feared. Taal Volcano, also located on Luzon, is one of the Decade Volcanoes.

The islands typically have narrow coastal plains and numerous swift-running streams. Every island has sand beaches, but few open onto spacious lowlands. There are few large plains or navigable rivers. The longest river is the Cagayan River or Rio Grande de Cagayan in northern Luzon measuring 354 kilometers. In Mindanao, the longest river is the Mindanao River or Rio Grande de Mindanao which drains Maguindanao and other parts in western-central Mindanao. Agusan River drains eastern Mindanao.

Most of the islands used to be covered by tropical rainforests. However, illegal logging has reduced forest cover to less than 10% of the total land area.

DEMOGRAPHY

The Philippines is the world's 12th most populous country, with a population of over 90 million as of 2008.As of 2007, 8% of Filipinos are living abroad as migrant laborers. Roughly half reside on the island of Luzon. Manila, the capital, is the eleventh most populous metropolitan area in the world. The literacy rate was 92.6% in 2003, and about equal for males and females. Life expectancy is 71.23 years, with 73.6 years for females and 69.8 years for males. Population growth rate in 1995-2000 is 3.21% but then dramatically fell to 1.59% for 2005-2010.

Ethnic Groups

Majority of Philippine nationals are descended from the various Austronesian-speaking migrants who arrived in successive waves over a thousand years ago from Taiwan, genetically most closely related to the Ami tribe. The Malayo-Polynesian-speaking peoples, a branch of Austronesian, migrated to the Philippines and brought their knowledge of rice agriculture and ocean-sailing technology. Filipinos to this day are composed of various Malayo-Polynesian-speaking ethnic groups, including but not limited to the Visayans, the Tagalog, the Ilocano, the Moro, the Kapampangan, the Bicolano, the Pangasinense, the Igorot, the Lumad, the Mangyan, the Ibanag, the Badjao, the Ivatan, and the Palawan tribes. The Negritos, including the Aetas and the Ati, are considered as the aboriginal inhabitants of the Philippines though they are estimated to be fewer than 30,000 people (0.03%).

Filipinos of Chinese descent currently forms the largest non-Austronesian ethnic group, claiming about 1.5% of the population followed by Filipinos of Spanish descent. Other significant minorities include British, Americans, Japanese, Asian Indians, Koreans, Arabs and Indonesians. Chinese mestizos are those in the Philippines of mixed Chinese and either indigenous Filipino or Spanish (or both) ancestry. They make up between 10-20% of the country's total population.

Throughout the country's history, various ethnic groups as well as immigrants and colonizers have intermarried, producing Filipino mestizos. These mestizos, apart from being of mixed indigenous Austronesian and European ancestry, can be descended from any ethnic foreign forebears. The percentage of Filipinos with foreign ancestry is unknown since there are no credible sources for the percentage of Philippine mestizos residing in the Philippines. The number of Filipino mestizos that reside outside the Philippines is also unknown. However, due to major historical factors, such as the Spanish colonization, the American occupation, and Chinese immigration after World War II; many Filipino mestizos that reside in the Philippines are now of Spanish, American and Chinese descent.

CULTURE

Filipino culture is a fusion of pre-Hispanic indigenous Austronesian civilizations of the Philippines mixed with Hispanic and American. It has also been influenced by Chinese, Arab, and Indianized cultures.

The Hispanic influences in Filipino culture are largely derived from the culture of Spain as a result of over three centuries of Spanish colonial rule. These Hispanic influences are most evident in literature, folk music, folk dance, language, food, art and religion, such as Roman Catholic Church religious festivals. Interestingly, there was relatively little Mexican influence in the Philippines, despite the ties to a Mexican-based administration and the galleon trade. Noticeably, the Spanish colonialists preferred Iberian dishes, such as arroz valenciana, to those of the Mexican Indians (adobo preparation is the only exception as the tomato, corn, avocado, and potato in adobo were all introduced from Mexico).

Filipinos hold major festivities known as barrio fiestas to commemorate their patron saints. One of the most visible Hispanic legacies is the prevalence of Spanish surnames among Filipinos. This peculiarity, unique among the people of Asia, came as a result of a colonial decree for the systematic distribution of family names and implementation of the Spanish naming system on the inhabitants of the Philippines. A Spanish name and surname among the majority of Filipinos does not always denote Spanish ancestry.

Names of countless streets, towns and provinces are in Spanish. Spanish architecture also made a major imprint in the Philippines. This can be seen especially in the country's churches, government buildings and universities. Many Hispanic style houses and buildings are being preserved, like the Spanish colonial town in Vigan City, for protection and conservation. The kalesa is a horse-driven carriage introduced by the Spaniards and was a major mode of transportation during the colonial times. It is still being used today. Filipino cuisine is also heavily influenced by Spanish cuisine.

The use of English language in the Philippines is contemporaneous and is America's visible legacy. The most commonly played sports in the Philippines are basketball and billiards. There is also a wide influence of American Pop cultural trends, such as the love of fast-food and movies; many street corners boast fast-food outlets. Aside from the American commercial giants such as McDonald's, Pizza Hut, Burger King, KFC, and Shakey's Pizza, local fast-food chains have also sprung up, including Goldilocks, Jollibee, Greenwich Pizza (acquired by Jollibee in 1994), and Chowking (acquired by Jollibee in 2000). Modern day Filipinos also listen to contemporary American music and watch American movies. However, Original Pilipino Music (also known as OPM) and Philippine movies are also widely appreciated.

Filipinos honor national heroes whose works and deeds contributed to the shaping of the Filipino nation. José Rizal is the most celebrated *ilustrado,* a Spanish-speaking reformist visionary whose writings contributed greatly in nurturing a sense of national identity and awareness. His novels *Noli Me Tangere* and *El Filibusterismo* originally written in Spanish, are required readings for Filipino students, and provide vignettes of colonial life during the period of Spanish rule.

As with many cultures, music (which includes traditional music) and leisure activities are an important aspect of the Filipino society. Various sports are also enjoyed, including boxing, basketball, badminton, billiards, football (soccer) and ten-pin bowling being popular games in the country.

POLITICS AND GOVERNANCE OF PHILIPPINES

The political system in the Philippines takes place in an organized framework of a presidential, representative, and democratic republic whereby the president is both the head of state and the head of government within a pluriform multi-party system. This system revolves around three separate and sovereign yet interdependent branches: the legislative branch (the law-making body), the executive branch (the law-enforcing body), and the judicial branch (the law-interpreting body). Executive power is exercised by the government under the leadership of the president. Legislative power is vested in both the government and the two-chamber congress — the Senate (the upper chamber) and the House of Representatives (the lower chamber). Judicial power is vested in the courts with the Supreme Court of the Philippines as the highest judicial body.

National Government of the Philippines

Executive Branch

The executive branch is headed by the President, Gloria Macapagal-Arroyo (party affiliation: Kampi/Lakas-CMD) 20 January 2001, who functions as both the head of state and the head of government. The president is also the Commander-in-Chief of the Armed Forces of the Philippines. The president is elected by popular vote to a term of 6 years. The president, then, appoints (and may fire) his/her cabinet members whom he/she presides over. The executive seat of government is administered officially from Malacañang Palace–also the official residence of the president–in the capital City of Manila. The President may no longer run for re-election, unless he/she becomes president through constitutional succession and has served for no more than 4 years as president.

The second highest official, Vice-President Noli de Castro (party affiliation: Lakas-CMD/Independent) 30 June 2004, is also elected by popular vote. The vice-president is second in line to succession should the president resign, be impeached or die in office. The vice-president usually, though not always, may be a member of the president's cabinet. If there is a vacancy in the position of Vice President, the President will appoint any member of Congress (usually a party member) as new Vice President. The appointment will be validated by a three-fourths vote of Congress voting separately.

Legislative Branch

The bicameral Philippine legislature, the Congress, consists of the Senate and the House of Representatives; members of both are elected by popular vote. The Senate is elected at large. There are currently 24 senators. Of a possible 250 members of the House of Representatives, 206 are elected from the single-member districts. The remainder of the House seats are designated for sectoral representatives elected at large through a complex "party list" system, hinging on the party receiving at least 2% to 6% of the national vote total. The upper house is located in Pasay City, while the lower house is located in Quezon City. The district and sectoral representatives are elected with a term of three years. They can be reelected but they are no longer eligible to run for a fourth consecutive term.

The senators are elected to a term of six years. They can be reelected but they are no longer eligible to run for a third consecutive term. The House of Representatives may opt to pass a resolution for a vacancy of a legislative seat that will pave way for a special election. The winner of the special election will serve the unfinished term of the previous district representative; this will be considered as one elective term. The same rule applies in the Senate however it only applies if the seat is vacated before a regular legislative election. This case applies when Senator Teofisto Guingona was appointed Vice President before the May 2001 election. Senator Gregorio Honasan was in the 13th position in the Senatorial election and he served the unfinished term of Guingona. Honasan is no longer eligible to run for the 2004 elections. The case did not apply in 1998 when Gloria Arroyo was elected as Vice President and in 2004 when Noli de Castro was elected as Vice President.

When Gloria Macapagal-Arroyo assumed the Presidency, her Lakas-CMD party also regained its dominant position in Congress. The party leads the 187 member Sunshine Coalition, composed of several major and minor parties such as her party, Lakas-CMD, the Liberal Party, the Nacionalista Party, the Nationalist People's Coalition, PDP-Laban, Aksyon Demokratiko, REPORMA-LM, PROMDI, and others. In addition, Arroyo established her own party KAMPI. In the Senate, the pro-administration coalition lost its majority in the May 2007 elections.

Members of the Philippine Congress tend to have weak party loyalties and change party affiliation easily. In October 2003, the Sunshine Coalition dissolved over Pres.

Gloria Macapagal-Arroyo's decision to seek election for the presidency, which she assumed when as vice-president, she succeeded Joseph Estrada following the EDSA 2 Revolution of 2001.

ECONOMY

The Philippines is a newly industrialized country with an economy anchored on agriculture but with substantial contributions from manufacturing, mining, remittances from overseas Filipinos and service industries such as tourism and, increasingly, business process outsourcing. The Philippines is listed in the roster of "Next Eleven" economies.

Historically, the Philippine economy has largely been anchored on the Manila galleon during the Spanish era, and bilateral trade with the United States during the American era. Pro-Filipino economic policies were first implemented during the tenure of Carlos P. Garcia with the "Filipino First" policy. By the 1960s, the Philippine economy was regarded as the second-largest in Asia, next only to Japan. However, the presidency of Ferdinand Marcos would prove disastrous to the Philippine economy, sliding the country into severe economic recession, only to recover starting in the 1990s with a program of economic liberalization and the breaking of Marcos-era monopolies and the system of cronyism under Fidel V. Ramos.

The Asian Financial Crisis affected the Philippine economy to an extent, resulting in a lingering decline of the value of the Philippine peso and falls in the stock market, although the extent to which it was affected is not as severe as that of its Asian neighbors. This is largely due to the fiscal conservatism of the Philippine government partly as a result of decades of monitoring and fiscal supervision from the International Monetary Fund, in comparison to the massive spending of its neighbors on the rapid acceleration of economic growth. By 2004, the Philippine economy experienced six-percent growth in gross domestic product and 7.3% in 2007, in line with the "7, 8, 9" project of the government to accelerate GDP growth by 2009.

In a bid to further strengthen the Philippine economy, President Gloria Macapagal-Arroyo pledged to make the Philippines a developed country by 2020. As part of this goal, she instituted five economic "super regions" to concentrate on the economic strengths of various regions of the Philippines, as well as the implementation of tax reforms, continued privatization of state assets, and the building-up of infrastructure in various areas of the Philippines.

Despite the growing economy, the Philippines will have to address several chronic problems in the future. Strategies for streamlining the economy include improvements of infrastructure, more efficient tax systems to bolster government revenues, furthering deregulation and privatization of the economy, and increasing trade integration within the region and across the world. The Philippine economy is also heavily reliant on remittances as a source of foreign currency, surpassing even foreign direct investment. China and India have emerged as major economic competitors, siphoning away investors who would otherwise have invested in the Philippines, particularly telecommunications companies. Regional development is also somewhat uneven, with Luzon and Metro Manila in particular gaining most of the new economic growth at the expense of the other regions, although the government has taken steps to distribute economic growth by promoting investment in other areas of the Philippines.

The Philippines is a founding member of the Asian Development Bank, playing home to its headquarters. It is also a member of the World Bank, the IMF, the Asia Pacific Economic Cooperation (APEC), the World Trade Organization (WTO), the Colombo Plan, and the G-77, among others.

8

THAILAND

The Kingdom of Thailand is an independent country which lies in the heart of Southeast Asia. The country is bordered to the north by Laos and Burma, to the east by Laos and Cambodia, to the south by the Gulf of Thailand and Malaysia, and to the west by the Andaman Sea and Burma. The capital and largest city of Thailand is Bangkok. It is also the country's centre of political, commercial, industrial and cultural activities. Bangkok is known in Thai as "Krung Thep Mahanakorn", or, more colloquially, "Krung Thep".

Thailand is considered to be the world's 50th largest country in terms of total area, with a surface area of approximately 513,000 km^2 (198,000 sq mi), and the world's 20th largest country in terms of population with approximately 63 million people. The population consists 80% of Thais, 10% of Chinese, and 3% of Malay. The rest are minorities such as Mons, Khmers, and various hill tribes. The country's official spoken and written language is Thai.

Thailand is one of the most strongly Buddhist countries in the world. The national religion is Theravada Buddhism which is practiced by more than 95% of all Thais (2002). The cultures and traditions in Thailand are significantly influenced by those of India, China, Cambodia, as well as various countries in Southeast Asia. As a result, seniority plays an important role in the country's cultures. Respect for the elders is essential to Thai's spiritual practices as well as daily lifestyles. Thais are also well-known for their friendliness and hospitality, leading to the country's so called reputation as the "Land of Smiles".

Thailand is a constitutional monarchy with His Majesty King Bhumibol Adulyadej, or King Rama IX, the ninth king of the Chakri Dynasty, as the present king. The King has reigned for more than half a century, making him the longest reigning Thai monarch. His Majesty the King is recognised as the Head of State, the Head of the Armed Forces, the Upholder of the Buddhist religion, and the Upholder of all religions. Due to the government of the Monarch, Thailand is the only country in Southeast Asia that has never been colonized by a European power.

GEOGRAPHY

Thailand's 514,000 square kilometers lie in the middle of mainland Southeast Asia. The nation's axial position influenced many aspects of Thailand's society and culture—it controls the only land route from Asia to Malaysia and Singapore.

The most conspicuous features of Thailand's terrain are high mountains, a central plain, and an upland plateau. Mountains cover much of northern Thailand and extend along the Myanmar border down through the Kra Isthmus and the Malay Peninsula. The central plain is a lowland area drained by the Chao Phraya River and its tributaries, the country's principal river system, which feeds into the delta at the head of the Bay of Bangkok. The Chao Phraya system drains about one-third of the nation's territory. In the northeastern part of the country the Khorat Plateau, a region of gently rolling low hills and shallow lakes, drains into the Mekong through the Mun River. The Mekong system empties into the South China Sea and includes a series of canals and dams.

Together, the Chao Phraya and Mekong systems sustain Thailand's agricultural economy by supporting wet-rice cultivation and providing waterways for the transport of goods and people. In contrast, the distinguishing natural features of peninsular Thailand are long coastlines, offshore islands, and diminishing mangrove swamps.

Climate

Most of Thailand has a Tropical wet and dry or savanna climate (*Aw*) according to the Köppen climate classification, while the South and the eastern tip of the East have a tropical monsoon climate (*Am*); countrywide, temperatures normally range from an average annual high of 38 °C (100 F) to a low of 19 °C (66 F). During the dry season, the temperature rises dramatically in the second half of March, spiking to well over 40°C in some areas by mid April when the Sun passes the Zenith. Southwest monsoons that arrive between May and July (except in the South) signal the advent of the rainy season (*ridu fon*), which lasts into October and the cloud covering reduces the temperature again but the high humidity is experienced as 'hot and sticky'. November and December mark the onset of the dry season and night temperatures on high ground can occasionally drop to a light frost. Temperatures begin to climb in January, and a hot sun parches the landscape.

The dry season is shortest in the South because of the proximity of the sea to all parts of the Malay Peninsula. With only minor exceptions, every area of the country receives adequate rainfall, but the duration of the rainy season and the amount of rain vary substantially from region to region and with altitude. The Northeast experiences a long dry season although the dry 2007/2008 season lasted only from late November through mid March. Its red,(laterite) dense clayey soils retain water well, which limits their agricultural potential for many crops but is ideal for keeping the water in the paddy fields and local village reservoirs. The well drained, loose sandy alluvium of the Mekong flood plain is very fertile, the main crops being tomatoes on an industrial scale, tobacco, and pineapples.

GOVERNMENT AND POLITICS

The government of Thailand has 3 branches: executive, legislative, and judicial.

Executive Branch

The king has little direct power under the constitution but is a symbol of national identity and unity. The present monarch has a great deal of popular respect and moral authority, which has been used to resolve political crises.

The head of government is the Prime Minister. Under the constitution, the Prime Minister must be a Member of Parliament. Cabinet members do not have to be Members of Parliament. The legislature could hold a vote of no-confidence against the Premier and members of his Cabinet if it had sufficient votes.

Legislative Branch

Under the new 2007 Constitution, the bicameral Thai legislature is called the National Assembly or informally, the Parliament. It consists of a House of Representatives (sapha phuthaen ratsadon) of 480 seats and a Senate of 150 seats.

The House of Representatives is made up of 400 members from constituency elections and 80 members from "proportional representation", as termed in the Constitution. However, the correct term for Thailand's "proportional representation" is actually parallel voting or Mixed Member Majoritarian (MMM), where the 80 seats are divided, to different political parties, according to the proportion of the "proportional representation" votes, each party receives, in the 8 election districts (10 seats per district).

The Senate is made up of 76 elected members (one for each province) and the rest (74) are selected from nominated candidates, from the academic sector, the public sector, the private sector, the professional sector and other sectors, by the Senates Selection Committee. Members of House of Representatives serve four-year terms, while Senators serve six-year terms.

Judicial Branch

Supreme Court, judges appointed by the monarch. All courts are not under the Thai Ministry of Justice according to 1997 constitution section 249. There is also an independent Constitutional Court. There is a Court of Appeals, divided into districts and three (3) judges compose a court. Research judges assist the sitting judges. Judges must take an examination and two different examinations are given: one exam is for judges trained in Thailand and a different examination is given for judges who graduate from foreign law schools. Trial courts of the first instance (civil, criminal and kwaeng) are also staffed by judges. Labor Court judges are not necessarily lawyers and work for the ministry of Labor.

There is also the IPCIT Court for intellectual property and international trade. There is no stenographic record of any trial court proceedings and all court proceedings are composed by the trial judge. There is no discovery of evidence or witnesses in trial court. The criminally accused are entitled to have a court-appointed certified translator present in court if they cannot afford one. Appeals must be filed with the trial court within thirty (30) days of the judge reading, signing and issuing the verdict. There are no juries in trials. Only Thai citizens can be admitted to the Bar and can practice before the courts.

The Asian Human Rights Commission called the Thai legal system a "mess" and called for a drastic overhaul of Thailand's criminal procedures. It cited the rampant use of forced confessions, and the fact that even a senior justice ministry official admitted that 30% of cases went to court with no evidence. It also criticized the judiciary for failing to ensure that trials are conducted speedily, citing the case of four Thai men accused of plotting to kill a Supreme Court president. The accused appeared in court 461 times before 91 different judges since proceedings began in 1993.

Legal System

Thailand's legal system blends principles of traditional Thai and Western laws; the western sourced laws are often misused and corrupted and the traditional 'Thai' laws are the product of Hindu-brahmin laws used by the Khmer Empire. The Constitutional Court of Thailand has jurisdiction over certain constitutional issues. The Courts of Justice have jurisdiction over criminal and civil cases and are organized in three tiers: Courts of First Instance, the Court of Appeals, and the Supreme Court of Justice. There are no stenographic records kept by the trial court and the record is composed of what the judge decides. There is no discovery in the Thai legal system. Slander and libel are not civil torts in Thailand but criminal offenses.

Attorneys must carry their current, yellow, bar card when in court and may be required to produce it on challenge. Administrative courts have jurisdiction over suits between private parties and the government, and cases in which one government entity is suing another. In Thailand's southern border provinces, where Muslims constitute the majority of the population, Provincial Islamic Committees have limited jurisdiction over probate, family, marriage, and divorce cases. Thailands legal system has been often criticised by other countries for having penalties of life in prison or even death for crimes such as drug possession or smuggling, while having lenient penalties for crimes such as terrorism and marital abuse resulting in spousal death.

Local Government

Thailand is divided into seventy-six provinces (*changwat*, singular and plural). The Ministry of the Interior appoints governors for all but one province–the metropolis of greater Bangkok, where the governor is popularly elected.

THAI CULTURE

The culture of Thailand incorporates a great deal of influence from India, China, Cambodia, and the rest of Southeast Asia. Thailand's main theology Theravada Buddhism is central to modern Thai identity and belief. In practice, Thai Buddhism has evolved over time to include many regional beliefs originating from Hinduism, animism as well as ancestor worship. In areas in the southernmost parts of Thailand, Islam is prevalent. Several different ethnic groups, many of which are marginalized, populate Thailand. Some of these groups overlap into Burma, Laos, Cambodia, and Malaysia and have maintained a distinctly traditional way of life despite strong Thai cultural influence. Overseas Chinese also form a significant part of Thai society, particularly in and around Bangkok. Their successful integration into Thai society has allowed for this group to hold positions of economic and political power, the most noteworthy of these being the Thai Prime Minister, Thaksin Shinawatra, who held power from 2001 until 19 September 2006 when he was ousted by a military coup d'état.

Like most Asian cultures, respect towards ancestors is an essential part of Thai spiritual practice. Thais have a strong sense of hospitality and generosity, but also a strong sense of social hierarchy. Seniority is an important concept in Thai culture. Elders have by tradition ruled in family decisions or ceremonies.

The traditional Thai greeting, the *wai*, is generally offered first by the youngest of the two people meeting, with their hands pressed together, fingertips pointing upwards as the head is bowed to touch their face to the hands, usually coinciding with the spoken word "Sawat-dii khrap" for male speakers, and "Sawat-dii ka" for females. The elder then is to respond afterwards in the same way. Social status and position, such as in government, will also have an influence on who performs the *wai* first. For example, although one may be considerably older than a provincial governor, when meeting it is usually the visitor who pays respect first. When children leave to go to school, they are taught to *wai* to their parents to represent their respect for them. They do the same when they come back. The wai is a sign of respect and reverence for another, similar to the namaste greeting of India.

Muay Thai, or Thai boxing, is the national sport in Thailand and its native martial art call "Muay". In the past "Muay" was taught to Royal soldiers for combat on battlefield if unarmed. After they retired from the army, these soldiers often became Buddhist monks and stayed at the temples. Most of the Thai people's lives are closely tied to Buddhism and temples; they often send their sons to be educated with the monks. "Muay" is also one of the subjects taught in the temples..

Muay Thai achieved popularity all over the world in the 1990s. Although similar martial arts styles exist in other southeast Asian countries, few enjoy the recognition that Muay Thai has received with its full-contact rules allowing strikes including elbows, throws and knees. Football (soccer), however, has possibly overtaken Muay Thai's position as most widely viewed and liked sport in contemporary Thai society and it is not uncommon to see Thais cheering their favourite English Premier League teams on television and walking around in replica kits. Another widely enjoyed pastime, and once a competitive sport, is kite flying.

Taboos in Thailand include touching someone's head or pointing with the feet, as the head is considered the most sacred and the foot the dirtiest part of the body. Stepping over someone, or over food, is considered insulting. However, Thai culture as in many other Asian cultures, is succumbing to the influence of globalization with some of the traditional taboos slowly fading away with time.

Books and other documents are the most revered of secular objects. One should not slide a book across a table or place it on the floor.

Thai cuisine blends five fundamental tastes: sweet, spicy, sour, bitter and salty. Some common ingredients used in Thai cuisine include garlic, chillies, lime juice, lemon grass, and fish sauce. The staple food in Thailand is rice, particularly jasmine variety rice (also known as Hom Mali rice) which is included in almost every meal. Thailand is the world's largest exporter of rice, and Thais domestically consume over 100 kg of milled rice per person per year. Over 5000 varieties of rice from Thailand are preserved in the rice gene bank of the International Rice Research Institute (IRRI), based in the Philippines. The King of Thailand is the official patron of IRRI.

Thai society has been influenced in recent years by its widely-available multi-language press and media. There are numerous English, Thai and Chinese newspapers in circulation; most Thai popular magazines use English headlines as a chic glamor factor. Most large businesses in Bangkok operate in English as well as other languages. Thailand is the largest newspaper market in South East Asia with an estimated circulation of at least 13 million copies daily in 2003. Even upcountry, out of Bangkok, media flourishes. For example, according to Thailand's Public Relations Department Media

Directory 2003-2004, the nineteen provinces of northeast Thailand themselves hosted 116 newspapers in addition to radio, TV and cable.

DEMOGRAPH OF THAILAND

Language

The official language of Thailand is the Thai language, a Tai-Kadai language closely related to Lao, Shan in Burma, and numerous smaller languages spoken in an arc from Hainan and Yunan south to the Malaysian border. It is the principal language of education and government and spoken throughout the country. The standard is based on the dialect of the Central Thai people, and it is written in the Thai alphabet, an abugida script that evolved from the Khmer script. Several other dialects exist, and coincide with the regional designations. Southern Thai is spoken in the southern provinces, and Northern Thai is spoken in the provinces that were formally part of the independent kingdom of Lannathai.

Thailand is also host to several other minority languages, the largest of which is the Lao dialect of Isan spoken in the northeastern provinces. Although sometimes considered a Thai dialect, it is a Lao dialect, and the region in where it is traditionally spoken was historically part of the Lao kingdom of Lan Xang. In the far south, Yawi, a dialect of Malay, is the primary language of the Malay Muslims. Chinese dialects are also spoken by the large Chinese population, Teochew being the dialect best represented.

Numerous tribal languages are also spoken, including those belonging to the Mon-Khmer family, such as Mon, Khmer, Viet, Mlabri; Austronesian family, such as Cham, Moken, and Orang Asli, Sino-Tibetan family such as Hmong, Lawa, Akhan, and Karen; and other Tai-Kadai languages such as Nyaw, Phu Thai, and Saek. English is a mandatory school subject, but the number of fluent speakers remains very low, especially outside the cities.

Religion

According to the last census (2000) 95% of Thais are Buddhists of the Theravada tradition. Muslims are the second largest religious group in Thailand at 4.6%. Thailand's southernmost provinces–Pattani, Yala, Narathiwat and part of Songkhla Chumphon have dominant Muslim populations, consisting of both ethnic Thai and Malay. Most often Muslims live in separate communities from non-Muslims. The southern tip of Thailand is mostly ethnic Malays. Christians, mainly Catholics, represent 0.75% of the population. A tiny but influential community of Sikhs in Thailand and some Hindus also live in the country's cities, and are heavily engaged in retail commerce. There is also a small Jewish community in Thailand, dating back to the 17th century. Since

2001, Muslim activists, generally described by the Thai government as terrorists or separatists, have rallied against the central government because of alleged corruption and ethnic bias on the part of officials.

ECONOMY

The economy of Thailand is an emerging economy which is heavily export-dependent, with exports accounting for more than two thirds of GDP. The exchange rate is Baht 33.00/ usd. Thailand has a GDP worth $8.5 trillion Baht (PPP), or US$ 627 billion (PPP). This classifies Thailand as the 2nd largest economy in Southeast Asia after Indonesia. Despite this, Thailand ranks midway in the wealth spread in Southeast Asia as it is the 4th richest nation according to GDP per capita, after Singapore, Brunei and Malaysia. It functions as an anchor economy for the neighboring developing economies of Laos, Burma, and Cambodia. Thailand's recovery from the 1997-1998 Asian financial crisis depended mainly on exports, among various other factors. Thailand ranks high among the world's automotive export industries along with manufacturing of electronic goods.

Most of Thailand's labour force is working in agriculture. However, the relative contribution of agriculture to GDP has declined while exports of goods and services have increased. Tourism revenues are on the rise. With the instability surrounding the recent coup and the military rule, however, the GDP growth of Thailand has settled at around 4-5% from previous highs of 5-7% under the previous civilian administration, as investor and consumer confidence has been degraded somewhat due to political uncertainty. The incumbent elected civilian administration under Samak Sundaravej in power since January 29, 2008 states that the economy will have grown by 5.5% to 6% by the end of 2008. Due to rising oil and food prices, the annual inflation rate for 2008 shot up to 9.2% in July; a 10-year high, but it will unlikely reach double digit rates later this year as oil and food prices are stabilizing.

Industries

Agriculture, Forestry, and Fishing

In 2007 agriculture, forestry, and fishing contributed only 11.4% percent to GDP. Thailand is the world's leading exporter of rice and a major exporter of shrimp. Other crops include coconuts, corn, rubber, soybeans, sugarcane and tapioca. In 1985 Thailand officially designated 25 percent of the nation's land area for protected forests and 15 percent for timber production. Protected forests have been set aside for conservation and recreation, while production forests are available for the forestry industry. Between 1992 and 2001, exports of logs and sawn timber increased from 50,000 cubic meters to 2 million cubic meters per year. The regional avian flu outbreak led to a contraction of Thailand's agricultural sector during 2004, and the tsunami disaster of December 26,

2004, devastated the west coast fisheries industry. In 2005 and 2006 agricultural GDP was stated to have contracted by 10 percent.

Mining and Minerals

Thailand's major minerals include fluorite, gypsum, lead, lignite, natural gas, rubber, tantalum, tin and tungsten. The tin mining industry has declined sharply since 1985, and so Thailand has become a net importer of tin. As of 2008, the main mineral export was gypsum. Thailand is the world's second largest exporter of gypsum after Canada, even though government policy limits gypsum exports to prevent price cuts. In 2003 Thailand produced more than 40 types of minerals with an annual value of about US$740 million. However, more than 80 percent of these minerals were consumed domestically. In September 2003, in order to encourage foreign investment in the mining industry, the government relaxed severe restrictions on mining by foreign companies and reduced mineral royalties payable to the state.

Industry and Manufacturing

In 2007 industry contributed 43.9% of gross domestic product (GDP) but employed only 14% of the workforce. This proportion is the opposite of the one applying to agriculture. Industry expanded at an average annual rate of 3.4 percent during the 1995–2005 period. The most important subsector of industry is manufacturing, which accounted for 34.5 percent of GDP in 2004. Thailand is becoming a center of automobile manufacturing for the Association of Southeast Asian Nations (ASEAN) market. By 2004 automobile production had reached 930,000 units, more than twice as much as in 2001. Two automakers active in Thailand are Toyota and Ford. The expansion of the automotive industry has led to a boom in domestic steel production. Thailand's electronics industry faces competition from Malaysia and Singapore, while its textile industry faces competition from China and Vietnam.

Energy

In 2004 Thailand's total energy consumption was estimated at 3.4 quadrillion British thermal units, representing about 0.7 percent of total world energy consumption. Thailand is a net importer of oil and natural gas, but the government is promoting the use of ethanol to reduce imports of petroleum and the gasoline additive methyl tertiary butyl ether. In 2005 daily oil consumption of 838,000 barrels per day (133,200 m^3/d) exceeded domestic production of 306,000 barrels per day (48,700 m^3/d). Thailand's four oil refineries have a combined capacity of 703,100 barrels per day (111,780 m^3/d). Thailand's government is considering establishing a regional oil processing and transportation hub, serving the needs of south-central China. In 2004 natural gas consumption of 1,055 billion cubic feet (2.99×10 m) exceeded domestic production of

790 billion cubic feet (2.2×10 m). Also in 2004, estimated coal consumption of 30.4 million short tons exceeded coal production of 22.1 million short tons. As of January 2007, proven oil reserves totaled 290 million barrels (46,000,000 m), and proven natural gas reserves were 14.8 trillion cubic feet (420 km). In 2003 recoverable coal reserves totaled 1,492.5 million short tons.

In 2005 Thailand consumed about 117.7 billion kilowatt-hours of electricity. Electricity consumption rose by 4.7 percent in 2006 to 133 billion kilowatt-hours. According to the state electricity utility, the Electricity Generating Authority of Thailand, power consumption by residential consumers has been increasing because of more favorable rates given to residential customers over the industry and business sectors. Thailand's state-controlled electric utility and petroleum monopolies are undergoing restructuring.

Services

In 2007 the services sector, which ranges from tourism to banking and finance, contributed 44.7% of gross domestic product and employed 37 percent of the workforce.

Tourism

Tourism makes a larger contribution to Thailand's economy (typically about 6 percent of gross domestic product) than that of any other Asian nation. Most tourists come to Thailand for various reasons — mostly for the beaches and relaxation, although with the recent insurgency in the South, Bangkok has seen a large increase in tourism over the past 4 years. Also, a sharp increase in American tourists has contributed largely to Thailand's economy even though the Baht is gaining strength to the dollar. In 2004 some 11 million tourists visited Thailand. However, terrorism in southern Thailand and in Indonesia and natural disasters, most notably the December 2004 tsunami, have taken their toll on tourism. One of the negative side effects of Thailand's tourism industry is a burgeoning sex tourism industry and a related threat from human immunodeficiency virus/acquired immune deficiency syndrome (HIV/AIDS).

Banking and Finances

Dangerous levels of nonperforming assets at Thai banks helped trigger the attack on the Thai baht by currency speculators that led to the Asian financial crisis in 1997–1998. By 2003 nonperforming assets had been cut in half to about 30 percent. Despite a return to profitability, however, Thailand's banks continue to struggle with the legacy of the financial crisis in the form of unrealized losses and inadequate capital. Therefore, the government is considering various reforms, including establishing an integrated financial regulatory agency that would free up the Bank of Thailand to focus on monetary policy. In addition, the Thai government is attempting to strengthen the financial sector through the consolidation of commercial, state-owned, and foreign-owned institutions. Specifically, the government's Financial Sector Reform Master Plan, which was first introduced in early 2004, provides tax breaks to financial institutions that engage in mergers and acquisitions. The reform program has been deemed successful by outside experts. In 2007, there were three state-owned commercial banks and five state-owned specialized banks, 15 Thai commercial banks, and 17 foreign banks in Thailand.

The Bank of Thailand sought to stem the flow of foreign funds into the country in December 2006. This led within one day to the largest drop in stock prices on the Stock Exchange of Thailand since the 1997 Asian financial crisis. The massive selling by foreign investors amounted more than US$708 million.

9

VIETNAM

Vietnam, officially the Socialist Republic of Vietnam, is the easternmost country on the Indochina Peninsula in Southeast Asia. It is bordered by China to the north, Laos to the northwest, Cambodia to the southwest, and the South China Sea to the east. With a population of over 86 million, Vietnam is the 13th most populous country in the world.

Vietnam was under Chinese control for a thousand years before becoming a nation-state in the 10th century. Successive dynasties flourished along with geographic and political expansion deeper into Southeast Asia, until it was colonized by the French in the mid-19th century. Efforts to resist the French eventually led to their expulsion from the country in the mid-20th century, leaving a nation divided politically into two countries. Bitter fighting between the two sides continued during the Vietnam War, ending with a communist victory in 1975.

Emerging from a long and bitter war, the war-ravaged nation was politically isolated. The government's centrally-planned economic decisions hindered post-war reconstruction and its treatment of the losing side engendered more resentment than reconciliation. In 1986, it instituted economic and political reforms and began a path towards international reintegration. By 2000, it had established diplomatic relations with most nations. Its economic growth had been among the highest in the world in the past decade. These efforts culminated in Vietnam joining the World Trade Organization in 2007 and its successful bid to become a non-permanent member of the United Nations Security Council in 2008.

GEOGRAPHY OF VIETNAM

Vietnam is approximately 331,688 km² (128,066 sq mi) in area (not including Hoang Sa and Truong Sa islands), larger than Italy and almost the size of Germany. The perimeter of the country running along its international boundaries is 4,639 km (2,883 mi). The topography consists of hills and densely forested mountains, with level land covering no more than 20%. Mountains account for 40% of the area, with smaller hills accounting for 40% and tropical forests 42%. The northern part of the country consists mostly of highlands and the Red River Delta. Phan Xi Păng, located in Lào Cai province, is the highest mountain in Vietnam at 3,143 m (10,312 ft). The south is divided into coastal lowlands, Annamite Chain peaks, extensive forests, and poor soil. Comprising five relatively flat plateaus of basalt soil, the highlands account for 16% of the country's arable land and 22% of its total forested land.

The delta of the Red River (also known as the Sông HÓng), a flat, triangular region of 15,000 square kilometers, is smaller but more intensely developed and more densely populated than the Mekong River Delta. Once an inlet of the Gulf of Tonkin, it has been filled in by the enormous alluvial deposits of the rivers over a period of millennia, and it advances one hundred meters into the Gulf annually. The Mekong delta, covering about 40,000 square kilometers, is a low-level plain not more than three meters above sea level at any point and criss-crossed by a maze of canals and rivers. So much sediment is carried by the Mekong's various branches and tributaries that the delta advances sixty to eighty meters into the sea every year.

Because of differences in latitude and the marked variety of topographical relief, the climate tends to vary considerably from place to place. During the winter or dry season, extending roughly from November to April, the monsoon winds usually blow from the northeast along the China coast and across the Gulf of Tonkin, picking up considerable moisture; consequently the winter season in most parts of the country is dry only by comparison with the rainy or summer season. The average annual temperature is generally higher in the plains than in the mountains and plateaus and in the south than in the north. Temperatures in the southern plains (Ho Chi Minh City and the Mekong Delta) varies less, going between 21 and 28 degree Celsius (70 and 82.5 °F) over the course of a year. The seasons in the mountains and plateaus and in the north are much more dramatic, and temperatures may vary from 5 degree Celsius (41 °F) in December and January to 37 degree Celsius (98.6 °F) in July and August.

DEMOGRAPHY

Originating in what is now southern China and northern Vietnam, the Vietnamese people pushed southward over two millennia to occupy the entire eastern seacoast of the Indochinese Peninsula. Ethnic Vietnamese, or Viet (known officially as Kinh), live in the lowlands and speak the Vietnamese language. This group dominates much of the cultural and political landscape of Vietnam.

The Vietnamese government recognizes 54 ethnic groups, of which the Viet is the largest; according to official Vietnamese figures (1999 census), ethnic Vietnamese account for 86% of the nation's population. The ethnic Vietnamese inhabit a little less than half of Vietnam, while the ethnic minorities inhabit the majority of Vietnam's land (albeit the least fertile parts of the country).

The Khmer Krom are found in the delta of the Mekong River, in the south of Vietnam, where they form in many areas the majority of the rural population. They live in an area which was previously part of Cambodia and which Vietnam conquered in the 17th and 18th centuries. Official Vietnamese figures put the Khmer Krom at 1.3 million people.

Vietnam's approximately 1 million ethnic Chinese, concentrated mostly in southern Vietnam, constitute one of Vietnam's largest minority groups. Long important in the Vietnamese economy, Vietnamese of Chinese ancestry have been active in rice trading, milling, real estate, and banking in the south and shopkeeping, stevedoring, and mining in the north. Restrictions on economic activity following reunification in 1975 and the subsequent but unrelated general deterioration in Vietnamese-Chinese relations sent chills through the Chinese-Vietnamese community.

The relation between China and Vietnam also declined in this period, with Vietnam siding with the Soviet Union against China in the Chinese-Soviet split. Tensions peaked when Vietnam invaded Cambodia, an ally of China, to depose Pol Pot, resulting in a Chinese invasion of Vietnam in 1979. In 1978-79, some 450,000 ethnic Chinese left Vietnam by boat as refugees (many officially encouraged and assisted) or were expelled across the land border with China. However in recent years the government has performed an about turn and is encouraging overseas Hoa to return and invest.

The central highland peoples commonly termed Degar or Montagnards (mountain people) comprise two main ethnolinguistic groups—Malayo-Polynesian and Mon-Khmer. About 30 groups of various cultures and dialects are spread over the highland territory. Other minority groups include the Cham—remnants of the once-mighty Champa Kingdom, conquered by the Vietnamese in the 15th century, Hmong, and Tai ("Thái").

Vietnamese is the official language of the country. It is a language pertaining to the Austroasiatic language family, a language family also including Khmer, Mon, etc. Vietnamese was spoken by 65.8 million people in Vietnam at the 1999 census. Another 1.6 million Vietnamese speakers are found outside of Vietnam. Thus Vietnamese is the most spoken language of the Austroasiatic family, being spoken by three times more people than the second most spoken language of the family, Khmer. Both languages, however, are extremely different: under the influence of Chinese, Vietnamese has become a tonal language, while Khmer has remained non-tonal. Vietnamese was heavily influenced by Chinese and a great part of the Vietnamese vocabulary is Chinese, while Khmer was heavily influenced by Sanskrit and Pali and a great part of its vocabulary is now made up of Indian words, so that both languages look very dissimilar on the surface. Since the early 20th century, the Vietnamese have used a Romanized script introduced by the French.

CULTURE

The Culture of Vietnam is one of the oldest of such in the Asia Pacific region. In terms of prehistory, most Vietnamese historians consider the ancient Dong Son culture to be one of the defining aspects of early Vietnamese civilization.

Long periods of domination and interaction with its northern neighbor, China, has resulted in Vietnam's historic inclusion as part of the East Asian Cultural Sphere, known widely as Chinese Cultural Sphere. Historically, passing the imperial Mandarin exams was the only means for Vietnamese people to socially advance themselves.

Following independence from China in the 10th century AD, Vietnam began a southward expansion that saw the annexation of territories formerly belonging to the Champa civilization (now Central Vietnam) and parts of the Khmer empire (today South Vietnam) which resulted in minor regional variances in Vietnam's culture due to exposure to these different groups.

In the socialist era, the cultural life of Vietnam has been deeply influenced by government-controlled media and the cultural influences of socialist programs. For many decades, foreign cultural influences were shunned and emphasis placed on appreciating and sharing the culture of communist nations such as the Soviet Union, China, Cuba and others. Since the 1990s, Vietnam has seen a greater exposure to Southeast Asian, European and American culture and media.

Marriage

In the past, both men and women were expected to be married at quite young ages (by today's standards). Marriages were generally arranged by the parents and extended family, with the children having little to no say in the matter.

In modern Vietnam, this has changed completely as people choose their own marriage-partners based on love, and in consideration primarily to their own needs and wants.

The traditional Vietnamese wedding is one of the most important of traditional Vietnamese occasions. Regardless of westernization, many of the age-old customs practiced in a traditional Vietnamese wedding continue to be celebrated by both Vietnamese in Vietnam and overseas, often combining both western and eastern elements

Religion and Philosophy

Historically, the so-called *Tam Giáo* ("triple religion"), characterizing the East Asian intricate mixture between Mahayana Buddhism, Confucianism, and Taoism has always had a large impact on Vietnamese society and philosophy. Of the three, Vietnamese Buddhism has always been the most popular with commoners.

Besides the "triple religion", Vietnamese life was also profoundly influenced by the practice of ancestor worship as well as native animism. Most Vietnamese people, regardless of religious denomination, practice ancestor worship and have an ancestor altar at their home or business, a testament to the emphasis Vietnamese culture places on filial duty.

Along with obligations to clan and family, education has always played a vital role in Vietnamese culture. In the old days, scholars were placed at the top of society. Men not born of noble blood could only wish to elevate their status by means of studying for a rigorous Imperial examination which could potentially open doors to a position in the government, granting them power and prestige as Mandarin officials.

Cuisine

Vietnamese cuisine is extremely diverse, often divided into three main categories, each pertaining to Vietnam's three main regions (north, central and south). It uses very little oil and many vegetables, and is mainly based on rice, soy sauce, and fish sauce. Its characteristic flavors are sweet (sugar), spicy (serrano peppers), sour (lime), nuoc mam (fish sauce), and flavored by a variety of mint and basil.

Vietnam also has a large variety of noodles and noodle soups. Different regions invented different types of noodles, varying in shapes, tastes, colours, etc. One of the nation's most famous type of noodles is phß (pronounced "fuh"), a type of noodle soup originating in North Vietnam, which consists of rice noodles and beef soup (sometimes chicken soup) with several other ingredients such as bean sprouts and scallions (spring onions). It is often eaten for breakfast, but also makes a satisfying lunch or light dinner. The boiling stock, fragrant with spices and sauces, is poured over the noodles and vegetables, poaching the paper-thin slices of raw beef just before serving. Phß is meant to be savored, incorporating several different flavors: the sweet flavor of beef, sour lemons, salty fish sauce, and fresh vegetables.

Currently, Vietnamese cuisine has been gaining popularity and can be found widely in many other countries such as the United States, Australia, Canada, South Korea, Laos, Japan, China, Malaysia, and France. Vietnamese cuisine is recognized for its strict, sometimes choosy selection of ingredients. A chef preparing authentic Vietnamese cuisine may incorporate the ingredients provided in these countries, but generally will prefer ingredients native to Vietnam.

Clothing

In feudal Vietnam, clothing was one of the most important marks of social status and strict dress codes were enforced. Commoners had a limited choice of similarly plain and simple clothes for every day use, as well as being limited in the colors they were allowed to use. For a period, commoners were not allowed to wear clothes with dyes other than black, brown or white (with the exception of special occasions such as festivals), but in actuality these rules could change often based upon the whims of the current ruler.

The Áo té thân or "4-part dress" is one such example of an ancient dress widely worn by commoner women, along with the Áo bodice which accompanied it. Peasants across the country also gradually came to wear silk pajama-like costumes, known as "Áo cánh" in the north and Áo bà ba in the south.

The headgear of peasants often included a plain piece of cloth wrapped around the head, or the stereotypical Nón lá (conical hat). For footwear peasants would often go barefoot whereas sandals and shoes were reserved for the aristocracy and royalty.

Monarchs had the exclusive right to wear the color gold, while nobles wore red or purple. Each member of the royal court had an assortment of different formal gowns they would wear at a particular ceremony, or for a particular occasion. The rules governing the fashion of the royal court could change dynasty by dynasty, thus Costumes of the Vietnamese court were quite diverse.

The most popular and widely-recognized Vietnamese national costume is the Áo Dài, which is worn nowadays mostly by women, although men do wear Áo dài on special occasions such as weddings and funerals. Áo dài is similar to the Chinese Qipao, consisting of a long gown with a slit on both sides, worn over silk pants. It is elegant in style and comfortable to wear, and likely derived in the 18th century or in the royal court of Hui. White Áo dài is the required uniform for girls in many high schools across Vietnam. Some female office workers (e.g. receptionists, secretaries, tour guides) are also required to wear Áo dài. Áo Dài was once worn by both genders but today it is worn mainly by females, except for certain important traditional culture-related occasions where some men do wear it.

In daily life, the traditional Vietnamese styles are now replaced by Western styles. Traditional clothing is worn instead on special occasions, with the exception of the white Áo dài commonly seen with high school girls in Vietnam.

GOVERNMENT AND POLITICS

The Socialist Republic of Vietnam is a single-party state. A new state constitution was approved in April 1992, replacing the 1975 version. The central role of the

Communist Party was reasserted in all organs of government, politics and society. Only political organizations affiliated with or endorsed by the Communist Party are permitted to contest elections. These include the Vietnamese Fatherland Front, worker and trade unionist parties. Although the state remains officially committed to socialism as its defining creed, the ideology's importance has substantially diminished since the 1990s. The President of Vietnam is the titular head of state and the nominal commander in chief of the military of Vietnam, chairing the Council on National Defense and Security. The Prime Minister of Vietnam Nguyen Tan Dung is the head of government, presiding over a council of ministers composed of 3 deputy prime ministers and the heads of 26 ministries and commissions.

The National Assembly of Vietnam is the unicameral legislature of the government, composed of 498 members. It is superior to both the executive and judicial branches. All members of the council of ministers are derived from the National Assembly. The Supreme People's Court of Vietnam, which is the highest court of appeal in the nation, is also answerable to the National Assembly. Beneath the Supreme People's Court stand the provincial municipal courts and the local courts. Military courts are also a powerful branch of the judiciary with special jurisdiction in matters of national security. All organs of Vietnam's government are controlled by the Communist Party. Most government appointees are members of the party. The General Secretary of the Communist Party is perhaps one of the most important political leaders in the nation, controlling the party's national organization and state appointments, as well as setting policy.

The Vietnam People's Army is the official name for the combined military services of Vietnam, which is organized along the lines of China's People's Liberation Army. The VPA is further subdivided into the Vietnamese People's Ground Forces (including Strategic Rear Forces and Border Defense Forces), the Vietnam People's Navy, the Vietnam People's Air Force and the coast guard. Through Vietnam's recent history, the VPA has actively been involved in Vietnam's workforce to develop the economy of Vietnam, in order to coordinate national defense and the economy. The VPA is involved in such areas as industry, agriculture, forestry, fishery and telecommunications. The total strength of the VPA is close to 500,000 officers and enlisted members. The government also organizes and maintains provincial militias and police forces. The role of the military in public life has steadily been reduced since the 1980s.

ECONOMY

Vietnam's economy is developing economy. Through history, Vietnam was among agricultural center of the world and soon had some commercial port. Over the past 20 years, Vietnam has made the shift from a central command planning -based economy to socialist oriented mixed market economy. Over that period, the economy has experienced rapid growth. Nowadays, Vietnam is in the period of integrating into world's economy, as a part of globalization. Although, almost Vietnamese enterprises are SMEs with some nationwide trademarks such as VNPT, Vinamilk, Trung Nguyen, Kinh Do and others but Vietnam has been raising as an image of world's leading agricultural exporter and a bright foreign investment attraction destination in East and Southeast Asia. With the enhancing of managing skills and the potential young workforce, Vietnam is hoped to reach average developed country up to 2020 as well as keeping the sustain in society and environment.

Mining and Minerals

In 2003 mining and quarrying accounted for a 9.4 percent share of gross domestic product (GDP); the sector employed 0.7 percent of the workforce. Petroleum and coal are the main mineral exports. Also mined are antimony, bauxite, chromium, gold, iron, natural phosphates, tin, and zinc.

Industry and Manufacturing

Although industry contributed 40.1 percent of gross domestic product (GDP) in 2004, it employed only 12.9 percent of the workforce. In 2000, 22.4 percent of industrial production was attributable to non-state activities. During 1994–2004, industrial GDP grew at an average annual rate of 10.3 percent. Manufacturing contributed 20.3 percent of GDP in 2004, while employing 10.2 percent of the workforce. During 1994–2004, manufacturing GDP grew at an average annual rate of 11.2 percent. The top manufacturing sectors—food processing, cigarettes and tobacco, textiles, chemicals, and electrical goods—experienced rapid growth. Almost a third of manufacturing and retail activity is concentrated in Ho Chi Minh City.

Energy

Petroleum is the main source of commercial energy, followed by coal, which contributes about 25 percent of the country's energy (excluding biomass). Vietnam's oil reserves are in the range of 270–500 million tons. Oil production rose rapidly to 403,300 barrels per day (64,120 m^3/d) in 2004, but output is believed to have peaked and is expected to decline gradually. Vietnam's anthracite coal reserves are estimated at 3.7 billion tons. Coal production was almost 19 million tons in 2003, compared with 9.6 million tons in 1999. Vietnam's potential natural gas reserves are 1.3 trillion cubic meters. In 2002 Vietnam brought ashore 2.26 billion cubic meters of natural gas. Hydroelectric power is another source of energy. In 2004 Vietnam began to build a nuclear power plant with Russian assistance.

Crude oil is Vietnam's leading export, totaling 17 million tons in 2002; in 2004 crude oil represented 22 percent of all export earnings. Petroleum exports are in the form of crude petroleum because Vietnam has a very limited refining capacity. Vietnam's only operational refinery, a facility at Cat Hai near Ho Chi Minh City, has a capacity of only 800 barrels per day (130 m^3/d). Refined petroleum accounted for 10.2 percent of total imports in 2002.

Services and Tourism

In 2004 services accounted for 38.2 percent of gross domestic product (GDP). During 1994–2004, GDP attributable to the services sector grew at an average annual rate of 6.0 percent. In 2004 Vietnam received 2.9 million international arrivals, up from 2.4 million the previous year. The annual increase represented a strong rebound from a slight decline in 2003 attributable to the severe acute respiratory syndrome (SARS) epidemic in Asia. From 1999 to 2004, tourism rose by 63 percent. Most of the visitors in 2004—27 percent—came from China, with 8–9 percent each coming from the United States, Japan, and South Korea. The Vietnam National Administration of Tourism is following a long-term plan to diversify the tourism industry, which brings needed foreign exchange into the country.

Banking and Finance

Vietnam's first stock exchange, known as the Ho Chi Minh City Securities Trading Center, was established in July 2000. By the spring of 2005, the number of companies listed on the exchange had reached 28, representing a total market capitalization of only US$270 million. In March 2005, Vietnam opened an over-the-counter exchange, known as the Hanoi Securities Trading Center. The purpose of the second exchange is to expedite the process of equitization (partial privatization) of state-owned enterprises. Although these exchanges are still very small, officials have set the goal of expanding their combined market capitalization to 10 percent of gross domestic product by 2010 and gradually phasing out restrictions on foreign ownership of shares. In September 2005, Vietnam's prime minister announced that the limit on foreign share ownership would rise from 30 percent to 49 percent.

Vietnam's banks suffer from low public confidence, regulatory and managerial weakness, high levels of non-performing loans (NPL), non-compliance with the Basel capital standards, and the absence of international auditing. Since 1992 Vietnam's banking system has consisted of a combination of state-owned, joint-stock, joint-venture, and foreign banks, but the state-owned commercial banks predominate, and they suffer from high levels of NPL, most of them to state-owned enterprises. Consequently, in September 2005 Vietnam decided to equitize all five state-owned banks—a change from previous plans to equitize only two of them. In addition, Vietnam plans to boost the transparency of its financial system by establishing a credit-rating agency and performance standards for joint-stock banks. Large foreign banks are balancing their strong interest in serving multinationals in Vietnam and frustration with continuing restrictions on their activities. Although Vietnam is a cash-based society, 300 to 400 automated teller machines (ATMs) have been installed, and about 350,000 debit cards are in circulation.

10

SINGAPORE

Singapore, officially the Republic of Singapore, is an island country located at the southern tip of the Malay Peninsula. It lies 137 kilometres (85 mi) north of the equator, south of the Malaysian state of Johor and north of Indonesia's Riau Islands. At 707.1 km (273.0 sq mi), Singapore is one of three remaining true city-states in the world. It is the smallest nation in Southeast Asia.

Prior to European settlement, the island now known as Singapore was the site of a Malay fishing village at the mouth of the Singapore River. Several hundred indigenous Orang Laut people also lived along the nearby coast, rivers and on smaller islands. In 1819 the British East India Company established a trading post on the island, which was used thereafter as a strategic trading post along the spice route. Singapore would become one of the most important commercial and military centres of the British Empire, and the hub of British power in Southeast Asia. The city was occupied by the Japanese during World War II, which Winston Churchill called "Britain's greatest defeat". Singapore reverted to British rule immediately postwar, in 1945. Eighteen years later the city, having achieved independence from Britain, merged with Malaya, Sabah and Sarawak to form Malaysia. However, less than two years later it seceded from the federation and became an independent republic on 9 August 1965. Singapore joined the United Nations on September 21 that same year.

Since independence, Singapore's standard of living has been on the rise. Foreign direct investment and a state-led drive to industrialization based on plans drawn up by the Dutch economist Albert Winsemius have created a modern economy focused on electronics manufacturing, petrochemicals, tourism and financial services alongside traditional entrepôt trade. Singapore is the 6th wealthiest country in the world in terms of GDP per capita. The small nation has foreign exchange reserves of more than US$177 billion.

The population of Singapore is approximately 4.59 million. Though Singapore is highly cosmopolitan and diverse, ethnic Chinese form the majority of the population. English is the administrative language of the country. The Constitution of the Republic of Singapore established the nation's political system as a representative democracy, while the country is recognized as a parliamentary republic. The People's Action Party (PAP) dominates the politica! process and has won control of Parliament in every election since self-government in 1959.

GOVERNMENT AND POLITICS

Singapore is a parliamentary democracy with a Westminster system of unicameral parliamentary government representing different constituencies. The bulk of the executive powers rests with the Cabinet, headed by the Prime Minister, currently Lee Hsien Loong. The office of President of Singapore, historically a ceremonial one, was granted some veto powers as of 1991 for a few key decisions such as the use of the national reserves and the appointment of judiciary positions. Although the position is to be elected by popular vote, only the 1993 election has been contested to date. The legislative branch of government is the Parliament.

Parliamentary elections in Singapore are plurality-based for group representation constituencies since the Parliamentary Elections Act was modified in 1991.

The Members of Parliament (MPs) consist of either elected, non-constituency or nominated Members. The majority of the Members of Parliament are elected into Parliament at a General Election on a first-past-the-post basis and represent either Single Member or Group Representation Constituencies (GRCs).

The elected Members of Parliament act as a bridge between the community and the Government by ensuring that the concerns of their constituents are heard in the Parliament. The present Parliament has 94 Members of Parliament consisting of 84 elected Members of Parliament, one NCMP and nine Nominated members of Parliament.

- Elected Members, In Group Representation Constituencies, political parties field a team of between three to six candidates. At least one candidate in the team must belong to a minority race. This requirement ensures that parties contesting the elections in Group Representation Constituencies are multi-racial so that minority races will be represented in Parliament. Presently there are 14 Group Representation Constituencies and 9 Single Member constituencies.
- Non-Constituency Members,This is to ensure that there will be a minimum number of opposition representatives in Parliament and that views other than the Government's can be expressed in Parliament.

- Nominated Members, up to nine Nominated Members of Parliament (NMPs) was made in 1990 to ensure a wide representation of community views in Parliament. Nominated Members of Parliament are appointed by the President of Singapore for a term of two and a half years on the recommendation of a Special Select Committee of Parliament chaired by the Speaker. Nominated Members of Parliament are not connected to any political parties.

Politics in Singapore have been controlled by the People's Action Party (PAP) since self-government was attained. In consequence, foreign political analysts and several opposition parties like the Workers' Party of Singapore, the Singapore Democratic Party (SDP) and the Singapore Democratic Alliance (SDA) have argued that Singapore is essentially a one-party state. Many analysts consider Singapore to be an illiberal or procedural democracy rather than a true democracy. The Economist Intelligence Unit describes Singapore as a "hybrid regime" of democratic and authoritarian elements. Freedom House ranks the country as "partly free". Though general elections are free from irregularities and vote rigging, the PAP has been criticized for manipulating the political system through its use of censorship, gerrymandering, and civil libel suits against opposition politicians. Francis Seow, the exiled former Solicitor-General of Singapore, is a prominent critic. Seow and opposition politicians such as J.B. Jeyaretnam and Chee Soon Juan claim that Singapore courts favour the PAP government, and there is no separation of powers.

Singapore has a successful and transparent market economy. Government-linked companies are dominant in various sectors of the local economy, such as media, utilities, and public transport. Singapore has consistently been rated as the least corrupt country in Asia and among the world's ten most free from corruption by Transparency International.

Although Singapore's laws are inherited from British and British Indian laws, including many elements of English common law, the PAP has also consistently rejected liberal democratic values, which it typifies as Western and states there should not be a 'one-size-fits-all' solution to a democracy. There are no jury trials. Laws restricting the freedom of speech are justified by claims that they are intended to prohibit speech that may breed ill will or cause disharmony within Singapore's multiracial, multi-religious society. For example, in September 2005, three bloggers were convicted of sedition for posting racist remarks targeting minorities. Some offences can lead to heavy fines or caning and there are laws which allow capital punishment in Singapore for first-degree murder and drug trafficking. Amnesty International has criticised Singapore for having "possibly the highest execution rate in the world" per capita. The Singapore government argues that there is no international consensus on the appropriateness of the death penalty and that Singapore has the sovereign right to determine its own judicial system and impose capital punishment for the most serious crimes.

GEOGRAPHY

Singapore consists of 63 islands, including mainland Singapore. There are two man-made connections to Johor, Malaysia — Johor-Singapore Causeway in the north, and Tuas Second Link in the west. Jurong Island, Pulau Tekong, Pulau Ubin and Sentosa are the largest of Singapore's many smaller islands. The highest natural point of Singapore is Bukit Timah Hill at 166 m (545 ft).

The south of Singapore, around the mouth of the Singapore River and what is now the Downtown Core, used to be the only concentrated urban area, while the rest of the land was either undeveloped tropical rainforest or used for agriculture. Since the 1960s, the government has constructed new residential towns in outlying areas, resulting in an entirely built-up urban landscape. The Urban Redevelopment Authority was established on 1 April 1974, responsible for urban planning.

Singapore has on-going land reclamation projects with earth obtained from its own hills, the sea-bed, and neighbouring countries. As a result, Singapore's land area grew from 581.5 km (224.5 sq mi) in the 1960s to 704 km (271.8 sq mi) today, and may grow by another 100 km^2 (38.6 sq mi) by 2030. The projects sometimes involve some of the smaller islands being merged together through land reclamation in order to form larger, more functional islands, such as in the case of Jurong Island.

Under the Köppen climate classification system, Singapore has a tropical rainforest climate with no distinctive seasons. Its climate is characterized by uniform temperature and pressure, high humidity, and abundant rainfall. Temperatures range from 22 °C to 34 °C (72° to 93 °F). On average, the relative humidity is around 90 percent in the morning and 60 percent in the afternoon. During prolonged heavy rain, relative humidity often reaches 100 percent. The lowest and highest temperatures recorded in its maritime history are 18.4 °C (65.1 °F) and 37.8 °C (100.0 °F) respectively. June and July are the hottest months, while November and December make up the wetter monsoon season. From August to October, there is often haze, sometimes severe enough to prompt public health warnings, due to bushfires in neighbouring Indonesia. Singapore does not observe daylight saving time or a summer time zone change. The length of the day is nearly constant year round due to the country's location near the equator.

About 23 percent of Singapore's land area consists of forest and nature reserves. Urbanization has eliminated many areas of former primary rainforest, with the only remaining area of primary rainforest being Bukit Timah Nature Reserve. A variety of parks are maintained with human intervention, such as the Singapore Botanic Gardens.

DEMOGRAPHY

According to government statistics, the population of Singapore as of 2007 was 4.59 million, of whom 3.58 million were Singaporean citizens and permanent residents (termed "Singapore Residents"). Various Chinese ethnic groups formed 75.2% of Singapore's residents, Malays 13.6%, Indians 8.8%, while Eurasians and other groups formed 2.4%.

In 2006 the crude birth rate stood at 10.1 per 1000, a very low level attributed to birth control policies, and the crude death rate was also one of the lowest in the world at 4.3 per 1000. The total population growth was 4.4% with Singapore residents growth at 1.8%. The higher percentage growth rate is largely from net immigration, but also increasing life expectancy. Singapore is the second-most densely populated independent country in the world after Monaco, excluding Macau and Hong Kong, which are special administrative regions of the People's Republic of China. In 1957, Singapore's population was approximately 1.45 million, and there was a relatively high birth rate. Aware of the country's extremely limited natural resources and small territory, the government introduced birth control policies in the late 1960s. In the late 1990s, the population was ageing, with fewer people entering the labour market and a shortage of skilled workers. In a dramatic reversal of policy, the Singapore government introduced a "baby bonus" scheme in 2001 (enhanced in August 2004) that encouraged couples to have more children.

In 2006, the total fertility rate was only 1.26 children per woman, the 3rd lowest in the world and well below the 2.10 needed to replace the population. In 2006, 38,317 babies were born, compared to around 37,600 in 2005. This number, however, is not sufficient to maintain the population's growth. To overcome this problem, the government is encouraging foreigners to immigrate to Singapore. These large numbers of immigrants have kept Singapore's population from declining.

Religion

Singapore is a multi-religious country. According to *Statistics Singapore,* around 51 percent of resident Singaporeans (excluding significant numbers of visitors and migrant workers) practice Buddhism and Taoism. About 15 percent, mostly Chinese, Eurasians, and Indians, practice Christianity–a broad classification including Catholicism, Protestantism and other denominations. Muslims constitute 14 percent, of whom Malays account for the majority with a substantial number of Indian Muslims and Chinese Muslims. Smaller minorities practice Sikhism, Hinduism, the Bahá'í Faith and others, according to the 2000 census.

Some religious materials and practices are banned in Singapore. The Jehovah's Witnesses, for example, are prohibited from distributing religious materials and are sometimes jailed for their conscientious refusals to serve in the Singaporean military. About 15 percent of the population declared no religious affiliation.

CULTURE

Singapore is a mixture of an indigenous Malay population with a third generation Chinese majority, as well as Indian and Arab immigrants with some intermarriages. There also exist significant Eurasian and *Peranakan* (known also as 'Straits Chinese') communities.

Cuisine

Singaporean cuisine is an example of diversity and cultural diffusion in Singapore, with a fusion of Chinese, Indian, Malay and Tamil influences. In Singapore's hawker centres, traditionally Malay hawker stalls selling halal food may serve halal versions of traditionally Tamil food. Chinese food stalls may introduce indigenous Malay ingredients or cooking techniques. This continues to make the cuisine of Singapore a significant cultural attraction.

Local foods are diverse, ranging from Hainanese chicken rice to satay. Singaporeans also enjoy a wide variety of seafood including crabs, clams, squid, and oysters. One such dish is stingray barbecued and served on banana leaf and with *sambal* or chili.

Amongst locals, popular dishes include bak chor mee, mee poh, sambal stingray, laksa, nasi lemak, chili crab and satay. All of which, can be found at local hawker centres around Singapore.

Performing Arts

Since the 1990s, the government has been striving to promote Singapore as a centre for arts and culture, and to transform the country into a cosmopolitan 'gateway between the East and West'. The highlight of these efforts was the construction of Esplanade, a centre for performing arts that opened on October 12, 2002.

An annual arts festival is also organised by the National Arts Council that incorporates theatre arts, dance, music and visual arts, among other possibilities.

A first Singapore Biennale took place in 2006 to showcase contemporary art from around the world. The next one will be in 2008 which will feature Southeast Asian works.

ECONOMY

Singapore has a highly developed market-based economy, which historically revolves around extended entrepot trade. Along with Hong Kong, South Korea and Taiwan,

Singapore is one of the Four Asian Tigers. The economy depends heavily on exports refining imported goods, especially in manufacturing. Manufacturing constituted 26 percent of Singapore's GDP in 2005. The manufacturing industry is well-diversified into electronics, petroleum refining, chemicals, mechanical engineering and biomedical sciences manufacturing. In 2006, Singapore produced about 10 percent of the world's foundry wafer output. Singapore is the busiest port in the world in terms of tonnage shipped. Singapore is the world's fourth largest foreign exchange trading centre after London, New York City and Tokyo.

Singapore has been rated as the most business-friendly economy in the world, with thousands of foreign expatriates working in multi-national corporations. The city-state also employs tens of thousands of foreign blue-collared workers around the world.

As a result of global recession and a slump in the technology sector, the country's GDP contracted 2.2 percent in 2001. The Economic Review Committee (ERC) was set up in December 2001, and recommended several policy changes with a view to revitalising the economy. Singapore has since recovered from the recession, largely due to improvements in the world economy; the Singaporean economy itself grew by 8.3 percent in 2004, 6.4 percent in 2005 and 7.9 percent in 2006. In the first half of Year 2007, the economy grew by 7.6 percent. The growth forecast for the whole year is expected to be between 7 percent to 8 percent, up from the original estimation of 5 percent to 7 percent. On August 19 2007, Prime Minister Lee Hsien Loong announced in his National Day Rally Speech that Singapore's economy is expected to grow by at least 4-6 percent annually over the next 5-10 years.

The per capita GDP in 2006 was US$29,474. As of September 2007, the unemployment rate is 1.7 percent, which is the lowest in a decade, having improved to around pre-Asian crisis level. Employment continued to grow strongly as the economy maintained its rapid expansion. In the first three quarters of 2007, 171,500 new jobs were created, which is close to the 176,000 for the whole of 2006. For the whole of 2007, Singapore's economy has grown 7.5 percent and drew in a record S$16 billion of fixed asset investments in manufacturing and projects generating S$3 billion of total business spending in services. The government expects the Singapore economy to grow by 4.5 percent to 6.5 percent in 2008.

Singapore introduced a Goods and Services Tax (GST) with an initial rate of 3 percent on 1 April 1994 substantially increasing government revenue by S$1.6 billion and stabilizing government finances. The taxable GST was increased to 4 percent in 2003, to 5 percent in 2004, and to 7 percent on 1st July 2007.

Singapore is a popular travel destination, making tourism one of its largest industries. About 9.7 million tourists visited Singapore in 2006. The Orchard Road shopping district is one of Singapore's most well-known and popular tourist draws. To attract more tourists, the government decided to legalise gambling and to allow two casino resorts (euphemistically called Integrated Resorts) to be developed at Marina South and Sentosa in 2005. To compete with regional rivals like Hong Kong, Tokyo and Shanghai, the government has announced that the city area would be transformed into a more exciting place by lighting up the civic and commercial buildings. Cuisine has also been heavily promoted as an attraction for tourists, with the Singapore Food Festival in July organized annually to celebrate Singapore's cuisine.

Singapore is fast positioning itself as a medical tourism hub — about 200,000 foreigners seek medical care in the country each year and Singapore medical services aim to serve one million foreign patients annually by 2012 and generate USD 3 billion in revenue. The government expects that the initiative could create an estimated 13,000 new jobs within the health industries.

Under the Infocomm Development Authority of Singapore (IDA), Wireless@SG is a government initiative to build Singapore's infocomm infrastructure. Working through IDA's Call-for-Collaboration, SingTel, iCell and QMax deploy a municipal wireless network throughout Singapore. Since late 2006, users have enjoyed free wireless access through Wi-Fi under the "basic-tier" package offered by all three operators for 3 years.

11

BRUNEI

Brunei Darussalam, officially the State of Brunei, Abode of Peace, is a country located on the north coast of the island of Borneo, in Southeast Asia. Apart from its coastline with the South China Sea it is completely surrounded by the state of Sarawak, Malaysia, and in fact it is separated into two parts by Limbang, which is part of Sarawak.

Brunei, the remnant of a very powerful sultanate, regained its independence from the United Kingdom on 1 January 1984.

GEOGRAPHY

Brunei Darussalam consists of two unconnected parts with a total area of 5,766 sq. kilometers (2,226 sq. miles). 97% of the population lives in the larger western part, while only about 10,000 live in the mountainous eastern part (the district of Temburong). The total population of Brunei Darussalam is about 400,000 of which around 130,000 live in the capital Bandar Seri Begawan. Other major towns are the port town of Muara, the oil producing town of Seria and its neighboring town, Kuala Belait. In the Belait district, the Panaga area is home to large numbers of expatriates due to Royal Dutch Shell and British Army housing and recreational facilities. The well-known Panaga Club is situated here. Jerudong Park, a well known amusement park, is located on the west of Bandar Seri Begawan.

Climate

Bandar Seri Begawan has a humid subtropical climate. The average annual temperature is 23.6 °C (74.5 °F), with a summer average of 29.4 °C (84.9 °F) and a winter average of 12.0 °C (52.8 °F).

DEMOGRAPHY

Like neighbouring countries, Brunei is a Malay-dominated country. Many cultural and linguistic differences make Brunei Malays distinct from the larger Malay populations in nearby Malaysia and Indonesia, even though they are ethnically related and share the Muslim religion.

Brunei has a hereditary nobility with the title Pengiran these are, more often than not, related to the Sultan by blood. The Sultan can award to commoners the title Pehin, the equivalent of a life peerage awarded in the United Kingdom. The Sultan also can award his subjects the Dato, the equivalent of a knighthood in the United Kingdom, and Datin, the equivalent of a damehood.

Bruneians adhere to the practice of using complete full names with all titles, including the title Haji (for men) or Hajjah (for women) for those who have made the Haj pilgrimage to Mecca. Many Brunei Malay women wear the tudong, a traditional head covering. Men wear the songkok, a traditional Malay cap. Men who have completed the Haj wear a white songkok.

The requirements to attain Brunei citizenship include passing tests in Malay culture, customs, and language. Stateless permanent residents of Brunei are given International Certificates of Identity, which allow them to travel overseas. The majority of Brunei's Chinese are permanent residents, and many are stateless.

Petroleum wealth allows the Brunei Government to provide the population with one of Asia's finest health care systems. The Brunei Medical and Health Department introduced the region's first government "flying doctor service" in early 1965. Malaria has been eradicated, and cholera is virtually nonexistent. There are three general hospitals—in Bandar Seri Begawan, Tutong, and Kuala Belait—and there are numerous health clinics throughout the country.

Education starts with preschool, followed by 6 years of primary education and up to 6 years of secondary education. Nine years of education are mandatory. Most of Brunei's college students attend universities and other institutions abroad, but approximately 2,542 study at the University of Brunei Darussalam. Opened in 1985, the university has a faculty of over 300 instructors and is located on a sprawling campus at Tungku, overlooking the South China Sea.

The official language is Malay, but English is widely understood and used in business. Other languages spoken are several Chinese dialects, Iban, and a number of native dialects. Islam is the official religion, but religious freedom is guaranteed under the constitution.

CULTURE

The culture of Brunei is predominantly Malay, with heavy influences from Hinduism and Islam, but is seen as more conservative than Malaysia. The culture is also influenced by the demographics of the country: two-thirds of the population are Malay, and the remainder consists of Chinese, Indians and indigenous Malays Brunei also has a large number of foreign workers, including Indonesian and Filipino domestic workers, labourers from Thailand, Indonesia and the Indian subcontinent (particularly India and Bangladesh), and American and British professionals working in industry and education.

Prohibition of Alcohol

The sale and public consumption of alcohol is banned. Foreigners and non-Muslims are allowed to bring in 12 cans of beer and two bottles of other alcohol (e.g., wine or spirits; no distinction is made for alcohol content). This limit used to apply to every entry; in 2007, however, this was changed to one limit every 48 hours. After the introduction of prohibition in the early 1990s, all pubs and nightclubs were forced to close; however, several types of restaurants allegedly still offer illicit alcohol sometimes served in teapots.

POLITICS AND GOVERNMENT

The politics of Brunei take place in a framework of an absolute monarchy, whereby the Sultan of Brunei is both head of state and head of government. Executive power is exercised by the government. Brunei has a Legislative Council with 20 appointed members, that only has consultative tasks. Under Brunei's 1959 constitution, His Majesty Paduka Seri Baginda Sultan Haji Hassanal Bolkiah Mu'izzaddin Waddaulah, is the head of state with full executive authority, including emergency powers since 1962. The Sultan's role is enshrined in the national philosophy known as Melayu Islam Beraja (MIB), or Malay Islamic Monarchy. The country has been under hypothetical martial law since a rebellion occurred in the early 1960s and was put down by British troops from Singapore.

Executive Branch

Sultan Hassanal Bolkiah of Brunei, whose title has passed within the same dynasty since the 15th century, is the head of state and head of government in Brunei. The Sultan is assisted and advised by five councils, which he appoints. A Council of Ministers, or cabinet, which currently consists of nine members (including the Sultan himself), assists in the administration of the government.

Legislative Branch

Under the 1959 constitution there was an elected Legislative Council, or *Majlis Masyuarat Negeri,* but only one election has ever been held, in 1962. Soon after that election, the assembly was dissolved following the declaration of a state of emergency, which saw the banning of the Brunei People's Party. In 1970 the Council was changed to an appointed body by decree of the Sultan. In 2004 the Sultan announced that for the next parliament, fifteen of the 20 seats would be elected. However, no date for the election has been set.

The Legislative Council currently consists of 20 appointed members, and has only consultative powers. Although there are no elections, the following legal parties exist:

- Brunei National Solidarity Party (PPKB)
- Brunei People's Awareness Party (PAKAR)
- National Development Party (Brunei) (NDP)

Former parties include:

- Brunei National Democratic Party (BNDP)
- Brunei People's Party (Parti Rakyat Brunei)

ECONOMY

The Asian financial crisis in 1997 and 1998, coupled with fluctuations in the price of oil have created uncertainty and instability in Brunei's economy. In addition, the 1998 collapse of the AMEDEO Corporation, Brunei's largest construction firm whose projects helped fuel the domestic economy, caused the country to slip into a mild recession.

Brunei is the third-largest oil producer in Southeast Asia, averaging about 180,000 barrels (29,000 m^3) a day. It also is the fourth-largest producer of liquefied natural gas in the world. Brunei's gross domestic product (GDP) soared with the petroleum price increases of the 1970s to a peak of $5.7 billion in 1980. It declined slightly in each of the next 5 years, then fell by almost 30% in 1986.

This drop was caused by a combination of sharply lower petroleum prices in world markets and voluntary production cuts in Brunei. The GDP recovered somewhat since 1986, growing by 12% in 1987, 1% in 1988, and 9% in 1989. In recent years, GDP growth was 3.5% in 1996, 4.0% in 1997, 1.0% in 1998, and an estimated 2.5% in 1999. However, the 1999 GDP was still only about $4.5 billion, well below the 1980 peak.

In the 1970s, Brunei invested sharply increasing revenues from petroleum exports and maintained government spending at a low and constant rate. Consequently, the government was able to build its foreign reserves and invest them around the world to help provide for future generations. Part of the reserve earnings were reportedly also used to help finance the government's annual budget deficit. Since 1986, however, petroleum revenues have decreased, and government spending has increased. The government has been running a budget deficit since 1988. The disappearance of a revenue surplus has made Brunei's economy more vulnerable to petroleum price fluctuations.

Brunei Shell Petroleum (BSP), a joint venture owned in equal shares by the Brunei Government and the Royal Dutch/Shell group of companies, is the chief oil and gas production company in Brunei. It also operates the country's only refinery. BSP and four sister companies constitute the largest employer in Brunei after the government. BSP's small refinery has a distillation capacity of 10,000 barrels (1,600 m^3) per day. This satisfies domestic demand for most petroleum products.

The French oil company ELF Aquitaine, became active in petroleum exploration in Brunei in the 1980s. Known as Elf Petroleum Asia BV, it has discovered commercially exploitable quantities of oil and gas in three of the four wells drilled since 1987, including a particularly promising discovery announced in early 1990. Recently, UNOCAL, partnered with New Zealand's Fletcher Challenge has been granted concessions for oil exploration. Brunei is preparing to tender concessions for deep water oil and gas exploration.

Brunei's oil production peaked in 1979 at over 240,000 barrels (38,000 m^3) per day. Since then it has been deliberately cut back to extend the life of oil reserves and improve recovery rates. Petroleum production is currently averaging some 200,000 barrels (32,000 m^3) per day. Japan has traditionally been the main customer for Brunei's oil exports, but its share dropped from 45% of the total in 1982 to 19% in 1998. In contrast, oil exports to South Korea increased from only 8% of the total in 1982 to 29% in 1998. Other major customers include Taiwan (6%), and the countries of ASEAN (27%). Brunei's oil exports to the United States accounted for 17% of the total exported.

Almost all of Brunei's natural gas is liquefied at Brunei Liquefied Natural Gas (LNG) plant, which opened in 1972 and is one of the largest LNG plants in the world. Over 82% of Brunei's LNG produced is sold to Japan under a long-term agreement renewed in 1993. The agreement calls for Brunei to provide over 5 million tons of LNG per year to three Japanese utilities. The Japanese company, Mitsubishi, is a joint venture partner with Shell and the Brunei Government in Brunei LNG, Brunei Coldgas, and Brunei Shell Tankers, which together produce the LNG and supply it to Japan. Since 1995, Brunei has supplied more than 700,000 tons of LNG to the Korea Gas Corporation as well. In 1999, Brunei's natural gas production reached 90 cargoes per day. A small amount of natural gas is used for domestic power generation. Brunei is the fourth-largest exporter of LNG in the Asia-Pacific region behind Indonesia, Malaysia, and Australia.

Brunei's proven oil and gas reserves are sufficient until at least 2015, and planned deep sea exploration is expected to find significant new reserves. The government sought in the past decade to diversify the economy with limited success. Oil and gas and government spending still account for most of Brunei's economic activity. Brunei's non-petroleum industries include agriculture, forestry, fishing, and banking.

The government regulates the immigration of foreign labor out of concern it might disrupt Brunei's society. Work permits for foreigners are issued only for short periods and must be continually renewed. Despite these restrictions, foreigners make up a significant portion of the work force. The government reported a total work force of 122,800 in 1999, with an unemployment rate of 5.5%.

Oil and natural gas account for almost all exports. Since only a few products other than petroleum are produced locally, a wide variety of items must be imported. Brunei statistics show Singapore as the largest point of origin of imports, accounting for 25% in 1997. However, this figure includes some transshipments, since most of Brunei's imports transit Singapore. Japan and Malaysia were the second-largest suppliers. As in many other countries, Japanese products dominate local markets for motor vehicles, construction equipment, electronic goods, and household appliances. The United States was the third-largest supplier of imports to Brunei in 1998.

Brunei's substantial foreign reserves are managed by the Brunei Investment Agency (BIA), an arm of the Ministry of Finance. BIA's guiding principle is to increase the real value of Brunei's foreign reserves while pursuing a diverse investment strategy, with holdings in the United States, Japan, western Europe, and the Association of South East Asian Nations (ASEAN) countries.

The Brunei Government actively encourages more foreign investment. New enterprises that meet certain criteria can receive pioneer status, exempting profits from income tax for up to 5 years, depending on the amount of capital invested. The normal corporate income tax rate is 30%. There is no personal income tax or capital gains tax.

One of the government's most important priorities is to encourage the development of Brunei Malays as leaders of industry and commerce. There are no specific restrictions of foreign equity ownership, but local participation, both shared capital and management, is encouraged. Such participation helps when tendering for contracts with the government or Brunei Shell Petroleum.

Companies in Brunei must either be incorporated locally or registered as a branch of a foreign company and must be registered with the Registrar of Companies. Public companies must have a minimum of seven shareholders. Private companies must have a minimum of two but not more than 50 shareholders. At least half of the directors in a company must be residents of Brunei.

The government owns a cattle farm in Australia that supplies most of the country's beef. At 2,262 square miles (5,859 km^2), this ranch is larger than Brunei itself. Eggs and chickens are largely produced locally, but most of Brunei's other food needs must be imported. Agriculture and fisheries are among the industrial sectors that the government has selected for highest priority in its efforts to diversify the economy.

Recently the government has announced plans for Brunei to become an International Offshore Financial Center as well as a Center for Islamic Banking. Brunei is keen on the development of Small and Medium Enterprises and also is investigating the possibility of establishing a "cyber park" to develop an information technology industry. Brunei also hopes to foster tourism through its "Visit Brunei 2009" campaign.

12

EAST TIMOR

East Timor, also known as Timor-Leste (officially the Democratic Republic of Timor-Leste) is a country in Southeast Asia. It comprises the eastern half of the island of Timor, the nearby islands of Atauro and Jaco, and Oecussi-Ambeno, an exclave on the northwestern side of the island, within Indonesian West Timor. The small country of 15,410 km^2 (5,400 sq mi) is located about 640 km (400 mi) northwest of Darwin, Australia.

East Timor was colonized by Portugal in the 16th century, and was known as Portuguese Timor until Portugal's decolonization of the country. In late 1975 East Timor declared its independence but was invaded and occupied by Indonesia later that year, and declared that country's 27th province the following year. In 1999, following the United Nations-sponsored act of self-determination, Indonesia relinquished control of the territory and East Timor became the first new sovereign state of the twenty-first century on May 20, 2002. East Timor is one of only two predominantly Roman Catholic countries in Asia, the other being the Philippines.

East Timor is a lower-middle-income economy. Its Human Development Index (HDI) corresponds to a medium degree of human development and places East Timor 150th among the world's states.

POLITICS AND GOVERNMENT

Politics of East Timor takes place in a framework of a parliamentary representative democratic republic, whereby the Prime Minister of East Timor is the head of government, and of a multi-party system. Executive power is exercised by the government. Legislative power is vested in both the government and the National Parliament. The Judiciary is independent of the executive and the legislature. The

Timorese constitution was modelled on that of Portugal. The country is still in the process of building its administration and governmental institutions.

Executive Branch

The Head of state of the East Timorese republic is the president, who is elected by popular vote for a five-year term and whose role is largely symbolic, though he is able to veto some legislation. Following elections, the president appoints as the prime minister, the leader of the majority party or majority coalition. As head of government the prime minister presides over the Council of State or cabinet.

Legislative Branch

The unicameral Timorese National Parliament (*Parlamento Nacional*) has 88 members, 13 elected in single seat constituencies and 75 elected by proportional representation for a five-year term. The number of seats can vary from a minimum of 52 to a maximum of 65, though it exceptionally has 88 members at present, due to this being its first term of office. The East Timorese constitution was modelled on that of Portugal. The country is still in the process of building its administration and governmental institutions.

Judicial Branch

The Supreme Court of Justice has one judge appointed by the National Parliament and the rest appointed by the Superior Council for the Judiciary.

GEOGRAPHY

Located in southeast Asia, the island of Timor is part of the Malay archipelago, and is the largest and easternmost of the Lesser Sunda Islands. To the north of the mountainous island are the Ombai Strait, Wetar Strait and the greater Banda Sea, to the south the Timor Sea separates the island from Australia, while to the west lies the Indonesian Province of East Nusa Tenggara. The highest point of East Timor is Mount Ramelau (also known as Mount Tatamailau) at 2,963 meters (9,721 ft).

The local climate is tropical and generally hot and humid, characterised by distinct rainy and dry seasons. The capital, largest city and main port is Dili, and the second-largest city is the eastern town of Baucau.

The easternmost area of Timor-Leste consists of the Paitchau Range and Iralalaro area. This area has been proposed as to be the first conservation area in Timor-Leste as it contains the last remaining Tropical Dry forested area within the country as well as hosts a number of unique plant and animal species and is sparsely populated. The Northern coast is characterized by a number of important reef systems that have been determined as being at risk.

DEMOGRAPHY

The population of East Timor is about one million. It has grown considerably recently, because of a high birth rate, but also because of the return of refugees. The population is especially concentrated in the area around Dili.

The Timorese are called Maubere collectively by some of their political organizations, an originally derogatory name turned into a name of pride by Fretilin. They consist of a number of distinct ethnic groups, most of whom are of mixed Malayo-Polynesian and Melanesian/Papuan descent. The largest Malayo-Polynesian ethnic groups are the Tetum (or Tetun) (100,000), primarily in the north coast and around Dili; the Mambae (80,000), in the central mountains; the Tukudede (63,170), in the area around Maubara and Liquiçá; the Galoli (50,000), between the tribes of Mambae and Makasae; the Kemak (50,000) in north-central Timor island; and the Baikeno (20,000), in the area around Pante Macassar. The main tribes of predominantly Papuan origin include the Bunak (50,000), in the central interior of Timor island; the Fataluku (30,000), at the eastern tip of the island near Lospalos; and the Makasae, toward the eastern end of the island.

In addition, like other former Portuguese colonies where interracial marriage was common, there is a smaller population of people of mixed Timorese and Portuguese origin, known in Portuguese as *mestiços*. The East Timorese *mestiço* best-known internationally is José Ramos-Horta, the spokesman for the resistance movement in exile, and now President of East Timor. Mário Viegas Carrascalão, Indonesia's appointed governor between 1987 and 1992, is also a *mestiço*. East Timor also has a small Chinese minority, most of whom are Hakka. Most left after the Indonesian invasion, with most moving to Australia although many Sino-Timorese have returned, including Pedro Lay, the Minister for Infrastructure.

CULTURE

The Culture of East Timor reflects numerous cultural influences, including Portuguese, Roman Catholic and Malay, on the indigenous Austronesian cultures in East Timor.

Literature

Easily the most famous East Timorese author is Xanana Gusmão, the leader of the Timorese resistance organization Fretilin, and now the president of independent East Timor. He wrote two books during the struggle for independence. Also a poet and painter, he produced works describing the culture, values, and skills of the Timorese people. Other important writers of Timor are: Luís Cardoso, Fernando Sylvan, Ponte Pedrinha, Jorge Barros Duarte, Crisódio Araujo, Jorge Lauten, Francisco Borja da Costa, Afonso Busa Metan and Fitun Fuik.

Religion

East Timor has been nominally Catholic since early in the Portuguese colonial period. The Catholic faith became a central part of East Timorese culture during the Indonesian occupation between 1975 and 1999. While under Portuguese rule, the East Timorese had mostly been animist, sometimes integrated with minimal Catholic ritual, the number of Catholics dramatically increased under Indonesian rule. This was for several reasons: Indonesia was predominantly Muslim; the Indonesian state required adherence to one of five officially recognised religions and did not recognise traditional beliefs; and because the Catholic church, which remained directly responsible to the Vatican throughout Indonesian rule, became a refuge for East Timorese seeking sanctuary from persecution.

The 'Apostolic Administrator' (*de facto* Bishop) of the Diocese of Dili, Monsignor Martinho da Costa Lopes, began speaking out against human rights abuses by the Indonesian security forces, including rape, torture, murder, and disappearances. Following pressure from Jakarta, he stepped down in 1983 and was replaced by the younger priest, Monsignor Carlos Filipe Ximenes Belo, who Indonesia thought would be more loyal. However, he too began speaking out, not only against human rights abuses, but the issue of self-determination, writing an open letter to the Secretary General of the United Nations, calling for a referendum. In 1996 he was awarded the Nobel Peace Prize, along with exiled leader José Ramos-Horta, now the country's President.

In spite of accusations by the Suharto regime that East Timor's independence movement, Fretilin, was communist, many of its leaders had trained to be priests, and their philosophy probably owed more to the Catholic liberation theology of Latin America than to Marxism.

However, in spite of the majority of the country's people now being Catholics, there is freedom of religion in the new secular republic, and the former Prime Minister Marí Alkatiri, is a Muslim of Yemeni descent.

ECONOMY

In late 1999, about 70% of the economic infrastructure of East Timor was destroyed by Indonesian troops and anti-independence militias, and 260,000 people fled westward. From 2002 to 2005, an international program led by the United Nations, manned by civilian advisers, 5,000 peacekeepers (8,000 at peak) and 1,300 police officers, substantially reconstructed the infrastructure. By mid-2002, all but about 50,000 of the refugees had returned.

One promising long-term project is the joint development with Australia of petroleum and natural gas resources in the waters southeast of Timor. The Portuguese colonial administration granted concessions to Oceanic Exploration Corporation to develop the deposits, however, this was curtailed by the Indonesian invasion in 1976. The resources were divided between Indonesia and Australia with the Timor Gap Treaty in 1989. The treaty established guidelines for joint exploitation of seabed resources in the area of the "gap" left by then-Portuguese Timor in the maritime boundary agreed between the two countries in 1972. Revenues from the "joint" area were to be divided 50%-50%. Woodside Petroleum and ConocoPhillips began development of some resources in the Timor Gap on behalf of the two governments in 1992.

East Timor inherited no permanent maritime boundaries when it attained independence, repudiating the Timor Gap Treaty as illegal. A provisional agreement (the Timor Sea Treaty, signed when East Timor became independent on 20 May 2002) defined a Joint Petroleum Development Area (JPDA), and awarded 90% of revenues from existing projects in that area to East Timor and 10% to Australia. The first significant new development in the JPDA since Timorese independence is the largest petroleum resource in the Timor Sea, the Greater Sunrise gas field. Its exploitation was the subject of separate agreements in 2003 and 2005. Only 20% of the field lies within the JPDA and the rest in waters not subject to the treaty (though claimed by both countries). The initial, temporary agreement gave 82% of revenues to Australia and only 18% to East Timor.

The Government of East Timor has sought to negotiate a definite boundary with Australia at the halfway line between the countries, in accordance with the United Nations Convention on the Law of the Sea. The Government of Australia preferred to establish the boundary at the end of the wide Australian continental shelf, as agreed with Indonesia in 1972 and 1991. Normally a dispute such as this could be referred to the International Court of Justice or the International Tribunal for the Law of the Sea for an impartial decision, but the Australian government had withdrawn itself from these international jurisdictions (solely on matters relating to maritime boundaries) shortly before Timorese independence. Nevertheless, under public and diplomatic pressure, the Australian government offered instead a last-minute concession on Greater Sunrise gas field royalties alone. On July 7, 2005, an agreement was signed under which both countries would set aside the dispute over the maritime boundary, and East Timor would receive 50% of the revenues (estimated at A$26 billion or about US$20 billion over the lifetime of the project) from the Greater Sunrise development. Other developments within waters claimed by East Timor but outside the JPDA (Laminaria-Corallina and Buffalo) continue to be exploited unilaterally by Australia, however.

In 2007 bad harvest lead to deaths in several parts of Timor-Leste. In November 2007 eleven subdistricts still needed food supply by international aid. East Timor also has a large and potentially lucrative coffee industry, which sells organic coffee to numerous Fair Trade retailers and on the open market. Currently three foreign banks have a branch in Dili: Australia's ANZ, Portugal's Banco Nacional Ultramarino, and Indonesia's Bank Mandiri. There are no Patent Laws in East Timor.

13

INDIA AND SOUTHEAST ASIA RELATIONS

ASSOCIATION OF SOUTHEAST ASIAN NATIONS

The Association of Southeast Asian Nations, commonly referred to as ASEAN, is a geo-political and economic organization of 10 countries located in Southeast Asia, which was formed on August 8, 1967 by Indonesia, Malaysia, the Philippines, Singapore and Thailand. Its aims include the acceleration of economic growth, social progress, cultural development among its members, the protection of the peace and stability of the region, and to provide opportunities for member countries to discuss differences peacefully.

In 2005, the bloc spanned over 1.1 billion acres with a combined GDP (Nominal/PPP) of about USD$896.5 billion/$2.728 billion growing at an average rate of around 5.6% per annum. Nominal GDP had grown to $1,073.9 billion in 2006.

ASEAN was preceded by an organization called the Association of Southeast Asia, commonly called ASA, an alliance consisting of the Philippines, Malaysia, and Thailand that was formed in 1961. The bloc itself, however, was established on August 8, 1967, when foreign ministers of five countries – Indonesia, Malaysia, the Philippines, Singapore, and Thailand – met at the Thai Department of Foreign Affairs building in Bangkok and signed the ASEAN Declaration, more commonly known as the Bangkok Declaration. The five foreign ministers – Adam Malik of Indonesia, Narciso Ramos of the Philippines, Abdul Razak of Malaysia, S. Rajaratnam of Singapore, and Thanat Khoman of Thailand – are considered as the organization's Founding Fathers.

The motivations for the birth of ASEAN were the desire for a stable external environment (so that its members' governing elite could concentrate on nation building), the common fear of communism, reduced faith in or mistrust of external powers in the 1960s, as well as the aspiration for national economic development; not to mention

Indonesia's ambition to become a regional hegemon through regional cooperation and the hope on the part of Malaysia and Singapore to constrain Indonesia and bring it into a more cooperative framework. Unlike the European Union, ASEAN was designed to serve nationalism.

In 1976, the Melanesian state of Papua New Guinea was accorded observer status. Throughout the 1970s, the organization embarked on a program of economic cooperation, following the Bali Summit of 1976. This foundered in the mid-1980s and was only revived around 1991 due to a Thai proposal for a regional free trade area. The bloc then grew when Brunei Darussalam became the sixth member after it joined on January 8, 1984, barely a week after the country became independent on January 1.

During the 1990s, the bloc experienced an increase in both membership as well as in the drive for further integration. In 1990, Malaysia proposed the creation of an East Asia Economic Caucus composing the then-members of ASEAN as well as the People's Republic of China, Japan, and South Korea, with the intention of counterbalancing the growing influence of the United States in the APEC as well as in the Asian region as a whole. This proposal, however, failed since it faced heavy opposition from Japan and the United States.

Despite this failure, member states continued to work for further integration. In 1992, the Common Effective Preferential Tariff (CEPT) scheme was signed as a schedule for phasing tariffs and as a goal to increase the *region's competitive advantage as a production base geared for the world market*. This law would act as the framework for the ASEAN Free Trade Area.

On July 28, 1995, Vietnam became the seventh member. Laos and Myanmar joined two years later in July 23, 1997. Cambodia was to have joined together with Laos and Myanmar, but was deferred due to the country's internal political struggle. The country later joined on April 30, 1999, following the stabilization of its government.

At the turn of the 21st century, issues shifted to involve a more environmental prospective. The organization started to discuss environmental agreements. These included the signing of the ASEAN Agreement on Transboundary Haze Pollution in 2002 as an attempt to control haze pollution in Southeast Asia. Unfortunately, this was unsuccessful due to the outbreaks of the 2005 Malaysian haze and the 2006 Southeast Asian haze. Other environmental treaties introduced by the organization include the Cebu Declaration on East Asian Energy Security, the ASEAN-Wildlife Enforcement Network in 2005, and the Asia-Pacific Partnership on Clean Development and Climate, both of which are responses to Global Warming and the negative effects of climate change.

Through the Bali Concord II in 2003, ASEAN has subscribed to the notion of democratic peace, which means all member countries believe democratic processes will promote regional peace and stability. Also the non-democratic members all agreed that it was something all member states should aspire to.

The leaders of each country, particularly Mahathir Mohamad of Malaysia, also felt the need to further integrate the region. Beginning in 1997, the bloc began creating organizations within its framework with the intention of achieving this goal. ASEAN Plus Three was the first of these and was created to improve existing ties with the People's Republic of China, Japan, and South Korea. This was followed by the even larger East Asia Summit, which included these countries as well as India, Australia, and New Zealand. This new grouping acted as a prerequisite for the planned East Asia Community, which was supposedly patterned after the now-defunct European Community. The ASEAN Eminent Persons Group was created to study the possible successes and failures of this policy as well as the possibility of drafting an ASEAN Charter.

In 2006, ASEAN was given observer status at the United Nations General Assembly. As a response, the organization awarded the status of "dialogue partner" to the United Nations. Furthermore, on July 23 that year, José Ramos-Horta, then Prime Minister of East Timor, signed a formal request for membership and expected the accession process to last at least five years before the then-observer state became a full member.

In 2007, ASEAN celebrated its 40th anniversary since its inception, and 30 years of diplomatic relations with the United States.

On August 26, 2007, ASEAN stated that it aims to complete all its free trade agreements with China, Japan, South Korea, India, Australia and New Zealand by 2013, in line with the establishment of the ASEAN Economic Community by 2015.

In November 2007 the ASEAN members signed the ASEAN Charter, a constitution governing relations among the ASEAN members and establishing ASEAN itself as an international legal entity.

In the 1960s, the push for decolonization promoted the sovereignty of Indonesia, Malaysia, the Philippines and Singapore, among others. Since nation building is often messy and vulnerable to foreign intervention, the governing elite wanted to be free to implement independent policies with the knowledge that neighbors would refrain from interfering in their domestic affairs. Territorially small members such as Singapore and Brunei were consciously fearful of force and coercive measures from much bigger neighbors like Indonesia and Malaysia. As a result, non-interference, consensus, non-use of force and non-confrontation became the key principles of the organization.

On the surface, the process of consultations and consensus is supposed to be a democratic approach to decision making, but the ASEAN process has been managed through close interpersonal contacts among the top leaders only, who often share a reluctance to institutionalize and legalize co-operation which can undermine their regime's control over the conduct of regional co-operation.

All of these features, namely non-interference, informality, minimal institutionalization, consultation and consensus, non-use of force and non-confrontation have constituted what is called the ASEAN Way.

Since the late 1990s, many scholars have argued that the principle of non-interference has blunted ASEAN efforts in handling the problem of Myanmar, human rights abuses and haze pollution in the region. Meanwhile, with the consensus-based approach, every member in fact has a veto and decisions are usually reduced to the lowest common denominator. There has been a widespread belief that ASEAN members should have a less rigid view on these two cardinal principles when they wish to be seen as a cohesive and relevant community.

Policies

Apart from consultations and consensus, ASEAN's agenda-setting and decision-making processes can be usefully understood in terms of the so-called Track I and Track II. Track I refers to the practice of diplomacy among government channels. The participants stand as representatives of their respective states and reflect the official positions of their governments during negotiations and discussions. All official decisions are made in Track I. Track II on the other hand refers to diplomatic activities that are unofficial and includes participants from both government and non-government institutions such as the academic, economic communities and NGOs. This track enables governments to discuss controversial issues and test new ideas without making official statements or binding commitments, and, if necessary, backtrack on positions.

Although Track II dialogues are sometimes cited as examples of the involvement of civil society in regional decision-making process by governments and other second track actors, NGOs have rarely got access to this track, meanwhile participants from the academic community are a dozen think-tanks. However, these think-tanks are, in most cases, very much linked to their respective governments, and dependent on government funding for their academic and policy-relevant activities. Their recommendations, especially in economic integration, are often closer to ASEAN's decisions than the rest of civil society's positions.

The track that acts as a forum for civil society in Southeast Asia is called Track III, which is essentially people-to-people diplomacy undertaken mainly by CSOs. Track III networks claim to represent communities and people who are largely marginalised from political power centers and unable to achieve positive change without outside assistance. This track tries to influence government policies indirectly by lobbying, generating pressure through the media. Third-track actors also organise and/or attend meetings as well as conferences to get access to Track I officials.

While Track II meetings and interactions with Track I actors have increased and intensified, rarely has the rest of civil society had the opportunity to interface with Track II. Those with Track I have been even rarer. In other words, the participation of the big majority of CSOs has been excluded from ASEAN's agenda-setting and decision-making.

Looking at the three tracks, it is clear that until now, ASEAN has been run by government officials who, as far as ASEAN matters are concerned, are accountable only to their governments and not the people. In a lecture on the occasion of ASEAN's 38th anniversary, the incumbent Indonesian President Dr. Susilo Bambang Yudhoyono admitted:

"All the decisions about treaties and free trade areas, about declarations and plans of action, are made by Heads of Government, ministers and senior officials. And the fact that among the masses, there is little knowledge, let alone appreciation, of the large initiatives that ASEAN is taking on their behalf."

Meetings

ASEAN Summit

The organization holds meetings, known as the ASEAN Summit, where heads of government of each member meet to discuss and resolve regional issues, as well as to conduct other meetings with other countries outside of the bloc with the intention of promoting external relations.

The ASEAN Leaders' Formal Summit was first held in Bali, Indonesia in 1976. Its third meeting was held in Manila in 1987 and during this meeting, it was decided that the leaders would meet every five years. Consequently, the fourth meeting was held in Singapore in 1992 where the leaders again agreed to meet more frequently, deciding to hold the summit every three years. In 2001, it was decided to meet annually to address urgent issues affecting the region. Member nations were assigned to be the summit host in alphabetical order except in the case of Myanmar which dropped its 2006 hosting rights in 2004 due to pressure from the United States and the European Union.

Regional Forum

The ASEAN Regional Forum (ARF) is a formal, official, multilateral dialogue in Asia Pacific region. As of July 2007, it is consisted of 27 participants. ARF objectives are to foster dialogue and consultation, and promote confidence-building and preventive diplomacy in the region. The ARF met for the first time in 1994. The current participants in the ARF are as follows: all the ASEAN members, Australia, Bangladesh, Canada, the People's Republic of China, the European Union, India, Japan, North Korea, South Korea, Mongolia, New Zealand, Pakistan, Papua New Guinea, Russia, Timor-Leste, United States and Sri Lanka. The Republic of China (also known as Taiwan) has been excluded since the establishment of the ARF, and issues regarding the Taiwan Strait is neither discussed at the ARF meetings nor stated in the ARF Chairman's Statements.

Other Meetings

Aside from the ones above, other regular meetings are also held. These include the annual ASEAN Ministerial Meeting as well as other smaller committees, such as the Southeast Asian Fisheries Development Center. Meetings mostly focus on specific topics, such as defense or the environment, and are attended by Ministers, instead of heads of government.

Plus Three

The ASEAN Plus Three is a meeting between ASEAN, the People's Republic of China, Japan, and South Korea, and is primarily held during each ASEAN Summit.

Asia-Europe Meeting

The Asia-Europe Meeting (ASEM) is an informal dialogue process initiated in 1996, bringing together the European Union and the ASEAN Plus Three groupings.

Russia Summit

The ASEAN-Russia Summit is a meeting between leaders of member states and the President of Russia.

Economic Community

ASEAN has emphasized regional cooperation in the "three pillars" of security, sociocultural and economic integration. The regional grouping has made the most progress in economic integration, aiming to create an ASEAN Economic Community (AEC) by 2015. The AEC would have a combined population of over 566 million and a GDP exceeding US$ 1.173 trillion.

Free Trade Area

The foundation of the AEC is the ASEAN Free Trade Area (AFTA), a common external preferential tariff scheme to promote the free flow of goods within ASEAN. The ASEAN Free Trade Area (AFTA) is an agreement by the member nations of ASEAN concerning local manufacturing in all ASEAN countries. The AFTA agreement was signed on January 28, 1992 in Singapore. When the AFTA agreement was originally signed, ASEAN had six members, namely, Brunei, Indonesia, Malaysia, the Philippines, Singapore and Thailand. Vietnam joined in 1995, Laos and Myanmar in 1997, and Cambodia in 1999. The latecomers have not fully met the AFTA's obligations, but they are officially considered part of the AFTA as they were required to sign the agreement upon entry into ASEAN, and were given longer time frames in which to meet AFTA's tariff reduction obligations.

Investment Area

The AIA will encourage the free flow of investment within ASEAN. The main principles of the AIA are as follows:

- All industries are to be opened up for investment, with exclusions to be phased out according to schedules
- National treatment is granted immediately to ASEAN investors with few exclusions
- Elimination of investment impediments
- Streamlining of investment process and procedures
- Enhancing transparency
- Undertaking investment facilitation measures

Full realization of the AIA with the removal of temporary exclusion lists in manufacturing agriculture, fisheries, forestry and mining is scheduled by 2010 for most ASEAN members and by 2015 for the CLMV countries (Cambodia, Lao PDR, Myanmar, and Viet Nam).

Trade in Services

An ASEAN Framework Agreement on Trade in Services was adopted at the ASEAN Summit in Bangkok in December 1995. Under the agreement, ASEAN members are negotiating intra-regional services liberalization in several sectors, including air transport, business services, construction, financial services, maritime transport, telecommunications and tourism. Although some sectors have liberalized faster, such as air transport, other sectors remain subject to continued negotiation. Efforts to expand the scope of the Framework Agreement also remain subject to continued negotiations.

Single Aviation Market

The ASEAN Single Aviation Market (SAM), proposed by the ASEAN Air Transport Working Group, supported by the ASEAN Senior Transport Officials Meeting, and endorsed by the ASEAN Transport Ministers, will introduce an open-sky arrangement to the region by 2015. Not only will the ASEAN SAM be expected to fully liberalize air travel between its Member States, it is also expected that SAM will further enhance tourism, trade, investment and services flows between Member States. Beginning January 1, 2009, there will be full liberalization of air freight services in the region, as well as removal of third and fourth freedom restrictions between capital cities of Member States for air passengers services. By January 1, 2011, there will be liberalization of fifth freedom traffic rights between all capital cities.

Cultural Activities

The organization hosts cultural activities in an attempt to further integrate the region. These include sports and educational activities as well as writing awards. Examples of these include the ASEAN University Network and the Singapore-sponsored ASEAN Scholarship.

S.E.A. Write Award

The S.E.A. Write Award is a literary award given to Southeast Asian poets and writers annually since 1979. The award is either given for a specific work or as a recognition of an author's lifetime achievement. Works that are honored vary and have included poetry, short stories, novels, plays, folklore as well as scholarly and religious works. Ceremonies are held in Bangkok and is presided by a member of the Thai royal family.

ASAIHL

ASAIHL or the Association of Southeast Asian Institutions of Higher Learning is a non-governmental organization founded in 1956 that strives to strengthen higher learning institutions, espescially in teaching, research, and public service, with the intention of cultivating a sense of regional identity and interdependence.

Heritage Parks

ASEAN Heritage Parks is a list of nature parks launched 1984 and relaunched in 2004. It aims to protect the region's natural treasures. There are now 35 such protected areas, including the Tubbataha Reef Marine Park and the Kinabalu National Park.

INDIA-ASEAN RELATIONS

India has had close cultural and economic ties with Southeast Asian countries throughout history. ASEAN's political and strategic importance in the larger Asia-Pacific region and its potential to become a major partner of India in the area of trade and investment have encouraged India to seek closer linkages with these countries. After

1991 however, a conscious effort was begun to reach out to these countries as part of our 'Look East' policy'. The fact that the Southeast Asian countries had consolidated themselves into a dynamic regional grouping, ASEAN, accelerated our efforts. With the eastward expansion of ASEAN to include Myanmar, India and ASEAN are no longer just maritime neighbours but share a land boundary of over 1600 km.

India became a Sectoral Dialogue Partner of ASEAN in 1992 and Full Dialogue Partner in 1996. The Dialogue Partnership with ASEAN has enabled India to significantly deepen its relationship with its member countries. ASEAN's other full Dialogue Partners are Australia, Canada, China, European Union, Japan, New Zealand, Republic of Korea, Russia and USA. The Dialogue process is meant to complement and augment India's bilateral relations with its Southeast Asian neighbours, as well as its interaction with ASEAN countries under the framework of sub-regional (BIMST-EC and MGC), regional (IOR ARC) and inter-regional (G 15) cooperation initiatives.

Dialogue Mechanisms

The mechanisms for ASEAN-India dialogue have hitherto consisted of (i) the ASEAN Post Ministerial Conferences (PMC), in the form of the ASEAN+10 (meeting of ASEAN with 10 Dialogue Partners together) and ASEAN+1 (individual meeting of ASEAN with each dialogue Partner) interactions; (ii) ASEAN-India Senior Officials' Meeting (iii) ASEAN-India Joint Cooperation Committee (JCC); and (iv) the ASEAN-India Working Group. There are also specialised Working Groups in the various areas where ASEAN and India are cooperating: Science and Technology, Trade & Investment, and Transport & Infrastructure. As Full Dialogue Partner, since 1996, India has been participating at the ministerial level in the ASEAN Post Ministerial Conferences (PMC), held in end-July every year, after the main ASEAN Ministerial Meeting. In November 2001, the ASEAN-India relationship was upgraded to summit level. Thus, to this list would now have to be added the ASEAN-India Summit.

Trade and Investment Relations

Our exports to ASEAN include oil meals, gems and jewellery, meat and meat preparations, cotton yarn, fabrics, made-ups, engineering goods, transport equipment, machinery and instruments, electronic goods, marine products, fruits and vegetables, rice, drugs and pharmaceuticals, chemicals, etc. Our imports mainly consist of artificial resins, plastic material, natural rubber, wood and wood products, electronic goods, non-ferrous metals, metaliferous ores and metal scrap, organic chemicals, edible oils, coal, fertilisers, etc. ASEAN-India trade in 2001-02 was about US$ 7.8 billion, over 3 times the 1993-94 trade figure of US$ 2.5 billion. India's exports to ASEAN were US$ 3.5 billion while imports came to about US$ 4.3 billion.

With economic liberalisation, businesses in ASEAN are increasingly undertaking Foreign Direct Investment (FDI) in India in crucial infrastructure sectors such as telecommunications, fuels, hotel and tourism services, heavy industry, chemicals, fertilisers, as also in trading, textiles, paper and pulp, and food processing. ASEAN – especially Malaysia, Singapore, and Thailand, has become a major source of FDI into India. From a negligible amount in 1991, cumulative approved FDI (Jan 1991 – May 2002) from ASEAN was over Rs.14,000 crores (US$ 4 billion) in May 2002; this represents of share of 6.1% in the total FDI approved by India in this period. Actual inflow of FDI from ASEAN during this period (January 1991 – May 2002) was, however, more modest: US$ 620 million, representing 3.4% of total FDI flows in to India. It is our priority to increase investment flows between India and ASEAN. We hope that the Business Summit will be a significant step in this direction.

Functional Cooperation

Currently, India is closely collaborating with ASEAN countries in various fields such as trade and investment, science and technology, tourism, human resource development and transport & infrastructure. Cooperation with ASEAN countries in various sectors is either through joint projects, e.g., joint study in the HRD sector or through research, training and attachment of experts from India and ASEAN countries. ASEAN has greatly appreciated the premium placed by EAM (in an intervention at the PMC 2000) on the actual delivery on proposals and agreed projects. In Science & Technology, ASEAN and India have a broad-based programme of cooperation, which includes information technology, biotechnology, advanced materials, space applications, etc.

In information technology, a training programme in advanced software techniques for 94 ASEAN candidates at NIIT organised by India in 2000 was greatly appreciated by ASEAN; they requested that such training programmes be organised on an annual basis. In response, 50 out of the additional 100 HRD training places being offered annually to ASEAN, would be used for IT courses. An ASEAN-India Digital Archive (AIDA) project is also being set up. Multi-media representation of common phrases & terms in the various ASEAN languages, Hindi and English has already been provided. We have suggested that future activities under the AIDA project be carefully reviewed and properly designed to enhance the utility of the archive. India also proposes to train candidates from CLMV countries in High-End Networking.

In biotechnology, cooperation includes projects in plant and animal biotechnology and establishment of an ASEAN-India Bioinformatics Network. Besides, it has been decided at the highest level to establish an India-ASEAN Institute of Biotechnology

(IAIB) in Jakarta, for carrying out R&D in identified areas of relevance. The IAIB would also aim to commercialise the results of R&D activities. While cooperation in plant biotechnology has already commenced, expert-level discussions are underway in animal biotechnology. It is expected that the IAIB would start functioning from November 2002. In bioinformatics, as a result of discussions held at the expert level, the necessary modalities have been worked out for the project, in which the private sector would also be involved. In advanced materials, projects in rare earth magnets and thermal and wear resistant surface coatings have been completed. It is proposed to expand these project, with a focus on the realisation of commercial benefits.

In space technology, the areas identified for cooperation in the initial stages include capacity-building, including training, formal education, on-the-job attachment and exchange of scientists, besides use of Indian Remote Sensing (IRS) data for environmental management such as forest fire monitoring, marine and coastal management. Training of ASEAN scientists in India is expected to start sometime soon.

India also participated in the 6th ASEAN Science and Technology Week, held in Brunei in September 2001. There were some 300 participants, from both ASEAN as well as the Dialogue Partners. Besides presenting papers in a number of areas, at the S&T exhibition India displayed about fifty products developed and commercialised indigenously: e.g., natural dyes, high technology titanium products, composite materials and ceramics, etc. It afforded India a good platform for disseminating information about its technological achievements and capabilities.

In trade and investment, a joint ASEAN-India study on 'AFTA-India Linkages for the Enhancement of Trade and Investment' has been taken up because it was felt that there was considerable unrealised potential in respect of ASEAN-India trade and investment ties. At a meeting of our Commerce and Industry Minister with his ASEAN counterparts, held on 15th September 2002 back-to-back with at the ASEAN Economic Ministers' Meeting in Brunei, an India-AFTA Regional Trade and Investment Area (RTIA) was endorsed as a long term objective, and it was agreed to set up India-ASEAN Economic Linkages Task Force to follow up on the recommendations of the joint expert study. The Task Force has also been mandated to prepare a draft framework agreement for enhancing India-ASEAN trade and economic cooperation, which would be submitted to the next meeting of the Indian and ASEAN economic ministers in Phnom Penh in October 2003. Also, an India-ASEAN Business Summit is being held in New Delhi and Hyderabad on 17 & 18 October 2002 respectively. The event would bring together the senior level political leadership in the areas of trade and economy, top business executives, industrialists, senior officials, etc., and should constitute a useful input for the ASEAN-India Summit.

In tourism, India is keen to cooperate with ASEAN by leveraging its complementarities to ASEAN tourist circuits in international tourism markets for promoting two-way tourist flows. The active cultural and commercial ties that India has had throughout history with the Mekong Basin Area can be used to advantage. In particular, the Buddhist pilgrimage sites in India, e.g., Bodh Gaya, are of special interest to ASEAN. It is proposed to publish a Tourism Investment Guide covering investment opportunities within both ASEAN and India, and with a separate section on pilgrimage tourism. Besides, the very useful mechanism of informal consultations between our tourism authorities and the National Tourism Organisations of ASEAN countries needs to be reactivated.

The first meeting of the Working Group on transport and infrastructure was held in Indonesia in September 2002, following discussions between ASEAN transport officials and our ministries of Shipping, Road Transport and Highways, and Railways to identify the areas for cooperation in these sectors. It was agreed in principle that ASEAN-India cooperation in this sector could be achieved at the institutional and private sector levels. In this regard, the meeting exchanged views regarding the specific areas of mutual interest and possible cooperation in railways, roads, shipping, inland waterways, ports, maritime training, etc., and the modalities for funding ASEAN-India transport projects. In particular, India offered to impart training to the railway personnel of CLMV countries. The meeting also encouraged member countries of ASEAN to hold internal consultations on further possible areas for cooperation with India and submit their proposals to India through the ASEAN Secretariat. Besides, it was agreed that apart from bilateral cooperation between the individual ASEAN countries and India, ASEAN should, as a regional grouping, develop joint regional projects with India.

In human resource development (HRD), India has offered 100 seats in various training courses at reputed Indian institutions for development of human resources. Of these, while 50 will be utilised for IT training, the other will be in areas such as management, banking & finance, urban development, education planning, labour relations, etc.. The 100 are in addition to the approximately 250 places offered to ASEAN countries bilaterally under the ITEC Programme. A joint ASEAN-India study on Indian and ASEAN capabilities and complementarities in HRD has been conducted. At a joint workshop for identifying practical ways and means for implementing the recommendations of the study endorsed by the ASEAN-India JCC, it was agreed to focus on management and technical education. Universities and other institutions for technical and higher education in ASEAN and their Indian counterparts are keen to enhance their linkages by working together under the supervision of the AUN and relevant Indian authorities. In this regard, India is examining a proposals submitted by ASEAN in respect of a 'Preliminary Visit for ASEAN-India Academic Exchanges' and English language training for CLMV countries.

An ASEAN-India Eminent Persons' Lecture Series has been launched with the objective of promoting awareness about the reality and potential of the ASEAN-India relations, under which, eminent leaders and opinion makers, senior academics and media personalities, technologists and captains of trade and industry give public lectures on different aspects of ASEAN-India economic, political, cultural and security ties. To increase the efficacy of future lectures, suitable topics and themes focussing on ASEAN-India cooperation would be identified. It has also been decided to set up a network of think tanks in India and ASEAN. At the 4th ASEAN-India Working Group, ASEAN suggested that a draft outline for a concept paper on 'ASEAN-India Vision 2020', covering economic, social and developmental issues relevant to ASEAN-India cooperation be drawn up; this would be of assistance in identifying the relevant institutions in ASEAN that might form part of this network. The concept paper on ASEAN-India Vision 2020 is to be released at the ASEAN India Summit and constitute a track-II input into the Summit.

India is very keen to broaden and deepen functional cooperation in diverse fields with ASEAN, especially with a focus on the Initiatives for ASEAN Integration (IAI), launched by ASEAN to bridge the intra-ASEAN developmental gap, especially between the four new ASEAN entrants, Cambodia, Lao PDR, Myanmar and Vietnam (CLMV countries), and the other six. This has been expressed by India in meetings with ASEAN at various levels. At the PMC 10+1 meeting in Hanoi in July 2001, India offered assistance and cooperation in projects relating to ICT & computer literacy, HRD, space technology – including use of space imagery for flood forecasting and control, commercialisation of indigenous technologies, cooperation among SMEs, English teaching, health and pharmaceuticals, tropical medicine, telemedicine, development and manufacturing of generic medicines, computer literacy, distance & interactive learning through multimedia techniques, cooperation in long-distance education through Indira Gandhi National Open University, biotechnology, training of government officials, further projects in advanced materials, commercialisation of indigenously developed technologies, and technology competitiveness. Initial soundings are being made through our missions in the CLMV countries for setting up an advanced training centre in one of the CLMV capitals for imparting vocational training in the mechanical trades, including some initial training in English language to enable the trainees could understand the courses. This training centre is expected to cost some US$ 1.6 crores (16 million), with the land, etc. being made available by the CLMV country in which the Centre would be set up. Besides, we are looking at the possibility of giving unilateral tariff concessions in selected items for imports from these countries. India also expressed keenness to be involved in developmental projects in the Greater Mekong Sub-region.

India's keenness to cooperate in diverse areas and its focus on the IAI have been appreciated by ASEAN as a sign of India's commitment to ASEAN and its processes.

The ideas put forward by India for furthering functional cooperation were further discussed at the 4th ASEAN-India JCC Meeting, held on 24-26 January 2002, and briefly at the ASEAN-India SOM in March 2002. ASEAN expressed particular interest in cooperation in HRD, IT and biotechnology.

ASEAN-India Summits

Indian economy and collectively ten ASEAN members are large and dynamic markets. They are undertaking reforms to deepen their integration within and outside the region. Although the India-ASEAN trade and economic relations have grown over the past decade in an impressive manner, the immense potential of cooperation and synergies remain to be exploited. They could fruitfully share technology, capital, human talent, developmental experiences and coordinated their positions in international forums such as WTO negotiation. India-ASEAN partnership could also be an important building bloc of the emerging broader regional economic cooperation in Asia viz. an Asian Economic Community built in a phased manner.

The original signatories of ASEAN Declaration at Bangkok in 1967, were Indonesia, Malaysia, the Philippines, Singapore and Thailand. Later, after the cold war ended, the grouping was joined by Cambodia, Lao PDR, Myanmar, Vietnam (CLMV) and Brunei Darussalam. ASEAN has four Summit level Dialogue Partners, i.e., China, Japan, ROK and India. In addition, it has a number of Dialogue and sectoral Dialogue Partners as well.

India's focus on a strengthened and multi-faceted relationship with ASEAN is an outcome of the significant changes in the world's political and economic scenario since the early 1990s and India's own march towards economic liberalisation. India's search for economic space has resulted in our *'Look East'* policy. ASEAN's economic, political and strategic importance in the larger Asia-Pacific Region and its potential to become a major partner of India in trade and investment is a significant factor in our policy paradigms. ASEAN's steady expansion westward to include Myanmar has also brought it to our land boundaries. It now provides a land bridge for India to connect with the Asia-Pacific-centred economic crosscurrents shaping the 21st century market place. ASEAN seeks access to India's professional and technical strengths. Our traditional friendship with the CLMV countries also makes India a valuable ally for promoting the Initiative for ASEAN Integration (IAI).

India and ASEAN have convergence in their security perspectives. We have vital stakes in peace and stability in the region, including the security of the sea-lanes of the Indian Ocean for smooth flow of raw materials, merchandise and energy supplies. Since 1996, India has been an active participant in the ASEAN Regional Forum (ARF).

Our policy of entrenching our relations with ASEAN is not a 'stand alone'- we have developed other policy initiatives in the region to support our relations with ASEAN. In order to develop a continuum, we are actively engaged in the Mekong-Ganga-Cooperation (MGC) which brings together India and five ASEAN countries, Cambodia, Lao PDR, Myanmar, Thailand and Vietnam. Another significant pillar of our "Look East" approach is BIMSTEC which brings together India with Nepal, Bhutan,

Bangladesh, Sri Lanka, Myanmar and Thailand. In addition to providing a forum for functional cooperation, a BIMSTEC FTA is also under negotiation.

India became a Sectoral Dialogue Partner of ASEAN in 1992 and Full Dialogue Partner in 1996. The political level mechanisms for ASEAN-India dialogue consist of the annual ASEAN-India Summit and an annual Foreign Ministers Meeting. These political level interactions are further strengthened through the Senior Officials' Meeting as also specialised working groups in the various functional areas: Science & Technology, Health, Trade & Investment, and Transport & Infrastructure.

Trade and Investment

Our sustained efforts to engage with ASEAN in the last one decade have shown commensurate results. ASEAN-India trade in 2003-4 was about US$ 15 billion, an increase of approximately 350% over the 1993-94 trade figures. The balance of trade is in favour of ASEAN. There remains significant potential to further expand these ties. For a total population of approx. 1.5 billion people and with a combined GDP of US$1.5 trillion, a trade turnover of approx. US$ 15 billion is grossly inadequate. At the 2nd India-ASEAN Business Summit held in New Delhi and Mumbai in 2003, a target of US$ 15 billion by 2005 and US$ 30 billion for India ASEAN trade by 2007 was set out. The target of US$ 30 billion was reiterated by Prime Minister at the 3rd ASEAN-India Summit held in Vientiane on November 30, 2004. Our exports to ASEAN member countries include oil meals, gems and jewellery, meat and meat preparations, cotton yarn, fabrics, machinery, rice, drugs and pharmaceuticals, chemicals, etc. Our imports mainly consist of artificial resins, plastic material, natural rubber, wood and wood products, electronic goods, organic chemicals, edible oils, fertilisers, etc.

ASEAN countries, particularly, Malaysia, Singapore and Thailand, are also increasingly investing in India in sectors such as telecommunications, fuels, hotel and tourism services, heavy industry, chemicals, fertilizers, textiles, paper and pulp, and food processing.

Functional Co-operation

ASEAN-India cooperation covers a wide field, including Trade & Investment, Science & Technology, (including IT, Biotechnology, Advanced Materials, Space Sciences and their applications, etc), Tourism, Human Resource Development, Transport &

Infrastructure, and Health and Pharmaceuticals. In HRD, in the context of the Initiative for ASEAN Integration (IAI), India has imparted training to ASEAN member countries, especially Cambodia, Lao PDR, Myanmar and Vietnam (CLMV). We have undertaken training courses for 48 CLMV personnel for Railway training in Civil Infrastructure (17 participants), Signalling Operations (14 participants), and Railway Management (17 participants). In cooperation with Singapore, we have organized English language Training courses for CLMV countries in their respective capitals. We have also established the Lao-India Entrepreneurship Development Centre in Vientiane, which was inaugurated by EAM on the eve of the Third ASEAN-India Summit. Similar EDCs will also be established in Phnom Penh, Hanoi and Yangon in 2005.

1st ASEAN-India Summit (Phnom Penh, 5 November 2002)

The 1st ASEAN-India Summit was the culmination of our sustained efforts to upgrade our dialogue partnership with ASEAN, to bring it at par with those of the PRC, ROK and Japan. At the Summit, India called for an ASEAN-India FTA within a 10-year time frame. We also announced our willingness to extend special and differential trade treatment to ASEAN countries based on their level of development, to improve their market access to India. We said that India was committed to aligning its peak tariffs to East Asian levels by 2005.

The then Prime Minister's statement at the Summit identified the following other areas of co-operation: R&D in Agriculture, Biotechnology, and Health and Pharmaceuticals with a view to their commercial exploitation, co-operation in Space Technology, including joint launch and manufacture of communication and remote sensing satellites and strengthening physical connectivity through new rail, road and air linkages. Stressing the need for greater people to people contacts, steps towards easier travel for students, businessmen and tourists were also identified as priority areas. We also announced our support to projects under the Initiative for ASEAN Integration (IAI).

2nd ASEAN-India Summit (Bali, 8 October 2003)

The 2nd ASEAN-India Summit was a significant landmark in India-ASEAN relations. At the 2nd ASEAN-India Summit in Bali, on 8 October 2003, India and ASEAN concluded the following three documents:

(i) The *Frame work Agreement for Comprehensive Economic Cooperation* signed by leaders of the ASEAN and India,

(ii) The accession document to the *ASEAN Treaty of Amity and Cooperation, signed by the Minister of External Affairs, and*

(iii) adoption of the *Joint Declaration on Cooperation in Combating International Terrorism.*

The Framework Agreement envisages the establishment of an Indo-ASEAN Regional Trade and Investment Area, which includes a Free Trade Area in goods, services and investment. Negotiations on the Free Trade Area in goods are expected to commence in January 2004 and be completed by June 2005. The negotiated FTA would come into force from January 2006.

For trade in services and investments, the negotiations on the respective agreements shall commence in 2005 and be concluded by 2007.The Framework Agreement includes an Early Harvest Programme (EHP) on trade in goods towards progressive tariff reduction on 105 agreed items. Tariff elimination/reduction shall be completed by Brunei, Indonesia, Malaysia, Philippines, Singapore, Thailand and India by October 2007 and by Cambodia, Laos, Myanmar and Vietnam by October 2010. In addition, India has also given unilateral tariff-concessions to Cambodia, Laos, Myanmar and Vietnam on 111 items. The Agreement provides the roadmap for negotiating a Free Trade Area Agreement with the ASEAN. An ASEAN-India Trade Negotiating Committee (TNC) has been established to carry out the programme of negotiations.

The *Joint Declaration on Cooperation in Combating International Terrorism* envisages cooperation in i) exchange of information, ii) legal and enforcement matters, iii) institutional capacity augmentation, and iv) training.

India accession to the *Treaty of Amity and Cooperation in Southeast Asia* signifies India's commitment to work with the ASEAN countries in maintaining regional peace and stability.

In his statement, the then Prime Minister proposed a new road map for India-ASEAN relationship, leading eventually to an Asian Community. He also laid emphasis on better connectivity to reap requisite benefits from our geographical contiguity.

We also proposed to organise an India-ASEAN Motor car Rally as a demonstration of India's geographical contiguity with ASEAN and to draw attention for the need to better road connectivity between India and ASEAN.

3rd ASEAN-India Summit (Vientiane, 29-30 November 2004)

Prime Minister attended 3rd India-ASEAN Summit in Vientiane on November 29-30, 2004. He held bilateral discussions with his counterparts from Australia, China, Indonesia, Japan, Laos, Singapore and Vietnam.

The following specific proposals were made by the Prime Minister:

(i) India will replenish India-ASEAN Cooperation Fund by contributing US$2.5 million.

(ii) A workshop of policy makers, senior officers and business representatives to be held in India in the first quarter of 2005 to evolve a concept paper on Asian Economic Community.

(iii) Extension of the proposed optical fibre link along India-Myanmar-Thailand highway to all ASEAN countries.

(iv) Sharing with ASEAN the newly developed integrated system of Text to Speech and Text to Braille (Shruti Drishti) and assisting ASEAN to set up suitable Net Portal for this purpose.

(v) Launch of satellites and micro satellites from ASEAN member countries at concessional terms.

(vi) Concessional lines of credit up to US$200 million to eligible ASEAN member countries.

(vii) Joint Research and Development of Medicines.

(viii) Joint stockpiling of rarely used drugs.

(ix) Exchange of germplasm of tropical fruits and vegetables.

Outcome of the Summit

PM signed an agreement on "India-ASEAN Partnership for Peace, Progress and Shared Prosperity". A detailed Plan of Action providing for enhanced cooperation in diverse areas is annexed to the agreement. Some key features of this Agreement are:

(i) Cooperate in strengthening the UN system, including support for early reforms of the United Nations and the Bretton Woods institutions to make them more democratic and responsive to the priorities of its member states particularly, the developing countries;

(ii) Cooperate in other multilateral fora, in particular the WTO, for greater equity and greater benefits from globalisation for the developing countries;

(iii) Cooperate in combating the menace of international terrorism and other transnational crimes such as trafficking in drugs, arms smuggling, human trafficking particularly in women and children, cyber crimes, international economic crimes, environmental crimes, sea piracy and money laundering, through effective institutional linkages and programmes of cooperation giving priority to information exchange and capacity building;

(iv) Collaborate in areas of general and complete disarmament, and in the nonproliferation of weapons of mass destruction under strict and effective international control;

(v) Give high priority to development of regional infrastructure and road, rail, sea and air transportation links to increase physical connectivity that would facilitate greater movement of goods and people;

(vi) Facilitate travel and tourism between ASEAN and India by developing links of tourist centres to enhance synergies of tourism destinations;

(vii) Promote cooperation in science and technology, in particular information technology and biotechnology, including through joint research and development and commercialization of new technologies;

(viii) Work through both conventional and innovative trade and economic arrangements, and full implementation of the ASEAN-India Free Trade Area by 2011 for ASEAN-5 and India, 2016 for the Philippines and India and by 2011 by India and 2016 by the 4 new ASEAN Members Countries, including the early implementation of the Early Harvest Programme, to achieve freer movement of goods, services, investment, and cooperation in other economic areas;

(ix) Reiterate full support for the implementation of the Declaration of ASEAN Concord II, leading to the formation of a more integrated ASEAN Community comprising the ASEAN Security Community, the ASEAN Economic Community and the ASEAN Socio-Cultural Community;

(x) Promote cooperation in human resource development, through capacity building, strengthening of institutions, training and entrepreneurship development focussing on small and medium enterprises;

India ASEAN Free Trade Area (FTA)

Agreement was reached during the Summit on Interim Rules of Origin (ROO) for the Early Harvest Program (EHP) of the India-ASEAN Free Trade Area (FTA). The Interim ROO will be based on a general rule of 40% value addition with ASEAN proposed list of minimal process, subject to a reasonably short list of products where product specific rules will be negotiated. The EHP will be implemented from April 1, 2005. Negotiations will now also commence on the FTA in goods. The establishment of the FTA is envisaged in the Framework Agreement for Comprehensive Economic Cooperation which was signed during the 2nd Summit. The EHP is expected to contribute to achieving the target of US$30 billion in India-ASEAN trade by 2007. The present level of trade is approximately US$ 15 billion.

Asian Economic Community and East Asia Summit

The suggestion of an Asian Economic Community, which would bring together the ASEAN 10, Japan, China and ROK, had been made by India at the second India-ASEAN Summit held at Bali in 2003. During the third Summit, Prime Minister proposed the holding of a workshop in India in the first quarter of 2005 to evolve a concept paper on this subject. Policy makers, senior officials and industry representatives would be invited to participate in the workshop.

The idea of an Asian Economic Community, in broad terms, is of community constituting an 'arc of advantage', over which there would be a large scale movement of people, capital, ideas, and creativity. Such a community would be roughly the size of the European Union in terms of income, and bigger than NAFTA in terms of trade. It would account for half the world's population, and it would hold foreign exchange reserves exceeding those of the EU and NAFTA put together.

Several ASEAN countries have supported India's participation in the first East Asia Summit to be held in Kuala Lumpur end 2005, Indonesia and Singapore being the foremost among them. India conforms to the three criteria laid down by ASEAN for participation in the EAS. A formal decision on the matter is to be announced at the AMM due for July, 2005.

India ASEAN Car Rally

PM and ASEAN leaders flagged off the second leg of the India-ASEAN car rally in Vientiane on November 30. The first leg had been flagged off by PM at Guwahati on November 22. The Rally will conclude at Batam, Indonesia on December 11. The rally lasting for a period of 20 days will travel through 11 countries covering approximately 8,000 kms. It has evoked considerable public interest in ASEAN countries. Each ASEAN member, (except the Philippines), has sent two cars to join the car rally. PM's suggestion that the Rally be organised on a regular basis was noted by ASEAN leaders. The key objectives of organizing the Rally are:

- To demonstrate the proximity of India with the ASEAN countries
- To create public awareness of India-ASEAN relations
- To promote connectivity, especially road transport
- To enhance trade, investment, tourism and people to people links between India and the ASEAN countries

Assessment

The 3rd India-ASEAN Summit marks a maturing of the relationship. The Summit showed that there is mutual recognition that strengthened India-ASEAN relations, which are rooted in deep historical and cultural ties, serves the interests of both India and ASEAN. The mutual desire to move ahead rapidly is also clear. India's growing economic strength and active independent role in world affairs impels ASEAN to seek greater engagement with us. We would now be following up on initiatives taken at the Summit to keep up the momentum of the relationship.

BIBLIOGRAPHY

Abu-l-Fazl (1972-1973) *The Akbar Nama,* 3 volumes tr. Delhi: H. Beveridge.

Agoncillo, Teodoro A. and Milagros C. Guerrero (1977) *History of the Filipino People,* Quezon City.

Andaya, Barbara Watson and Leonard Y. Andaya (2001) *A History of Malaysia* Honolulu.

Andaya, Leonard Y. (1975) *The Kingdom of Johor 1641-1728,* Kuala Lumpur.

Gregory L. Possehl (ed.) (1979) *Ancient Cities of the Indus,* Durham.

Apte, V. M. (1954) *Social and Religious Life in the Grihya Sutras,* Bombay.
Arnold, Edwin (1969) *The Light of Asia,* Wheaton.

Barwise, J. M. and N. J. White (2002) *A Traveller's History of Southeast Asia,* New York.

Nicholas, Tarling (ed.) (1992) *The Cambridge History of Southeast Asia,* 2 vols. Cambridge.

Chakrabongse, Chula (1967) Lords *of Life: A History of the Kings of Thailand,* London.

Chandler, David (1996) A *History of Cambodia,* Boulder.

Chandler, David P. *et al,* (1987) *In Search of Southeast Asia: A Modern History.* Honolulu.

Chapuis, Oscar (1995) *A History of Vietnam from Hong Bang to Tu Duc,* Westport.

Basham, A. L. (1954) *The Wonder That Was India,* New York.

Bhattacharji, Sukumari (1984) Literature *in the Vedic Age,* 2 vols. Calcutta.

Warren, H.C. (1896) *Buddhism in Translations* tr. New York.

Goddard, Dwight (ed.) (1938) A *Buddhist Bible,* Thetford.

Burgess, James (1913) *The Chronology of Modern India,* Edinburgh.

Rapson, E.J. (ed.) (1922) The *Cambridge History of India, vol. 1: Ancient India,* Cambridge.

Majumdar, R.C. (ed.) (1954) The Classical *Age*, Bombay.

Sastri Nilkantha, K.A. (ed.) (1957) A *Comprehensive History of India, vol. 2: The Mauryas & Satavahanas 325 B.C.-A.D.* Bombay.

Banerjee, A.C. and D.K. Ghosh (ed.) (1978) A *Comprehensive History of India, vol. 9: (1712-1772),* New Delhi.

Datta, K.K. and V.A. Narain (ed.) (1985) A *Comprehensive History of India, vol. 11: (1818-1858),* New Delhi.

Coomeraswamy, Ananda K. (1928) *Buddha and the Gospel of Buddhism*, London.

Chatterji, Suniti Kumar (ed.) (1958) The *Cultural Heritage of India, vol. 1: The Early Phases*, Calcutta.

Bhattacharyya, Haridas (ed.) (1956) The *Cultural Heritage of India, vol. 4: The Religions*, Calcutta.

Cunningham, Joseph Davey (1915) *A History of the Sikhs*, Delhi.

Dasgupta, Surendranath, (1922) *A History of Indian Philosophy*, vols.1 and 2. Delhi.

De Silva, Chandra Richard (1997) Sri *Lanka: A History*, New Delhi.

De Silva, K. M. (1981) *A History of Sri Lanka*, London.

Dunn, Ross E. (1986) *The Adventures of Ibn Battuta*,Berkeley.

Dutt, Romesh Chunder (1981) A *History of Civilization in Ancient India*, Calcutta.

Edwardes, Michael (1967) *British India 1772-1947*, New York.

Eliade, Mircea (1969) *Yoga Immortality and Freedom* tr. Princeton.

Geiger, Wilhelm (1960) *Culture of Ceylon in Medieval Times*, Wiesbaden.

Anderson, G.L. (ed.) (1966) The *Genius of the Oriental Theater*, New York.

Ghoshal, U. N. (1966) A *History of Indian Political Ideas*, London.

Ghosh, Manomohan (1968) *A History of Cambodia*, Calcutta.

Hall, D. G. E. (1981) *A History of South-East Asia*, New York.

James, Lawrence (1998) *Raj: The Making and Unmaking of British India*, New York.

Kautilya, *Arthasastra* (1915) tr. Mysore: R. Shamasastry.

John Bastin and Robin W. Winks (ed.) (1966) *Malaysia: Selected Historical Readings*, London.

Manich, M. L. (1970) *History of Anglo-Thai Relations*, Bangkok.

Manich, M. L. (1967) *History of Laos (including the history of Lannathai, Chiengmai)* Bangkok.

Manich, M. L. (1970) *History of Thailand & Cambodia*, Bangkok.

Marsden, William (1966) *The History of Sumatra*, New York.

Molina, Antonio M. (1960) *The Philippines Through the Centuries*, vol. 1, Manila.

Morga, Antonio de (1907) *History of the Philippines*, 2 volumes. Cleveland.

Moorhead, F. J. (1957) *A History of Malaya and Her Neighbors*, Volume 1. London.

Moorhead, F. J. (1963) *A History of Malaya*, Volume 2. Kuala Lumpur.

Myint-U, Thant (2001) *The Making of Modern Burma*, Cambridge.

Kennedy, J. (1970) *A History of Malaya*, London.

Koenig, William J. (1990) *The Burmese Polity, 1752-1819,* Ann Arbor.

Lieberman, Victor (2003) *Strange Parallels Southeast Asia in Global Context, c. 800-1830.* Cambridge.

Majumdar, R. C. *et al.* (1960) *An Advanced History of India,* London.

Malik, Hafeez (1980) *Sir Sayyid Ahmad Khan and Muslim Modernization in India and Pakistan,* New York.

Mill, James and Horace Hayman Wilson (1848) *The History of British India,* 9 volumes. London.

Moon, Penderel (1989) *The British Conquest and Dominion of India,* London.

Nguyen-Van-Thai and Nguyen-Van-Mung (1958) *A Short History of Vietnam,*Saigon.

Percival Spear, (ed.) (1958), The *Oxford History of India* Oxford.

Radhakrishnan, S. (1931) *Indian Philosophy,* vol. 2. London.

Rawson, Philip (1967) *The Art of Southeast Asia,* New York.

Reid, Anthony (1988) *Southeast Asia in the Age of Commerce 1450-1680, vol. 1: The Lands below the Winds.* New Haven.

Reid, Anthony (1993) *Southeast Asia in the Age of Commerce 1450-1680, vol. 2: Expansion and Crisis,* New Haven.

Ricklefs, M. C. (1993) *A History of Modern Indonesia since c. 1300.* Stanford.
Sanwal, B. D. (1965) *Nepal and the East India Company,* New York.

Sar Desai, D. R. (1997) *Southeast Asia: Past & Present,* Boulder.

Sastri Nilkantha, K.A. (ed.) (1967) Age of the Nandas and Mauryas, Delhi.
Marr David G. and A. C. Milner (ed.) (1986) *Southeast Asia in the 9th to 14th Centuries* Singapore.

Patricia Herbert and Anthony Milner (ed.) (1989) *Southeast Asia: Languages and Literatures,* Honolulu.

Shakabpa, Tsepon W. D. (1967) *Tibet: A Political History,* New Haven.

Smith, Vincent A., J. B. Harrison, and Percival Spear (1958) *The Oxford History of India,* Oxford.

Stein, R. A. (1972) *Tibetan Civilization* tr. J. E. S. Driver. Stanford.

Tate, D. J. M. (1971) *The Making of Modern South-east Asia, vol. 1: The European Conquest,* New York.

Taylor, Jean Gelman (2003) *Indonesia: Peoples and Histories,* New Haven.

Thapar, Romila (1978) *Ancient Indian Social History,* New Delhi.

Thapar, Romila (1966) *A History of India,* vol.1. Baltimore.

Vlekke, Bernard H. M. (1959) *Nusantara: A History of Indonesia,* Chicago.

Williams, Lea E. (1976) *Southeast Asia: A History,* New York.

Winstedt, Richard (1961) *A History of Classical Malay Literature,* Kuala Lumpur.

Wood, W. A. R. (1933) *A History of Siam from the Earliest Times to the Year A.D. 1781,* Bangkok.

Wyatt, David K.(2003) *Thailand: A Short History,* New Haven.

Walker, Benjamin (1968) *The Hindu World,* 2 vols. New York.

Lin Yutang (ed.) (1942) The *Wisdom of China and India,* New York.

Woodruff, Philip (1953) *The Men Who Ruled India, vol. 1: The Founders.* London.

Woodruff, Philip (1954) *The Men Who Ruled India, vol. 2: The Guardians.* New York.

Zuñiga, Joaquin Martinez de (1966) *An Historical View of the Philippine Islands* tr. John Maver, Manila.

INDEX